A DICTIONARY OF PICTORIAL SUBJECTS FROM CLASSICAL LITERATURE

A DICTIONARY OF PICTORIAL SUBJECTS FROM CLASSICAL LITERATURE

A Guide to Their Identification in Works of Art

PERCY PRESTON

CHARLES SCRIBNER'S SONS • *NEW YORK*

Library of Congress Cataloging in Publication Data

Preston, Percy.
  A dictionary of pictorial subjects from classical
literature.

  Bibliography: p.
  1. Mythology, Classical, in art. 2. Mythology,
Classical—Dictionaries. I. Title.
N7760.P68 1983   704.9′47′0938   83-4470
ISBN 0-684-17913-X

1 3 5 7 9 11 13 15 17 19 F/C 20 18 16 14 12 10 8 6 4 2

PRINTED IN THE UNITED STATES OF AMERICA.

To Frances

ACKNOWLEDGMENTS

WITHOUT the encouragement of Professor Rensselaer W. Lee, this project would not have been undertaken, nor could it have been carried out without the suggestions of John R. Martin and W. Robert Connor of the Princeton faculty, of Frances F. Jones of the Princeton Art Museum, Charles Scribner III, and the assistance of the staffs of Marquand and Firestone Libraries. Charles Scribner, Jr., and Jacques Barzun have given me much good advice about selecting and arranging the material. The unique problems of editing and layout, for which there was no precedent to guide them, have been admirably solved by Marshall De Bruhl, Director of the Reference Book Division, and Janet Hornberger, the Production Supervisor. To my editor, Christiane Deschamps, I am especially indebted for the severe scrutiny she gave to the text. Lynda Emery did a splendid job of typing a difficult manuscript. The errors and shortcomings that remain are mine. I am sincerely grateful for the contributions of all the above.

CONTENTS

INTRODUCTION

THIS volume is the outgrowth of an observation by my daughter that there seemed to be a gap in the resource material available to students and scholars interested in pictures of classical subjects. She was on the staff of a museum at the time and had come upon a sixteenth-century painting in the style of Veronese that was labeled *Apollo and Daphne* but did not accord with her recollection of that myth. Her curiosity aroused, she searched the libraries of Boston and Cambridge for help; but unable to identify any figure, she could not use standard dictionaries of mythology because they are all arranged according to proper names. Thinking that the subject might be another of Ovid's "Metamorphoses," she turned to that poem, where in the tenth book she came to the passage describing the birth of Adonis, which was clearly what this painting illustrated. Although she found the answer, she nevertheless recognized that, had the source *not* been Ovid, she would have been at a loss as to where she could search further on her own. She suggested to me, a retired classics teacher with some familiarity with Western art, that it might be interesting as well as useful to produce something that would help solve problems of this sort.

My interest was immediately engaged. The first step clearly was to find out whether or not such a work already existed—perhaps as a by-product of German lexicography. My search of libraries and interviews with art historians, classicists, and other humanists led me to believe that there was no such book and that one would be welcomed. How to go about it was the next consideration. I would have to present classical myth and legend in such a way that someone looking at a work of art based on these subjects could discover—by reference to this dictionary—who the figures were and where additional information about the scene could be found.

It became clear that what is needed is an index to mythology that can be entered by way of the particulars of an artist's rendering of a myth. By particulars are meant the objects, the creatures, the essential, distinguishing features of a figure, or a figure's various activities in a given scene. Accordingly, the headings of this dictionary–index include such terms as "Axe," "Bear," "Warrior," or "Seduction," rather than proper names.

Such an index could not be compiled by inspecting existing works of art, given the vast number of them; it could be done, I concluded, only by working from the other medium in which these myths survive, namely, literature. My method has been to read the works with an eye for material of intrinsic visual interest, enough perhaps to have inspired an artist to have depicted the scene. I then selected from the visual impression made by the text the particulars that could be used as headings.

An example of how the book can be used is provided by the painting mislabeled *Apollo and Daphne*. In it three women are shown, one holding a baby, the other two showing great interest in it. Behind them is a tree, in the lower part of which the upper part of a woman's body is dimly seen. "Baby" and "Tree" are more suitable headings to turn to than "Woman" or "Human Figure," since adult human figures appear in a majority of paintings and are usually not of themselves distinguishing particulars. Under "Baby" we find subheadings that describe various vicissitudes that befall babies, of which "Birth of" and "Held by mother or nurse" are promising. Under "Birth of" we read that "Adonis is delivered from the tree into which pregnant Myrrha (Smyrna) has been transformed"; this seems to describe the scene, with the dim figure in the shadows being the clue that the tree was once a woman. If we enter by way of "Tree" and suspect a metamorphosis because of the dim figure, the subhead "Changed into trees" will lead us to Myrrha, but if we miss that clue, we will come to "Gives birth to baby Adonis," where a version other than Ovid's is also recorded.

In any case, the theme of the picture is apparent. To identify the women and to learn the circumstances of the marvelous event, we have to look up the citations given. If the works cited are not readily available, we may turn to Adonis in a dictionary such as Smith's or Roscher's (see the Bibliography). There we learn that Lucina assisted at the birth and that the baby passed into the care of some Naiads, which identifies the women; we also learn why Myrrha was pregnant and had been metamorphosed.

The subheadings as a rule focus on what is visually distinctive in a scene or a group of scenes. However, when the main head is itself the visual link between entries or a subhead in the margin links them, they are arranged by the names of the most prominent figures. Examples of this are under "Ascension," "Boat," and "Centaur."

Another function of the book is to help someone who is doing research on certain topics, for example, "Centaurs in Myth" or "The Symbolism of Snakes" by assembling in one place many citations that could be consulted. The book may also provide the forgotten name of someone involved in a remembered incident, as that of the woman who, by tossing a golden apple into the midst of the guests at a wedding, set in motion the chain of events that led to the Trojan War, or of the king who acquired the ears of an ass. Likewise it can occasionally clarify an allusion, such as "Bed of Procrustes."

Because it was impractical to cover all the literature of classical myth and legend, from Homer and Hesiod to the grammarians and mythographers of the

Middle Ages, I have concentrated on the important works of the classical period and early Roman Empire, though reaching beyond to include the works of Apollodorus and of novelists like Heliodorus, whose romances occasionally provided subjects for artists. Authors who have been indexed completely are marked by an asterisk in the List of Works Cited (see page xvii). The other works listed there contain scenes of interest missing from the chief sources or variations of the original tradition, to which I have been led by notes and commentary in my texts and by references in dictionaries (see the Bibliography). And since artists have drawn much from Greek and Roman history as well as mythology, I have included historical scenes of special interest.

I have not striven for complete comprehensiveness. It seemed unnecessary to include every combat of the Trojan War, since it is unlikely that those of lesser warriors would have attracted an artist's notice. Similarly, the begetting of progeny has not been entered here when it is reported simply to keep the genealogical record straight, without the circumstantial detail giving it pictorial interest.

Another limitation is imposed by the loss of much Greek and Roman literature, rendering our knowledge of the classical myths incomplete. The plots of Euripides' lost plays and the outlines of the lost epics of the Trojan and Theban Cycles are to a considerable extent known through fragments and synopses or quotation in the works of later writers. But some scenes that artists have illustrated (mostly on Greek vases) are not in existing literary sources, and therefore no clues to their identification can be found in this volume.

When Roman writers retold or embellished Greek myths and legends, they often substituted the name of the Latin deity of similar nature or a Latinized form of the Greek name. Because this book often cites a Greek source and also a Latin version, which uses the Latin form of a deity's name, I had to decide whether to give both names. To write "Zeus (Jupiter)" wherever the overlapping occurred seemed undesirably repetitive, so I have used the Greek name only. Greek names are used even when the only source cited uses the Latin, because it could be confusing to change from one to the other. Thus, when Aeneas' mother appears in scenes that are not part of Greek mythic tradition, as in the *Aeneid,* she is referred to as Aphrodite. (In the case of Aphrodite-Venus, the usage adopted can also be defended by pointing out that Vergil presents Venus as having the nature of Aphrodite and not at all that of the obscure Italian deity of uncertain pedigree.) Roman equivalents of Greek names are given on page xv. If one is referred to a passage such as *Met.* 9.292f. and there expects to find the name Eileithyia and instead finds Lucina, he will be reassured to learn from the table that they are the same divinity.

Latin names are used occasionally in the entries in which attributes are given. This reflects the transformation of the gods of Homer and Hesiod at a later time—

when Latin had become the universal language of the West—into deities with broadened powers and therefore with additional and sometimes different attributes than those assigned to them by the Greeks.

For the most part the attributes have been taken from Smith, Hirt, de Tervarent, and Cartari (see Bibliography). Attributes can help to identify a figure in a work of art, but one should remember that they are not invariably presented by the artist.

A proper name in parentheses is an alternative name, for example, Myrrha (Smyrna), or it identifies a figure, more often a deity, who has taken or been given a different form or likeness, for example, Mentor (Athena), a beggar (Odysseus). It may also be a translation of a name, for example, Lussa (Madness).

Artistic license must be taken into account by anyone using this volume, since an artist does not feel bound to represent faithfully a scene he has taken from the mythological tradition. The setting may be changed from the forest where, in the *Aeneid,* Aeneas receives his new armor, to the seashore, where Jordaens has placed it; or, Orpheus may be clothed in contemporary dress and be playing a mandolin or violin instead of a lyre. Most often artistic license is a matter of substituting one thing, such as a weapon, for another.

An attempt to deal with this propensity is made in two ways. Sometimes I anticipate an artist's modification by, for example, stating that Tullia drives over her father's body in a chariot, rather than in the less dramatic vehicle that Livy mentions. This incident therefore appears under both "Wagon" and "Chariot." But, more often, cross-references are given without repeating the entry. For example, under "Beggar" the reader will find (see also **Castaway; Old Man**). These are also given when an object might be confused with something else; a stone might be mistaken for an apple, ball, egg, or loaf of bread, all of which are suggested as things to look up if "Stone" does not produce what is wanted.

Fifty-one line drawings are scattered throughout the text. These may help the reader to identify objects and creatures encountered in a work of art. Because the variety of form in which classical subjects have been represented is far too great to reproduce here, readers are directed to Smith's or to Daremberg and Saglio's dictionary of antiquities (see Bibliography) for more extensive illustrations.

PERCY PRESTON

GREEK NAMES WITH ROMAN EQUIVALENTS

Greek	Roman	Greek	Roman
Aphrodite	Venus	Gaea, Gaia, Ge	Terra, Tellus
Ares	Mars	Hades, Pluto	Pluto, Dis, Orcus
Artemis	Diana	Hebe	Juventas (Youth)
Athena, Pallas	Minerva, Pallas	Helius, Phoebus, Titan	Sol, Phoebus
Charites	Gratiae (Graces)		
Chloris	Flora	Hephaestus	Vulcan
Cronus	Saturnus	Hera	Juno
Cybele, Rhea	Ops	Hestia	Vesta
Demeter	Ceres	Hypnos	Somnus (Sleep)
Dionysus, Bacchus, Bromius, Evius	Bacchus, Liber, Lyaeus	Leto	Latona
		Moirai	Parcae (Fates)
		Neoptolemus	Pyrrhus
		Nike	Victoria
Dioscuri		Nyx	Nox (Night)
Castor	Castor	Palaemon	Portunus
Polydeuces	Pollux	Persephone, Cora, Kore	Proserpina
Eileithyia	Lucina		
Eirene	Pax	Phoebe	Luna (Moon)
Elpis	Spes (Hope)	Poseidon	Neptune
Enyo	Bellona	Selene	Luna
Eos	Aurora (Dawn)	Thanatos	Mors (Death)
Erinyes, Eumenides	Furiae, Dirae (Furies)	Tyche	Fortuna
		Zeus	Jupiter
Eris	Discordia		

LIST OF WORKS CITED

*Marks the works that have been indexed completely

Aelian	Claudius Aelianus, *Varia Historia*	Cat.	Catullus (Poems of)
Aen.	*Vergil, *Aeneid*	Cic.	Cicero
Aes.	*Aeschylus	*de Div.*	*de Divinatione*
Agam.	*Agamemnon*	*de Off.*	*de Officiis*
Choëph.	*Choëphoroe (Libation Bearers)*	*de Sen.*	*de Senectute*
		Tusc.	*Tusculan Disputations*
Eumen.	*Eumenides*	Cypria	*Poem of Cyprus* (a poem of the Epic Cycle, of which Proclus' epitome is found in Photius, q.v.)
Pers.	*Persians*		
Prom.	*Prometheus Bound*		
Seven	*Seven Against Thebes*		
Suppl.	*Suppliant Women*		
Aesop	*Fables* (numbering is that of B. E. Perry, *Aesopica* [1952])	Dares	Dares Phrygius, *The Fall of Troy*
Aeth.	*Heliodorus, *Aethiopica*	Dictys	Dictys Cretensis, *The Trojan War*
Amores	Ovid, *Amores*	Dio	Dio Cassius, *Roman History*
Ant. Lib.	Antoninus Liberalis, *Metamorphoses*	Diod. Sic.	Diodorus Siculus, *Bibliotheca Historica*
Appian	*Roman History*	Diog. Laërt.	Diogenes Laërtius, *Lives of the Philosophers*
Apuleius	*Metamorphoses*		
Aratus, *Phainomena*	Aratus, *Phainomena*	*Ecl.*	Vergil, *Eclogues (Bucolics)*
Argo.	*Apollonius Rhodius, *Argonautica*	*Ep.*	*Apollodorus, *Epitome*
Aristophanes	Aristophanes, *Lysistrata, Knights*	Eur.	*Euripides
		Alc.	*Alcestis*
Arrian	*Anabasis of Alexander*	*Andro.*	*Andromache*
Ars Amat.	Ovid, *Ars Amatoria*	*Bacch.*	*Bacchae*
Athenaeus	*Deipnosophistai*	*Cycl.*	*Cyclops*
Bacchylides	*Odes*	*Elec.*	*Electra*
Caesar	Julius Caesar	*Hec.*	*Hecuba*
B.C.	*Bellum Civile*	*Hel.*	*Helen*
B.G.	*Bellum Gallicum*	*Her.*	*Heracles*
Callimachus, *Baths of Pallas*	Callimachus, *Baths of Pallas*	*Heracleidae*	*(Children of Heracles)*

xvii

Hipp.	*Hippolytus*
Ion	*Ion*
Iph. Aul.	*Iphigeneia in Aulis*
Iph. Taur.	*Iphigeneia in Tauris*
Med.	*Medea*
Orest.	*Orestes*
Phoen.	*Phoenissae*
	(Phoenician Maidens)
Rhes.	*Rhesus*
Suppl.	*Suppliant Women*
Troad.	*Troades (Trojan Women)*
[fragment of. . . .	Contents of the fragments of lost plays are summarized in Rose, *A Handbook of Greek Literature* (1960), pp. 202–208]
Eust.	Eustathius, *ad Homerum*
ad Il.	*ad Iliadem*
ad Od.	*ad Odysseam*
Fab.	*Hyginus, Fabulae
Fasti	*Ovid, *Fasti*
Frag. Hist. Graec.	C. and T. Müller, *Fragmenta Historicorum Graecorum*
Frontinus, *Strategemata*	Frontinus, *Strategemata*
Galen, *de Temperamentis*	Galen, *de Temperamentis*
Georg.	Vergil, *Georgics*
Herod.	Herodotus, *Persian Wars*
Heroïdes	*Ovid, *Heroïdes*
Hes.	*Hesiod
Eoiai	*Catalogue of Women* (numbering as in Oxford Classical Text)

Sh. Her.	*Shield of Heracles*
Theog.	*Theogony*
W. & D.	*Works and Days*
H.	*Hymn (Homeric)
to Dem.	*to Demeter* (#2)
to Ap.	*to Apollo* (#3)
to Her.	*to Hermes* (#4)
to Aph.	*to Aphrodite* (#5)
to Dion.	*to Dionysus* (#7)
to Pan	*to Pan* (#19)
Hor. *Odes*	Horace, *Odes*
Il.	*Homer, *Iliad*
Ilias Mikra }	*Little Iliad* } (poems of the Epic Cycle, of which Proclus' epitomes are found in Photius, q.v.)
Iliupersis }	*Sack of Troy* }
Justin	M. J. Justinus, abridgment of Trogus, *Variae Philippicae*
Juv.	Juvenal, *Satires*
Lib.	*Apollodorus, *Library*
Livy	*History of Rome*
Epitome	(Abstracts of the books of the above)
Longus	*Daphnis and Chloë*
Lucian *Dial. Deo.*	*Dialogi Deorum*
Met.	*Ovid, *Metamorphoses*
Moschus, *Epigram* 7	In Palatine and Greek (Loeb edn.) Anthology, 16.200
Nat. Hist.	Pliny, *Natural History*
Nep.	Nepos
Epam.	*Epaminondas*
Han.	*Hannibal*

Nonnus	*Dionysiaca*	Pind.	Pindar
Nostoi	*Returns* (a poem of the Epic Cycle, of which an epitome by Proclus is found in Photius, q.v.)	*Isth.*	*Isthmian Odes*
		Nem.	*Nemean Odes*
		Ol.	*Olympian Odes*
		Pyth.	*Pythian Odes*
Od.	*Homer, Odyssey*		
Paus.	*Pausanias, Description of Greece*	Plato, *Protagoras*	Plato, *Protagoras*
Philostratus	*Imagines (Eikones)*	Pliny the Younger	*Letters*
Photius	Photius, *Bibliotheca,* Bekker, ed.	Plut.	*Plutarch, Parallel Lives*

1-Theseus; 2-Romulus; 3-Lycurgus; 4-Numa Pompilius; 5-Solon; 6-Publicola (Poplicola); 7-Themistocles; 8-Camillus; 9-Pericles; 10-Fabius Maximus; 11-Alcibiades; 12-Coriolanus; 13-Timoleon; 14-Aemilius Paulus; 15-Pelopidas; 16-Marcellus; 17-Aristides; 18-Cato Major (the Censor); 19-Philopoemen; 20-Flamininus; 21-Pyrrhus; 22-Marius; 23-Lysander; 24-Sulla; 25-Cimon; 26-Lucullus; 27-Nicias; 28-Crassus; 29(30)-Eumenes; 30(29)-Sartorius; 31-Agesilaüs; 32-Pompey; 33-Alexander; 34-Caesar; 35-Phocion; 36-Cato of Utica (the Younger); 37-Agis; 38-Cleomenes; 39-Tiberius Gracchus; 40-Gaius Gracchus; 41-Demosthenes; 42-Cicero; 43-Demetrius; 44-Antony; 45-Dion; 46-Marcus Brutus; 47-Artaxerxes; 48-Aratus; 49-Galba; 50-Otho

Plut.	Plutarch	Ptolem. Heph.	Ptolemaeus Hephaestus, quoted in Photius, *Bibliotheca*, Bekker, ed.
Moralia	(Numbering as in Stephanus and Loeb editions)		
Parallela Minora		Q. Curt.	Quintus Curtius, *History of Alexander*
Quaestiones Graecae		Quint. *Inst.*	Quintilian, *Institutiones*
Poet. Astr.	*Hyginus, Poetica Astronomica*	Quint. Smy.	Quintus Smyrnaeus, *Posthomerica*
Polybius	*Roman History*	*Res Gestae Divi Augusti*	*Deeds of the Divine Augustus*
Powell	J. U. Powell, ed., *New Chapters in the History of Greek Literature*, 3rd series	Rose	H. J. Rose, *A Handbook of Greek Literature* (1960)
Proclus	*Chrestomatheia* (a lost work of which extracts are found in Photius, q.v.)	Schol.	Scholiast
		ad Argo.	*on Argonautica*
		ad Homerum	*on Homer*
Ps.-Cal.	*Pseudo-Callisthenes, History of Alexander* (Armenian version)	*ad Il.*	*on The Iliad*
		ad Lycophrona	*on Lycophron,*

ad Lycophrona	Alexandra (Cassandra)
ad Od.	on The Odyssey
Sen.	*Seneca
Agam.	Agamemnon
Her. Fur.	Hercules Furens
Her. Oet.	Hercules Oetaeus
Med.	Medea
Oed.	Oedipus
Phaed.	Phaedra
Phoen.	Phoenissae
Thy.	Thyestes
Tro.	Troades
Serv.	*Servius, Commentary on Vergil
ad Aen.	ad Aeneida
ad Ecl.	ad Eclogas (Bucolica)
ad Georg.	ad Georgica
Soph.	*Sophocles
Ajax	Ajax
Ant.	Antigone
Elec.	Electra
Ich.	Ichneutae (Trackers)
Oed. Col.	Oedipus at Colonus

Oed. Tyr.	Oedipus Tyrannus (The King)
Phil.	Philoctetes
Trach.	Trachiniae (Women of Trachis)
Statius, Thebaïd	Statius, Thebaïd
Strabo	Geographica
Suet.	Suetonius
Aug.	Augustus (Book 2)
Caes.	Caesar (Book 1)
Nero	Nero (Book 6)
Tac.	Tacitus
An.	Annals
Hist.	Histories
Theocritus	Bucolics (Idylls)
Thucy.	Thucydides, Peloponnesian War
Val. Max.	Valerius Maximus, de Factis
Velleius Paterculus	History of Rome
Xen.	Xenophon
Anab.	Anabasis
Cyro.	Cyropaedia
Mem.	Memorabilia

ILLUSTRATIONS

SOURCES used for the illustrations in this volume include: Catherine B. Avery, *The New Century Classical Handbook* (New York, 1962); Karl A. Baumeister, *Denkmäler des klassischen Altertums,* 3 vols. (Munich–Leipzig, 1885–1889); Daremberg and Saglio, *Dictionnaire des antiquités grecques et romaines,* 5 vols. (Paris, 1877–1919); Percy Gardner, *A Grammar of Greek Art* (New York–London, 1905); Charles Mills Gayley, *The Classic Myths in English Literature and in Art* (Boston, 1893. Rev. 1911); Pierre Gusman, *Pompei* (London, 1900); Jane Ellen Harrison and Dugald Sutheland Maccoll, *Greek Vase Paintings* (London, 1894); Thomas Hope, *Costumes of the Greeks and Romans* (New York [Dover Publications, Inc.], 1962); Harry Thurston Peck, *Harper's Dictionary of Classical Literature and Antiquities* (New York, 1896. Repr. 1923, 1965); Wilhelm Heinrich Roscher, *Ausführliches Lexikon der griechischen und römischen Mythologie,* 6 vols. and supp. (Leipzig, 1884–1937. Repr. 1965); and William Smith, *A Dictionary of Greek and Roman Antiquities* (London, 1842. Repr. 1977).

Boldface number indicates location of illustration in this text

1. Athena wearing the aegis (Daremberg and Saglio, vol. I, fig. 143) **1**
2. Orestes killing Neoptolemus at Delphi (Daremberg and Saglio, vol. IV, fig. 5405) **3**
3. Baby Zeus and the goat Amaltheia; Rhea and the Curetes (Baumeister, vol. III, fig. 2391) **18**
4. A Canephoros with a basket of sacred objects (Hope, fig. 215) **22**
5. Procrustes, his bed, and Theseus (Baumeister, vol. I, fig. 327) **25**
6. Ganymede and the eagle (Gayley, fig. 45) **30**
7. Charon ferrying the dead to Hades (Baumeister, vol. I, fig. 415) **38**
8. Theseus killing the Minotaur (Gardner, fig. 62) **50**
9. Rhea hands a stone wrapped in baby clothes to Cronus (Baumeister, vol. II, fig. 862) **51**
10. A herald with his caduceus (Smith, p. 218) **53**
11. Achilles in the care of Cheiron (Baumeister, vol. I, fig. 5) **64**
12. Triptolemus driving Demeter's chariot (Baumeister, vol. III, fig. 1959) **69**
13. Danaë and baby Perseus are put into a chest by King Acrisius and a servant (Harrison and Maccoll, fig. 34) **71**
14. Heracles, with club and bow, in Helius' golden goblet (Daremberg and Saglio, vol. III, fig. 3763) **73**
15. Cybele wearing a mural crown (Smith, p. 360) **84**
16. Cyclopes at work (Daremberg and Saglio, vol. I, fig. 2258) **85**
17. A woman with cymbals (Smith, p. 381) **86**
18. Poseidon with attributes: trident and dolphin (Avery, p. 923) **92**
19. Zeus fighting Giants (Baumeister, vol. III, fig. 1791) **107**
20. A flute player and a wine pourer (Gardner, fig. 53) **117**

A DICTIONARY OF
PICTORIAL SUBJECTS
FROM CLASSICAL
LITERATURE

ABDUCTION

(See **Captive; Chariot; Flight; God; Sea Deity; Seduction; Wings.**)

ABYSS

(See **Chasm.**)

AEGIS

The shield of Zeus, frequently lent to ATHENA, whose attribute it became. It is a goatskin worn on the left arm or over the breast, often tasseled or with a fringe of snakes and with a Gorgon's head in its middle. It became stylized as a bronze breastplate and in this form was adopted by Roman emperors. Another tradition holds that it is the skin of the Giant Pallas, whom Athena killed and flayed.

ATHENA WEARING THE AEGIS

Worn by ATHENA as she incites the Greeks to battle (*Il.* 2.445f) and rides in a chariot with Hera (*Il.* 5.738f).

Brandished by APOLLO to intimidate the Greek warriors (*Il.* 15.306f) and as he breaks down the wall of the Greek camp for Hector et al. (*Il.* 5.355f); by ATHENA to terrify the suitors of Penelope as Odysseus begins to destroy them (*Od.* 22.297f); by ZEUS to terrify the Greeks (*Il.* 17.593f) and to separate Athena and her girl companion Pallas before their friendly bout becomes serious, but this causes Pallas to be distracted and fatally wounded by Athena (*Lib.* 3.12.3).

Given by ZEUS to Apollo (*Il.* 15.229f).

Placed by APOLLO over Hector's corpse (*Il.* 24.18f); by ATHENA over the shoulders of Achilles (*Il.* 18.203f); on the statue of her friend Pallas (*Lib.* 3.12.3).

An Aegis-like object is removed by ION from a cradle or casket, as Creüsa watches (Eur. *Ion* 1417f).

ALLEGORICAL FIGURES

(See also **Bird: Allegorical, Unspecified; Chariot; Corpse; [Dragged]; Fabulous Beings and Creatures; Fates; Furies; Graces; Muses; Old Man; Old Woman; River God; Sea Deity; Shouting; Underworld; Water; Wings.**)

The more important allegorical figures encountered in literature and visual art are Deimos (Terror), Dike (Justice), Elpis (Hope), Eris (Discord), Horae (Seasons), Hubris (Violence), Hypnos (Sleep), Momus (Mockery), Nemesis (Retribution), Nike (Victory), Oneiros (Dream), Peitho (Persuasion), Phobos (Flight), Somnium (Dream), Thanatos (Death).

ATE (Heedlessness) rushes rashly ahead, followed slowly by the Litae (Prayers), old women with eyes askew who try to repair the harm Ate does (*Il.* 9.502f); she is flung from heaven by Zeus (*Il.* 19.126f).

LUSSA (Madness) and IRIS come to drive Heracles mad, causing him to kill his wife and sons (Eur. *Her.* 815f).

VOLUPTAS (Pleasure) and VIRTUS (Virtue), two attractive women, represent a choice Heracles has to make (Xen. *Mem.* 2.1.21; cf. Hes. *W. & D.* 286f, where the paths of wickedness and virtue are contrasted, and Cic. *de Off.* 1.32, where Heracles is faced with the choice between the roads of virtue and pleasure).

ALTAR

(See also **Hearth; Priest; Priestess; Suppliant; Temple; Tomb.**)

With fire on it: attribute of Aesculapius. With weapons and a cube on it: Mars.

ANIMAL SACRIFICE

Boar or pig. Sacrificed by AENEAS; he offers a sow and her litter to Hera before setting off up the Tiber (*Aen.* 8.81f); by AGAMEMNON, on the occasion of his reconciliation with Achilles and the return of Briseïs to him (*Il.* 19.252f); by CIRCE, as she purifies Jason and Medea of the murder of Medea's brother (*Argo.* 4.704f).

Bull or heifer. Sacrificed by AENEAS, preparing to found a city for the refugee Trojans (*Aen.* 3.19f) and before leaving Delos for Crete (*Aen.* 3.118f); by ARISTAEUS, on four altars, seeking to propitiate the shade of Eurydice (*Georg.* 4.538f); by DIDO, who pours a libation between its horns preparatory to reading its entrails (*Aen.* 4.56f); by MENELAÜS, on the ship that carries him and Helen away from Egypt (Eur. *Hel.* 1581f); by NESTOR; he offers a heifer whose horns are gilded before the ceremony (*Od.* 3.430f); by ORESTES and AEGISTHUS; they read the auspices from its viscera (Eur. *Elec.* 784f); by the SIBYL, at the entrance to Hades, as Aeneas sacrifices a sheep (*Aen.* 6.243f); by THEAGENES and CHARICLEIA; they fall in love as she

ORESTES KILLING NEOPTOLEMUS AT DELPHI

hands him a torch (*Aeth.* 3); by the WARRIORS who are about to assault the gates of Thebes (Aes. *Seven* 43f).

Horse. Sacrificed by CRASSUS, before his forces engage Spartacus' army (Plut. 28.11); by PELOPIDAS, before the battle of Leuctra (Plut. 15.18); by TYNDAREÜS, as Helen's suitors swear to defend her marriage with whichever one of them she selects (Paus. 3.20.9).

Ram. (See **Ram.**)

Sheep or lamb. Sacrificed by AENEAS, before sailing from Delos (*Aen.* 3.118f); by AGAMEMNON and PRIAM, to establish a truce during the combat of Paris and Menelaüs (*Il.* 3.271f); by JASON, to Hecate, who comes to accept the offering (*Argo.* 3.1031f, 3.1207f); by ODYSSEUS, at a pit from which ghosts are to appear (*Od.* 11.23f); by PROETUS' DAUGHTERS, to Hera, to cure their madness (Bacchylides 10.106f).

Unspecified. Sacrificed by AENEAS, at the tomb of Polydorus (*Aen.* 3.62f).

HUMAN SACRIFICE

Men. GUESTS of the horned women of Amathus are butchered on the altar of Jupiter Hospes (*Met.* 10.224f). HERACLES, about to be sacrificed by Busiris, breaks his bonds and kills Busiris (*Lib.* 2.5.11; *Fab.* 31). IDOMENEUS' SON, by his father (Serv. *ad Aen.* 3.121, 11.264). Three PERSIANS, by Themistocles, before the battle of Salamis (Plut. 7.13). THASIUS (Phrasius), by Busiris, to bring rain to Egypt (*Fab.* 56; *Lib.* 2.5.11). Twelve TROJANS, by Achilles, at the pyre of Patroclus (*Il.* 23.175f). Evidence of the practice is found by Orestes and Pylades (Eur. *Iph. Taur.* 66f).

Women. CALLIRHOË is about to be sacrificed when the priest, Coresus, kills himself; she does likewise (Paus. 7.21.1). CHTHONIA, to Poseidon; her sisters kill themselves (*Fab.* 46). DEMOPHON's DAUGHTERS, by Mastusius, who offers their blood in a cup to their father (*Poet. Astr.* 2.40). ERECHTHEUS' DAUGHTER, by her father; her sisters kill themselves (*Lib.* 3.15.4). HYACINTHUS' DAUGHTERS, to avert a plague in Athens (*Lib.* 3.15.8). IPHIGENEIA is lifted to the altar (Aes. *Agam.* 223f) and sacrificed by Agamemnon (Eur. *Elec.* 1020f). POLYXENA, as demanded by the ghost of Achilles (Eur. *Hec.* 107f, 521f; Eur. *Troad.* 622f; *Met.* 13.441f; *Fab.* 110).

Man and woman. The lovers MELANIPPUS and COMAITHO are sacrificed to Artemis (Paus. 7.19.2). PHRIXUS and HELLE, brother and sister, are rescued from the altar in a mist (Nephele) and escape to the sky on a golden ram (*Fasti* 3.857f; *Lib.* 1.9.1; *Fab.* 3).

Children. Two EGYPTIANS are sacrificed by Menelaüs (Herod. 2.119).

ANIMAL INSTEAD OF HUMAN VICTIM

A deer for Iphigeneia, by Artemis, who carries her off (Eur. *Iph. Aul.* 1581f; Eur. *Iph. Taur.* 28f; *Met.* 12.29; *Fab.* 98).

A goat for a boy, by Dionysus (Paus. 9.8.1).

A ram for Phrixus, by Nephele, who carries him off (*Lib.* 1.9.1; cf. *Fasti* 3.857f, where Phrixus and Helle escape on a golden ram; also *Fab.* 2, where Phrixus is saved by a slave's intervention).

VIOLATED BY MURDER OR SUICIDE

Of a man. ACHILLES and ANTILOCHUS are killed in Apollo's shrine by Paris et al. (Dares 34; Dictys 4.11). LYCUS, by Heracles (Eur. *Heracleidae* 712f). NEOPTOLEMUS, by Orestes et al. (Eur. *Andro.* 1118f; *Aen.* 3.330f). Aged OENEUS, by the sons of Agrius (*Lib.* 1.8.6). POLITES, by Neoptolemus (Pyrrhus), before Priam and Hecuba (*Aen.* 2.512f). PRIAM, by Neoptolemus after he has killed Polites (*Ep.* 5.21; *Aen.* 2.544f). One of two men sent to assassinate TIMOLEON; the other begs to be spared (Plut. 13.16). TROÏLUS, by Achilles in a sanctuary of Apollo (*Ep.* 3.32).

Of a woman. EURYDICE kills herself when she learns her son is a suicide (Soph. *Ant.* 1301f). HERACLIA and her daughters are killed by revolutionaries (Livy 24.26). SIDERO, by her stepson Pelias, at Hera's shrine (*Lib.* 1.9.8).

Of children. MEDEA's, by the Corinthians, whose king, Creon, Medea has poisoned (*Lib.* 1.9.28; Schol. on Eur. *Med.* 273). THYESTES' SONS, by Atreus (*Ep.* 2.13; Sen. *Thy.* 744f).

Of an officiant. AEGISTHUS, by Orestes (Eur. *Elec.* 774f). AGAMEMNON and CASSANDRA, by Clytemnestra and Aegisthus, with an axe (*Fab.* 117). ATREUS, while sacrificing on the shore, by Aegisthus (*Fab.* 88). BUSIRIS, by Heracles, who was himself on the point of being sacrificed (*Lib.* 2.5.11; *Fab.* 31). SYCHAEUS, Dido's husband, by her brother Pygmalion (*Aen.* 1.343f). TATIUS, king of the Sabines, by the Lavinians (Livy 1.14).

By an officiant. ALCATHOÜS kills his son with a log when he interrupts the sacrifice (Paus. 1.42.7). JASON, when attacked by Apsyrtus, kills him (*Fab.* 23). TELEPHON kills King Polyphontes instead of the victim provided (*Fab.* 137).

PLACE OF SANCTUARY OR HIDING

For a man. AJAX OÏLEUS takes refuge from the Greeks who are angered by his rape of Cassandra (*Ep.* 5.23; *Iliupersis* 1). ODYSSEUS hides while spying in Troy (Eur. *Rhes.* 507f). ORESTES and PYLADES hide from, then confront, Electra, who comes carrying a water jar (Eur. *Elec.* 107f, 215f). PARIS takes refuge from Deïphobus; Cassandra reveals to them that they are brothers (*Fab.* 91). PHINEAS hides from Perseus (*Met.* 5.30f).

For a woman. ANDROMACHE is threatened by Menelaüs, who is holding her baby, and also by Hermione et al. (Eur. *Andro.* 42f, 309f). CREÜSA is threatened by Ion and armed Delphians (Eur. *Ion* 1250f). HELEN is taken from an altar by Theseus and Peirithoüs (*Fab.* 79); she seeks asylum at King Proteus' tomb (Eur. *Hel.* 63f, 797f); she takes refuge as Troy is falling, and is spared when Aphrodite stays Aeneas from killing her (*Aen.* 2.576f). (Cf. EILEITHYIA, who is not seeking asylum, but is sitting on an altar with legs and fingers crossed to delay Alcmene's delivery of Heracles and Iphicles [*Met.* 9.285f].)

For a group. AETHRA, Adrastus, et al. are found by Theseus (Eur. *Suppl.* 88f). Old AMPHITRYON, Megara, and her children, by Heracles; they are threatened by Lycus; Heracles rescues them (Eur. *Her.* 46f, 514f). DANAÜS and his DAUGHTERS, refugees from Egypt, seek asylum in a sacred grove; they are found by King Pelasgus (Aes. *Suppl.* 176f). IOLAÜS and the children of Heracles are threatened by Copreus, who seizes Iolaüs (Eur. *Heracleidae* 48f). PRIAM, HECUBA, and their DAUGHTERS await the Greeks (*Aen.* 2.499f).

For a baby. ANIUS, placed by Rhoeo on Apollo's altar (Diod. Sic. 5.62.2).

VARIOUS RITES PERFORMED

By men. ADRASTUS offers a suppliant's branch as he prays for Athenian help in burying those killed at Thebes (*Lib.* 3.7.1). AENEAS sacrifices while Diomedes gives the Palladium to Nautes (Serv. *ad Aen.* 2.166, 3.407f); he honors Anchises at his tomb as a snake appears (*Aen.* 5.49f); he prays to Heracles and the Penates before departing from Evander's city with Pallas' troop (*Aen.* 8.541f); he and Turnus sacrifice at the same altar before their combat, and King Latinus solemnizes the terms agreed upon (*Aen.* 12.166f); while sacrificing, Aeneas falls into the Numicius and becomes a god (Serv. *ad Aen.* 4.620f). As ALEXANDER sacrifices, an eagle transfers the offering to another altar (Ps.-Cal. 89, 91). The tribune ATEIUS performs magical rites and curses Crassus because he is undertaking the Parthian campaign illegally (Plut. 28.16). CALASIRIS sanctifies the oath that Theagenes swears to Charicleia (*Aeth.* 4); he extracts from the altar fire a ring with which to redeem her from Nausicles (*Aeth.* 5). CHRYSES begs Apollo to punish Agamemnon and the Greeks (*Il.* 1.33f) and thanks Apollo for the return of his daughter by Odysseus (*Il.* 1.446f). The ETHIOPIAN KING marries Theagenes and Charicleia (*Aeth.* 10). FABIUS DORSO carries sacred objects through a crowd of invading Gauls to an altar (Livy 5.46). HAMILCAR has his son Hannibal swear eternal hatred for Rome (Livy 21.1; Nep. *Han.* 2). HERACLES, while engaged in sacrifice, is tormented by a poisoned robe (Soph. *Trach.* 755f; *Met.* 9.159f); he is pestered by flies (Paus. 5.14.1); he is purified by Thespius for the murder of his children (*Lib.* 2.4.12) and by Eumolpus for the murder of Centaurs (*Lib.* 2.5.12); he is inducted into the Eleusinian mysteries (*Lib.* 2.5.12); he and King Evander sacrifice, thereby confirming a prophecy of Rome's greatness (Livy 1.7). HIPPOLYTUS lays flowers on and prays at Artemis' altar, neglecting that of Aphrodite (Eur. *Hipp.* 72f, 1092f). IARBAS, an African king, prays to Zeus, who responds by sending Hermes to Aeneas (*Aen.* 4.198f). ORESTES, accompanied by Pylades, places a lock of hair on the altar before Agamemnon's tomb; they hide as Electra approaches (Aes. *Choëph.* 1f). PELIAS, while at the altar, observes that Jason wears but one sandal (*Argo.* 1.5f; *Fab.* 12). PERSEUS sacrifices before claiming Andromeda (*Met.* 4.753f). PRIAM and AGAMEMNON solemnize a truce (*Il.* 3.264f). A PRIEST and children at an altar beg Oedipus to alleviate a plague, as Creon enters (Soph. *Oed. Tyr.* 1f). TELEMACHUS is sacrificing when he is joined by the fugitive THEOCLYMENUS (*Od.* 15.222f).

By women. ALCESTIS prays to Hestia to care for her children after she dies (Eur. *Alc.* 162f). ANDROMACHE, at twin altars, is approached by Aeneas et al. (*Aen.* 3.300f). CIRCE purifies Jason and Medea of the murder of her brother (*Argo.* 4.576f, 4.662f; *Lib.* 1.9.24). CLYTEMNESTRA is praying to Apollo, with Electra in attendance, as an old man arrives (Soph. *Elec.* 637f). CYDIPPE, while attending a sacrifice, reads the writing on an apple, which has been tossed into the shrine by Acontius and handed to her by her nurse; she then throws it away (*Heroïdes* 20, 21; the same story is told of Ctesylla and Hermocrates in Ant. Lib. 1). DIDO pours a libation on a heifer's head and inspects its entrails (*Aen.* 4.56f); she observes portents of death (*Aen.* 4.450f) and prays to three-faced Hecate (*Aen.* 4.504f). ELECTRA is found at the tomb of Agamemnon by Orestes and Pylades (Aes. *Choëph.* 84f; Soph. *Elec.* 1098f). HELEN is abducted from Artemis' altar by Theseus and Peirithoüs (*Fab.* 79). HERSE et al., in procession and at an altar, are observed by Hermes, who becomes enamored of Herse (*Met.* 2.711f). MAIDENS engaged in sacrifice are captured by pirates, along with Hymenaeus (Serv. *ad Aen.* 4.99). MEDEA, at Hecate's altar, gives Jason magic herbs (*Met.* 7.74f); she prepares a magic brew with which to rejuvenate old Aeson's body (*Met.* 7.179f, 7.234f; Sen. *Med.* 733f). PELOPIA, sacrificing and leading a dance, is watched lecherously by Thyestes (*Fab.* 88). PENELOPE prays to Athena while her suitors carouse (*Od.* 4.759f). PROETUS' DAUGHTERS sacrifice to Artemis and are cured of their madness (Bacchylides 38[x], 82f). ROMAN WOMEN perform the ritual of Bona Dea, which is invaded by Clodius, dressed as a woman (Plut. 34.10, 42.28). THEBAN WOMEN, while sacrificing to Leto, are interrupted by Niobe (*Met.* 6.165f). While TROJAN WOMEN are performing a rite, Achilles falls in love with Polyxena (Dictys 3.2; Dares 27).

By a couple. CHARICLEIA and THEAGENES meet at an altar and fall in love (*Aeth.* 3). DEUCALION and PYRRHA pray to Themis and receive her instructions (*Met.* 1.371f). PRIAM and HECUBA pray to Zeus before he sets out to recover Hector's body; they see an eagle (*Il.* 24.302f).

By a group. AENEAS, Latinus, Turnus, and their followers solemnize a truce (*Aen.* 12.161f). ARGONAUTS sacrifice before departure (*Argo.* 1.404f); with the Doliones, they celebrate the burial of Cyzicus (*Argo.* 1.1057f). HELEN's SUITORS seal with a burnt offering their oath to defend her marriage (Eur. *Iph. Aul.* 58f; *Lib.* 3.10.9). ROMANS interrupt a rite in Veii by bursting in from an underground passage (Plut. 8.5). TROJANS, on reaching Italy, pray to Athena and sacrifice to Hera (*Aen.* 3.543f); they sacrifice to Zeus at Actium and hold games (*Aen.* 3.278f); they celebrate a funeral for Polydorus (*Aen.* 3.62f) and for Anchises (*Aen.* 3.708f, 5.72f).

RITES EVOKING THE DEAD

From Hades. Are performed by CREON and a priest (Sen. *Her. Oet.* 584f). After sacrificing, ODYSSEUS calls heroines and heroes from a pit (*Od.* 11.23f).

From a tomb. DARIUS' QUEEN calls him forth (Aes. *Pers.* 606f).

OTHER SCENES

A snake, emerging from an altar, devours nestling birds and their mother (*Il.* 2.308f; *Met.* 12.11f); another tastes offerings on the altar at Anchises' tomb (*Aen.* 5.84f).

Fire (a firebrand) is taken from the altar at Delphi by Electra, with which she attacks Iphigeneia; Orestes intervenes (*Fab.* 122). Fire blazes from the offering as auspices are taken before Salamis (Plut. 7.13).

Three altars, on one a toad, on another a snake, on the third a fox, are symbols of the different realms assumed by Temenus, by Chresphontes, and by Procles and Eurysthenes together (*Lib.* 2.8.5).

AMAZON

(See **Warrior.**)

ANIMAL

(See also the particular species and **Altar, Animal Sacrifice.**)

Spoils of the hunt: attribute of Autumnus. Wild animals: Dionysus; Eros. Wild animals emerging from Minos' body attack the woman he is seducing (*Lib.* 3.15.1).

Animal shape assumed. By the Olympian GODS to escape from the monster Typhoeus (*Met.* 5.325f; *Lib.* 1.6.3); by various LESSER DEITIES (e.g., Proteus, Thetis, Metis, Nereus, Acheloüs, and Periclymenus) to escape from someone's grasp (see **Bonds** and **Wrestling**) or from a net or snare (see **Captive** and **Net**).

Men turned into animals. MEN who have been caught by Circe; they are chained or caged (*Aen.* 7.15f); they fawn on Odysseus' men (*Met.* 14.254f; *Od.* 10.212f) and are restored to human form by Circe's wand (*Met.* 14.297f). Men are changed into sheep, cattle, and wolves by Poseidon, who himself becomes a ram (*Fab.* 188). ODYSSEUS' men, when they visit Circe (*Met.* 14.276; *Ep.* 7.15; *Od.* 10.316f). PICUS' retinue, by Circe, who makes Picus himself a woodpecker (*Met.* 14.412f).

Attracted by the music of ARION (*Fasti* 2.79f); of ORPHEUS (*Met.* 10.86f; *Argo.* 1.26f).

Created by DIONYSUS to frighten the sailors, who have kidnapped him, into leaping overboard, where they become dolphins (*Met.* 3.666f).

Hybrid. The pets of Circe (*Argo.* 4.672f). Hybrids may also be a convention representing the ability of certain deities to assume various forms. (See also **Monster, Hybrid; Wrestling.**)

ANIMAL EARS

(See **Ears.**)

ANIMAL HEAD

The appropriate sacrifice to Praxidice and her daughters.

Horned, on a male body: attribute of Cephisus (see also **Bull's Head**). Three different on a female body: Artemis-Hecate-Selene: Three different on a male body: Saturnus.

ANIMAL SKIN

(See **Skin.**)

ANTS

M<small>YRMEX</small> is changed into an ant by Athena for claiming to have invented the plow (Serv. *ad Aen.* 4.402; *Fab.* 52).

Become men when an oak (Zeus) answers A<small>EACUS</small>' prayer that the population of Aegina, which a plague has destroyed, be replaced (*Met.* 7.624f; cf. *Fab.* 52 and Serv. *ad Aen.* 2.7, which do not mention Zeus' form as an oak).

Separate a pile of mixed grain for P<small>SYCHE</small> (Apuleius 9).

Fill the mouth of youthful M<small>IDAS</small> with grain (Cic. *de Div.* 1.36).

ANVIL

(See also **Arms and Armor; Forge.**)

Attribute of Hephaestus.

H<small>ERA</small> is punished by Zeus by being hung in the sky with two anvils tied to her feet (*Il.* 15.18).

APOTHEOSIS

(See **Ascension.**)

APPLE

(See also **Ball; Pomegranate; Stone.**)

Attribute of Aphrodite; Hercules; Hygeia.

M<small>ELUS</small>, after hanging himself because of Adonis' death, is transformed into an apple (Serv. *ad Ecl.* 8.37).

Given or shown to C<small>HLOË</small> by Daphnis, who climbs a tree to get it (Longus 3); to C<small>YDIPPE</small>, as she stands at an altar; she reads what her rejected suitor Acontius has written on it, and throws it away (*Heroïdes* 20, 21; a similar story is told of Ctesylla in Ant. Lib. 1).

Golden. A<small>PHRODITE</small> gives three to Hippomenes (to Melanion, according to *Lib.* 3.9.2), which he tosses before Atalanta during their race; unable to resist picking them up, she is defeated (*Met.* 10.649f; *Fab.* 185). E<small>RIS</small> (Discord) tosses one among the divine guests at the wedding of Peleus and Thetis; being claimed by Hera, Athena, and Aphrodite, it and the three goddesses are taken by Hermes to Mt. Ida, where the shepherd Paris considers the bribes they offer him and awards the apple to Aphrodite (*Ep.* 3.2; *Fab.* 92).

GAEA gives (a branch or tree of?) golden apples to Hera and Zeus at their wedding; the Hesperides become their custodians (*Lib.* 2.15.11; *Poet. Astr.* 2.3). HERACLES picks the apples of the Hesperides after killing the guardian dragon; alternatively, Atlas fetches them for him while he supports the sky in Atlas' place; he gives them to Eurystheus or to Athena, who returns them to the Hesperides (*Argo.* 4.1396f; *Lib.* 2.15.11; *Fab.* 30; *Met.* 9.130). PERSEUS visits Atlas to get the apples that are in his care (*Met.* 4.631f).

ARCH

Framing a figure, it may be a conventionalized representation of a cave.

ARM

(See also **Monster.**)

Upraised arms: attribute of Hera Hypercheiria (her surname as a protective deity).

A severed arm comes off in the hand of the Persian king's daughter when she clutches at a thief (Herod. 2.121).

Many-armed figures. AJAX OÏLEUS was believed by some to have three arms because of the dexterity with which he handled his weapons (Serv. *ad Aen.* 1.41). BRIAREÜS (Aegaeon) is brought to Olympus by Thetis to quell a revolt against Zeus (*Il.* 1.396f; *Aen.* 10.565f). COTTUS, BRIAREÜS, and GYES (The Hundred-handed) aid the gods against the Titans (Hes. *Theog.* 147f, 664f; *Lib.* 1.1.1); they guard the Titans' prison (Hes. *Theog.* 734f; *Lib.* 1.2.1), and are imprisoned underground by Ouranos (Hes. *Theog.* 150f, 617f). EURYTUS and CTEATUS (Moliones or Actoriones; twins with one body, or two bodies joined, each with his own head and arms) defeat Nestor in a chariot race (*Il.* 23.638f) and are killed in a fight by Heracles (*Lib.* 2.7.2). Six-armed GIANTS attack Heracles and the Argonauts (*Argo.* 1.942f, 1.989f). Six arms may also be an attribute of Hecate.

ARMS AND ARMOR
(See also **Helmet; Shield; Sword; Warrior; Weapon.**)

Attribute of Ares; Athena; Eirene; Enyo; Hercules; Nike; Virtus. Being burned: Honos.

Donned by ACHILLES, as he prepares to defend Iphigeneia from angry soldiers (Eur. *Iph. Aul.* 1358f) and as he prepares to rejoin the battle after

Patroclus' death (*Il.* 19.364f); by AGAMEMNON, before the fight at the Greek wall and ships (*Il.* 11.15f); by ATHENA, while Hera harnesses their chariot team (*Il.* 8.350f); by HECTOR, after he removes them from Patroclus' body (*Il.* 17.193f); by HERACLES, before fighting against Ares and Cycnus (Hes. *Sh. Her.* 122f); by old IOLAÜS, who is helped into his armor so that he can defend the children of Heracles (Eur. *Heracleidae* 721f); by JASON, after sprinkling them with Medea's magic, and before he undertakes to harness Aeëtes' fire-breathing bulls (*Argo.* 3.1246f); by old NESTOR, after Agamemnon awakens him (*Il.* 10.131f); by PARIS, before his single combat with Menelaüs (*Il.* 3.328f); by PATROCLUS, who is borrowing Achilles' armor (*Il.* 16.130f); by TURNUS, before fighting the Trojans and Aeneas (*Aen.* 11.486f, 12.87f).

Made by Hephaestus for ACHILLES, at Thetis' request (*Il.* 18.468f); for AENEAS, at Aphrodite's request (*Aen.* 8.439f); and for MEMNON at Eos' request (Serv. *ad Aen.* 1.751; *Aen.* 8.443f).

Presented by APHRODITE to Aeneas, in a wood (*Aen.* 8.608f); by ATHENA to Heracles (*Lib.* 2.4.11); by HEPHAESTUS to Heracles (*Lib.* 2.4.11) and to Thetis (*Il.* 18.614); by THETIS (and Nereïds, *Fab.* 106) to Achilles (*Il.* 19.1f). The armor of Achilles, claimed by Odysseus and Ajax, is awarded by the Greek chieftains to Odysseus (*Met.* 13.382f; *Od.* 11.543f; *Ep.* 5.6; *Fab.* 107), who subsequently gives it to Neoptolemus (*Ep.* 5.11).

Exchanged by DIOMEDES and GLAUCUS when they discover that they are guest-friends (*Il.* 6.232f).

Stripped from a dead warrior. (See **Corpse** [Stripped].)

Taken by ATHENA from Ares (*Il.* 15.123f).

Concealed in Turnus' house and there discovered (Livy 1.51).

Carried. ROMULUS in a procession carries Acron's armor on a pole (Plut. 2.16). TELEMACHUS and a beggar (Odysseus), under Athena's supervision, carry arms from the hall where the suitors are carousing (*Od.* 19.29f).

In the sky portend victory for AENEAS and his allies (*Aen.* 8.528f); portend CAESAR's murder (*Met.* 15.783f).

Placed in or by a tree. AENEAS dedicates the arms of Mezentius to Ares (*Aen.* 11.5f). APHRODITE sets down the arms she has brought to Aeneas (*Aen.* 8.608f). MARCELLUS (Plut. 16.7–8) and ROMULUS (Livy 1.10) dedicate armor to Zeus.

ARROW

(See also **Bow and Arrow; Feather; Fighting; Hunter; Huntress; Killing; Wounded Figure.**)

Attribute of Abaris (riding upon it); Aphrodite; Apollo; Artemis; Destinus.

Wounds. ACHILLES in his heel; withdrawing it, he bleeds to death (Quint. Smy. 3.80f, 3.135f). AENEAS as he tries to stop a battle; it resists extraction until Aphrodite tries (*Aen.* 12.319f, 12.400f). ALEXANDER, who shows the wound to those about him (Plut. 33.28); in another battle, after he is taken to safety, it is extracted (Plut. 33.64). APHRODITE on her breast as she fondles Eros, causing her to love Adonis (*Met.* 10.519f). A CENTAUR (q.v.). DIOMEDES in the shoulder; Athena heals him after it is pulled out (*Il.* 5.111f); in the foot; he extracts it with Odysseus' help (*Il.* 11.375f). EURY-PYLUS in the thigh; Patroclus aids him (*Il.* 11.804f, 11.842f, 15.309f). HADES, whom Heracles has shot; he goes to Olympus to be treated by Paeëon (*Il.* 5.395f); HERA on the breast (*Il.* 5.392f). MENELAÜS superficially, since Athena has averted it from a fatal spot; Agamemnon assists him (*Il.* 4.127f). PARIS, who seeks Oenone's help but is rejected; she repents too late to save him (*Lib.* 3.12.6). PHILOCTETES by falling on his foot (Serv. *ad Aen.* 3.402).

Presented to the twin babies APOLLO and ARTEMIS by Hephaestus (*Fab.* 140); to DARIUS by a Scythian herald—five of them, along with a bird, a frog, and a mouse (Herod. 4.131); to PHILOCTETES by Heracles, as a reward for igniting his pyre (*Fab.* 102).

Dipped in the Hydra's blood by HERACLES (*Fab.* 30; *Lib.* 2.5.2).

ASCENSION

(See also **Flying.**)

ASTRAEA, goddess of justice, forsakes the sinful earth (*Met.* 1.149f).

CAESAR's soul is taken from his body by Aphrodite (*Met.* 15.843f).

HELEN rises from a cave (Eur. *Hel.* 605f) or is carried by Apollo above the avenging swords of Orestes and Pylades (Eur. *Orest.* 1496f, 1625f).

HERACLES rises to heaven from his pyre (*Lib.* 2.7.7; *Met.* 9.259f; Sen. *Her. Oet.* 2048f).

HERSILIA, her hair ablaze, is taken by Iris to join her husband Romulus (*Met.* 14.846f).

ROMULUS is taken to heaven during a storm (Plut. 2.27, 4.2; Livy 1.16); he is carried up by Ares in his chariot (*Met.* 14.818f).

SEMELE is brought to Olympus from the underworld by her son Dionysus (*Lib.* 8.5.3).

ASS

(See also **Ears; Horse.**)

Attribute of Dionysus; Epona; Priapus; Silenus.

Carries DIONYSUS across a swamp without touching the water (*Poet. Astr.* 2.23).

Supports SILENUS, who is reaching into a tree for honey; it kicks him when bees attack (*Fasti* 3.747f).

Eats a rope as fast as OKNOS plaits it (Paus. 10.29.2).

Kicks and kills a LION, a disturbing portent for Alexander (Plut. 33.73).

Braying, wakes the nymph LOTIS (Vesta) in time for her to escape from lecherous Priapus (*Fasti* 1.4.5f, 6.331f); several terrify the GIANTS, causing them to flee from the gods (*Poet. Astr.* 2.23).

AXE

(See also **Beheading; Killing; Lictor; Sword.**)

Attribute of Hephaestus.

Used by ERYSICHTHON on a sacred oak, from which he draws blood; he beheads the man who interferes (*Met.* 8.741f); by HALLIRRHOTHIUS to chop down Athena's olive tree; he is decapitated when the blade comes off the handle (Serv. *ad Georg.* 1.18); by HEPHAESTUS to free Athena from within the head of Zeus (*Lib.* 1.3.6); by PARAEBIUS' FATHER to fell a tree, despite a nymph's protest (*Argo.* 2.474f); by PHILOPOEMEN to chop firewood on the order of a woman who has mistaken him for a common soldier (Plut. 19.2); by TENES to cut the ropes that moor Cycnus' ship (Paus. 10.14.2).

Used as a weapon by AEPYTUS to kill Polyphontes instead of sacrificial victims (*Fab.* 137); by the ASSASSIN of Tarquin I (Livy 1.40); by CLYTEMNESTRA (and Aegisthus?) to kill Agamemnon (Soph. *Elec.* 97f, 192f); by LYCURGUS, driven mad by Dionysus, to lop off his son's limbs (*Lib.* 3.5.1) and to kill his wife and son (*Fab.* 132); by MEROPE to try to kill her son, thinking him to be someone else; she is prevented by an old man (*Fab.* 137); by TEREUS, trying to catch and kill Procne and Philomela, who escape by becoming birds, as does Tereus in order to continue the pursuit (*Lib.* 3.14.8).

Retrieved from a river by HERMES for a woodcutter (Aesop 173).

Axe-heads are aligned by TELEMACHUS in such a way that Odysseus can shoot an arrow through the handle-holes of all of them (*Od.* 19.572, 21.118f, 21.404f).

BABY

(See also **Boy; Bundle; Eating; Girl; Human Figure, Small-scale; Suppliant.**)

DIONYSUS is sometimes represented as a baby, often in the care of Hermes.

HERACLES strangles the snakes sent by Hera, while his twin Iphicles flees (*Lib.* 2.4.8).

PROCA is attacked and badly torn by owls, but is rescued by his parents and healed by Crane (*Fasti* 6.131f).

ZEUS changes Laius et al. into birds as punishment for stealing honey (Ant. Lib. 19).

Birth of. ADONIS is delivered from the tree into which pregnant Myrrha (Smyrna) has been transformed (*Met.* 10.503f; *Fab.* 58; Serv. *ad Aen.* 5.72; Serv. *ad Ecl.* 10.18). ALEXANDER is born to Olympias, attended by the magician Nectanebos, who perhaps appears in the form of a snake (Ps.-Cal. 25–27). AMPHION and ZETHUS are born to fugitive Antiope at a road's fork (*Fab.* 7). APOLLO and ARTEMIS are born to Leto, who is grasping a palm tree and is being attended by Eileithyia (*Lib.* 1.4.1; *H. to Ap.* 3.115f; *Fab.* 140; cf. Serv. *ad Aen.* 3.73, where Artemis is said to have assisted at the birth of her twin). ARCAS is pulled from the body of a bear (Callisto), which Artemis has shot (Paus. 8.3.6). ASCLEPIUS is snatched from the body of Coronis as she lies on a burning pyre (*Met.* 2.628f; Paus. 2.26.5). CASTOR and POLYDEUCES, sons of Tyndareüs, are born to Leda (*Od.* 11.298f; cf. *Lib.* 3.10.6, which states that Castor and Clytemnestra are the offspring of Leda by Tyndareüs, and that Polydeuces and Helen are her children by Zeus, in the form of a swan). CHARICLEIA is born with white skin because at the moment of conception her mother, the black Ethiopian queen, could see a picture of white-skinned Andromeda (*Aeth.* 2, 4). DIONYSUS emerges from the thigh of Zeus (*Lib.* 3.4.3; *Met.* 3.308f); he is taken from Semele's body after she dies from the awesome sight of Zeus in all his splendor, or from his thunderbolt (*Met.* 3.297f; *Lib.* 3.4.3; *Fab.* 167; Eur. *Bacch.* 95f). Snake-legged ERICHTHONIUS springs from the seed of Hephaestus when he fails in his attempt to seduce Athena (*Fab.* 166). EURYSTHEUS is born prematurely to the wife of Sthenelus by Hera's contrivance (*Il.* 19.144f). HEPHAESTUS is born to Hera (Hes.

Theog. 927f) from her thigh (Serv. *ad Aen.* 8.454). HERACLES is delivered from Alcmene when the midwife Galanthis tricks Eileithyia into relaxing the spell that delays the birth, after which Galanthis is changed into a weasel (*Met.* 9.314f); he and his twin Iphicles are born to Alcmene (*Lib.* 2.4.8). HERMES is born to Maia in a cave, where he is laid on a winnowing fan (*Lib.* 3.10.2). MELEAGER is born to Althaea, who is attended by the three Fates (*Fab.* 171, 174). ORION grows from a bull's hide that has been urinated on and then buried (see **Urinating**). PAN, with all his goatish characteristics, is born to Penelope whom Hermes in the form of a goat has seduced (Serv. *ad Aen.* 2.44; see also **Satyr**).

At the breast. Attribute of Hera, as goddess of childbirth. ARES' SON nurses at Aerope's breast, although she has died giving birth to him (Paus. 8.44.8). HERACLES is nursed by Hera, at Athena's behest (Diod. Sic. 4.9.6); he is placed at sleeping Hera's breast by Athena; the milk spilled at her awakening becomes the Milky Way (*Poet. Astr.* 2.43). TRIPTOLEMUS is nursed by Demeter (*Fab.* 147).

Nursed or fed by an animal. By a BEAR: Atalanta (*Lib.* 3.9.2) and Paris, who is found by a shepherd (*Lib.* 3.12.5). BEES: Zeus (Serv. *ad Georg.* 4.15; Serv. *ad Aen.* 3.104). A COW: Harpalyce, after her mother dies (*Fab.* 193), and the twins of Melanippe and Poseidon (*Fab.* 186). A DEER: Telephus, son of Auge and Heracles, and Parthenopaeus, together or separately (*Fab.* 99; *Lib.* 2.7.4). A DOG: Cyrus (Herod. 1.122). A GOAT: Aegisthus, after being found by shepherds (*Fab.* 87, 88); Asclepius, who is guarded by a dog when a thunderbolt reveals his divinity (Paus. 2.26.4); Attis (Paus. 7.17.5); and Zeus (Diod. Sic. 5.703; *Fasti* 5.111; *Poet. Astr.* 2.13). A LEOPARD: Cybele (Diod. Sic. 3.58). A MARE: Camilla (*Aen.* 11.570f); Harpalyce, after her mother dies (*Fab.* 193); and Hippothoön, son of Alope and Poseidon, on two occasions; the first time he is richly dressed (*Fab.* 187). A PANTHER: one of Aura's twins; the other she dismembers and eats (Nonnus 48.910). A SHEEP: Poseidon, after being left in a sheepfold by Rhea (Paus. 8.8.2). SNAKES: Iamus, son of Evadne and Apollo (Pind. *Ol.* 6.27f). A WOLF: Miletus, son of Apollo and Acacallis (Ant. Lib. 30); Romulus and Remus, whom a shepherd finds (Plut. 2.4.7); and the twins of Philonome, after a river god rescues them (Plut. *Parallela Minora* 36). A WOODPECKER: Romulus and Remus (*Fasti* 3.5.4).

Held by mother or nurse. ACHILLES is held up by a Centaur, Cheiron's wife, for his father Peleus to see as the *Argo* sails by (*Argo.* 1.533f). AICHMAGORAS and his mother Phialo, who is tied up, are rescued by Heracles, whom a jay has led to them (Paus. 8.12.3–4). AMPHISSOS clings to

Dryope as she is turned into a tree (*Met.* 9.338f). APOLLO and ARTEMIS are carried by Leto as she flees from Hera and encounters rustics at a pool (*Met.* 6.337f). ASTYANAX is terrified by Hector's helmet but laughs when it is removed (*Il.* 6.466f). HYPNOS is held by Nyx (Hes. *Theog.* 756f; she carries Thanatos as well, Paus. 5.18.1). MELEAGER is held by Althaea, in the presence of the Fates (*Lib.* 1.8.2). OPHELTES is held by Hypsipyle, who rattles a sistrum and sings to him (Eur. *Hypsipyle,* fragment, see Rose, p. 200). ORESTES is held by Iphigeneia, as she begs Agamemnon for her life (Eur. *Iph. Aul.* 1243f). PLUTUS is held by Tyche or Eirene, representing wealth at its source (Paus. 9.16.1). SABINE WOMEN, holding their babies, intervene in the battle between their husbands and brothers (Plut. 2.19). Aeolus discovers the baby (UNNAMED) begotten by his son and daughter in the arms of its nurse, who is hidden under branches (*Heroïdes* 11.69f).

Tended or fostered. ACHILLES, by Phoenix (*Il.* 9.485f). AENEAS, by nymphs (*H. to Aph.* 5.256f). CHARILAÜS, by King Lycurgus, whom he captivates (Plut. 3.3). DIONYSUS, by the nymphs of Nysa in their cave (*Met.* 3.313f; Paus. 3.24.3–4); he is fed honey by Macris (*Argo.* 4.1131f) and washed in a spring by his nurses (Plut. 23.28). EPAPHUS, after being stolen from Io, is found by her in the care of the Queen of Byblus (*Lib.* 2.1.3). HERMAPHRODITUS, son of Hermes and Aphrodite, by nymphs in a cave (*Met.* 4.288f). PYRRHUS, by King Glaucias, whose heart he wins (Plut. 21.3). TRIPTOLEMUS is cuddled, kissed, and cured of his illness by an old woman (Demeter) (*Fasti* 4.538f). ZEUS, by nymphs (and a goat?), protected by armed Curetes (*Lib.* 1.1.6; *Fasti* 5.111f); by a youth and nymphs (Serv. *ad Aen.* 1.394); by nymphs who bathe him (Paus. 4.33.1).

Given into the care of another. ADONIS, in a chest, is given to Persephone by Aphrodite (*Lib.* 3.14.4). AMPHILOCHUS and TISIPHONE, to King Creon by their father Alcmaeon (*Lib.* 3.7.7). BABIES, to the Centaur Cheiron (see **Centaur**). CYRUS, to a herdsman and his wife (Herod. 1.109f). DEMOPHOÖN, to the goddess Demeter by his mother (*H. to Dem.* 184f). DIONYSUS, to Zeus, who sews him into his thigh (*Lib.* 3.4.3; *Met.* 3.297f; *Fab.* 167); to the nymphs of Nysa by Hermes (*Met.* 3.313f; Diod. Sic. 4.2.3, cf. 3.70.1–2, where Athena and Aristaeus assist the nymphs with their charge); to Ino and Acamas by Hermes (*Lib.* 3.4.3); to Ino by the Hyades after they rescue him from Lycurgus (*Poet. Astr.* 2.21). ERICHTHONIUS, in a chest, to the daughters of Cecrops by Athena (*Lib.* 3.14.6; Eur. *Ion* 265f). ODYSSEUS to his grandfather Autolycus by his nurse Eurycleia (*Od.* 19.399f). OEDIPUS, to a herdsman by Jocasta, and to a shepherd by the herdsman (Soph. *Oed. Tyr.* 1142f). ORESTES, to Strophius by Electra (*Ep.* 6.24; *Fab.* 119). ROMULUS and

BABY ZEUS AND THE GOAT AMALTHEIA; RHEA AND
THE CURETES

REMUS, to Larentia by her husband Faustulus (Livy 1.4; Plut. 2.4). TWIN boys to Theano by shepherds, and to King Metapontes by Theano (*Fab.* 186). ZEUS, to the nymphs of Mt. Dicte by his mother Rhea (*Lib.* 1.1.6).

Taken or held by a man. ASTYANAX is taken from Andromache in a wagon by Talthybius (Eur. *Troad.* 774f); from Andromache by Odysseus (Serv. *ad Aen.* 3.489) or from his nurse by Neoptolemus (*Ilias Mikra* 14; Schol. *ad Lycophrona* 1268). CYPSELUS, son of King Aëtion, is innocently given by his mother Labda to some men who have come to kill him; his smiles soften their hearts (Herod. 5.92). EPAPHUS is taken from Io by the Curetes on Hera's order (*Lib.* 2.1.3); cf. *Fasti* 6.513f, where it is Thyiads (Maenads) who attempt the kidnapping but are routed by Heracles. HIPPOTHOÜS, Alope's son, is brought by two shepherds, with identifying garments, to King Cercyon (*Fab.* 187). ORESTES is taken from his cradle by a beggar (Telephus), who threatens Clytemnestra and Agamemnon with their son's death unless they heed his plea (*Fab.* 101; fragment of Eur. *Telephus,* see Rose, p. 207). TELEMACHUS is taken from Penelope by Palamedes and threatened with death (*Ep.* 3.7).

Rescued by flight. APOLLO and ARTEMIS are saved from Hera by their mother Leto (*Met.* 6.346f). CAMILLA, with whom her father flees from his enemies, is hurled over a stream lashed to his spear; he then swims across (*Aen.* 11.539f). PYRRHUS' attendants save him from pursuing soldiers by crossing a river on a raft (Plut. 21.2).

Dropped, laid down, or hidden. ARCHEMORUS (Opheltes) is laid on the ground by Hypsipyle, where a snake kills him (*Lib.* 3.6.4; *Fab.* 74). CYPSELUS is hidden from assassins in a corn bin by his mother Labda (Herod. 5.92). HERMES, when he sneezes, is dropped to the ground by Apollo (*H. to Her.* 293f). TELEMACHUS is laid by Palamedes before Odysseus' plow, which a horse and an ox are pulling (*Ep.* 3.7 n. 2, Loeb edn.). TELEPHON is hidden from an assassin by Merope, who later escapes with him (*Fab.* 137). (See also **Altar, Chest, Cradle,** and **Winnowing Fan** for babies placed there.)

Exposed. (See also "Nursed or fed by an animal," above.) AEGISTHUS, by Pelopia; he is found by shepherds (*Fab.* 87, 88). AMPHION and ZETHUS, by Antiope; shepherds find them (*Lib.* 3.5.5). CAECULUS, who is found by water-carriers at a fire or hearth (Serv. *ad Aen.* 7.678f). CANACE'S BABY is left to die or to be the prey of wolves (*Heroïdes* 11.83f). CHARICLEIA; she is found by an Ethiopian (*Aeth.* 2, 4). DAPHNIS, son of Hermes; shepherds find him (Serv. *ad Ecl.* 5.20). ION, by Creüsa in a cave guarded by snakes; Hermes leaves him at Apollo's temple at Delphi, where a priestess finds him (Eur. *Ion.* 32f). OEDIPUS, with his feet pierced; he is found by a shepherd (Soph. *Oed. Tyr.* 1349f; Eur. *Phoen.* 21f, 801f; *Lib.* 3.5.7) or on the shore by Periboea (*Fab.* 66). PARIS; he is found by shepherds (*Fab.* 91). PELIAS and NELEUS, by Tyro; one twin is accidentally kicked by the horse of the man who finds them (*Lib.* 1.9.8). PSAMATHE'S BABY; it is killed by dogs (Paus. 1.43.7). (UNNAMED), to appease the Teumessian fox (*Lib.* 2.4.7).

Held in fire to be made immortal. ACHILLES, by Thetis; when Peleus interferes, Thetis throws her baby to the ground and angrily departs (*Argo.* 4.866f; *Lib.* 3.13.6; *Fab.* 147). DEMOPHON, by his nurse (Demeter); his mother interferes (*Lib.* 1.5.1; *H. to Dem.* 239f). TRIPTOLEMUS, by his nurse (Demeter); his mother snatches him out or his father interferes (*Fab.* 147; *Fasti* 4.549f; Serv. *ad Georg.* 1.19).

Thrown into or taken from fire. ASCLEPIUS is taken by Hermes from the burning body of Coronis (Paus. 2.26.5). DIONYSUS is taken from Semele's blazing body by Zeus (*Fasti* 3.503f; *Fab.* 167) or by Hermes (*Fab.* 179; *Argo.* 4.1134 f). MEGARA'S SONS are hurled into a fire by their mad father Heracles (*Lib.* 2.4.12).

Thrown or held in water. ACHILLES is dipped into the Styx by Thetis, to make him invulnerable (Serv. *ad Aen.* 1.57). EUMOLPUS is thrown into the sea by his mother Chione and rescued by his father Poseidon (*Lib.* 3.15.4).

RHESUS is thrown into the river of his father, the god Strymon, by his mother, the Muse Euterpe (Eur. *Rhes.* 926f). The TWIN SONS of Ares are thrown into the river Erymanthus by Philonome but are saved by its resident deity (Plut. *Parallela Minora* 36).

Hurled to death. ASTYANAX, from the walls of Troy (*Ep.* 5.23; *Met.* 13.415), by Odysseus (Eur. *Troad.* 774f; Serv. *ad Aen.* 3.489) or by Neoptolemus (*Ilias Mikra* 14; Schol. *ad Lycophrona* 1268). CANACE'S BABY is thrown by Aeolus to his dogs when he learns it is the child of his own son and daughter (*Heroïdes* 11 ; *Fab.* 238). CLYTEMNESTRA'S BABY is torn from her breast and dashed to the ground by Agamemnon after he has killed her husband Tantalus (Eur. *Iph. Aul.* 1149f). LEARCHUS is dashed against a rock by his mad father Athamas (*Met.* 4.515f).

Killed. (See also **Killing; Sword.**) LEARCHUS is shot with an arrow by his mad father Athamas (*Lib.* 1.9.2). ONE of her twins is dismembered by their mad mother Aura, who then leaps into the sea (Nonnus 260). TWINS are killed by their mother Themisto, who mistakes them for Ino's children; she afterward kills herself (*Fab.* 1–5).

BACCHANTS

(See **Mad Women; Maenads.**)

BAG

(See also **Bundle; Wineskin.**)

Attribute of Aeolus.

Containing winds is given to ODYSSEUS by Aeolus; Odysseus' sailors open it while he sleeps, and a violent storm arises (*Od.* 10.19f; *Met.* 14.233f).

In which to carry Medusa's head is given to PERSEUS by the three Phorcides, along with winged sandals and a hat to make him invisible (*Lib.* 2.4.2).

BALD-HEADED

(See **Head.**)

BALL

(See also **Apple; Globe; Stone.**)

Two balls: attribute of Jupiter.

Offered to ALEXANDER, along with a letter, a thong, and a chest, by an embassy from Darius (Ps.-Cal. 103–106); to EROS by Aphrodite to induce him to shoot an arrow at Medea (*Argo.* 3.132).

Played with by ALEXANDER and his friends (Plut. 33.39); by DANCERS at Alcinoüs' banquet for Odysseus (*Od.* 8.370f); by the boy GLAUCUS, causing him to fall into a jar of honey (*Fab.* 136); by NAUSICAÄ and her friends on a beach (*Od.* 6.99f).

BANNER

Carried by a nude man on horseback fleeing from Fate: attribute of Fortuna.
Carried in battle (see **Standard**).

BANQUET

(See **Drinking; Eating.**)

BARBARIAN

(See also **Fighting.**)

GAULS, invading Greece, attack Delphi and are routed by lightning, a shower of stones, and the Delphians, aided by several ghostly heroes (Paus. 1.4.4, 10.23.3); they become intoxicated when introduced to wine by Arron (Plut. 8.15). Invading Italy, they enter Rome where the senators calmly await them; one of the Gauls touches the beard of M. Papirius, who strikes back and is killed; they sack and burn the city; they steal up the Capitoline Hill and are repelled when discovered; their chief Brennus adds his sword to the scales as tribute is being weighed; they are ordered by Camillus to depart (Plut. 8.22f; Livy 5.41f). VERCINGETORIX rides into the Roman siege-works at Alesia to surrender to Caesar (Plut. 34.30).

BARREL

(See also **Vessel.**)

Forms DIOGENES' shelter, to which Alexander pays a visit (Plut. 33.14).

BASKET

Of fruits: attribute of Demeter (Ceres). Carried on the head: a Canephoros (a virgin assisting at certain rites).

A CANEPHOROS WITH A BASKET OF SACRED OBJECTS

BAT

Attribute of Diana; Nox.

MINYAS' DAUGHTERS are transformed into bats as they weave and spin; and their tapestries are changed into vines because they ignore Dionysus (*Met.* 4.389f).

BATHING

(See also **Sea; Swimming; Washing; Water.**)

This commonplace subject in art is often unrelated to a particular incident.

GODDESSES OR NYMPHS

Surprised. APHRODITE by Erymanthus, who is attacked by a boar (Apollo) (Ptolem. Heph. 1.306). ARETHUSA by the river god Alpheius, from whom she flees (*Met.* 5.585f). ARTEMIS and her nymphs by the hunter Actaeon, who is turned into a stag (*Met.* 3.155f; *Lib.* 3.4.2). ATHENA and CHARICLO by the seer Teiresias, whom they punish with blindness (*Lib.* 3.6.7).

Make a discovery that CALLISTO, one of Artemis' nymphs, is pregnant, for which she is banished (*Met.* 2.460f); that one of Daphne's companions is a man (LEUCIPPUS), whom they immediately kill with their hunting spears (Paus. 8.20.2).

Lose a sandal to an eagle. APHRODITE (*Poet. Astr.* 2.16). RHODOPIS (Strabo 17.1.33; Aelian 13.33).

Punished. AURA, one of Artemis' company, makes an unflattering remark about her patron while they are bathing, for which she is made to submit to Dionysus (Nonnus 48.335f). SCYLLA finds dogs' heads sprouting from her waist because she has won the love of Glaucus away from the goddess Circe (*Met.* 14.51f; *Fab.* 199; cf. Serv. *ad Aen.* 3.420, where it is suggested that Poseidon punished her for preferring Glaucus to himself).

MEN

In sea or stream. ALEXANDER, in the Cydnus River (Plut. 33.19); MIDAS, in the Pactolus River (*Fab.* 191; cf. *Met.* 11.134f, where he is showered by a spring—also in order to rid himself of the "golden touch "); ODYSSEUS (*Od.* 6.223f, 7.295f); ODYSSEUS and DIOMEDES (*Il.* 10.572f).

In a tub. AGAMEMNON, where he is killed by Clytemnestra (Aes. *Agam.* 1107f; Aes. *Choëph.* 1070f; Aes. *Eumen.* 461f, 633f). MINOS, where he is drenched with boiling water or pitch by the daughters of Cocalus (*Ep.* 1.15, n. 5, Loeb edn.). ODYSSEUS, where he is attended by Circe and her maids (*Od.* 10.358f), by Eurynome, after the slaughter of the suitors (*Od.* 23.153f), by Calypso (*Od.* 5.264), and by maids in the palace of Alcinoüs (*Od.* 8.433f).

BEACON

(See **Fire; Light; Torch.**)

BEAR

Nurses baby ATALANTA (*Lib.* 3.9.2); baby PARIS (*Lib.* 3.12.5).

CALLISTO (Helice; Serv. *ad Georg.* 1.138) is changed into a bear by Zeus to conceal his seduction of her (or she is changed by a jealous Hera). She is shot by Artemis at Hera's command and delivered by Zeus of baby Arcas as she dies. In another version she is attended by Hermes when she gives birth to Arcas, who later hunts her down. Both she and her son become constellations (*Fab.* 177; *Poet. Astr.* 2.1.4; *Lib.* 3.8.2; *Met.* 2.477f; Paus. 8.3.6).

In this form, the river god CRIMISUS seduces Egesta (Serv. *ad Aen.* 1.550).

BEARD

Attribute of Boreas; the Indian Dionysus; Hephaestus; Heracles; Odysseus; Zeus.

Of "watery" appearance: attribute of personifications of the ocean, rivers, rain-carrying winds (especially Notus; *Met.* 1.264f); and of the minor sea god Glaucus.

Worn by a woman: attribute of Venus (Serv. *ad Aen.* 2.632 mentions a statue of Venus Barbata on Cyprus that was worshiped by men dressed as women and by women dressed as men); also, attribute of a priestess of Athena at Pedasia (Herod. 1.175, 8.104).

BEARSKIN

(See **Skin, of Animal.**)

BED

(See also **Dying Figure; Litter; Seduction; Sleeping Figure.**)

Type of bed. Sleeping HELIUS, the sun god, is transported in a golden bed from his setting to his rising (Athenaeus 11.470). MEDEA and JASON's bridal bed is fleece-covered (*Argo.* 4.1141f). PENELOPE and ODYSSEUS' bed has an olive trunk, still rooted, for a post (*Od.* 23.183f).

Women approaching a bed. ANNA PERENNA, disguised as Athena, is led by Ares; he is much chagrined when he discovers that his intended bride is an aged crone who mocks him (*Fasti* 3.677f). NYCTIMENE steals into her father's bed; upon leaving it, she becomes an owl (*Met.* 2.589f; *Fab.* 204). SMYRNA is led to her father's bed by her nurse (*Fab.* 204).

Place of sickness or death. ALEXANDER trustingly drinks medicine as his physician reads a letter that accuses him of planning Alexander's death (Plut. 33.19; Ps.-Cal. 155f); he drinks poisoned medicine (Arrian 7.27.1); dying, he is visited by his officers (Plut. 33.76; Arrian 7.26.1) and soldiers (Ps.-Cal. 270); he gives the hand of Roxane, his wife, to Perdiccas (Ps.-Cal.

279). ANTIOCHUS is visited by Queen Stratonike and a physician (Plut. 43.38). GERMANICUS, attended by his wife and friends, dies (Tac. *An.* 2.71, 72). ORESTES, being nursed by Electra, is visited by Furies (Eur. *Orest.* 211f). TIBARINI HUSBANDS take to their beds when their wives are about to give birth, and are cared for by them (*Argo.* 2.1011f).

Place of punishment or violence. AGRIPPINA is murdered by Nero's soldiers (Tac. *An.* 14.5.8). A GOD who has broken an oath sworn by the waters of the Styx is made to lie abed in a coma for a year (Hes. *Theog.* 793f). LUCRETIA is raped by Tarquin (Livy 1.58; *Fasti* 2.792f). PROCRUSTES' guest is fitted to his bed by being stretched or trimmed (*Ep.* 1.4; *Fab.* 38; Plut. 1.11).

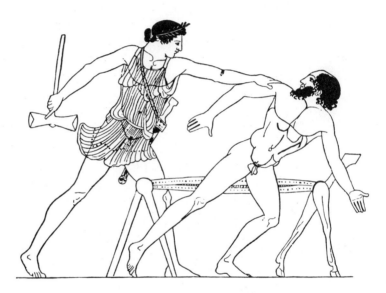

PROCRUSTES, HIS BED, AND THESEUS

BEES

Attribute of Artemis of Ephesus.

A swarm alights in the top of a laurel tree; this portends to King LATINUS and the Latins the coming of the Trojans to Italy (*Aen.* 7.59f).

Are born from the carcasses of animals sacrificed by ARISTAEUS (*Georg.* 4.58f) or from a calf buried by him (*Fasti* 1.377f); from the body of old MELISSA, a devotee of Demeter, after she has been killed by angry women (Serv. *ad Aen.* 1.430).

Bring honey to baby ZEUS (*Georg.* 4.149f; Serv. *ad Georg.* 3.104, 4.15) and provide the honey that Macris feeds to baby DIONYSUS (*Argo.* 4.1131f).

Sting EROS, who is raiding their hive; Aphrodite then comforts him (Theocritus 19); LAIUS et al., whom Zeus then changes into birds (Ant. Lib. 19); and SILENUS, who is standing on his donkey reaching for their honey (*Fasti* 3.737f).

Are chased by an owl, which signifies to the seer POLYIDUS that Minos' son is to be found in a jar of honey (*Fab.* 136).

In this form, PERICLYMENUS attempts to escape from the grasp of Heracles (*Lib.* 1.9.9).

BEGGAR

(See also **Castaway; Old Man.**)

ODYSSEUS, disguised as a beggar, steals into Troy, where he meets Helen, kills some sentries, and steals the Palladium (*Od.* 4.244f; *Ep.* 5.13; Eur. *Rhes.* 501f, 710f); he is recognized by Helen and begs Hecuba for his life (Eur. *Hec.* 240f); he is transformed by Athena with her staff into a beggar (*Od.* 13.429f, 16.454f; all following citations are from the *Odyssey*); he is welcomed by the swineherd Eumaeus and given food (17.345f); meets his son Telemachus in Eumaeus' hut (16.42f); is reviled and kicked by the goatherd Melantheus (17.197f); is provoked by another beggar, Arnaeus, whom he knocks down (18.8f); finds carousing suitors of Penelope in possession of his palace (17.336f, 20.257f, 24.151f); begs for food (20.365f); talks to the maids and suitors (18.311f, 18.343f); is struck by objects thrown at him (17.409f, 17.462f, 18.394f, 20.299f); his scar is recognized by his old nurse Eurycleia when she washes his feet (19.386f); he prays to Zeus who thunders from a clear sky, an omen that is interpreted by a woman working at a mill (20.97f); he reveals his identity to the faithful servants (21.190f); strings his bow and slays the suitors (bks. 20–22 pass., 24.147f); sits with Penelope, who is still uncertain of his identity (23.88f).

TELEPHUS holds baby Orestes hostage, threatening to kill him unless his wound is healed by Achilles (fragment of Eur. *Telephus,* see Rose, p. 207).

BEHEADING

(See also **Axe; Head.**)

AJAX OÏLEUS beheads Imbrius and flings the head at Hector's feet (*Il.* 13.201f).

DIOMEDES beheads the spy Dolon (*Il.* 10.454f; *Met.* 13.243f).

ERYSICHTHON beheads the man who tries to stop him from chopping a tree (*Met.* 8.768f).

FLAMININUS (or another man at his order) beheads a condemned prisoner at a party simply to satisfy a young friend's whim (Plut. 20.18; at 18.17 Plutarch tells the same story about L. Quintius).

HERACLES beheads the opponent of his friend Daphnis after he has saved Daphnis from defeat in a reaping contest (Serv. *ad Ecl.* 8.68).

HERMES beheads many-eyed Argus, the guard of a heifer (Io), after lulling him to sleep (*Met.* 1.715f).

HYLLUS (Iolaüs) beheads Eurystheus (*Lib.* 2.8.1).

LICTORS, by Brutus' order, execute Brutus' traitorous sons (Plut. 6.6; Livy 2.4.5) and the disobedient son of Torquatus (Livy 8.7).

ODYSSEUS beheads Leiodes, one of Penelope's suitors, despite his plea for mercy (*Od.* 22.326f).

OENOMAÜS beheads a suitor of his daughter after overtaking the chariot in which they are fleeing (*Ep.* 2.5).

PERSEUS, using his shield as a mirror and guided by Athena, beheads sleeping Medusa (*Lib.* 2.4.2–3).

TORQUATUS beheads his son for engaging in single combat against his order (Val. Max. 2.7.6, 6.9.1).

BELLOWS

(See also **Bag.**)

Attribute of Aeolus.

BELT

A belt at the waist (ZONA) is an attribute of Aphrodite and of Ares. It may be worn by either sex. A sword belt (BALTEUS) hangs diagonally from the shoulder.

ZONA

Given by AJAX to Hector, who presents his sword in return after their inconclusive combat (*Il.* 7.303f); by APHRODITE to Hera, to enable her to seduce Zeus (*Il.* 14.214f); by HERACLES to Eurystheus for his wife Admete (*Lib.*

2.5.9; *Fab.* 30); by HIPPOLYTE, the Amazon queen, to Heracles as ransom for Melanippe (*Argo.* 2.966f).

Taken by HERACLES from Hippolyte's body after he kills her (*Fab.* 30; *Lib.* 2.5.9) or from her after he takes her captive (Diod. Sic. 2.46.4).

Found. DEMETER finds the belt of her abducted daughter Persephone in a pool (*Met.* 5.468f).

BALTEUS *Given* by HECTOR to Ajax along with sword and scabbard in exchange for Ajax's scarlet zona (*Il.* 7.303f).

Taken from the body of PALLAS by Turnus after their fight (*Aen.* 10.495f).

Worn by the shade of HERACLES when he converses with Odysseus (*Od.* 11.601f); by TURNUS in combat with Aeneas; the sight of this balteus (taken from Pallas and now on Turnus' shoulder) causes Aeneas to reject his plea for mercy (*Aen.* 12.941f).

BIRD

(See also **Bat; Butterfly.**)

ALLEGORICAL Feathered FAMA has many eyes, ears, and tongues with which to gather and spread rumors (*Aen.* 4.173f, 4.298f, 7.104f).

COCK Attribute of Aesculapius; Apollo; Athena; Aurora; Eros; Helius; Hermes.

Is plucked by DIOGENES and shown to his pupils (Diog. Laërt. 6.2.40).

CORMORANT AESACUS, after leaping into the sea from grief at Hesperia's death, is turned into a cormorant by Tethys (*Met.* 11.783f).

CRANE The Pygmy queen GERANA is turned into a crane by Hera (*Met.* 6.90f).

PYGMIES fight with cranes (*Il.* 3.3f).

CROW Attribute of Apollo; Athena; a Fury (q.v.).

Changed into this form. APOLLO, to escape from the Giant Typhoeus (*Met.* 5.329); ARNE, because she betrayed her city for gold (*Met.* 7.466f); CORONIS, daughter of Coroneus, while trying to flee from Poseidon, is transformed by Athena and becomes her companion (*Met.* 2.569f).

In flight. Crows lead ALEXANDER and his retinue to Ammon's temple in the Libyan desert (Plut. 33.27); one falls stunned by shouting in the Roman Forum (Plut. 32.25) and several are felled by the din raised at the Isthmian games when Flaminius declares peace (Plut. 20.10).

Carries a bowl to collect figs for APOLLO and returns with a snake (*Fasti* 2.251f); to fetch water for Apollo's sacrifice but tarries to eat figs before returning (*Poet. Astr.* 2.40).

Speaking, tattles to APOLLO about his beloved Coronis' faithlessness to him (*Met.* 2.631f); reports to ATHENA that the chest she has given to Cecrops' daughters to guard has been opened and a baby and a snake found within (*Met.* 2.557f; *Fab.* 166); tells the seer MOPSUS not to accompany Jason to his tryst with Medea (*Argo.* 3.927f).

CUCKOO

In this form, ZEUS seduces Hera during a storm (Paus. 2.17.4, 2.36.3; Schol. on Theocritus 15.64).

DOVE

Changed into this form. ANIUS' DAUGHTERS by Dionysus, to free them from enslavement by the Greeks attacking Troy (*Met.* 13.673f). PELEIA, after hanging herself from grief for Adonis (Serv. *ad Ecl.* 8.37).

In flight, precedes the *Argo* between the "Dark Rocks" (Symplegades) (*Argo.* 2.317f, 2.555f; *Lib.* 1.9.22; *Fab.* 19); rises from the body of ALCIDAMAS' DAUGHTER (*Met.* 7.369f); pursued by a hawk, takes refuge in JASON's lap as the hawk smashes into the ship (*Argo.* 3.540f); two doves lead AENEAS and the Sibyl to a golden fleece that hangs in a tree (*Aen.* 6.190f).

Speaking, tell HERACLES the prophecies of an oracular oak (Soph. *Trach.* 169f); orders a WOODSMAN to stop cutting an oracular oak (Serv. *ad Aen.* 3.466).

Are held by ACHILLES in order to lure Troïlus into his grasp (Serv. *ad Aen.* 1.474).

Is tied as a target for archers (*Il.* 23.852f; *Aen.* 5.487).

Dies after drinking wine that ION has poured from his cup (Eur. *Ion* 1192f).

EAGLE

Attribute of Apollo; Ceres; Fidius; Zeus.

Changed into this form. A BOY, favorite of Zeus, by jealous Hera (Serv. *ad Aen.* 1.394f). PERICLYMENUS, by Poseidon to save him from Heracles (*Fab.* 10). A SNAKE (Nectanebos), after he has made Olympias pregnant with Alexander (Ps.-Cal. 21).

In this form, APHRODITE pursues a swan (Zeus), which takes refuge in the lap of Nemesis (*Poet. Astr.* 2.8); Periclymenus attacks Heracles, who then shoots him (*Met.* 12.559f); Zeus embraces Asteria (*Met.* 6.105).

Carries off or drops a BABY (Zeus) to rescue him from Cronus (Serv. *ad Aen.* 1.394); a BOY (Ganymede) to serve the gods (*Met.* 10.155f; *Lib.* 3.12.2; *Aen.* 5.250f); the CAP from the head of Lucumo (he is in a carriage with his wife), and then replaces it (Livy 1.34); a DOVE, above Priam at an altar (Quint. Smy. 1.196f), and above Penelope's suitors (*Od.* 20.242f); a FAWN (*Il.* 8.245f); a GOOSE, as Telemachus prepares to sail (*Od.* 15.160f); a JAR that it fills from the Styx, guarded by dragons, and brings to Psyche (Apuleius 9); the OFFERING that Alexander is about to sacrifice (Ps.-Cal. 89, 91); a SANDAL, while Aphrodite is bathing, and gives it to Hermes (*Poet. Astr.* 2.16); also one belonging to Rhodopis, as she too bathes, to give to the Egyptian king (Strabo 17.1.33; Aelian 13.33); a SNAKE, which it drops among the Trojans as they prepare to assault the Greek camp (*Il.* 12.200f); a SWAN and is attacked by other swans (*Aen.* 12.247f); a TORTOISE, on Aeschylus' bald pate (Val. Max. 9.12b.2).

Fighting. Two eagles fight in the air above Penelope's suitors (*Od.* 2.146f). One eagle is attacked and routed by a falcon above the Persian queen, as she stands at Phoebus' altar (Aes. *Pers.* 205f).

Shot by Heracles. PERICLYMENUS, who, in the form of an eagle, has attacked him (*Met.* 12.559f). The TORMENTOR of Prometheus (Hes. *Theog.* 521f; *Fab.* 31, 54, 144; *Lib.* 1.7.2, 2.5.11).

Flies over ALEXANDER while he is addressing his army (Plut. 33.33); over the *Argo* (*Argo.* 2.1251f); over HERACLES as he prays that Telamon be given a son (*Lib.* 3.12.7); over PRIAM as he drives from Troy to ransom Hec-

GANYMEDE AND THE EAGLE

tor's body from Achilles (*Il.* 24.315f); over the TROJAN and GREEK armies (*Il.* 13.821f).

Pursues a swan (Zeus) on his way to seduce Leda (Eur. *Hel.* 18f).

Tears at PROMETHEUS, who is chained to a cliff (Aes. *Prom.* 1022f).

An eagle-like bird, the Phoenix, dies in its nest, and from its body a young one is born (*Met.* 15.391f); the young bird brings its dead parent, covered with myrrh, to the Egyptian Temple of the Sun for burial (Herod. 2.73).

GOOSE

In this form, NEMESIS mates with a swan (Zeus) (*Lib.* 3.10.7).

Flees from CORA (Persephone) and Hercyna; when it is pulled from its hiding place, a spring gushes forth (Paus. 9.39.2); from old PHILEMON and BAUCIS, who wish to serve it to their guests (Zeus and Hermes) (*Met.* 8.684f).

Geese, with their cackling, alert the ROMANS to the Gauls who are climbing the Capitoline (Livy 5.47; Plut. 8.27); are clothed in finery to honor their saving the Capitoline, while the ineffective watchdogs are crucified (Serv. *ad Aen.* 8.652).

GUINEA HEN

MELEAGER's sorrowing sisters become guinea hens (*Fab.* 174; *Met.* 8.543f).

GULL

CEŸX is turned into a gull and his wife Alcyone into a halcyon (*Lib.* 1.7.4).

HALCYON

ALCYONE, upon finding Ceÿx drowned, leaps into the sea and becomes a halcyon, as does Ceÿx at Alcyone's caress; they nest on a calm sea (*Fab.* 65; *Met.* 11.731f).

Flying over sleeping JASON, speaks to Mopsus and Acastus (*Argo.* 1.1080).

HAWK

DAEDALION is changed into a hawk by Apollo when he throws himself from a cliff out of grief for his daughter Chione (*Met.* 11.339f; *Fab.* 200).

Pursues a dove, which takes refuge in JASON's lap (*Argo.* 3.540f).

Fighting. A hawk fights an eagle above the Queen of Persia as she stands at Phoebus' altar (Aes. *Pers.* 205f). Seven hawks attack two vultures, watched by Darius et al. (Herod. 3.76).

Carrying a DOVE flies over Telemachus' ship (*Od.* 15.525f); the ENTRAILS of a bull that Briareüs is about to sacrifice, brings them to Zeus (*Fasti* 3.799f); a NIGHTINGALE (in a fable illustrating that "might is right," Hes. *W. & D.* 203f).

HERON   Flies to encourage ODYSSEUS and DIOMEDES (an omen sent by Athena) (*Il.* 10.274f); from the ashes of TURNUS' city Ardea (*Met.* 14.573f).

HOOPOE   In this form, TEREUS pursues a nightingale and a swallow (Philomela and Procne) (*Met.* 6.666f; *Fab.* 45; *Lib.* 3.14.8).

IBIS   In this form, HERMES escapes from the monster Typhoeus (*Met.* 5.331).

JAY   By its screaming, attracts HERACLES to the place where Phialo with her baby is tied (Paus. 8.12.3).

KINGFISHER   (See **Halcyon.**)

MAGPIE   PIERUS' DAUGHTERS, after the one of them chosen to compete with the Muse Calliope in singing is judged the loser, are changed into magpies (*Met.* 5.305f, 5.662f); they perch in a tree over the heads of Athena and the Muses (*Met.* 5.294f).

NIGHTINGALE   *Changed into this form.* AËDON, who has unwittingly killed her son (*Od.* 19.518f); PHILOMELA, who flees with a swallow (Procne) from a hoopoe (Tereus) (*Met.* 6.666f; *Fab.* 45; *Lib.* 3.14.8).

OSPREY   *Changed into this form.* ATHENA, who after addressing Nestor and Telemachus, flies away (*Od.* 3.371f); NISUS attacks Scylla in the water by Minos' ship, and she becomes a bird (*Met.* 8.142f) or a fish (*Fab.* 198).

OWL   Attribute of Athena; Mors; Nox; Somnus. It may portend evil or some dire event.

    Changed into this form. ASCALAPHUS, by Demeter (*Lib.* 2.5.12) or by Persephone, who sprinkles him with water (*Met.* 5.543f); NYCTIMENE, after visiting her father's bed or being seduced by him (*Met.* 2.589f; *Fab.* 204).

    Perching on a rooftop as DIDO prepares to kill herself (*Aen.* 4.462f); warns MYRRHA as she is being led by her nurse to her father's bed (*Met.* 10.452f); on a pillar to which OTUS and EPHIALTES are bound with snakes (*Fab.* 28); in the bridal chamber of PROCNE and TEREUS, where Furies also are present (*Met.* 6.430f).

    In flight. An owl drives away bees, an omen that enables the seer POLYIDUS to find Minos' son in a jar of honey (*Fab.* 136); owls attack PROCAS' infant son but are driven off by Crane's magic (*Fasti* 6.131f); an owl goes to THEMISTOCLES' ship among the Greek fleet at Salamis (Plut. 7.12); an owl hovers over TURNUS and beats on his shield (*Aen.* 12.881f).

PARTRIDGE   A falling BOY, pushed from a height by Daedalus, is changed into a partridge by Athena (*Met.* 8.250).

Watches DAEDALUS bury Icarus (*Met.* 8.236f).

PEACOCK   Attribute of Hera.

HERA decorates the tail of a peacock with the eyes of Argus (*Met.* 1.722f).

PELICAN   POLYTECHNUS is changed into a pelican (Ant. Lib. 11).

QUAIL   Attribute of Artemis.

ASTERIA dives into the sea to escape Zeus and is changed into a quail (*Lib.* 1.4.1), which Zeus then transforms into the island of Delos (*Fab.* 53).

In this form, ZEUS seduces Leto (Serv. *ad Aen.* 3.72).

Flies out from ALCIBIADES' robe as a crowd is applauding him (Plut. 11.10).

RAVEN   (See **Crow.**)

SPARROW   Attribute of Aphrodite.

LESBIA's pet sparrow pecks her finger playfully, arousing Catullus' envy (Cat. 2).

Is devoured by a snake along with her eight young, a number (nine) that forecasts the years the Greeks will fight at Troy before they capture it in the tenth (*Il.* 2.309f).

STORK   Attribute of Fides; Pietas.

ANTIGONE is changed into a stork by Hera (*Met.* 6.93f).

SWALLOW   Attribute of Aphrodite.

PROCNE is changed into a swallow. She flees with her sister Philomela (a nightingale) from a hoopoe (Tereus) (*Met.* 6.666f; *Fab.* 45; *Lib.* 3.14.8).

In this form, Athena watches the battle of Odysseus et al. against Penelope's suitors (*Od.* 22.239f).

Flies or perches above sleeping Alexander and awakens him (Arrian 1.25.6).

SWAN	Attribute of Aphrodite; Apollo; Clio; Erato; Fortuna (riding upon a swan).

CYGNUS is changed into a swan in order to escape from Achilles, who is strangling him (*Met.* 12.72f).

In this form, ZEUS mates with Leda (*Met.* 6.111; *Fab.* 77; *Lib.* 3.10.6) and with a goose (Nemesis) (*Lib.* 3.10.7); pursued by an eagle (Aphrodite), he takes refuge in the lap of Nemesis (*Poet. Astr.* 2.8), or in the arms of Leda (Eur. *Hel.* 18f).

In flight. A swan attacks an eagle that is grasping another swan (*Aen.* 12.247f). Twelve swans are scattered by an eagle, as a huntress (Aphrodite) and Aeneas look on (*Aen.* 1.39f).

VULTURE

Attribute of Pluto.

Fighting with hawks (see **Hawk**).

In this form, APOLLO and ATHENA perch in a tree watching warriors fighting (*Il.* 7.58f).

Several feed on the ever-renewed liver of gigantic TITYOS, in chains in Hades (*Od.* 11.576f; *Aen.* 6.594f; *Met.* 4.457f).

Twelve are seen by ROMULUS, six by REMUS as they practice divination, each on a different hill (Plut. 2.9; Livy 1.7).

Speaks to the seer MELAMPUS as he sacrifices bulls (*Lib.* 1.9.12).

Wearing collars, vultures are mascots of MARIUS' soldiers (Plut. 22.17).

WOODPECKER

Attribute of Mars; Picus.

PICUS is changed into a woodpecker by Circe, after being led to her by a phantom boar (*Met.* 14.386f, 16.558f).

Brings food to babies ROMULUS and REMUS (Plut. 1.2.7; *Fasti* 3.54).

UNSPECIFIED

With a woman's head (see **Harpies; Sirens**).

Changed into this form. ANTHUS, after being torn apart by horses (Ant. Lib. 7); COMBE, enabling her to escape death at the hands of her sons (*Met.* 7.382f); LAIUS et al., trying to steal honey from baby Zeus (Ant. Lib. 19); MEMNON's comrades, when they visit his tomb (Serv. *ad Aen.* 1.751); SCYLLA, while swimming after Minos' ship and being attacked by an osprey (*Met.* 8.142f); THEBAN WOMEN, distressed by Ino's leap into the sea; others of them are turned to stone (*Met.* 4.543f).

In this form, CAENUS escapes from the trees piled on him by Centaurs (*Met.* 12.510f); HYPNOS, perched in a tree, watches Zeus make love to Hera

(*Il.* 14.286f); POSEIDON seduces the nymph Medusa in Athena's shrine (*Met.* 4.798f, 6.119f); THETIS tries to escape from the grasp of Peleus (*Met.* 11.243).

In flight. A bird drops a stone on ALEXANDER's head as he performs a sacrifice (Arrian 2.26.4). Several lead Alexander and his retinue across Libya to Ammon's temple (Arrian 3.3.6). Birds rise from MEMNON's pyre and fall back into the flames (*Met.* 13.604f); fall into a lake that has been made noxious because of PHAËTHON's fall into it (*Argo.* 4.596f), or because it lies at the entrance to the underworld (*Aen.* 6.237f); are observed by GORDIUS as he is plowing (Justin 11.7.5) and by the priest-king NUMA (Plut. 4.7). One is shot by ANTENOR and falls at the spot where he is to build a city (Serv. *ad Aen.* 1.242). STYMPHALIAN birds, using feathers as arrows, attack the Argonauts and are driven off by the noise of shouting, rattles, and the clashing of spears on shields (*Argo.* 2.1033f; *Fab.* 20); they are put to flight by Heracles with a bronze rattle or castanets (*Argo.* 2.1052f; *Lib.* 2.5.6).

A white bird observes the seduction of Apollo's beloved Coronis, daughter of Phlegyas, by a youth of Thessaly; when it reports this to Apollo, he turns it black (*Met.* 2.535f, 2.631f).

A four-legged bird carries Oceanus to visit Prometheus, who is in chains in the Caucasus (Aes. *Prom.* 286f, 397f).

Birds eat the flour with which ALEXANDER has marked out the walls of Alexandria (Plut. 33.26); sing to the seer TEIRESIAS, to whom Athena has given understanding of their song (*Lib.* 3.6.7); come before ZEUS to be judged for beauty (Aesop 101).

BIRD-FOOTED

Attribute of the Sirens (q.v.) and of the daughters of Stymphalus (Paus. 8.22.7).

BIRTHMARK

Spear-shaped, identifies to King Creon his grandson (*Fab.* 72; fragment of Eur. *Antig.*, see Rose, p. 203).

BLACK SKIN

(See **Dark Skin.**)

BLINDFOLD

(See also **Eye.**)

Attribute of Eros; Fortuna; Furor; Justitia.

BLIND MAN

(See **Eye.**)

BLOOD

(See also **Wounded Figure.**)

From the body of ACHILLES, flows from his heel when he removes Paris' arrow (Quint. Smy. 3.80f); of ACIS, who has been buried beneath a rock, becomes the spring of a horned river god (*Met.* 13.885f); of ADONIS, wounded by a boar, is changed into flowers by Aphrodite (*Met.* 10.731f); of AJAX, who has fallen on his sword, becomes hyacinths (*Met.* 13.394f); of HYACINTHUS, whom Apollo's discus has killed, becomes a white flower (*Met.* 10.209f); of MEDUSA, dripping from her head, produces snakes (*Met.* 4.614f) and from her neck, the winged horse Pegasus (*Met.* 4.785f; *Lib.* 2.4.2); of the Centaur NESSUS, is given by him in a jar to Deïaneira after Heracles shoots him (*Lib.* 2.7.6); of OURANOS, castrated by Cronus, produces Furies or Giants (*Lib.* 1.1.4; Hes. *Theog.* 176f); of PYRAMUS, spurts aloft to stain mulberries red (*Met.* 4.121f); of SENECA and his wife, drains away from their wrists, while Seneca uses his final hour dictating to a scribe (Tac. *An.* 15.60); of gigantic TALOS, drains from his ankle as he tries to pelt the *Argo* with rocks (*Argo.* 4.1677f; *Lib.* 1.9.26).

Drips from shoots uprooted on Polydorus' grave by AENEAS (*Aen.* 3.27f); from flowers picked by DRYOPE, who is changed into a tree (*Met.* 9.342f).

Pool. CYRUS' head is placed in a pool of blood by his conqueror, Queen Tomyris (Herod. 1.214; Val. Max. 9.106.1).

BLOW

(See **Boxing; Fist; Hand.**)

BOAR

(See also **Altar, Animal Sacrifice; Pig.**)

Attribute of either Tydeus or Polyneices, with a lion symbolizing the other. These identifications may be made by their shield devices or other convention. By the manner of their fighting, Adrastus identifies them as the heroes whom an oracle has foretold will be his sons-in-law (Eur. *Suppl.* 140f; *Lib.* 3.6.1).

Grasped or carried. The Erymanthian Boar is caught in deep snow and carried to Mycenae by HERACLES (*Lib.* 2.5.4), who drops it to join the Argonauts (*Argo.* 1.126f). PROTEUS becomes a boar in his effort to break the grip of Aristaeus (*Georg.* 4.407) and of Menelaüs et al. (*Od.* 4.457).

In this form, APOLLO attacks Erymanthus because he has seen Aphrodite bathing (Ptolem. Heph. 1.306); ARES is attacked by the hunter Adonis, who is blasted by Zeus' thunderbolt (Serv. *ad Ecl.* 10.18).

Attacking or being attacked. ADONIS is wounded by a boar and dies in Aphrodite's arms; flowers spring from his blood (*Met.* 10.710f). ADRASTUS' spear misses a boar and hits Atys (Herod. 1.43–44). ALEXANDER is charged by a boar that Hermolaüs kills, to Alexander's irritation (Arrian 4.13.2). ATTIS et al. are killed by a boar (Paus. 7.17.5). The CALYDONIAN BOAR is brought to bay by Meleager et al. (*Met.* 8.329f); it kills Ancaeus, who attacks it with an axe (*Met.* 8.391f); Peleus hurls his spear at it but hits Eurytion (*Lib.* 3.13.2); Nestor escapes it by pole-vaulting into a tree (*Met.* 8.365f); Atalanta wounds it and Meleager kills it (*Met.* 8.380f; *Il.* 9.538f; *Lib.* 1.8.2). The ERYMANTHIAN BOAR is killed by Heracles (*Fab.* 30). HYAS is killed by a boar and his grieving sisters become stars (*Fab.* 192). IDAS et al. kill the boar that has killed Idmon (*Fab.* 14, 18; *Lib.* 1.9.23; *Argo.* 2.818f). ODYSSEUS is wounded while hunting with the sons of Autolycus but makes a kill (*Od.* 19.439f; Paus. 10.8.4).

Slashes a tree (Myrrha), which releases baby ADONIS, with whom she was pregnant at the time of her metamorphosis (Serv. *ad Ecl.* 10.18; Serv. *ad Aen.* 5.72).

Is yoked with a lion by ADMETUS, with Apollo's help, to the chariot in which he carries off Alcestis (*Fab.* 50, 51).

A phantom boar leads PICUS to Circe, who changes him into a woodpecker (*Met.* 14.358f).

BOAR'S HEAD

Forms a helmet that is stolen by AUTOLYCUS from Amyntor, worn by Meriones, and given to Odysseus (*Il.* 10.255f).

BOARSKIN

(See **Skin, of Animal.**)

BOAT

(See also **Chest; Raft; Sail; Ship.**)

Attribute of Fortuna; Isis.

ALEXANDER crosses the Hydaspes River on a stormy night (Plut. 33.60).

CAESAR attempts a stormy passage in a small boat (Plut. 34.44).

CHARON, the old ferryman of Hades, carries the dead across the Styx (*Aen.* 6.298f) and also Aeneas and the Sibyl (*Aen.* 6.385f); Heracles (*Aen.* 6.392); Psyche (Apuleius 9); Theseus and Peirithoüs (*Aen.* 6.393f); Theseus and Heracles (Sen. *Her. Fur.* 847f).

DAEDALUS and ICARUS, each in a small sailboat, escape from Minos' galley (Paus. 9.11.3); Daedalus spreads his robe to make a sail to aid their escape (Serv. *ad Aen.* 6.14).

DEITIES ferry Meliboea to her lover (Serv. *ad Aen.* 1.720).

DEUCALION and PYRRHA survive flood waters and land on Parnassus (*Met.* 1.316f).

EGESTA is set adrift by her father to save her from sacrifice to a sea monster (Serv. *ad Aen.* 5.30).

FLOOD SURVIVORS row among treetops and roofs (*Met.* 1.293f).

The golden goblet of HELIUS transports him and his horses from his setting to his rising (Athenaeus 9.39); he lends it to Heracles to transport the cattle of Geryon (*Lib.* 2.5.10).

CHARON FERRYING THE DEAD TO HADES

Jason et al. row across a river to Medea's aid (*Argo.* 4.67f).

Ugly Phaon transports Aphrodite, for which she makes him handsome; he becomes Sappho's ferryman (Aelian 12.18).

BODY

(See **Corpse; Sleeping Figure; Statue; Torso.**)

Double-bodied (see **Twins**). Triple-bodied (see **Head** [Three-headed]).

BONDS

(See also **Captive; Chain; Net; Seated Figure; Snake.**)

On the feet: attribute of Aphrodite Morpho (Paus. 3.15.11); Saturn. On the arms: Furor (sitting on armor, *Aen.* 1.294f).

Applied to men. Acoëtes, a votary of Dionysus, is chained and imprisoned by Pentheus, then magically set free (*Met.* 3.696f). Amycus is tied to a tree by Polydeuces (Schol. *ad Argo.* 2.98). Ares, who has been tied up by gigantic Otus and Ephialtes, is released by Hermes (*Il.* 5.385f; *Lib.* 1.7.4). Briareüs, Cottus, and Gyes (the "Hundred-handed") are imprisoned underground by their father Ouranos (Hes. *Theog.* 617f). The twin Cercopes are carried lashed head-down to a pole by Heracles (*Lib.* 2.6.3, n. 3, Loeb edn.). Daedalus is tied up by Minos, whose wife Pasiphaë frees him (*Fab.* 40). Democedes, a physician, is brought in chains from prison to heal Darius (Herod. 3.129, 3.130). Dionysus is brought with his hands tied before Pentheus (Eur. *Bacch.* 434f, 502f). The spy Dolon is tied to a tree by Odysseus and Diomedes, and killed on their return with the Palladium (Serv. *ad Aen.* 12.347). Eurystheus, after being captured by Iolaüs, is brought before Alcmene (Eur. *Heracleidae* 857). Sleeping Faunus (a Satyr-like deity) and Picus are bound by Numa (*Fasti* 3.299f). Heracles, after running amok, is restrained from further carnage by Amphitryon et al. (Eur. *Her.* 1009f); as he is about to be sacrificed, he breaks his bonds and kills the priest (*Lib.* 2.5.11). Heralds are sent bound back to Erginus by Heracles, with ears and noses cut off (*Lib.* 2.4.11). Melampus is chained and imprisoned by Phylacus (*Od.* 15.231f) or by Iphicles (*Od.* 11.288f). The sea deity Nereus is tied up by Heracles (*Lib.* 2.5.11). Odysseus is disarmed and tied up by Diomedes during their theft of the Palladium (Eust. *ad Il.* 10.531); he is tied to his ship's mast while it passes the Sirens (*Od.* 12.178f). Odysseus' crew is dragged aboard bound after eating lotus (*Od.* 9.98f). Orestes and

PYLADES are brought in bonds by guards before King Thoas and his priestess Iphigeneia, to be sacrificed (*Fab.* 120; Eur. *Iph. Taur.* 467f) and are marched in a procession led by Iphigeneia to a ship (Eur. *Iph. Taur.* 1205f). POLYTECHNUS is tied up, smeared with honey, and exposed to insects because he offended both the gods and his wife (Ant. Lib. 11). PROMETHEUS, chained to a cliff by Hermes, is tormented by an eagle (Hes. *Theog.* 521f; *Argo.* 2.1248f; *Lib.* 1.7.1); chained by Hephaestus, he is visited by various demons and creatures (Aes. *Prom.* 17f and pass.); he is visited by Zeus and released when Heracles shoots the eagle that has been tearing at his liver (*Fab.* 54, 144). PROTEUS is tied up by Menelaüs in order to extract information from him (*Fab.* 118) and by Aristaeus (*Georg.* 4.387f, 4.437f; *Fasti* 1.371f). Drunken SILENUS, in chains made of flowers, entertains the company with a song (*Ecl.* 6.16f); he is taken by rustics to King Midas (*Met.* 11.90f). SINON is led bound by shepherds to Priam at the Wooden Horse (*Aen.* 2.57f). Winged THANATOS is chained by Sisyphus and released by Ares (Eust. *ad Il.* 6.150; *Od.* 11.593). THESEUS and PEIRITHOÜS are tied up in the underworld, where they are tormented by Furies until they are rescued by Heracles (*Fab.* 79); they are imprisoned by the Thesprotian king (Paus. 1.17.4). Huge TITYOS is chained in the underworld and tormented by vultures or serpents (*Lib.* 1.4.1; *Met.* 4.457f; *Fab.* 55). Twelve TROJAN YOUTHS are bound by Achilles and slain by him at Patroclus' pyre (*Il.* 21.26f, 23.175f).

Applied to women. ANDROMACHE, her hands bound, and her son Molossus are threatened with death by Menelaüs, but set free by Peleus (Eur. *Andro.* 501f). ANDROMEDA is chained to a cliff as an offering to a sea monster; she is rescued by Perseus (*Met.* 4.672f; *Lib.* 2.4.3; *Fab.* 64). ANTIOPE, in chains and imprisoned by Dirce, is freed by Zeus (*Fab.* 7). HERA is suspended in air by Hephaestus with chains because she threw him from Olympus; made drunk by Dionysus, he releases her (*Fab.* 166). HESIONE, in a plight similar to Andromeda's (above), is saved by Heracles (*Met.* 11.211f; *Lib.* 2.59; *Fab.* 89). MAENADS' chains, applied by Pentheus, are caused to drop off by Dionysus (Eur. *Bacch.* 444f). TARCHETIUS' DAUGHTER and her maid are chained to a loom where they weave a web that is unraveled at night (Plut. 2.2).

Applied to a man and woman. APHRODITE and ARES are held fast in bed by Hephaestus' chain, to the amusement of other gods (*Fab.* 148). CHARICLEIA and THEAGENES are brought in chains before the Ethiopian king (*Aeth.* 9).

Applied to baby OEDIPUS, are removed from his feet by the shepherds who find him (Soph. *Oed. Tyr.* 1349f).

Applied to an animal form assumed by NEREUS as he tries to escape from Heracles (*Lib.* 2.5.11), or by PROTEUS trying to escape from Aristaeus (*Fasti* 1.371f; *Georg.* 4.387f, 4.437f).

BONE

Gathered for burial (see **Vessel, Funerary**).

PELOPS' shoulder bone is dredged from the sea in a net (Paus. 5.13.5).

BOOK

(See also **Box; Letter; Scroll; Writing.**)

The book referred to here may be depicted as a scroll or a codex (the modern form), depending on the date of the representation or on the artist's preference.

Attribute of Calliope; Clio; Clotho; Tempus.

ALEXANDER's copy of the *Iliad* is kept in a precious box and is frequently read by him (Plut. 33.26).

CAESAR reads about Alexander's achievements at an early age and weeps because he has not equalled them (Plut. 34.12).

VERGIL reads from the *Aeneid* to Augustus et al.; Octavia weeps at the mention of her son (Serv. *ad Aen.* 6.861).

BOOT

(See also **Sandal; Shoe.**)

Reaching the calf or knee: attribute of Artemis; Dionysus; Hermes; horsemen; hunters; Melpomene; tragic actors. With flaps: Thracians.

BOTTLE

(See **Vessel.**)

BOW

(See also **Arrow; Bow and Arrow; Hunter; Huntress.**)

Attribute of Apollo; Artemis; Camilla; Eros; Heracles; Locrians; Odysseus; Paris.

Given by APOLLO to Heracles (*Lib.* 2.4.11) and to Eurytus (*Od.* 8.223f; *Argo.* 1.88f); by the swineherd EUMAEUS to a beggar (Odysseus) in the presence of Penelope's suitors and Telemachus (*Od.* 21.359f); by HERACLES to a woman who is a serpent below the waist (Herod. 4.9) and to Philoctetes, in gratitude for igniting his pyre (*Lib.* 2.7.7; *Fab.* 36; Sen. *Her. Oet.* 1744f); by IPHITUS to Odysseus, who gives him a sword and spear in exchange (*Od.* 21.31f); by NEOPTOLEMUS to Philoctetes (Soph. *Phil.* 1286f); by PENELOPE to her suitors to test their strength (*Od.* 21.9f); by PHILOCTETES to Diomedes, Odysseus, and Neoptolemus (*Ep.* 5.8; Soph. *Phil.* 762f); by PHILOCTETES, when he dedicates Heracles' bow to Apollo (*Ep.* 6.15).

Stringing of a bow. SCYTHES, son of a woman who is part snake, strings the bow of his father Heracles after his brothers fail (Herod. 4.10). TELEMACHUS and several suitors fail to string Odysseus' bow (*Od.* 21.124f), which a beggar (Odysseus) is able to accomplish (*Od.* 21.376).

Carrying a bow. DOLON, a Trojan spy, is caught by Diomedes and Odysseus (*Il.* 10.333f). HERACLES' ghost converses with Odysseus (*Od.* 11.601f). ODYSSEUS raids the Trojan camp with Diomedes (*Il.* 10.260f). PARIS challenges the Greeks to single combat, and Menelaüs accepts (*Il.* 3.16f). PHILOCTETES, abandoned on Lemnos, is visited by Odysseus et al. (*Ep.* 3.27; Soph. *Phil.* 220f) and by the divine Heracles (Soph. *Phil.* 1408f).

Is snatched by HERA from Artemis and used to beat her (*Il.* 21.389f).

Mice eat the bowstrings of SCAMANDER's sleeping followers, which indicates that they are to found Troy on the spot (Serv. *ad Aen.* 3.108).

BOW AND ARROW

(See also **Arrow; Bow; Corpse; Fighting; Hunter; Huntress; Killing; Wounded Figure.**)

PEACEFUL USE

Archery is taught to HERACLES by Eurytus (*Lib.* 2.4.9).

Arrow shot into the air by ACESTES bursts into flame (*Aen.* 5.522f); by DARIUS, who is invoking Zeus' aid against Athens (Herod. 5.105).

Arrow shot at a target: ANTENOR hits a bird; it falls where he is to found a city (Serv. *ad Aen.* 1.242); APOLLO competes with Eurytus (*Argo.* 1.88f); COMPETITORS at games for Patroclus, and at those for Anchises, shoot at a dove tied to a mast or flying free (*Il.* 23.852f; *Aen.* 5.500f); HERACLES competes with the sons of Eurytus (*Lib.* 2.4.9); ODYSSEUS shoots an arrow through the handle-holes of a line of axe-heads (*Od.* 19.572f, 21.118f, 21.404f).

ALCO shoots the snake that is coiled around his son (Serv. *ad Ecl.* 5.11).

APOLLO shoots: ACHILLES, in the heel (Quint. Smy. 3.63; Soph. *Phil.* 334f; and *Fab.* 107, where he assumes the likeness of Paris); AMPHION, for attacking his shrine (*Fab.* 9); CORONIS, for being faithless to their love (*Met.* 2.603f); the CYCLOPES, because they forged the thunderbolt with which Zeus killed his son Asclepius (Eur. *Alc.* 5f; *Fab.* 49; *Poet. Astr.* 2.15); gigantic EPHIALTES, in an eye, as does Heracles (*Lib.* 1.6.2); EURYTUS, after beating him in an archery contest (*Argo.* 1.88f); GREEK WARRIORS encamped before Troy, because Agamemnon has taken Chryses, the daughter of his priest (*Il.* 1.48f); NIOBE's SONS, while they are exercising; one runs to help his brother, another prays for mercy (*Met.* 6.224f); huge OTUS and EPHIALTES as they attempt to storm Olympus (*Od.* 11.317f; *Fab.* 28); PHLEGYAS, for setting his temple afire (Serv. *ad Aen.* 6.618); PHRONTIS, the helmsman of Menelaüs' ship (*Od.* 3.278f); PYTHON (Delphyne), a great dragon (*Met.* 1.441f; *Fab.* 140; *Argo.* 2.703f); RHEXENOR (*Od.* 7.64f); gigantic TITYOS, as he carries off Leto (*Argo.* 1.759f).

APOLLO and ARTEMIS shoot: ELDERLY MORTALS, to bring them welcome death (*Od.* 15.409f); NIOBE's SONS and DAUGHTERS, respectively, sparing only Meliboea (Chloris), who prays to Leto (Paus. 2.21.10; *Fab.* 9; *Il.* 24.602f); gigantic TITYOS, as he carries off Leto (*Lib.* 1.4.1).

ARTEMIS shoots: ARIADNE, upon Dionysus' testimony against her (*Od.* 11.324f); BOUPHAGUS, for trying to rape her (Paus. 8.27.17); huntress CHIONE, because of her insolence (*Fab.* 200; *Met.* 11.324f); LAODAMEIA, because her father Bellerophon has lost favor with the gods (*Il.* 6.205f; Schol. ad loc.); NIOBE's DAUGHTERS, one of them in her mother's arms (*Met.* 6.286f); ORION, while he is swimming, because Apollo has challenged her to shoot at a distant object in the water that turns out to be Orion's head (*Poet. Astr.* 2.34); or because she is jealous of Eos' love for him, or because he offered violence to her (Artemis) or to another goddess (*Fab.* 195; *Poet. Astr.* 2.34; *Lib.* 1.4.5; *Od.* 5.121f); a WOMAN who has carried the boy Eumaeus away on a ship (*Od.* 15.477f).

ASCANIUS, from a rampart, hits the Latin warrior Romulus (*Aen.* 9.621f).

ATHAMAS, made mad by Hera, shoots one of his sons as Ino flees with the other (*Lib.* 1.9.2, 3.4.3; *Fab.* 5).

CHARICLEIA, from a ship, shoots at warriors on shore (*Aeth.* 5).

HERACLES shoots: the Giant ALCYONEUS, and drags him off (*Lib.* 1.6.1); CALAÏS and ZETES, the winged sons of Boreas (*Fab.* 14; *Lib.* 3.15.2); gigantic EPHIALTES, in one eye, as does Apollo (*Lib.* 1.6.2); HADES, who is then cured by Paeëon (*Il.* 5.395f); he draws his bow at HELIUS (the Sun) but does not shoot (*Lib.* 2.5.10); he shoots HERA in the breast (*Il.* 5.392f); LAOMEDON, after he takes Troy (*Lib.* 2.6.4); his wife MEGARA and their sons, in a fit of madness (Eur. *Her.* 922f; *Fab.* 32); MELEAGER's ghost, in Hades (Bacchylides 5.71f); the NEMEAN LION, without effect (*Lib.* 2.5.1); PERICLYMENUS, who has taken the form of an eagle (*Met.* 12.564f); the Giant PORPHYRION, for trying to violate Hera (*Lib.* 1.6.2); the STYMPHALIAN birds (*Lib.* 2.5.6).

ION shoots the birds that are defiling Apollo's shrine at Delphi (Eur. *Ion* 103f).

ODYSSEUS shoots down Penelope's suitors as they attack with swords and spears (*Od.* 22.1f, 22.79f).

OPIS, a nymph, shoots Arruns dead after he kills Camilla (*Aen.* 11.8.52f).

ORESTES aims at a Fury (Eur. *Orest.* 269f).

PANDARUS, instigated by Laodocus (Athena), from a hiding place hits Menelaüs, thereby breaking a truce (*Il.* 4.86f); he wounds Diomedes (*Il.* 5.95f).

PARIS shoots: .ACHILLES; the arrow is directed to his heel by Apollo (*Met.* 12.598f; *Ep.* 5.3; cf. *Fab.* 107, which records that it is Apollo in Paris' form who shoots Achilles; and Serv. *ad Aen.* 6.57, where it is said that Paris shoots from behind a statue of Apollo); DIOMEDES in the foot, from behind a pillar (*Il.* 11.375f); EUCHENOR in the neck (*Il.* 13.360f); EURYPYLUS in the thigh, as he is stripping a corpse (*Il.* 11.580f); MACHAON in the shoulder; Nestor and Idomeneus come to his aid (*Il.* 11.660f).

PERSIAN BOWMEN kill Alcibiades as he flees from a burning house (Plut. 11.39).

PHILOCTETES, abandoned on Lemnos, shoots game with the bow Heracles has given him (Soph. *Phil.* 287f); he aims at Odysseus, who runs away as Neoptolemus watches (Soph. *Phil.* 1298f); kills Paris (Soph. *Phil.* 1427f; *Lib.* 3.12.6; *Ep.* 5.9; Quint. Smy. 10.233f).

POEAS, shooting from the *Argo*, fells gigantic, brazen Talos by hitting him in the ankle (*Lib.* 1.9.26).

TEUCER shoots from the protection of Ajax' shield (*Il.* 8.266f); he aims at Hector but hits someone else (*Il.* 8.300f) and shoots another arrow at Hector, which Apollo diverts (*Il.* 8.309); at Trojans from Ajax's beached ship (*Il.* 15.442f) and at Hector, in vain, because his bowstring breaks (*Il.* 15.458f).

MISCHIEVOUS USE

EROS hits APOLLO with a gold-tipped arrow that arouses love and Daphne with one tipped with lead that deadens it (*Met.* 1.466f); hits HADES in his chariot, causing him to carry off Persephone (*Met.* 5.379f); shoots MEDEA, causing her to love Jason (*Argo.* 3.275f); aims at the dead dragon PYTHON that Apollo has just killed, whereupon Apollo mocks his puny weapon (*Met.* 1.454f).

BOWL

(See **Drinking; Vessel.**)

BOX

(See also **Chest; Cradle.**)

A box may be rectangular, as is usual for jewelry and money, or cylindrical for scrolls.

Attribute of Persephone (also with sceptre); women in a Dionysiac procession. Of books (scrolls): Clio.

Funerary: such receptacles are sometimes rectangular, but more usually of rounded form, made of earthenware or of metal. (See **Vessel, Funerary.**)

ALEXANDER keeps Homer's *Iliad* in a rich casket (Plut. 33.26).

PANDORA releases evils among men from the box or vessel given her by the gods (Hes. *W. & D.* 90f).

PHYLLIS gives a box to her departing husband Demophon; the awful object within (described only as holy) frightens him into flight when he opens it (*Ep.* 6.16, 6.17).

PSYCHE is enveloped in a dark cloud that emerges from the box given her by Persephone (Apuleius 9).

BOXING

ENTELLUS defeats Dares at the games for Anchises (*Aen.* 5.424f).

EPEIUS defeats Euryalus at the games for Patroclus (*Il.* 23.685f).

HERACLES knocks out Titias' teeth (*Argo.* 2.783f); he defeats Eryx (Sen. *Her. Fur.* 524f).

ODYSSEUS, playing the part of a beggar, beats another beggar who resents the competition for alms (*Od.* 18.90f).

POLYDEUCES beats huge Amycus as the Argonauts look on (*Argo.* 2.67f; *Lib.* 1.9.20; Theocritus 22.27f; *Fab.* 17).

BOY

(See also Baby; Captive; Children; Girl; Human Figure, Small-scale.)

Boy dressed as girl (see **Girl**).

AENEAS is reared by mountain nymphs (*H. to Aph.* 256f).

ASCANIUS, asleep, is carried off by Aphrodite (*Aen.* 1.691f).

CYRUS stands before King Astyages, accused by a noble Mede and his son; his noble birth is revealed (Herod. 1.115).

EROS, in the form of Ascanius, brings gifts to Queen Dido (*Aen.* 1.697f) and is fondled by her (*Aen.* 1.717f, 4.84f).

EUMAEUS is led aboard ship by his nurse (*Od.* 15.464f).

The GRACCHI are proudly introduced by their mother Cornelia to a friend (Val. Max. 4.4).

HANNIBAL, standing at an altar with his father Hamilcar, swears eternal enmity against Rome (Livy 21.1).

MOLOSSUS is grasped by Menelaüs while his mother Andromache takes asylum on an altar; he and his mother are threatened with death by Menelaüs, but are set free by Peleus (Eur. *Andro.* 309f, 501f).

ORESTES is protected from a blow from Aegisthus by an old servant (Eur. *Elec.* 16f).

BRANCH

(See also Herb; Suppliant; Wreath.)

Unspecified: attribute of Glaucus; Hypnos (sprinkling sleep with it); Mercury; with fruit on it, Pomona. Of ash: Nemesis. Of laurel: Apollo. Of myrtle: Aphrodite; Charites. Of olive: Anubis; Apollo; Athena; Concordia; Eirene; Pax; a suppliant (q.v.). Of palm: Anubis; Nike; Victoria. Of thorn: Crane (Carna) (*Fasti* 6.129).

ALEXANDER has branches dragged by cattle to raise dust and confuse the enemy (Ps.-Cal. 173).

APOLLO receives a branch of laurel from a wolf after he has dispatched Python (Serv. *ad Aen.* 4.377).

Holding a branch. ADRASTUS lays a branch on an altar (*Lib.* 3.7.1). AENEAS picks a golden bough, to which doves have led him (*Aen.* 6.136f, 6.201f) and, coming to the entrance of Elysium with the Sibyl, he affixes it at the threshold (*Aen.* 6.636f); near an altar he pulls up shoots of a shrub that drip blood (*Aen.* 3.24f). AGAMEMNON, in a dream of Clytemnestra, holds a sceptre that has sprouted (Soph. *Elec.* 417f). GAEA presents a branch with golden apples to Hera at her marriage to Zeus (*Poet. Astr.* 2.3). ION, using one as a broom, sweeps Apollo's shrine (Eur. *Ion* 112f). ODYSSEUS covers his nakedness when he encounters Nausicaä and her companions (*Od.* 6.127f). ORESTES, holding a bloody sword also, sits in Apollo's shrine where Furies lie sleeping; whereupon Apollo and Hermes appear (Aes. *Eumen.* 39f). PELIAS comes as a suppliant to Ceÿx (*Met.* 11.278). The SIBYL shows the boatman Charon a golden bough as she leads Aeneas into Hades (*Aen.* 6.405f).

BREAST

Multiple breasts: attribute of the Ephesian Artemis; Natura. Pendulous: the hag Invidia. With right breast bare: Virtus (armed).

Offered to an elderly person. A DAUGHTER feeds her imprisoned mother (Val. Max. 5.4a.7). PERO feeds her imprisoned father Mycon (Val. Max. 5.46.1). PIETAS may be so represented

Breasts are bared by HECUBA, who shows one for Hector to see as she tries to dissuade him from fighting Achilles (*Il.* 22.79f); by HELEN, causing Menelaüs to drop the sword with which he intended to kill her (*Ilias Mikra* 13; Aristophanes, *Lysistrata* 155 and scholia); by PHRYNE, a courtesan, before her judges, winning her acquittal (Athenaeus 13.590e; Quint. *Inst.* 2.15.9).

Milky Way is formed from milk spilled from the breast of HERA as she nurses Heracles or Hermes, according to Eratosthenes (*Poet. Astr.* 2.43); of RHEA, as she pretends to nurse the stone she has substituted for baby Zeus (*Poet. Astr.* 2.43).

BREASTPLATE

(See **Aegis; Arms and Armor.**)

BRIDGE

Crossed by the army of ALEXANDER at the Indus (Arrian 5.7.1f); of DARIUS at the Bosporus (Herod. 4.88) and the Danube (Herod. 4.97; also in his retreat, Herod. 140–141); of XERXES at the Hellespont (Herod. 7.55) and the Strymon, after burying alive several local boys and girls (Herod. 7.114).

Being defended. HORATIUS, at first with two others and then alone, holds back the Etruscans; when it is cut down behind him, he swims back to Rome (Plut. 6.16; Livy 2.10).

Set afire by blazing timbers, prevents the SABINES' escape from Rome (Livy 1.37).

BRIDLE

Attribute of Nemesis.

Invented by ATHENA; she bridles Pegasus for Bellerophon (Paus. 2.4.1).

BROOM

(See **Branch**.)

BUILDING

(See also **House; Stone; Wall**.)

The construction of CARTHAGE is observed by Aeneas and Achates (*Aen*. 1.421f); Aeneas, in oriental dress, supervises this construction when Hermes accosts him (*Aen*. 4.259).

TARQUIN carries out large building projects in Rome (Livy 1.56) as does Augustus (*Res Gestae Divi Augusti* 4.19–20).

BULL

(See also **Altar, Animal Sacrifice; Cattle; Cow; Plow**.)

Attribute of Apis; Mithras; Oceanus; river gods. It may also personify a river god, e.g., Cephisus (Eur. *Ion* 1261).

Changed into this form. The horned women of Amathus, guilty of human sacrifice, are metamorphosed by Aphrodite (*Met*. 10.222f).

In this form, ACHELOÜS wrestles Heracles for Deïaneira; Heracles tears off one of his horns (*Met*. 9.80f; *Fab*. 31; Soph. *Trach*. 507f); POSEIDON seduces Canace (*Met*. 6.115f); ZEUS joins a bevy of girls, from among whom he carries off Europa (*Met*. 2.847f; *Lib*. 3.3.1; *Fab*. 178; cf. *Lib*. 2.5.7, where Zeus sends a bull to effect the abduction); Zeus visits a cow (Io) (Aes. *Suppl*. 291f).

Killed by many-eyed Argus (*Lib.* 2.1.2); by Entellus, with his fist (*Aen.* 5.477f); by Heracles, who frees it from a cart, cooks and eats it (*Lib.* 2.5.11, 2.7.7); by Heracles with his club, as Ancaeus kills another with an axe to provide a feast for the Argonauts (*Argo.* 1.425f); by Heracles and another by Lepreus, after which they cook and eat them (Paus. 5.5.4); by Theseus, who has been sent by Aegeus to rid Marathon of a rampaging bull (*Fab.* 38; *Ep.* 1.5; Plut. 1.14).

Dead, from whose carcass (*Georg.* 4.295f) or carcasses bees emerge to replace Aristaeus' lost swarm (*Georg.* 4.538f).

Tamed or subdued. Heracles catches and brings the Cretan bull to Eurystheus (*Fab.* 30; *Lib.* 2.5.7). Jason resists the charge of fire-breathing bulls and harnesses them to a plow, with the help of Medea or the Dioscuri (*Argo.* 3.1289f; *Lib.* 1.9.23; *Met.* 7.104f; *Fab.* 22; cf. *Argo.* 3.413f, where Aeëtes performs the same feat). Theagenes, from horseback, subdues a bull (*Aeth.* 10). Theseus flings a bull over a building (Paus. 1.19.1).

From or in the sea. Joins the herd of Eryx in Sicily (*Lib.* 2.5.10). Tows Heracles across the Strait of Messina (Diod. Sic. 4.22.6). Comes to Minos to be sacrificed to Poseidon but is set free (*Lib.* 2.5.7, 3.1.3). Sent by Poseidon, frightens Hippolytus' chariot team, which bolts and drags him to his death (*Met.* 15.507f; *Fab.* 47; Eur. *Hipp.* 1203f; *Ep.* 1.19; Sen. *Phaed.* 1053f).

Plowing. Jason plows a field from which armed men grow (*Argo.* 3.1289f; *Lib.* 1.9.23; *Met.* 7.104f; *Fab.* 22). Maenads attack plow-oxen and kill them (*Met.* 11.30f). Prometheus instructs mankind to yoke oxen to the plow (Aes. *Prom.* 462f). Theiodamas is plowing when Heracles demands his ox and kills him when he is refused (*Argo.* 1.1213f).

Drags Dirce to her death after her sons tie her to it (*Fab.* 7, 8; *Lib.* 3.5.5).

Fights and kills Androgeüs (*Lib.* 3.15.7; Paus. 1.27.9); with a wolf, as Danaüs watches (Serv. *ad Aen.* 4.377).

Lies down at the place where Cadmus is to found Thebes; a crescent marks its hide (*Fab.* 178). A wounded bull on the site where Helenus is to found Buthrotum (Serv. *ad Aen.* 3.293).

Mates with an artificial cow that Daedalus has made and in which Pasiphaë is concealed (*Met.* 9.735f; *Lib.* 3.1.4; *Fab.* 40).

Of bronze, set over a fire, incinerates Phaleris' victims within; Phaleris suffers the same fate (Polybius 12.25; Diod. Sic. 9.20).

Pet bull belonging to Paris, is taken from him; he wins it back as a prize for athletic events (*Fab.* 91).

Created by Zeus, is criticized by MOMUS, who also finds fault with Prometheus' creation, a man, and Athena's house, for which he is expelled from Olympus (Aesop 100).

BULL'S HEAD

Attribute of Apollo (with one foot resting on it).

DIDO digs up a bull's head and a horse's head at the spot where she is to found Carthage (Serv. *ad Aen.* 1.443).

Bull-headed serpent is sacrificed by Briareüs (*Fasti* 3.799f).

Bull-headed man. ACHELOÜS wrestles Heracles for Deïaneira (Soph. *Trach.* 8f). The MINOTAUR eats victims (*Met.* 8.169f) and is killed by Theseus (*Lib.* 3.1.4; *Ep.* 1.9; *Fab.* 42; *Met.* 8.171). Brazen TALOS hurls rocks at the *Argo;* he dies when his blood gushes from his ankle as a result of Medea's magic or Poeas' arrow (*Lib.* 1.9.26). TAUROCEPHALUS (bull-headed) is a surname of Dionysus in Orphic mysteries.

BULL'S HIDE

(See **Skin, of Animal.**)

THESEUS KILLING THE MINOTAUR

BUNDLE

(See also **Bag; Loaf of Bread; Stone; Wineskin.**)

Of sticks: attribute of Mars.
Containing a stone instead of baby Zeus, is given to Cronus to swallow (Hes. *Theog.* 485f; *Lib.* 1.1.7; *Fab.* 139).

BURDEN

(See **Carrying.**)

BURIAL

(See also **Corpse; Pit; Pyre; Sarcophagus; Tomb; Vessel, Funerary.**)

Antigone is caught in the forbidden act of burying her brother Polyneices (Soph. *Ant.* 80f, 245f, 384f).
Live burial of Antigone, in the same grave as her brother's body (*Lib.* 3.7.1); of two couples, one of Gauls, one of Greeks, by the Romans (Plut. 16.3); of Leucothoë, by her father, even though she begs her lover Helius

Rhea hands a stone wrapped in baby clothes to
Cronus

to save her (*Met.* 4.23f); of PHILONOME, by her husband Cycnus, after stoning to death her accomplice in the false accusation she has made against her stepson (*Ep.* 3.25); of the VESTAL VIRGINS Minucia (Livy 8.15) and Opimia (Livy 22.57).

BUST

On a pedestal, with tridents below: attribute of Terminus. A three-headed bust symbolizes the diversity of Mercury's functions.

On the ground may represent the emergence of an autochthonous deity such as Aphrodite (Diod. Sic. 5.5), Persephone (Cora), Eros, Pandora, Pan, and Ariadne. It may be a stage in the growth of warriors who are sprouting from the dragon's teeth sowed by AEËTES (*Argo.* 3.413f); by CADMUS, with Athena's support (*Met.* 3.101f; *Lib.* 3.4.1; Eur. *Phoen.* 657f), or by JASON (*Argo.* 3.1377f). It may also represent the rising of the seer TAGES from the furrow plowed by Tarchon (*Met.* 15.552f), and the repeopling of the earth after the flood, from stones cast behind them by Deucalion and Pyrrha (*Met.* 1.381f; *Lib.* 1.72; *Fab.* 153).

BUTTERFLY

Attribute of the Horae. It may also represent a departing soul (see **Human Figure, Small-scale**).

CADUCEUS

(See also **Sceptre; Staff; Stick; Wand.**)

The caduceus was originally an olive branch with sprouting shoots, which evolved into a stylized device of two prongs entwined or forming a crescent at the staff's tip, and eventually into two snakes. Wings at the tip are a later embellishment. It is an attribute of heralds; Hermes; Iris; and, in its snake-entwined form only, of Asclepius.

Given to baby HERMES by Apollo (*H. to Her.* 529f) in exchange for his lyre (*H. to Her.* 496f) or his pipes (*Lib.* 3.10.2).

HERMES puts Chione to sleep with his wand in order to seduce her (*Met.* 11.307f). See also another attribute of Hermes, **Wings, On Hat or Sandals.**

Carried by JASON as he leaves the *Argo* with several companions to undergo the trial of harnessing the fire-breathing bulls (*Argo.* 3.196f).

A HERALD WITH HIS CADUCEUS

CALF

(See **Bull**; **Cow**.)

CAMEL

Introduced into battle by CYRUS to frighten Croesus' cavalry (Herod. 1.80).
A camel-headed lion or leopard is a Camelopard (see **Lion**).

CANDLE

(See **Light**.)

CAP

(See **Crown**; **Hat**.)

CAPTIVE

(See also **Bonds; Burial; Chariot; Flight; Killing; Seduction; Wrestling; Yoke**.)

Captivity, if not made obvious by restraints of some sort, may be represented simply by a convention, such as the grasping of an arm. No distinction is made, in the case of abducted women, between the willing and the unwilling captive, or between rescue and abduction.

The vehicle of abduction or other means by which it is being carried out is often not made clear in the literary source, but it is a feature of an abduction that the illustration must include. The deities, for whom a natural method of transport would be a chariot or aerial flight, can be determined by the attributions given under the **Chariot** and **Wings** entries. Mortal abductors may use a ship or a chariot, or may simply drag or carry off the captive.

A person pictured as a captive of love is an attribute of Eros.

Dead mortals, being led to or from the underworld (see **Underworld**).

ABDUCTION OF WOMEN   *By a deity.* AEGINA, by Zeus disguised as fire (*Lib.* 3.12.6; *Fab.* 42; Paus. 2.5.1, 2.29.2). AETHRA, by the Dioscuri, who give her to Helen as a slave (Plut. 1.34). ALCYONE, by Poseidon, as Zeus makes off with Taygete (Paus. 3.18.10). ARIADNE, by Dionysus, from Theseus in a ship (Paus. 10.29). The shepherdess CYRENE, by Apollo (*Argo.* 2.500f). HELEN, by Apollo, who is rescuing her from the threatening swords of Orestes and Pylades (Eur. *Orest.*

1496f); by the Dioscuri, her brothers, who rescue her from Theseus (Plut. 1.32; *Lib.* 3.10.7; cf. *Ep.* 1.23, which records that they also take Aethra from Theseus); by Hermes, while she is picking flowers; he takes her off to King Proteus in Egypt (Eur. *Hel.* 44f, 243f). LETO (Apollo's mother), by gigantic Tityos, whom Apollo shoots as he drags her off (*Argo.* 1.759f). LEUCE, by Hades; she is transformed into a poplar (Serv. *ad Ecl.* 7.61). OREITHYIA, by winged Boreas (*Met.* 6.706f). PERSEPHONE, by Hades in his chariot, while she is picking flowers with other girls; Hecate observes the abduction from her cave (*Met.* 5.391f; *H. to Dem.* 19f, 25f). PHOEBE and HILAIRA, by the Dioscuri (*Fasti* 5.699f). TAYGETE, by Zeus, as Poseidon carries off Alcyone (Paus. 3.18.10). THEOPHANE, by Poseidon (*Fab.* 188).

   By men (see also "Prisoners of war," below). AETHRA, by the sons of Theseus, is rescued from Troy and given to Demophon by Agamemnon (*Ep.* 5.22; Paus. 10.25.8). ANDROMACHE, by Menelaüs' soldiers, when she leaves Thetis' altar (Eur. *Andro.* 425f). ANTIOPE, by Epopeus (Paus. 2.6.1). The AMAZON ANTIOPE (Hippolyte), by Theseus, in his ship (Plut. 1.26; *Ep.* 1.16), or by Heracles, who takes her belt and gives her to Theseus (Diod. Sic. 2.46.4; *Fab.* 30). BRISEÏS, by Achilles, after he kills her husband and brothers (*Il.* 19.290f); she is taken by heralds from Achilles' quarters (*Il.* 1.326f) and back to Achilles with many gifts (*Il.* 19.242f). CHARICLEIA, by Theagenes et al. (actually it is an elopement) (*Aeth.* 4). The shepherdess CHLOË, by the cowherd Lampis (Longus 3). CLYTEMNESTRA, by Agamemnon after killing her husband and baby (Eur. *Iph. Aul.* 1149f) and by Aegisthus in Agamemnon's absence (*Od.* 3.272f). EUROPA, by Greek sailors (Herod. 1.2). HELEN, by Theseus (*Ep.* 1.23), by Theseus and Peirithoüs, while she is sacrificing to Artemis (Plut. 1.31), by Paris (*Fab.* 92; *Lib.* 3.12.6; *Ep.* 3.3; *Cypria* 1; Herod. 2.113f) and by Menelaüs after killing Deïphobus (*Ep.* 5.22). HERMIONE, by Orestes and Pylades, who hold her hostage (Eur. *Orest.* 1346f), or by Neoptolemus, taking her from her husband Orestes (Eur. *Orest.* 967f; *Ep.* 6.14; *Fab.* 123; *Heroïdes* 8.31), or by Orestes, after he kills Neoptolemus (*Fab.* 123). HESIONE, by Heracles, after he captures Troy; he bestows her on Telamon (*Lib.* 2.6.4; *Fab.* 89). The HESPERIDES, daughters of Atlas, by pirates; Heracles rescues them (Diod. Sic. 4.27.4). HYPSIPYLE, by pirates, as she flees from the women of Lemnos; she is sold to King Lycus as a slave (*Fab.* 15). HYRNETHO, by her brothers in a chariot, pursued by her husband Deïphontes (Paus. 2.28.3). IOLE, by Heracles, after killing her father Eurytus et al.; he gives her to Deïaneira (*Lib.* 2.7.7; Serv. *ad Aen.* 8.291; *Fab.* 35, 36). MARPESSA, by Idas in a "winged" chariot, pursued by Euenus (*Lib.* 1.7.8). MEDEA, by Greek sailors (Herod. 1.2). PANDAREOS' DAUGHTERS, by storm winds, who take them from the goddesses who have been caring for them and give them to the Furies (*Od.* 20.66f). PHILOMELA, by Tereus, who drags her into a hut and rapes her (*Met.* 6.519f). SABINE WOMEN, by the Romans, at a festival; a particularly attractive one is grabbed by rustics acting for (or pretending to act for) rich Talasius (Livy 1.9; Plut. 2.14–15). THEONOË, by pirates, who sell her to King Icarus (*Fab.* 190).

By a woman. ANTIOPE, by jealous Dirce (*Fab.* 8). LAVINIA, by her mad mother Amata; she is taken to a forest to keep her from marrying Aeneas (*Aen.* 7.385f).

WOMEN CAPTIVES

Buried alive (see **Burial**). Sacrificed (see **Altar**).

Prisoners of war. ANDROMACHE is taken by Neoptolemus, after her son Astyanax has been thrown from the wall of Troy (Eur. *Andro.* 12f; *Ep.* 5.23; Schol. *ad Lycophrona* 1268). CASSANDRA is dragged by Ajax Oïleus to Athena's shrine (Eur. *Troad.* 69f) or from the shrine, breaking her grasp on Athena's statue (*Iliupersis* 1), as Coroebus and other Trojans vainly try to rescue her (*Aen.* 2.403f); she is taken from Hecuba to Agamemnon's ship by Talthybius (Eur. *Troad.* 419, 455f) and by Agamemnon to Argos (Aes. *Agam.* 950f; *Ep.* 5.23). HECUBA is taken by Odysseus (*Ep.* 5.23). HELEN is dragged away from Hecuba and other Trojan captives by Menelaüs' soldiers (Eur. *Troad.* 895f). TROJAN WOMEN and CHILDREN are herded together as Troy burns (Eur. *Troad.* 1309f; *Met.* 13.410f; *Aen.* 2.763f).

Haled before authority. ALOPE is condemned to death by her father Cercyon, and her baby is taken (*Fab.* 187). ANDROMACHE, lured from Thetis' altar, is seized by servants and condemned to die by Menelaüs, who also holds her son Molossus; they beg for mercy and are saved when old Peleus comes (Eur. *Andro.* 425f, 501f). ANTIGONE is seized on Creon's order; blind Oedipus tries to aid her; Theseus has Antigone freed (Soph. *Oed. Col.* 826f); she is brought by soldiers before Creon, who condemns her to be buried alive (Soph. *Ant.* 385f, 882f); her sister Ismene is made to join her before Creon (Soph. *Ant.* 528f). A beautiful CAPTIVE is presented to Scipio in Africa; he returns her to her father (Polybius 10.19.3). CHARICLEIA is brought before the Ethiopian Princess Arsace and accused of poisoning Cybele (*Aeth.* 8). DARIUS' WIFE, MOTHER, and children are brought before Alexander but mistakenly make their obeisance to the more richly attired Hephestion (Q. Curt. 3.12; Arrian 2.12.6; Plut. 33.21 records that Alexander did not receive the women but sent an officer to reassure them). ELECTRA stands before Aegisthus after Agamemnon's murder (Sen. *Agam.* 1064f). HELEN and PARIS et al. are brought before King Proteus in Egypt (Herod. 2.115). IOLE et al. are brought by Lichas before Deïaneira (Soph. *Trach.* 225f). LEUCIPPE, dressed as a priest, is ordered to prison by her sister Theonoë (*Fab.* 190). MELANIPPE is blinded and imprisoned by her father; her babies by Poseidon are taken from her (*Fab.* 186). TIMOCLEA is brought before Alexander for killing one of his soldiers, and is pardoned because she had been raped (Plut. 33.12).

Imprisoned. ANTIGONE is sealed in a cave on Creon's order and left to die (Soph. *Ant.* 773f, 891f). ANTIOPE, pregnant by Zeus, is kept bound in a cell by jealous Dirce; she is released by Zeus (*Fab.* 7; *Lib.* 3.5.5 records that her imprisonment by Dirce occurred after her twins were born and that her escape from her bonds was miraculous). DANAË, shut in a tower to keep her from marrying, is visited by Zeus in the form of golden rain (*Met.* 4.611, 6.113; *Lib.* 2.4.1). ELECTRA is kept under house arrest by Aegisthus to prevent her marriage (Eur. *Elec.* 24f). HERA is held fast on a golden throne by invisible cords; Hephaestus has devised the trap; he releases her when Dionysus gets him drunk (Paus. 1.20.2; Serv. *ad Aen.* 8.454). LEUCIPPE, dressed as a priest, is about to be murdered by old Thestor; unable to do the deed, Thestor is going to kill himself when he and she discover they are father and daughter (*Fab.* 190). Blind MELANIPPE is rescued by her sons; her jailer is killed and her sight restored by Poseidon (*Fab.* 186). METOPE is blinded by her father Echetus and set the impossible task of grinding pieces of bronze into flour (*Argo.* 4.1093f). MYRENE is shut up by pirates who do not know she is their sister (Serv. *ad Aen.* 3.23). TARCHETIUS' DAUGHTER and her maid are made to weave by day; their work is unraveled by others at night (Plut. 2.2).

WOMEN AND MEN	ANTIGONE, HAEMON, and their son are ordered to execution by Creon, but are saved by divine intervention (fragment of Eur. *Antigone,* see Rose, p. 203). APHRODITE and ARES are trapped in bed by Hephaestus' golden net, to the amusement of the gods (*Od.* 8.266f; *Met.* 4.171f). CHARICLEIA and THEAGENES are captured by Ethiopian pirates (*Aeth.* 1); by Persian soldiers (*Aeth.* 5); are led in chains before the Ethiopian king (*Aeth.* 8–9). Seven MAIDS and seven YOUTHS, among them Theseus, are handed over as tribute to King Minos or his Cretan captain (Plut. 1.7; *Lib.* 3.15.5, 3.15.8; *Ep.* 1.7; *Poet. Astr.* 2.5).
ABDUCTION OR CAPTURE OF MEN	*By women.* CEPHALUS, a handsome hunter, by Eos (*Met.* 7.700f). CLODIUS, by devotees of Bona Dea during a secret rite, when they penetrate his woman's disguise (Plut. 34.10, 42.28). HYLAS, a friend of Heracles, by nymphs of a pool from which he has drawn water (Serv. *ad Ecl.* 6.43); he is drawn into the water by one of them (*Argo.* 1.1221f). NISUS, by Dionysus et al.,

dressed as Maenads (*Fab.* 131). PENTHEUS, by Maenads because he spied on their rites (*Met.* 3.710f). PHAËTHON, by Aphrodite, to be custodian of her temple (Hes. *Theog.* 988f). TITHONUS, by Eos (*H. to Aph.* 218f).

By men. AEGISTHUS, by Orestes and Pylades; they lead him indoors to kill him (Soph. *Elec.* 1491f). AMULIUS, tyrant of Alba Longa, by Romulus and Remus; they kill him (Plut. 2.8). CAESAR, by pirates, who treat him as a guest while they await ransom (Plut. 34.2). CREON, by Theseus' soldiers, to make him release Antigone and Oedipus (Soph. *Oed. Col.* 1025f). CHRYSIPPUS, a handsome youth, by Laius, in his chariot (*Lib.* 3.5.5; *Fab.* 85); by Theseus (*Fab.* 271). DAMON, held hostage and about to be executed, is saved by the arrival of his friend Pythias (Phintias) (Cic. *Tusc.* 5.22; cf. *Fab.* 257, in which the friends are called Moeros and Seluntius). DIONYSUS, by pirates (*H. to Dion.* 6f; *Lib.* 3.4.3; *Met.* 3.605f). DOLON, a Trojan spy, by Odysseus and Diomedes after a chase (*Il.* 10.374f). EURYALUS, by Rutulian horsemen; they kill him as Nisus rushes to his aid (*Aen.* 9.367f). The seer HELENUS is waylaid by Odysseus and taken to the Greek camp (Soph. *Phil.* 604f; *Ep.* 5.9). LYCAON, while cutting sticks, by Achilles, who holds him for ransom (*Il.* 21.34f). Old MARIUS, while hiding in a swamp, by soldiers (Plut. 22.38). One of ODYSSEUS' men is seized by the Cyclops Polyphemus preparatory to eating him (*Od.* 9.287f) and another by the king of the Laestrygonians with the same intention (*Od.* 10.166f). ORESTES and PYLADES as they wade ashore, by herdsmen (Eur. *Iph. Taur.* 240f). PANTHUS, a handsome priest of Delphi, by Antenor's son (Serv. *ad Aen.* 2.313). THESTOR, after being shipwrecked (*Fab.* 190). Twelve TROJAN YOUTHS, by Achilles, to sacrifice to Patroclus (*Il.* 21.26f, 23.175f).

Haled before authority. BRUTUS' traitorous sons are brought before him; he orders their execution (Plut. 6.5). HARMODIUS and ARISTOGEITON are seized as they approach the tyrant Phaleris; Aristogeiton escapes, and Harmodius bites his tongue off and spits it in the tyrant's face (*Fab.* 257). MEDUS is brought before King Perses, whom he has come to kill, and is sent to prison (*Fab.* 27). ORESTES and PYLADES are brought before the priestess Iphigeneia; she discovers that Orestes is her brother (Eur. *Iph. Taur.* 66f, 467f, 725f); they are brought before King Thoas (*Fab.* 120). A PERSIAN in Macedonian armor, trying to assassinate Alexander, is captured and set free (Ps.-Cal. 162). POROS, an Indian king, stands before his conqueror Alexander (Plut. 33.60). A PRIEST (Leucippe in disguise) is ordered to prison by her sister Theonoë, who does not recognize her (*Fab.* 190). REMUS is brought by shepherds before Numitor; rustic Faustulus produces the vessel in which Remus and his brother Romulus were set adrift, proving their parentage (Plut. 2.7). SILENUS is taken bound in garlands by Phrygian rustics to King

Midas (*Met.* 11.90f). THYESTES, seized by Agamemnon and Menelaüs at Delphi, is brought to Atreus and sent to prison (*Fab.* 88). TORQUATUS' SON is brought before his father by lictors and condemned to death for disobeying the order not to engage in single combat (Val. Max. 2.7.6, 6.9.1).

Imprisoned. APPIUS CLAUDIUS, after a trial; he kills himself in his cell (Livy 3.57–58). LYCURGUS, in a cave where he is left to die (Soph. *Ant.* 955f). MELAMPUS, by Phylacus, for stealing his cattle; the cell's roof collapses when Melampus leaves it (*Lib.* 1.9.12; *Od.* 15.231f). Blind OEDIPUS, by his sons Eteocles and Polyneices; he tries to kill himself (Eur. *Phoen.* 63f, 326f). OENEUS, by the sons of Agrius; Diomedes releases him (*Lib.* 1.8.6). A PRIEST (Leucippe in disguise) discovers that the old man, who has been sent to her cell to kill her, is her father Thestor (*Fab.* 190). THESEUS and PEIRITHOÜS are bound by snakes or simply stuck fast to their seats in Hades (*Ep.* 1.24 and n. 4, Loeb edn.); they (or Theseus alone, *Lib.* 2.5.12) are rescued by Heracles from torment by Furies when he comes to get Cerberus (*Fab.* 79); Theseus is imprisoned by the king of the Thesprotians after Peirithoüs is thrown to the king's dog Cerberus (Paus. 1.17.4; Plut. 1.31). ZEUS, in a cave by the monster Typhon, who disables him by removing his tendons, which Hermes and Aegipan later restore (*Lib.* 1.6.3). (See also "Haled before authority," above; **Cyclops;** and **Giant.**)

Caught in a net or trap. The Satyr FAUNUS and his father PICUS, by Numa; they assume various terrible forms (Plut. 4.15). One of two THIEVES in a treasure vault; to prevent identification, the other decapitates the trapped one and escapes (Herod. 2.121; a similar tale is told about Agamedes and Trophonius in Paus. 9.37.3).

CARPENTER'S SQUARE

Attribute of Nemesis.

CARRIAGE OR CART

(See **Chariot; Wagon.**)

CARRYING

A globe or some conventionalized representation of the heavens (see **Sky**). A corpse (see **Corpse**).

A warrior from battle. AENEAS is being carried by Aphrodite when Diomedes wounds her; she drops him, and Apollo picks him up (*Il.* 5.311f,

5.443f); he is carried out of reach of Achilles by Poseidon (*Il.* 20.321f). HEC-
TOR is taken out of Achilles' reach in a mist by Apollo (*Il.* 20.443f). HERA-
CLES, wounded in the attack on Cos, is rescued by Zeus (*Lib.* 2.7.1).

People carrying others. AENEAS carries his father and leads his son
from burning Troy (*Aen.* 2.707f). AGRIPPINA is carried to safety from a ship-
wreck (Tac. *An.* 14.5–8; Suet. *Nero* 34). ALCIBIADES carries his wife from
the divorce court through the marketplace to their home (Plut. 11.8). AMPHI-
NOMUS and ANAPIAS carry their aged parents through the fire and lava of
Etna (Val. Max. 5.4b; Paus. 10.28.2). HERACLES carries the twin Cercopes
upside down on a pole (*Lib.* 2.6.3, n. 3, Loeb edn.). JASON carries an old
woman (Hera) across a stream (*Argo.* 3.66f; *Fab.* 13, 22). Blind ORION carries, as his guide, one of the Cyclopes (Serv. *ad Aen.* 10.763), a boy (*Lib.*
1.4.3), or Cedalion, who guides him to Helius to be healed (*Poet. Astr.* 2.34).
(See also **Captive; Chariot; Flight; Seduction.**)

CASTAWAY

(See also **Beggar; Grieving; Sea; Seashore; Ship.**)

Reaching shore. AGRIPPINA reaches shore safely after her ship is
caused by her son Nero to founder (*Tac. An.* 14.5–8; Suet. *Nero* 34). AJAX
OïLEUS climbs from the sea onto a rock which Poseidon then splits (*Ep.* 6.6).
MENOETES climbs onto a rock after being jettisoned for incompetent helms-
manship in a boat race (*Aen.* 5.178f). ODYSSEUS, supported by Ino's veil,
floats ashore at Phaeacia, where he sleeps in a thicket and is awakened by
the noise of girls playing ball (*Od.* 5.451f, 6.110f, 7.278f). PALINURUS floats
to shore on his oar, only to be killed by rustics (*Aen.* 6.358f).

Marooned or rescued. ACHAEMENIDES, left behind when Odysseus
fled from the Cyclopes, is found by Aeneas (*Aen.* 3.588f; *Met.* 14.213f).
ANNA, Dido's sister, after her ship is wrecked, is found on the shore by
Aeneas and Achates (*Fasti* 3.601f). ARIADNE is abandoned by Theseus while
she sleeps (Cat. 64.52f; *Fab.* 43); she is rescued by Dionysus, who also subsequently deserts her (*Fasti* 3.469f; *Met.* 8.176f). MENELAÜS, shipwrecked
in Libya, comes to Proteus' palace or tomb (Eur. *Hel.* 408f) where he meets
Helen et al. (Eur. *Hel.* 541f). A MINSTREL, the guardian of Clytemnestra, is
left on a desert isle by Aegisthus (*Od.* 3.267f). PHILOCTETES is marooned by
Odysseus with only Heracles' bow to aid his survival (Soph. *Phil.* 1f; *Il.*
2.721f; *Ep.* 3.27); he is visited at his cave by Odysseus and Neoptolemus et
al. and leaves with them when Heracles intervenes (Soph. *Phil.* 220f, 975f,
1409f). PHRIXUS' four sons, after being shipwrecked, are rescued by the
Argonauts (*Argo.* 2.1121f; *Fab.* 21).

CAT

(See also **Lynx.**)

Attribute of Bubastis (identified with Artemis). She is frequently represented as a cat-headed woman.

In this form, ARTEMIS escapes from the monster Typhoeus (*Met.* 5.330).

CATTLE

(See also **Bull; Cow.**)

POSEIDON changes the people of Crimissa into cattle (*Fab.* 188).

Dragged backward into a cave. APOLLO's cattle, by Hermes (*H. to Her.* 76f, 205f; *Lib.* 3.10.2; *Met.* 2.685f). HERACLES' cattle, by Cacus (*Aen.* 8.205f; *Fasti* 1.543f).

Stolen or taken by ACHILLES, when Aeneas runs away (*Il.* 20.89f, 188f); by ALCYONEUS, one of the Giants, from Helius (*Lib.* 1.6.1); by AUTOLYCUS from Eurytus, are searched for by Heracles and Iphitus (*Lib.* 2.6.2), and from Sisyphus, who identifies them by a mark on a hoof (*Fab.* 201); by the DIOSCURI, IDAS and LYNCEUS; a quarrel ensues in which Idas kills Castor and Polydeuces kills Lynceus (*Lib.* 3.11.2); by HERACLES from three-headed Geryon; he carries them off over the sea in Helius' golden cup (*Lib.* 2.5.10; *Hes. Theog.* 289f) and delivers them to Eurystheus (*Lib.* 2.5.10); by HERMES from Neleus; Hermes bribes Neleus' servant Battus with the gift of a cow not to tell; he turns Battus to stone when he breaks his promise (*Met.* 2.687f); by MELAMPUS from Phylacus, for which he is imprisoned (*Lib.* 1.9.12; *Od.* 15.231f); by ODYSSEUS' men from Helius' herd are killed, cooked, and eaten (*Od.* 12.353f); by PEIRITHOÜS from Theseus, who forgives the raider; they become fast friends (Plut. 1.30); by the TAPHIANS from Electryon, whose sons attack the thieves (*Lib.* 2.4.6).

Tended by APOLLO for Admetus, whose cows he makes drop twins (Eur. *Alc.* 8f; *Lib.* 3.10.4) and for Laomedon, while Poseidon builds Troy's walls (*Il.* 11.448f); by NYMPHS for Helius (*Od.* 12.127f).

Slaughtered by AJAX in a fit of madness (Soph. *Ajax* 26f, 216f, 295f; *Fab.* 107; *Ep.* 5.6) by MAENADS after they rout the herdsman (Eur. *Bacch.* 735f); by ORESTES and PYLADES, who are driven by the Furies (Eur. *Iph. Taur.* 280f); by THEOPHANE's SUITORS; in return, Poseidon changes them into wolves (*Fab.* 188).

Fought over. AMPHITRYON kills Electryon (Hes. *Sh. Her.* 11f). IDAS kills Castor, and Polydeuces kills Lynceus (*Lib.* 3.11.2). ODYSSEUS is killed by the barbed spear of Telegonus, the son by Circe he had never seen (*Ep.* 7.36).

Graze in the meadow where PERSEPHONE and her friends are playing when a snow-white bull (Zeus) joins them; Hermes is their herder (*Met.* 2.843f).

Stampede. Cattle being driven by HERACLES scatter when they are attacked by flies sent by Hera (*Lib.* 2.5.10). Cattle with burning brush tied to their horns confuse Roman sentinels and allow Hannibal to escape (Livy 22.16; Plut. 10.6). Cattle raise a cloud of dust by dragging brush and confuse the enemy threatening Alexander (Ps.-Cal. 173).

CAULDRON

(See **Vessel.**)

CAVE

In vase painting, a cave is sometimes represented by an arch framing a figure.

Attribute of Aeternitas; Ceres; Mithras.

Born or reared in a cave. HERMAPHRODITUS is reared by the nymphs of Ida (*Met.* 4.288f). HERMES is born to Maia and laid on a winnowing fan (*Lib.* 3.10.2). ZEUS is born to Rhea, suckled by a goat, tended by nymphs, and protected by the Curetes (*Lib.* 1.1.6; Hes. *Theog.* 447f).

Abode or shelter of AEOLUS and the winds, of whom Hera asks a favor (*Aen.* 1.50f); of CACUS, a fire-breathing giant; it is decorated with human heads; Heracles invades it to recover his cattle (*Aen.* 8.193f, 8.251f); of CALYPSO, whom Hermes visits as she is weaving and Odysseus sits weeping on the shore (*Od.* 5.55f); she sets a meal before Odysseus (*Od.* 5.192f); of DEMETER, where she sits grieving for her lost Persephone; Pan and the Fates discover her (Paus. 8.42.2); of GREEKS returning from Troy who have been shipwrecked; they find a statue of Dionysus within (Paus. 2.23.1); of INVIDIA, a foul hag, whom Athena visits (*Met.* 2.760f); of PHILOCTETES, who has been marooned; Neoptolemus and Odysseus visit him (Soph. *Phil.* 15f and pass.); of POLYPHEMUS, a Cyclops, into which Odysseus and his men enter, to be trapped when Polyphemus stops the entrance with a boulder (*Od.* 9.216f), and before which Silenus and Satyrs are joined by Odysseus and his crew (Eur. *Cycl.* 85f); of the SIBYL of Cumae, which is cluttered with pages of her prophecies (*Aen.* 3.441f), and where Aeneas visits her (*Aen.* 6.42f; *Met.*

14.129f); of THETIS and the Nereïds, in the sea, where they lament the death of Patroclus (*Il.* 18.50f).

Used as a prison. ANTIGONE is left to die within a cave; when Creon relents and opens it, he finds her hanged and his son Haemon dead (Soph. *Ant.* 773f, 891f, 1100f). LYCURGUS, because of his persecution of Dionysus, is left to die (Soph. *Ant.* 955f). ZEUS is imprisoned by the monster Typhon and guarded by a dragon; Hermes and Aegipan rescue him (*Lib.* 1.6.3).

Lovemaking within. ATALANTA and HIPPOMENES offend Aphrodite by their lovemaking in Cybele's cave; they are turned into lions (*Met.* 10.689f). DIDO and AENEAS consummate their marriage (*Aen.* 4.123, 4.165f); JASON and MEDEA do likewise (*Argo.* 4.1128f; *Fab.* 23). ZEUS seduces Maia (*H. to Her.* 5f).

Gifts of the Phaeacians are hidden in a cave by Odysseus and Athena (*Od.* 13.366f).

Entrance to the underworld. AENEAS and the Sibyl approach and enter (*Aen.* 6.201f). The *Argo* sails by and lands near it (*Argo.* 2.784f). It is supported by silver columns (Hes. *Theog.* 775f).

CENTAUR

In earliest accounts Centaurs are described as hairy savages. After they acquired their man-horse nature they were represented as human with a horse's body and back legs attached. From the time of Pheidias they have been conceived as human to the waist with a horse's body and legs.

ORIGIN

CENTAURUS is born from a mist resembling Hera that Ixion has impregnated (*Fab.* 62; *Ep.* 1.20) or from the mating of Zeus, in the form of a horse, with Ixion's wife Dia (Serv. *ad Aen.* 8.293).

CHEIRON is born from the mating of Philyra, in the form of a mare, and Cronus, a stallion; Philyra is turned into a linden tree by Rhea, Cronus' wife (Serv. *ad Georg.* 3.93; *Fab.* 138).

ACTIVITIES

CENTAURS become intoxicated at Peirithoüs' wedding and try to carry off bride and bridesmaids, starting a battle with the Lapiths (*Met.* 12.210f; *Ep.* 1.21; *Od.* 21.295f; Hes. *Sh. Her.* 178f; Plut. 1.30), and they attack Caenus, whom they bury beneath uprooted trees (*Argo.* 1.59f; *Fab.* 14; *Ep.* 1.22); Caenus survives as a bird (*Met.* 12.510f). Ovid, in *Met.* 12.210–535, names fifty-six Centaurs who took part in the battle with the Lapiths and describes in detail many of the individual combats that took place.

CHEIRON is watched over by his mother Philyra (*Argo.* 2.1238f); he becomes the guardian of baby Achilles, brought to him by Peleus, and rears him with the help of nymphs (*Lib.* 3.13.6; *Argo.* 4.810f); he instructs Achilles in music (*Fasti* 5.385f); he becomes the guardian of Asclepius (*Met.* 2.628f; *Lib.* 3.10.3) of Apollo's son Aristaeus (*Argo.* 2.508f) and of the son of Jason and Medea (Hes. *Theog.* 1000f); he gives Peleus a spear made by Athena and Hephaestus (Schol. *ad Il.* 16.143; *Lib.* 3.13.5); he restores to Peleus his sword, enabling him to fight off some other Centaurs (*Lib.* 3.13.3); he wades into the sea to wave to the *Argo* as it passes, as his wife holds up baby Achilles for Peleus to see (*Argo.* 1.553f); he fashions a statue of their dead master for Actaeon's grieving dogs (*Lib.* 3.4.4); he restores Phoenix's sight (*Lib.* 3.13.8); he and Achilles are visited by Heracles (*Fasti* 5.387f); he is wounded in the knee by an arrow that Heracles had aimed at another Centaur (*Lib.* 2.5.3); he drops a poisoned arrow on his foot and dies, as Achilles weeps (*Fasti* 5.397f; *Poet. Astr.* 2.38).

EURYTION (Eurytus) claims as his bride Deïaneira (or Mnesimache, *Lib.* 2.5.5) and is killed by his rival Heracles (*Fab.* 31, 33); as he carries off Peirithoüs' bride Hippodameia, he is killed by Theseus with a cauldron (*Met.* 12.219f).

HYLAEUS is killed by Heracles, along with Pholus (*Aen.* 8.293); by Atalanta, for trying to violate her (*Lib.* 3.9.2); by Theseus, during the Centaur-Lapith fray (Serv. *ad Aen.* 8.294).

HYLONOME kills herself with the spear that slew her lover in the fight with the Lapiths (*Met.* 12.417f).

MELANIPPE escapes from her searching father Cheiron by becoming a mare and later a constellation (*Poet. Astr.* 2.18).

NESSUS carries Heracles' bride Deïaneira across a stream and tries to make off with her; dying, after being shot by Heracles, he gives some of his poisoned blood or his bloody robe to Deïaneira to use as a love charm (Soph. *Trach.* 555f; *Met.* 9.107f; *Lib.* 2.7.6; *Fab.* 31, 34; Sen. *Her. Oet.* 558f).

ACHILLES IN THE CARE OF CHEIRON

PHOLUS entertains Heracles in his cave; other Centaurs are attracted by the odor of wine and are repelled or slain by Heracles (*Lib.* 2.5.4); Pholus is killed by Heracles along with Hylaeus (*Aen.* 8.293f) or dies after dropping one of Heracles' poisoned arrows on his foot (*Lib.* 2.5.4).

PYLENOR and other Centaurs bathe the wounds inflicted by Heracles in a stream that becomes contaminated (*Met.* 15.218f; Paus. 5.5.10).

SEA CENTAURS

These Centaurs, called Hippocampi, have horses' heads and front legs, and serpent coils in place of back legs. They are an attribute of Amphitrite; Poseidon; Proteus (*Georg.* 4.389). Triton may be so represented.

CHAIN

(See also **Bonds; Captive; Net; Rope.**)

Attribute of Diana (Natura); Hercules (leading captives).
XERXES tries to chain the Hellespont (Aes. *Pers.* 745f).

CHAIR

(See also **Seated Figure; Throne.**)

POLYTECHNUS, in competition with Aëdon in their respective crafts, constructs a chair; but Aëdon finishes her weaving first (Ant. Lib. 11).

CHARIOT

(See also **Captive; Wagon.**)

A complicated knot tied on a chariot-pole is cut by Alexander at Gordium (Plut. 33.18; Arrian 1.1.7).

DRAWN BY HORSES

Four white horses: attribute of Helius; Phoebus Apollo; Zeus. Four black: Pluto. Two or four: Ares; Artemis; Demeter; Eos; Hera; Poseidon; Selene. On fire: Cupid.

One of ACHILLES' horses, having the gift of speech, addresses him as they set out to fight (*Il.* 19.400f).

Scythe-bearing chariots are used by Darius against Alexander (Ps.-Cal. 113–15, 186; Arrian 3.13.5).

Winged horses. Attribute of Thetis and sometimes of the deities named above. IDAS carries off Marpessa in a "winged chariot" given him by Poseidon; Euenus pursues him (*Lib.* 1.7.3). PELOPS receives from Poseidon a golden chariot drawn by winged horses that can be driven on water (Pind. *Ol.* 1.37[60]f, 71[114]f; *Ep.* 2.3) and in which he carries off Hippodameia, pursued by Oenomaüs (Paus. 5.17.7). PHAËTHON drives the sun-chariot; out of control, it scorches the earth, causing Zeus to strike him with a thunderbolt (*Met.* 2.119f).

Racing. ACHILLES, on foot, keeps up with a four-horse team (Eur. *Iph. Aul.* 206f). AETOLUS runs over Apis during the games for Azan (Paus. 5.1.8). ALEXANDER wins when his opponent crashes (Ps.-Cal. 53, 54). DIOMEDES wins the race at the games for Patroclus: during the race Apollo causes him to lose his whip, and Athena returns it to him after she wrecks Eumelus' chariot and Antilochus cuts off Menelaüs (*Il.* 23.352f). GLAUCUS loses a race, after which he is devoured by his horses (*Fab.* 250, 273.12; Paus. 6.20.19). NESTOR is defeated by the twin sons of Actor, the Moliones or Actoriones (These twins may have raced in two chariots, as one Scholiast conjectures, but most sources describe them as having two bodies joined, or as having one body, two heads, four arms, and four legs, in which case they would occupy a single chariot.) (*Il.* 23.638f; Schol. ad loc.).

In combat. Ordinary scenes of chariot fighting are virtually indistinguishable and are not included. The few that have an exceptional feature will be found elsewhere under the heading suggested by that feature.

Pursuing or fleeing. DEÏPHONTES overtakes Hyrnetho and her brothers (Paus. 2.28.3). EURYSTHEUS is overtaken and killed by Hyllus or Iolaüs (*Lib.* 2.8.1); he is overtaken and captured by Hyllus and Iolaüs, as Heracles and Hebe watch (Eur. *Heracleidae* 850f). EVENUS races a suitor for his daughter's hand and beheads him when he catches him (Eust. *ad Il.* 9.776; Schol. *ad Il.* 9.557). OENOMAÜS, driven by Myrtilus, overtakes and kills a suitor of his daughter Hippodameia (Paus. 8.15.10; *Fab.* 84; *Ep.* 2.5); when trying to spear Pelops, who is fleeing with Hippodameia, an axle breaks and he falls out (*Argo.* 1.752f); his chariot comes apart as he races Pelops and he is dragged to death (*Ep.* 2.7; *Fab.* 840).

Dragging a charioteer. HIPPOLYTUS, who has fallen out when his team bolts at the sight of a bull emerging from the sea (*Ep.* 1.19; Eur. *Hipp.* 1185f; *Met.* 15.521f; *Fab.* 47). OENOMAÜS, when his chariot falls apart (*Ep.* 2.7; see also "Pursuing or fleeing," above). TROÏLUS, after losing his balance while trying to escape from Achilles (*Aen.* 1.474f).

Dragging a corpse. HECTOR is dragged around Troy by Achilles (*Il.* 22.395f, 23.13f, 24.14f). METTIUS FUFETIUS is torn apart between two chariots (Livy 1.28). PENTHESILEIA is dragged by Diomedes (Dictys 43).

Driven over the body of APIS, by Aetolus, in a race (Paus. 5.1.8); of SERVIUS TULLIUS, by his daughter Tullia (Livy 1.48).

Driven or harnessed by divinities. APHRODITE and IRIS borrow Ares' chariot to escape from battle (*Il.* 5.353f). ARES comes to earth to fetch Romulus to heaven (*Met.* 14.818f; he drives his son Cycnus to a meeting with Heracles, Hes. *Sh. Her.* 57f). ATHENA, replacing Sthenelus, drives Diomedes into battle against Ares (*Il.* 5.835f); reaching out from her chariot, she turns Ares' spear away from Heracles (Hes. *Sh. Her.* 455f). DEIMOS (Terror) and PHOBOS (Flight) harness Ares' chariot (*Il.* 15.119f) and rescue Ares from Heracles (Hes. *Sh. Her.* 463f). HADES abducts Persephone (*Met.* 5.391f; *H. to Dem.* 19f) and strikes with his sceptre the water nymph Cyane, who tries to stop him (*Met.* 5.411f). HERA harnesses the horses while Athena arms herself, and drives Athena into battle (*Il.* 8.382f); she is helped with the harnessing by Hebe (*Il.* 5.720f). HERMES brings Persephone from Hades to Demeter (*H. to Dem.* 375f); he drives Priam's chariot, which is accompanied by a wagon full of ransom for Hector's body, to Achilles' quarters (*Il.* 24.440f). JUTURNA, after ejecting Turnus' driver and assuming his likeness, keeps her brother away from Aeneas, who is on foot (*Aen.* 12.468f). POSEIDON drives over the sea to calm a storm in which the Trojan ships of Aeneas are caught (*Aen.* 1.145f, 5.816f) and to go help the Greeks against Troy (*Il.* 13.23f).

Driven by mortals. AGAMEMNON arrives home with Cassandra, to be welcomed by Clytemnestra et al. (Aes. *Agam.* 738f). AMPHIARAÜS disappears into a chasm made by a thunderbolt (*Lib.* 3.6.8; Eur. *Suppl.* 500f; *Fab.* 68, 73). CLYTEMNESTRA, Iphigeneia, and baby Orestes come to Agamemnon at Aulis (Eur. *Iph. Aul.* 590f). HERACLES, driven by Iolaüs, and Cycnus, driven by his father Ares, meet and challenge one another (Hes. *Sh. Her.* 57f). Heracles' chariots and men are crushed by a stone hurled by the Giant Alcyoneus (Pind. *Nem.* 4.25f). LAIUS' car, or one of his horses, grazes Oedipus, who is on foot, at a narrow place or crossroads; in the resulting quarrel, Oedipus kills Laius (Soph. *Oed. Tyr.* 801f; Eur. *Phoen.* 37f; *Fab.* 67); or their chariots collide, with the same outcome (*Lib.* 3.5.7). PELASGUS comes upon Danaüs and his many daughters, in Egyptian dress, in a sacred grove (Aes. *Suppl.* 176f). PHAËTHON drives Phoebus' sun-chariot, from which he falls to earth when struck by a thunderbolt (*Met.* 2.150f; *Fab.* 152, 154). PRIAM drives his chariot behind a mule-drawn wagon carrying ransom for Hector's body (*Il.* 24.322f); where Priam and Idaeus, the wagoneer, stop to water their teams, a youth (Hermes) joins them and becomes Priam's driver to Achilles' hut, on the way to which he puts the Greek guards to sleep (*Il.* 24.440f); for the return, Hermes yokes the teams and accompanies the caravan part of the way to Troy (*Il.* 26.690f). RHESUS, driving his famed team of horses, arrives at Troy with his warriors, and is welcomed by Hector (Eur. *Rhes.* 300f). SAL-MONEUS drives over a bridge of brass, dragging bronze vessels and hurling torches to imitate thunder and lightning; Zeus blasts him with a real bolt (*Lib.* 1.9.7; *Aen.* 6.585f; *Fab.* 61). TELEMACHUS and PEISISTRATUS, in their search for Odysseus, take leave of Nestor (*Od.* 3.478f), and are welcomed by Menelaüs (*Od.* 4.20f), from whom they depart under the good omen of an eagle bearing a goose (*Od.* 15.144f). TURNUS decorates his chariot with the heads of two newly slain warriors (*Aen.* 12.509f). XERXES reviews his army from his chariot (Herod. 7.100).

DRAWN BY VARIOUS TEAMS

A boar and a lion: Apollo presents it to Admetus, who gives it to Pelias and in return wins from him the hand of Alcestis (*Lib.* 1.9.15; *Fab.* 50, 51).

Centaurs: attribute of Dionysus and Ariadne. Cocks: Hermes; Sol. Cow and ox: Cybele. Cows: Selene. Deer: Artemis; a priestess of Artemis (Paus. 7.18.7). Dogs: Hephaestus. Dolphins: Amphitrite.

Doves: attribute of Aphrodite. She comes to earth to fetch Aeneas to heaven (*Met.* 14.596f).

Dragons, frequently winged: Attribute of Cybele; Demeter; Medea; Oistros (Furor); Triptolemus. ANTHEAS takes the chariot of Triptolemus and falls from it (Paus. 7.18.2). DEMETER, carrying a torch, drives in search of Persephone (*Met.* 5.438f; *Fasti* 4.497f). MEDEA escapes from Jason (*Lib.* 1.9.28) with the bodies of their children (Eur. *Med.* 1317f); she travels afar to gather magic herbs (*Met.* 7.219f), escapes from the daughters of Pelias whom she has duped into killing their father (*Met.* 7.350f), returns to Colchis (*Fab.* 26), and comes to King Perses to free her imprisoned son Medus (*Fab.* 27). An OREAD (mountain nymph) drives in Demeter's chariot to bring Fames (Famine) to afflict Erysichthon (*Met.* 8.794f). TRIPTOLEMUS sows grain over the earth (*Met.* 5.642f; *Lib.* 1.5.2) and drives in a one-wheeled chariot to the Getae; when one of the dragons is killed by Carnabon, Demeter replaces it (*Poet. Astr.* 2.14).

Eagles: attribute of Zeus. Erotes (Cupids, Putti): Aphrodite. Goat and panther: Dionysus; Silenus. Hippocampi (see **Monster, Hybrid**): Amphitrite; Poseidon; Proteus.

Lions: attribute of Cybele (Rhea). ATALANTA and HIPPOMENES, after being changed into lions, are harnessed to Cybele's car (*Met.* 10.698f; *Fab.* 185).

Men: CLEOBIS and BITON yoke themselves to their mother's car and pull her to a temple ceremony (Herod. 1.31; Plut. 5.26).

TRIPTOLEMUS DRIVING DEMETER'S CHARIOT

Mules: attribute of Selene.

Oxen: attribute of Flora. CHARICLEIA, in an oxcart, hands a taper to Theagenes at the tomb of Neoptolemus, at which moment they fall in love (*Aeth.* 3).

Panthers: attribute of Dionysus. Peacocks: Hera. Seals: Proteus. Stags: Artemis. Storks: Demeter; Hermes.

Swans: attribute of Aphrodite; Apollo. APHRODITE comes to dying Adonis, who has been wounded by a boar (*Met.* 10.708f).

Tigers: attribute of Dionysus. He comes to rescue Ariadne, whom Theseus has deserted (*Ars. Amat.* 1.537f; *Ep.* 1.9).

Wolves: attribute of Ares.

Women: DARIUS, in a dream of his mother, harnesses two women, personifying Greece and Asia, to his chariot, which becomes overturned (Aes. *Pers.* 176f).

CHASM

(See also **Falling; Leaping; Pit; Well.**)

Disappearing into a chasm. ALTHAEMENES, after killing his aged parent whom he mistook for a member of a raiding party, learns the truth and disappears into a chasm (*Lib.* 3.2.2). AMPHIARAÜS drives his chariot into a chasm made by a thunderbolt (*Lib.* 3.6.8; *Fab.* 68, 73; Eur. *Suppl.* 500f). LAODICE escapes slavery to a Greek warrior when, in sight of all, she is swallowed by a chasm (*Ep.* 5.23). MARCUS CURTIUS rides his horse into a chasm in the Roman Forum in order to appease some hostile deity (Livy 7.6). THESEUS is pushed into an abyss by Lycomedes (*Ep.* 1.24). TROPHONIUS, carrying the head of his brother Agamedes, disappears into a chasm (Paus. 9.37.3).

CHECKERS OR CHESSMEN

Often represented by objects on a table or low box between two intent players. (See **Game.**)

CHEST

(See also **Boat; Box; Cradle; Sarcophagus; Vessel.**)

Containing people. Baby ADONIS is placed in a chest by Aphrodite and given to Persephone (*Lib.* 3.14.4). ARSINOË is put into a chest by her sons and given to Agapenor to be his slave (*Lib.* 3.7.5). Baby ERICHTHONIUS is found with a snake (or is himself part snake) in a chest that Athena has given to Cecrops' daughters (*Lib.* 3.14.6; Eur. *Ion* 265f); his presence is revealed by a crow (*Met.* 2.552f; *Fab.* 166).

Containing people is set afloat. AUGE with Telephus, her baby by Heracles, is set adrift by her father; she is found by Teuthras, who marries her (Paus. 8.4.9). DANAË with baby Perseus, by her father Acrisius; she is found by Dictys (*Lib.* 2.4.1; *Fab.* 63). DEUCALION and PYRRHA survive the flood and land on Mt. Parnassus (*Lib.* 1.7.2). RHOEO, pregnant by Apollo, by her father; she floats to Euboea or Delos, where Anius is born (Diod. Sic. 5.62.1). ROMULUS and REMUS, by a rustic or by servants of Amulius; they are found and nursed by a wolf (Livy 1.4; Plut. 2.3). SEMELE and baby DIONYSUS, by Cadmus; Semele is dead when the chest reaches shore and is

DANAË AND BABY PERSEUS ARE PUT INTO A CHEST
BY KING ACRISIUS AND A SERVANT

buried by the natives, who rear Dionysus (Paus. 3.24.3). TENES and HEMI-
THEA, brother and sister, by their father Cycnus upon a false accusation by
their stepmother; they float to Tenedos (*Ep.* 3.25; Paus. 10.14.2). Old
THOAS, by his daughter Hypsipyle, to save him from being murdered by the
women of Lemnos (*Argo.* 1.620f).

Containing various objects. ACHILLES takes his personal, precious
drinking cup from its elaborate chest (*Il.* 16.220f). ALEXANDER receives from
an embassy from Darius a chest containing a ball, a thong, and a letter (Ps.-
Cal. 103–106). ALTHAEA places the stick that betokens the span of her baby
Meleager's life into a chest after snatching it from the fire on her hearth; she
later lets it burn (*Lib.* 1.8.2; *Fab.* 174). ATREUS puts a golden lamb, which
he has killed, into a chest that his wife Aerope later gives to Thyestes, who
produces it and claims Atreus' kingdom (*Ep.* 2.11). EURYPHYLUS, in opening
the chest containing a statue of Dionysus, part of the booty taken at Troy, is
driven mad; he carries the chest to Delphi; later the chest is instrumental in
preventing the sacrifice of a boy and a girl and in restoring his sanity (Paus.
7.19.3). GLAUCE (Creüsa) puts on the poisoned robe and crown from the
chest given her by Medea's children; she burns to death, as does Creon when
he touches her (Eur. *Med.* 1153f; in *Fab.* 25 Jason also dies). HERACLES
puts on the robe, unwittingly made poisonous by Deïaneira, from the chest
brought to him by Lichas; he is tormented by it and tries to tear it off (Soph.
Trach. 660f, 756f). MEDEA opens her chest of drugs, intending to kill herself,
but her mind is changed by Hera (*Argo.* 3.802f).

CHILDREN

(See also **Baby; Boy; Girl.**)

Attribute of Pietas.

CHIMAERA

A lion-goat-snake hybrid, of which the goat element is sometimes represented by a goat's head sprouting from the lion's back. Hesiod describes the creature as a dragon with the heads of a lion, a goat, and a serpent.

BELLEROPHON, astride the winged horse Pegasus, kills the Chimaera (*Il.* 6.173f; *Fab.* 57; Hes. *Theog.* 319f; *Lib.* 2.3.1; Eur. *Ion* 201f; cf. *Il.* 6.178f, where Pegasus is not mentioned). (See also the note on **Horse** [Winged].)

CHITON

(See **Garment.**)

CLAY

(See **Mud.**)

CLIMBING

(See also **Ladder.**)

ALEXANDER leads the climb up the Rock of Aornos (Arrian 4.30.3).

ALEXANDER'S SOLDIERS, aided by ropes and pitons, ascend the vertical Rock of Sogdiana (Arrian 4.19.1f).

GAULS try to surprise the garrison on Rome's Capitoline Hill (Livy 5.47; Plut. 8.27).

CLOD

(See **Island; Rock; Stone.**)

CLOTHING

(See **Garment.**)

CLOUD

(See **Mist.**)

CLUB

(See also **Fighting; Hoe; Killing; Staff; Tools; Wand.**)

Attribute of Heracles.

HERACLES' club sprouts leaves while it leans against a statue of Hermes (Paus. 3.31.13).

OMPHALE carries Heracles' club, and arrays him in her garb, symbolizing his enslavement to her (*Fasti* 2.317f).

Used as a weapon by ALCATHOÜS against his son because he interrupts a sacrifice (Paus. 1.42.7); by AMPHITRYON, who throws it at a charging cow; the club bounces off its horns and kills Electryon (*Lib.* 2.4.6); by AREÏTHOÜS; he is outwitted by Lycurgus, who maneuvers him into a place too narrow to swing a club and then spears him (*Il.* 7.136f); by the BEBRYCES against the Argonauts (*Argo.* 2.98f); by the FATES against the Giants (*Lib.* 1.6.2); by HERACLES against the Giant Alcyoneus, who has crushed his men and chariots under a huge stone (Pind. *Nem.* 4.25f), the nine-headed Lernaean Hydra

HERACLES, WITH CLUB AND BOW, IN HELIUS' GOLD-
EN GOBLET

(*Lib.* 2.5.2), fire-breathing Cacus, who has stolen his cattle (*Fasti* 1.575f; Livy 1.7), the Nemean Lion (*Lib.* 2.5.1), a bull, as Ancaeus slays another with an axe (*Argo.* 1.425f), and against Eurytus, whose daughter Iole he takes (Sen. *Her. Oet.* 216f); by a MOB, which kills Tiberius Gracchus and many of his supporters (Plut. 39.19); by NERO'S SOLDIERS, against his mother Agrippina in her bed; Nero views her corpse (Tac. *An.* 14.8–9); by drunken SHEPHERDS against Icarius (*Fab.* 130; *Poet. Astr.* 2.4); by THESEUS, against Periphetes, from whom he has wrested it (*Lib.* 3.16.1; Plut. 1.8), against the Thebans in battle (Eur. *Suppl.* 713f) and several Centaurs during the fight with the Lapiths (*Met.* 12.342f); by TORQUATUS' MEN (lictors?) against his son, because he met a Gallic champion in single combat against orders (Serv. *ad Aen.* 6.824).

COAL

PORCIA swallows a hot coal to kill herself when she hears of Brutus' death (Plut. 46.53).

THEAGENES and CHARICLEIA, to prove their chastity to the Egyptian king and queen, stand in turn on a fiery brazier (*Aeth.* 10).

COCK

(See **Bird**.)

COFFIN

(See **Chest; Sarcophagus**.)

COLUMN

(See **Altar; Pillar; Stele; Temple; Tomb**.)

COMB

(See also **Toilette**.)

Attribute of a masculine Venus.

Used by the Cyclops POLYPHEMUS, seeking to win the favor of the sea nymph Galatea (*Met.* 13.764f); by the maid SCYLLA to comb Galatea's hair

(*Met.* 13.738); by SPARTAN SOLDIERS before the battle with the Persians at the pass of Thermopylae (Herod. 7.208).

COMBAT

(See **Fighting.**)

COMET

(See **Star.**)

COMPASS

Attribute of Saturn; Urania (with a sphere also).
   PERDIX, the nephew of Daedalus, invents the compass (*Met.* 8.247f).

CONCH

(See also **Cornucopia; Horn; Trumpet.**)

Attribute of Boreas; Glaucus; Triton; Tritons generally.
   DAEDALUS succeeds in passing a thread through a conch by tying it to an ant and boring a hole at the tip of the shell; the feat reveals to Minos that he has at last discovered Daedalus' whereabouts (*Ep.* 1.14).
   TRITON blows his conch to end the flood that Zeus and Poseidon have inflicted on mankind (*Met.* 1.332f); and to prove his superiority over Misenus, after which he plunges his competitor into the sea (*Aen.* 6.171f).

COOKING

(See **Eating; Fire; Vessel, Cooking.**)

CORMORANT

(See **Bird.**)

CORN EARS

(See also **Cornucopia; Wreath.**)

Attribute of Bonus Eventus; Demeter; Eirene; Horae; Iustitia; Ops; Pax; Triptolemus.

Grown by SPERMO, to whom Dionysus has given this power (*Met.* 13.632f; *Ep.* 3.10).

Lopped off or broken by THRASYBULUS in silent response to an envoy's question (Herod. 5.92).

Drip blood, portending HANNIBAL's invasion of Italy (Plut. 10.2).

Produced from inedible matter when touched by the daughters of ANIUS (*Met.* 13.652f).

CORNUCOPIA

(See also **Horn.**)

Attribute of Bacchus; Concordia; Copia; Gaea; a genius; Honos; Isis; Pax; Phoebus Apollo; Plutus; Priapus; Providentia; Sigalion; Themis; Tiber; Tyche; Vesta; Virtus. Emitting smoke: Somnium (Dream).

Made by AMALTHEIA from a horn of the goat that suckled baby Zeus (*Fasti* 5.115f); by NAIADS from the horn that Heracles tears from the head of a bull (Acheloüs) (*Met.* 9.85f).

Provides food for THESEUS and other guests of Acheloüs (*Met.* 9.89f); for baby ZEUS, who is being cared for by Amaltheia (*Fasti* 5.115f).

CORPSE

(See also **Altar; Blood; Burial; Dismembering; Dying Figure; Eating; Falling; Hanging; Killing; Sleeping Figure; Vessel, Cooking; Wounded Figure.**)

Found on the shore. AJAX OÏLEUS, by Thetis, who buries him (*Ep.* 6.6). CARPOS, by Calamus, who is turned by Zeus into reeds growing in the river in which his friend has drowned (Serv. *ad Ecl.* 5.48). CEŸX, by his wife Alcyone, who becomes a halcyon bird (*Met.* 11.710f). ICARUS, by Heracles, who buries him (*Lib.* 2.6.3). LEANDER, by his lover Hero (*Heroïdes* 19.199f); catching sight of the body from her tower, Hero leaps to her death (Serv. *ad Georg.* 3.258). MELICERTES, by Sisyphus, who buries him (Paus. 2.1.3). MISENUS, by Aeneas and Achates, after Triton drowned him for challenging him in trumpet playing (*Aen.* 6.362f). ORION, by Artemis, who had accidentally shot him in the head with an arrow while he was swimming (*Poet. Astr.* 2.34). PALINURUS is killed by local rustics after he swims ashore; his body is

left lying on the beach, and is later given burial (*Aen.* 6.362f). PERSIAN SAIL-
ORS by Themistocles et al. after the battle of Salamis (Plut. 7.18). POLYDO-
RUS, by his mother Hecuba, who has gone to the shore for water to wash her
daughter's body for burial (*Met.* 13.533f), or by servants, who bring the body
to Hecuba (Eur. *Hec.* 27f, 698f). POMPEY, headless, by his freedman Philip
and an old soldier, who wash and burn him (Plut. 32.80). PRIAM, headless,
unburied and untended (*Aen.* 2.547f). SCYLLA, after being thrown overboard
from Minos' ship, lies unburied and torn by sea birds (Paus. 2.34.7).

Found elsewhere. ADONIS, killed by a boar, by Aphrodite, while driving her chariot (*Met.* 10.708f). EURYDICE, a suicide, by her husband Creon,
as he returns with the body of their son (Soph. *Ant.* 1261f). ICARIUS, by his
daughter Erigone and her dog Maera, whereupon she hangs herself (*Lib.*
3.14.7). MEGARA and her sons, by Amphitryon et al., as Heracles, who has
killed them in a fit of madness, lies bound and asleep (Eur. *Her.* 1029f).
PARIS, wounded by an arrow, by Oenone who has come too late to heal him;
she hangs herself in remorse (*Lib.* 3.12.6). PHAEDRA, a suicide, with a letter
in her hand, by Theseus et al. (Eur. *Hipp.* 808f), and by Hippolytus (Eur.
Hipp. 905). PYRAMUS, who killed himself upon finding Thisbe's bloody robe,
by Thisbe, who then stabs herself (*Met.* 4.133f). THEANO's SONS, by their
mother, who then kills herself (*Fab.* 186).

Viewed by an enemy. AGRIPPINA, by her son Nero, who has had her
clubbed to death (Tac. *An.* 14.9; Suet. *Nero* 34). CYRUS, by Queen Tomyris;
she dips his head in blood to give him (symbolically) his fill of it (Herod.
1.214). DARIUS' WIFE, dead in childbirth, and Darius, killed in battle, are
viewed by a sorrowful Alexander (Plut. 33.30, 33.43). MARCELLUS, by Hannibal, respectfully (Plut. 16.30).

Displayed or revealed. AEGISTHUS, to Electra, by his assassins Orestes
and Pylades (Eur. *Elec.* 907f). AGAMEMNON and CASSANDRA, to the elders
of Argos, by their murderers Clytemnestra (Aes. *Agam.* 1372f) and Aegisthus (Aes. *Agam.* 1577f). CAESAR, to the Roman people by Antony (Plut.
44.14). CLYTEMNESTRA, when Aegisthus removes her shroud in the presence
of Electra, Orestes, and Pylades (Soph. *Elec.* 1466f). CLYTEMNESTRA and
AEGISTHUS, to the women of Argos, by Orestes, Pylades, and Electra (Eur.
Elec. 1165f), or by Orestes (and Pylades?) (Aes. *Choëph.* 972f). LUCRETIA,
a suicide after her rape by Tarquin, to the Roman people, by Brutus (Livy
1.59). MEDEA's CHILDREN, whom she has killed, to their father Jason; she
escapes in her dragon-drawn car (Sen. *Med.* 997f). PENTHEUS, headless and
mutilated, to his mother Agave by his grandfather Cadmus (Eur. *Bacch.*
1299f). VERGINIA, killed by her father to save her from Appius Claudius, to
the Roman people (Livy 3.48).

Embraced. CORONIS, by Apollo, remorseful at having killed her out of jealousy (*Met.* 2.612f). GLAUCE, by King Creon, who becomes stricken by the same poison that destroyed her (Eur. *Med.* 1204f). HESPERIA, by her suitor Aesacus, from whom she was fleeing when a snake bit her (*Met.* 11.777f). HYACINTHUS, by Apollo, whose discus has killed him (*Met.* 10.185f). LAUSUS, by Aeneas, remorseful at having killed him in battle (*Aen.* 10.830f). PATROCLUS, by Briseïs, sorrowful because of his past kindness to her (*Il.* 19.282f). POLYNEICES, by his sister Antigone, who resists Creon's efforts to pull her from him, the bodies of her mother, other brother, and blind Oedipus (Eur. *Phoen.* 1660f). PROCRIS, by her husband Cephalus, who has accidentally killed her during a hunt (*Met.* 7.842f). PYRAMUS, by Thisbe, after he has killed himself when he thought her dead (*Met.* 4.133f).

Mourned. ACHILLES, by his mother Thetis and other Nereïds (Quint. Smy. 3.595f). ADONIS, after a boar has killed him, by Aphrodite (*Met.* 10.708f). AJAX, who has fallen on his sword, by Tecmessa; she cuts a lock of his hair (Soph. *Ajax* 891f, 1171f). ALEXANDER mourns the death of a young soldier of the same name (Plut. 33.58). Baby ASTYANAX, lying on a shield, by Hecuba (Eur. *Troad.* 1120f, 1167f). HECTOR, after being brought back to Troy, by Andromache, Hecuba, et al. (*Il.* 24.719f). HEPHAESTION, by Alexander (Arrian 7.14.3). HYAS, who has been killed by a boar or a lion, is mourned by his sisters, who become the Pleiades (*Fab.* 192). LUCRETIA, after her suicide, by her husband and father; Brutus withdraws the knife (Livy 1.59). MELEAGER, by his sisters, who become birds, by his father, and by his mother, who kills herself (*Met.* 8.526f; *Lib.* 1.8.3). NIOBE'S SONS and DAUGHTERS, killed by the shafts of Apollo and Artemis, by their mother, who is turned to stone from which tears stream (*Met.* 6.301f). PALLAS, by Aeneas et al.; Aeneas places a robe to cover him on the journey home (*Aen.* 11.29f). PATROCLUS, by Achilles et al. (*Il.* 19.310f) and by Achilles' horses (*Il.* 17.426f). The Amazon PENTHESILEIA, by Achilles, who has killed her; he kills Thersites for jeering at his sorrow (*Ep.* 5.1). PENTHEUS, headless and mutilated, by his grandfather Cadmus and mother Agave (Eur. *Bacch.* 1298f). POLYDORUS, by his mother Hecuba and her handmaids, as Agamemnon appears (Eur. *Hec.* 681f). POLYNEICES and ETEOCLES, by their sister Antigone and mother Jocasta, who kills herself (Eur. *Phoen.* 1428f), by Antigone, Ismene, et al. (Aes. *Seven* 848). POLYNEICES, ETEOCLES, and JOCASTA, by blind Oedipus and Antigone, until Creon interferes (Eur. *Phoen.* 1480f). POLYXENA, who has been sacrificed to Achilles, by Hecuba (*Met.* 13.488f). RHESUS, by his mother, one of the Muses; she carries him off in her arms (Eur. *Rhes.* 895f). The SEVEN AGAINST THEBES, by their mothers, and by Thesus and Adrastus (Eur. *Suppl.* 795f).

Transformed. AJAX's blood produces flowers (*Met.* 13.394f). ALOPE's body is changed by Poseidon into a spring (*Fab.* 187). CEŸX's body becomes a halcyon when embraced by the bird that was his wife (*Met.* 11.731f). HYACINTHUS, killed by Boreas' discus, becomes a flower (Serv. *ad Ecl.* 3.13). MELISSA's body produces a swarm of bees (Serv. *ad. Aen.* 1.430). NARCISSUS' body disappears, and in its place his sisters find a flower (*Met.* 3.502f).

Washed and tended. ACHILLES, by Greek warriors, Thetis and other Nereïds (*Od.* 24.47f), or by Athena and warriors (Quint. Smy. 3.525f). AENEAS, by Aphrodite and the horned river god Numicius (*Met.* 11.602f). AJAX, by attendants directed by Teucer (Soph. *Ajax* 1403f). HECTOR, by Apollo and Aphrodite (*Il.* 23.184f), by Achilles' maidservants (*Il.* 24.582f). PATROCLUS, by Thetis (*Il.* 19.38f), by Achilles' comrades, after water has been heated (*Il.* 18.343f); they put locks of hair on the body and Achilles puts one into Patroclus' hands (*Il.* 23.135f, 23.152f). PHAËTHON, by the river god Eridanus; he is buried by nymphs (*Met.* 2.323f). SARPEDON, by Apollo, after which Sleep and Death take the body (*Il.* 16.667f).

Revived or rejuvenated. Old AESON has his throat cut by Medea and his blood replaced by her rejuvenating brew (*Met.* 7.251f). GLAUCUS, a child, by herbs applied by Polyidus, who has observed a snake use them to revive its dead mate (*Fab.* 136; *Lib.* 3.3.1) or by Asclepius in the same circumstances (*Poet. Astr.* 2.14). HEPHAESTUS, lifeless after his fall from Olympus, is revived by the women of Lemnos (*Il.* 1.590f). HIPPOLYTUS, by Asclepius (*Fab.* 49; *Poet. Astr.* 2.14) or by Asclepius and Artemis (Cynthia, Trivia) (*Met.* 15.531f; *Aen.* 7.765f). A WITCH's SON, killed in a battle, is made by her to rise and speak; Charicleia and the seer Calasiris are observers (*Aeth.* 6).

Carried. ACHILLES, out of battle, by Greek warriors (*Od.* 24.43f), by Odysseus (*Met.* 13.280f), by Ajax, protected by Odysseus (*Ep.* 5.4), by Thetis, from his pyre (*Aethiopis* 1, in Proclus 2). AEGISTHUS, by his killers Orestes and Pylades, to Electra (Eur. *Elec.* 880f). AJAX, by his small son et al. to burial, under Teucer's direction (Soph. *Ajax* 1403f). ALCESTIS, on a litter carried by servants, led by Admetus (Eur. *Alc.* 606f). ALCMENE, by Hermes, from her coffin and a stone substituted (Pherecydes in *Frag. Hist. Graec.* 1.82). DARIUS, by Alexander, in a splendid ceremony (Ps.-Cal. 198). ELPENOR, by Odysseus' men, to a pyre (*Od.* 12.8f). HAEMON, by Creon et al., on a bier to his palace where Creon finds his wife, the boy's mother, also dead (Soph. *Ant.* 1261f). HECTOR, by Achilles et al. onto a bier that is placed on a wagon (*Il.* 24.587f). ICARIUS, by the shepherds who have killed him; they drop him into a well (*Fab.* 130; *Poet. Astr.* 2.4). ICARUS, by Daedalus, to a tomb, watched by a bird (*Met.* 8.236f). Black MEMNON, by his mother

Eos (Dawn) (Serv. *ad Aen.* 1.493). MENOECUS, who has sacrificed himself to save Thebes, by Creon et al. (Eur. *Phoen.* 1310f). NEOPTOLEMUS on a litter carried by attendants, to his grandfather Peleus; Thetis appears (Eur. *Andro.* 1166f). ODYSSEUS, by Telegonus, his son by Circe, to his mother's island; he brings Penelope also (*Ep.* 7.37). PALLAS, on a shield, from battle, by his friends (*Aen.* 10.505f). PATROCLUS, from battle by other warriors, for whom the two Ajaxes hold off the Trojans (*Il.* 17.712f, 19.231f). POLYNEICES, by Antigone, to a grave (*Lib.* 3.7.1; in Soph. *Ant.* 246f she simply scatters dust on him to fulfill the ritual); by Antigone and Argia, who place him on the pyre with his brother (*Fab.* 72). RHESUS, by his mother, one of the Muses, to keep him from Hades (Eur. *Rhes.* 962f). SARPEDON, from battle, by Apollo (*Il.* 16.667f), and by Hypnos and Thanatos (*Il.* 16.671f). WARRIORS, fallen in battle, are snatched away by the Keres (female spirits of death) with their claws (Hes. *Sh. Her.* 248f).

Fought for. ACHILLES, by Ajax and Glaucus (*Ep.* 5.4). ALCATHOÜS, by Aeneas and Idomeneus, et al. (*Il.* 13.496f). CASTOR, by Polydeuces and Idas (*Fab.* 80). CYCNUS, by Ares and Heracles, the latter with Athena's help (Hes. *Sh. Her.* 434f). IPHIDAMAS, by Agamemnon and Coön (*Il.* 11.248f). PANDARUS, by Aeneas and Diomedes (*Il.* 5.297f). PATROCLUS, by the Ajaxes, Menelaüs, Hector, Aeneas, Euphorbus, et al. (*Il.* 17 pass., 18.155f). SARPEDON, by Patroclus, Menelaüs, the Ajaxes, Hector, Aeneas, Glaucus, et al. (*Il.* 16.548f).

Stripped of armor. ACHILLES, by Ajax (*Ep.* 5.4). CYCNUS, by Heracles (Hes. *Sh. Her.* 467f). HECTOR, by Achilles (*Il.* 22.367f). PALLAS, by Turnus (*Aen.* 10.495f). PATROCLUS, by Hector (*Il.* 17.125f). SARPEDON, by Patroclus (*Il.* 16.663f).

Dragged. HECTOR, behind Achilles' chariot (*Il.* 22.395f, 23.13f, 24.14f). ORTHRYONEUS, by the foot, by Idomeneus (*Il.* 13.389f). PATROCLUS, by Hippothoüs, with a belt (*Il.* 17.288f), and by Trojans and Greeks, tugging in opposite directions (*Il.* 17.389f). PENTHESILEIA, behind Diomedes' chariot (Dictys 4.3). POLYNEICES, by Antigone, to place it on the pyre with his brother Eteocles (Paus. 5.19.6, 9.25.2). A WARRIOR fallen in battle, by the feet, by Ker (a female spirit of death) (*Il.* 18.535f; Hes. *Sh. Her.* 156f). (For the dragging of living men or warriors, see **Chariot; Helmet.**)

Mistreated. HECTOR's corpse is stabbed with spears by Greek warriors who have gathered to view him (*Il.* 22.367f). PENTHESILEIA's eyes are gouged out by Thersites, for which Achilles kills him (Schol. *ad Lycophrona* 999). SERVIUS TULLIUS, over whose body his daughter drives her chariot or cart (Livy 1.48). (The withdrawing of the spear from Sarpedon's corpse by Patroclus [*Il.* 16.502f] and from Patroclus' corpse by Hector [*Il.* 16.862f] are hardly to be distinguished graphically from the stabbing of a corpse and accordingly are recorded here.)

Headless. PENTHEUS, the parts of whose dismembered body have been reassembled by Cadmus, is viewed by his mother Agave, who holds his head (Eur. *Bacch.* 1215f). POMPEY, after being beheaded on the shore, is placed on a pyre by his freedman Philip and an old soldier (Plut. 32.80). PRIAM's body lies untended on the shore (*Aen.* 2.547f). A THIEF's body is found in Rhampsinitus' treasure vault; it is publicly displayed, then removed when its guards become drunk (Herod. 2.121; a similar tale is told of the thief Agamedes in Hyreus' Treasury in Paus. 9.37.3).

COUCH

(See **Bed; Litter.**)

COW

(See also **Altar, Animal Sacrifice; Bull; Cattle.**)

In this form, HERA escapes from Typhoeus (*Met.* 5.330).

Changed into a cow by Zeus (*Met.* 1.6.10), IO is guarded by many-eyed Argus (Aes. *Prom.* 122f, 679f); she paws the ground trying to identify herself to her father and sisters (Aes. *Prom.* 642f), is rescued by Hermes whose pipes put Argus to sleep (Aes. *Prom.* 668f) or who kills Argus (*Fab.* 145), is tormented by a gadfly (*Lib.* 2.1.3) or by a Fury (*Met.* 1.724f), wanders or swims to the Scythians, Amazons, Gorgons, one-eyed horsemen (Arimaspians), Prometheus in chains, Ethiopians, and to Egypt (*Fab.* 145; *Lib.* 2.1.3; Aes. *Prom.* 561f), kneels to Zeus and is restored to human form (*Met.* 1.729f), and becomes the goddess Isis (*Fab.* 145).

Suckles HARPALYCE after her mother dies (*Fab.* 193); MELANIPPE's TWINS, who are found by herdsmen (*Fab.* 186).

Leads CADMUS to the destined site of Thebes and then lies down (*Met.* 3.10f; *Lib.* 3.4.1); ILUS to the site of Troy and then lies down (*Lib.* 3.12.3).

Attacks AMPHITRYON, whose club bounces off its head and kills Electryon (*Lib.* 2.4.6).

Stolen and cooked by HERMES, who invents fire for the purpose (*H. to Her.* 105f).

Offered as a bribe by HERMES to old Battus for his silence regarding the theft of Neleus' cattle; Battus is turned to stone when he proves false (*Met.* 2.687f).

Dead. From a calf's carcass bees emerge to replace ARISTAEUS' lost swarm (*Fasti* 1.377f).

Artificial. DAEDALUS constructs a cow that allows Minos' wife Pasiphaë inside to mate with a bull (*Lib.* 3.15.8; *Fab.* 40); the cow is mounted on wheels (*Lib.* 3.1.4).

CRAB

Attribute of Diana of the Ephesians.

Bites HERACLES' foot as he fights the Hydra (*Lib.* 2.5.2).

CRAB CLAW

Attribute of Amphitrite (appearing on her forehead).

CRADLE

(See also **Box; Chest.**)

Hanging in a tree, contains baby ZEUS (*Fab.* 139).

Given to CECROPS' DAUGHTERS by Athena, contains baby Erichthonius (Eur. *Ion* 265f; *Lib.* 3.14.6).

Shown by a PRIESTESS to Ion, as Creüsa, sitting at an altar, watches (Eur. *Ion* 1337f); by ION to Creüsa, along with its contents, a necklace, wreath, and coverlet, which establish that Ion is her son (Eur. *Ion* 1380f).

Contains baby HERMES, whom Apollo is accusing of stealing his cattle (*H. to Her.* 233f); from it Hermes departs to exercise his propensity for theft and invention; he returns to it for protection from Apollo (*H. to Her.* 20f, 150f, 235f).

CRANE

(See **Bird.**)

CRESCENT

(See also **Moon.**)

Attribute of Artemis; Lunus (with the horns extending from his shoulders); Selene.

Marks the bull that leads CADMUS to the site of Thebes (*Fab.* 178f).

CRICKET

(See **Grasshopper.**)

CRIPPLED MAN

(See also **Carrying; Wounded Figure.**)

ANCHISES was crippled by Zeus' thunderbolt for boasting of having loved Aphrodite (*Aen.* 2.648f; Serv. ad loc.; see also **Carrying**).

HEPHAESTUS, crippled by his fall from Olympus, is attended to by the women of Lemnos (*Lib.* 1.3.5; *Il.* 1.590f).

OEDIPUS is crippled as a result of being exposed as a baby with his feet bound (*Lib.* 3.5.7).

PHILOCTETES, crippled as a result of a poisoned foot, is marooned on an island because of the stench of his wound (*Ep.* 3.27; Soph. *Phil.* pass.).

THERSITES, lame in one foot, bow-legged(?), and hunchbacked, is beaten by Odysseus when he addresses the Greek chieftains (*Il.* 2.216f).

CROCODILE

Attribute of Anubis; Egypt; Egyptian Apollo; Nile; Sol; Typhon.

CROSS

Used to crucify. MURDERERS are executed by Alexander (Ps.-Cal. 202). The tyrant POLYCRATES is crucified by the Persian Oroetes (Herod. 3.125). The SAILORS from whom Arion escaped (see **Dolphin**) are crucified after Arion confronts them (*Fab.* 194). SELUNTIUS is about to be crucified when Moeros returns to save him (*Fab.* 257; cf. the similar story about Damon and Phintias in Cic. *de Off.* 3.10, *Tusc.* 5.22).

CROW

(See **Bird.**)

CROWN

(See also **Hat; Headband; Helmet; Wreath.**)

Occasional attribute of deities in general. Decorated with ships' beaks, deer, snakes: attributes of Agrippa (*Aen*. 8.682f); Nemesis (wingless; Paus. 1.33.3, 1.33.6); Persephone, respectively. Crescent shaped: attribute of Artemis; Selene. Worn by Isis (Io), to whom Telethusa prays that her daughter Iphis, whom she has raised as a boy, may actually become male (*Met*. 9.770f). Cylindrical: attribute of Pluto. Mural: attribute of Diana of Ephesus; Rhea (Cybele, Berecynthia, Dindymene); a personification of a city; Tyche. Flat and often large: attribute of a Canephoros (called a canistrum, it is worn by a maiden assisting at a certain rite). Held in the hand: attribute of Iris.

Given or offered to Abdolonimus, a gardener of royal descent, by Alexander, making him king of Sidon (Q. Curt. 4.1); to Ariadne, by Dionysus or Aphrodite; it becomes a constellation (*Poet. Astr*. 2.5; *Met*. 1.876f; *Fasti* 3.511f); to Caesar (who rejects it), by Antony, in the Forum before a crowd (Plut. 34.67); to Glauce (see "Poisoned," below); to some of his officers, by Alexander, for distinguished service (Arrian 7.5.4f); to Procris, by Pteleon, to win her favors (*Lib*. 3.15.1); to Semiramis, by Ninus, making her Queen of Asia for five days; whereupon she imprisons or kills him (Diod. Sic. 2.20; Arrian 7.1); to Theagenes, for winning a race, by Charicleia (*Aeth*. 4); to Theseus, by Thetis or Amphitrite, in the depths of the sea; Theseus returns to Minos' ship and shows it to him (*Poet. Astr*. 2.5).

Poisoned. Is made by Medea and given as a gift along with a robe to Glauce (Creüsa) by her small sons; Glauce is destroyed by it, as are those

Cybele wearing a mural crown

who touch her—Creon (Eur. *Med.* 1186; *Lib.* 1.9.28), or both Jason and Creon (*Fab.* 25).

CUCKOO

(See **Bird.**)

CUP

(See **Vessel.**)

CYCLOPS

A gigantic man with a single eye in his forehead.

One is carried by blind ORION to guide him (Serv. *ad Aen.* 10.763).

Polyphemus woos the nymph Galatea. He sings his love for her, which she overhears as she rests in the arms of Acis; she tosses apples at his flock; he surprises her with Acis, whom he buries with a huge rock as she escapes into the sea (*Met.* 13.764f; Theocritus 6, 11; Serv. *ad Ecl.* 7.37).

Polyphemus encounters Odysseus. He enters his cave with his sheep and finds Odysseus and his crew (in Euripides' *Cyclops,* Sileni manage the sheep and Polyphemus drives the Greeks into the cave, with Silenus following,

CYCLOPES AT WORK

Eur. *Cycl.* 36f, 345f); he devours two of the men and gets drunk on wine offered by Odysseus; his eye is put out as he sleeps; he fails to prevent the escape of the Greeks hanging beneath the sheep when they leave the cave; he hurls a huge rock at Odysseus' departing ship (*Od.* 9.231f; *Aen.* 3.616f; Eur. *Cycl.* 355f; *Met.* 14.181f).

Assistants of Hephaestus. Cyclopes are released from Tartarus when Zeus kills their jailer Campe (*Lib.* 1.2.1) or are released by Dionysus (Diod. Sic. 3.72.3; Hes. *Theog.* 501f); they forge thunderbolts for Zeus, armor and other weapons for other gods (*Argo.* 1.730f; *Aen.* 8.424f; *Lib.* 1.2.1; Hes. *Theog.* 138f); they are shot by Apollo for making the bolt that killed his son Asclepius (*Lib.* 3.10.4; Eur. *Alc.* 5f; *Fab.* 49; *Poet. Astr.* 2.15).

CYMBALS

Half spheres of metal, used in the worship of the earlier Greek and Roman deities, especially Dionysus-Bacchus, Hera-Juno, and Rhea (Cybele).

Attribute of Bacchants.

Clashed by HERACLES to scare off the Stymphalian birds (*Argo.* 2.1052f; *Lib.* 2.5.6).

A WOMAN WITH CYMBALS

DAGGER

(See **Knife.**)

DANCING

A pastime of the Muses.

ARGONAUTS dance during a sacrifice, beating their shields to drown out the ill-omened noise of wailing coming from a town (*Argo.* 1.1132f).

PHAEACIAN YOUTHS dance to the music of Demodocus (*Od.* 8.256f); two toss a ball as they dance (*Od.* 8.370f).

POLYMELE, as she dances with Artemis and other maidens, attracts Hermes' eye (*Il.* 16.181f).

PRIESTS called Salii leap into the air during their ritualistic procession (*Aen.* 8.663f).

DARK SKIN

Skin color is rarely mentioned as it is in the citations below. Consequently, the many scenes in which dark-skinned individuals appear will not be indexed here but elsewhere, on other evidence. Ethiopians are prominent chiefly in Heliodorus' *Aethiopica,* Egyptians in Herodotus and Aeschylus' *Suppliant Women,* Colchians in the *Argonautica.* Ariadne is described by Ovid as *fusca* (dark-colored) in *Fasti* 3.493.

Attribute of Colchians (Herod. 2.104); Egyptians (Aes. *Suppl.* 719); Ethiopians; Memnon (*Amores* 1.8.4; *Aen.* 1.489).

Ethiopian Queen CANDACE shows Alexander his portrait (Ps.-Cal. 240); Queen PERSINNA, at the moment of intercourse with her husband, the Ethiopian king, sees a picture of white-skinned Andromeda on the wall, which causes her daughter Charicleia to be born white (*Aeth.* 2, 4).

DEER

(See also **Fawn; Hunter.**)

Attribute of Artemis; Cybele; Erato.

SERTORIUS makes a deer into a pet (Paus. 29.11, 29.20).

Killed by AENEAS, to feed his hungry refugees after they are driven to Africa (*Aen.* 1.184f); by AGAMEMNON, thereby offending Artemis, who becalms the Greek fleet at Aulis (*Ep.* 3.21; Soph. *Elec.* 566f; *Fab.* 98); by ATHAMAS, is actually his son whom Hera has metamorphosed (*Lib.* 3.4.3); by CYPARISSUS unwittingly, is his own pet stag; grief-stricken, he is turned into a cypress tree (*Met.* 10.109f); by DOGS (see "Changed into," below); by ODYSSEUS to feed his hungry crew (*Od.* 10.156f).

Shot at but missed by AMYMONE, hitting a Satyr instead (*Lib.* 2.1.4); by OTUS and EPHIALTES; Apollo has sent the deer (or Artemis in the form of a deer, *Lib.* 1.7.4) between them, and the spear of each kills the other (*Fab.* 28); by PENTHESILEIA, killing Hippolyte instead (*Ep.* 5.1 and n. 4, Loeb edn.).

Changed into this form. ACTAEON is turned into a stag by Artemis, because he has seen her undressed for bathing; his own dogs then kill him (*Met.* 3.155f; *Fab.* 181; *Lib.* 3.4.4). ARGE, while chasing a stag, is turned by Helius into a doe because of her boastfulness (*Fab.* 205). A BULL is changed into a stag by Dionysus (*Met.* 7.358).

Hunted and captured. The CERYNITIAN HIND with golden horns is wounded by Heracles; Apollo and Artemis protest but are persuaded to allow him to carry it off to Eurystheus (*Lib.* 2.5.3; *Fab.* 30).

Provided as substitute by Artemis, for IPHIGENEIA, who is about to be sacrificed by Agamemnon (Eur. *Iph. Aul.* 1586f, *Iph. Taur.* 28f; *Met.* 12.32f; *Ep.* 3.22; *Fab.* 98).

Swimming, is pursued by SARON, who drowns (Paus. 2.30.7).

Nurses baby TELEPHUS, son of Auge and Heracles, and PARTHENO-PAEUS, together or separately (*Fab.* 99; *Lib.* 2.7.4).

DEER SKIN

(See **Skin, of Animal.**)

DEPARTURE

(See **Parting; Ship.**)

DIADEM

(See **Crown.**)

DICE

(See **Game.**)

DISCUS

(See also **Stone.**)

Causes death. APOLLO accidentally hits Hyacinthus, who becomes a flower (*Met.* 10.178f; *Lib.* 1.3.3; cf. Philostratus 1.23(24), which records that a jealous Zephyrus caused it to hit his rival). BOREAS kills Hyacinthus because he favors Apollo; he becomes a flower (Serv. *ad Ecl.* 3.63). HERMES accidentally kills Crocus, who becomes a flower (*Met.* 4.283f; Serv. *ad Georg.* 4.182). PELEUS kills Phocus intentionally (Paus. 2.29.7). PERSEUS kills Acrisius accidentally (*Lib.* 2.4.4; *Fab.* 63; Paus. 2.16.2). TELAMON kills his brother Phocus intentionally; his other brother Peleus helps hide the body (*Lib.* 3.12.6).

Thrown in competition by ODYSSEUS and PHAEACIAN youths (*Od.* 8.186f); by ORION and ARTEMIS (Lib. 1.4.5); by PENELOPE's SUITORS (*Od.* 4.625f).

DISH

(See **Vessel.**)

DISMEMBERING

DIONYSUS has Lycurgus torn apart by horses to which he is lashed (*Lib.* 3.5.1).

With knife or sword. ATREUS cuts up Thyestes' sons and serves them to their father to eat (*Ep.* 2.13; Sen. *Thy.* 818f). MEDEA cuts up her brother Apsyrtus and flings his limbs overboard to delay her father's pursuit of the *Argo* (*Lib.* 1.9.24). PELEUS cuts up Astydameia for causing the suicide of his wife (*Lib.* 3.13.7). PELIAS' DAUGHTERS butcher and cook their old father in order to rejuvenate him, according to Medea's instructions (*Lib.* 1.9.27; cf. *Fab.* 24 and *Met.* 7.348, where dismemberment is not mentioned). PROCNE and PHILOMELA cut up Itys to serve to his father Tereus (*Met.* 6.640f). TANTALUS cuts up Pelops to serve to the gods, who reassemble him (*Met.* 6.406f).

With bare hands. AURA in a fit of madness tears apart one of her babies, then leaps into the sea (Nonnus 48.848f). MAENADS tear to pieces

Orpheus (*Georg.* 4.520f; *Lib.* 1.3.2) and Pentheus, who has been spying on them from a tree (Eur. *Bacch.* 1077f; *Met.* 3.715f; *Lib.* 3.5.2). PELOPS kills and tears Stymphalus apart, incurring the gods' hostility (*Lib.* 3.12.6). The TITANS tear Dionysus apart; his heart is consumed by Zeus or Semele, in either case resulting in Semele's pregnancy and the rebirth of Dionysus (*Fab.* 167; Diod. Sic. 3.62.6).

By bent trees. ALEXANDER has Bessus torn apart for his treachery to Darius (Plut. 33.43). SINIS, a highwayman, waylays travelers and dismembers them; he meets the same fate at the hands of THESEUS (Paus. 2.1.4).

DISTAFF

Attribute of Athena's statue (the Palladium) (*Lib.* 3.12.3); Heracles, enslaved by Omphale (Sen. *Her. Oet.* 371f; Lucian *Dial. Deo.* 15 [13]); the Parcae (Cat. 64.311f).

DIVING

(See **Leaping.**)

DIVINITY

(See **God.**)

DOG

(See also **Hunter; Huntress; Wolf.**)

Attribute of Artemis; Asclepius; Hecate; Hygeia; Lares; Pomona; Vertumnus.

In this form, the river god CRIMISUS mates with Egesta (Serv. *ad Aen.* 1.550); HECUBA leaps into the sea from Odysseus' ship (Eur. *Hec.* 1259f; *Ep.* 5.23; *Met.* 13.567f, 13.620; *Fab.* 111).

Transformed. ACTAEON's dogs are turned into the Telchines, marine beings without feet and with fins for hands (Eust. *ad Il.* 9.771.55f).

With a baby. ASCLEPIUS is guarded by a dog and nursed by a goat; a thunderbolt reveals his divinity (Paus. 2.26.4). CYRUS is suckled by a bitch (Herod. 1.122).

Leading the way. ERIGONE is led by Maera to the body of her father

Icarius (*Lib.* 3.14.7); to his grave, where she hangs herself (*Fab.* 130; *Poet. Astr.* 2.4).

Friendly. ACTAEON's statue, which the Centaur Cheiron has made, is surrounded by his dogs (*Lib.* 3.4.4). A BEGGAR is recognized by old Argos as his long-absent master Odysseus; with a thump of his tail Argos dies (*Od.* 17.291f). TELEMACHUS is welcomed by several dogs as he approaches Eumaeus' hut, where a beggar (Odysseus) sits (*Od.* 16.4f).

Hostile. ACTAEON, changed into a stag because he saw Artemis bathing, is killed by his dogs (*Met.* 3.206f; *Lib.* 3.4.4; *Fab.* 181); in his own form he is killed after claiming to be a better hunter than Artemis (Eur. *Bacch.* 337f) or because Zeus resented his courting of Semele (*Lib.* 3.4.4). CANACE'S BABY is killed by the dogs to which it is thrown by her father Aeolus, when he discovers that Canace's brother is the father (*Heroïdes* 11). CATREUS, because of the barking of dogs, is not able to identify himself to the shepherds who, taking him for a pirate, kill him (*Lib.* 3.2.2). EURIPIDES is killed by the dogs of the Macedonian king (*Fab.* 247). ODYSSEUS, as a beggar, is threatened by the dogs outside Eumaeus' hut (*Od.* 14.29). OINOS, nephew of Heracles, repels a dog with a stone and is killed by the dog's owners; he is avenged by his uncle (*Lib.* 2.7.3; Paus. 3.15.4, 3.15.5). PEIRITHOÜS is torn to pieces by Aïdoneus' dog, which he calls Cerberus, and Theseus is made his prisoner (Plut. 1.31). PSAMATHE'S BABY is killed by dogs (Paus. 1.43.7).

Presented, with a spear, by ARTEMIS to Procris; the dog, Laelaps, is indefatigable and the spear is unerring; with the gift of these two things Procris becomes reconciled with her husband Cephalus (*Fab.* 189); by MINOS to Procris, with which he wins her favors (*Lib.* 3.15.1).

Running. CEPHALUS watches Procris' tireless Laelaps chase a fox destined never to be caught; Zeus changes both to stone (*Met.* 7.763f; *Lib.* 2.4.7).

In the sea. XANTHIPPUS' faithful dog swims after his ship to Salamis, where it expires (Plut. 7.10). (See also "In this form," above.)

Are crucified whereas geese are decked in finery, signifying their respective worth as sentinels on the Capitoline Hill (Serv. *ad Aen.* 8.652).

Mourned. TERTIA weeps for her dead puppy and is consoled by her father Aemilius Paulus (Plut. 14.10).

Has its tail cropped by ALCIBIADES to give Athenians something to gossip about (Plut. 11.9).

Made of gold by HEPHAESTUS, is stolen by Pandareos, given to Tantalus and recovered by Hermes (Schol. *ad Od.* 19.518, 20.66; *Ep.* 2.1, n. 2, Loeb edn.).

Two-headed ORTHOS, guarding triple-bodied Geryon's cattle, is killed by Heracles (*Lib.* 2.5.10; cf. Hes. *Theog.* 288f, where Orthos is not described as two-headed and Geryon is three-headed).

Three-headed (or fifty-headed, Hes. *Theog.* 311) CERBERUS is an attribute of Hades (the god and the place). He welcomes visitors to Hades and attacks those who try to leave (Hes. *Theog.* 767f); he is dragged or carried by Heracles from Hades and delivered to Eurystheus (*Met.* 7.408f; *Od.* 11.623f; *Fab.* 30; in *Lib.* 2.5.12 he is described as having snakes for a mane and tail); he greets Hera when she comes to ask the Furies to destroy Athamas (*Met.* 4.449f); he is put to sleep by the Sibyl and Aeneas (*Aen.* 6.417f) and by Psyche (Apuleius 9).

DOG'S HEAD

Attribute of Anubis.

Dogs' heads sprout from the waist of SCYLLA as she bathes in the sea; this is the result of Circe's enmity (*Met.* 14.51f; *Fab.* 199); SCYLLA snatches and devours men from Odysseus' ship (*Ep.* 7.21).

DOLPHIN

Attribute of Amor; Amphitrite; Arethusa; Arion; Dionysus; Poseidon; Venus.

POSEIDON WITH ATTRIBUTES: TRIDENT AND DOLPHIN

Changed into dolphins. The SAILORS who have jumped overboard to escape from the beasts that Dionysus, their captive, brings into being (*Met.* 3.666f), or from the bear and lion (Dionysus himself) that appear (*H. to Dion.* 44f).

In this form, APOLLO leaps aboard a ship; he later disembarks at Krisa and enters his shrine (*H. to Ap.* 397f); POSEIDON seduces Melantho (*Met.* 6.120).

Saved or aided by dolphins. ARION escapes from murderous sailors by leaping or being thrown overboard onto the back of a dolphin; the dolphin is later found dead on the shore and is given a burial (*Fasti* 2.95f; Herod. 1.24; Serv. *ad Ecl.* 8.55; *Fab.* 194). ENALUS, anticipating the imminent sacrifice of his beloved to Amphitrite, leaps with her into the sea; dolphins save them both (Plut. *Moralia* 163c, 984e). ICADIUS, a son of Apollo, after being shipwrecked (Serv. *ad Aen.* 3.332). Young MELICERTES and his mother Ino leap into the sea; he is carried to shore (Paus. 1.44.11). PHALANTHOS, after being shipwrecked, is carried to shore (Paus. 10.13.4). POSEIDON is led by a dolphin to Amphitrite's hiding place (Aratus, *Phainomena* 324f). THESEUS is conducted to Amphitrite, who gives him a ring and a wreath (*Poet. Astr.* 2.5; Bacchylides 16.97f).

DONKEY

(See **Ass.**)

DOOR

(See also **Gate.**)

Closed, with key inserted: attribute of two-faced Janus.

Open. Eos and Nyx, who carries baby Hypnos, pass each other in a portal; nearby stands Atlas holding up the sky (Hes. *Theog.* 748f).

Decorated with reliefs, is inspected by AENEAS (*Aen.* 6.20f); by PHAËTHON (*Met.* 2.1f).

With a picture of a horse drawn on it; the drawing serves to protect ANTENOR's house in Troy from molestation by the Greeks (Serv. *ad Aen.* 2.15).

Barred. Iphis haunts the door of hard-hearted Anaxarete and hangs himself from its beam (*Met.* 14.698f).

DOVE

(See **Bird.**)

DRAGGING

(See **Corpse; Helmet; Wagon.**)

DRAGON

(See also **Snake.**)

Since the sources do not always make a distinction between *dragon* and *snake,* it is made herein subjectively on the basis of the visual impression given by the text.

Dragon-tailed figure (see **Snake-headed** and **Snake-legged**). Attribute of Apollo.

Dragons draw the chariots of Demeter, Medea, and Triptolemus. One of Triptolemus' team is killed by Carnabon (*Poet. Astr.* 2.14). (See also **Chariot.**)

A sea monster attacks HERACLES, who escapes to a wall provided by Athena and the Trojans (*Il.* 20.144f); it swallows Heracles and then disgorges him (Schol. *ad Il.* 20.146f); is killed by HERACLES when he rescues Hesione (*Met.* 11.211f; *Fab.* 31, 89; *Lib.* 2.5.9); is killed by PERSEUS, borne on winged sandals to the rescue of Andromeda, who is chained to a cliff (*Met.* 4.689f; *Fab.* 64; *Lib.* 2.4.3; see also the note after the **Horse** [Winged] entry); emerging from the sea, causes HIPPOLYTUS' chariot team to bolt (Serv. *ad Aen.* 6.445); threatens HIPPOTES' DAUGHTER, whom a ship carries off to safety (Serv. *ad Aen.* 1.550). Two sea monsters swim to the shore, where the Trojan Horse stands; they attack LAOCOÖN and his sons (*Aen.* 2.203f).

The many-headed Lernaean Hydra is killed by HERACLES with the help of Iolaüs (Hes. *Theog.* 313f) with a sickle (Eur. *Ion* 190f) or with arrows and a club, while a crab attacks him; IOLAÜS cauterizes the severed necks (*Lib.* 2.5.2).

A destructive dragon that is ravaging the countryside is killed by Heracles, for which Queen Omphale showers him with gifts (*Poet. Astr.* 2.14).

Dragon acting as guardian of a BEARSKIN containing the tendons of Zeus, has been put on watch by the monster Typhoeus (the dragon is a half-bestial maiden named Delphyne); Hermes and Aegipan steal the sinews and restore them to Zeus (*Lib.* 1.6.3; cf. Nonnus 1.481f, where Cadmus gets the tendons back from Typhoeus); of the GOLDEN APPLES of the Hesperides, is killed by Heracles (*Lib.* 2.5.11; *Argo.* 4.1432f), and its corpse, being mourned by the Hesperides, is discovered by the Argonauts (*Argo.* 4.1396f); of the GOLDEN FLEECE, which Phrixus has placed in a shrine (*Fab.* 3) or which hangs in a tree (*Argo.* 2.404f), is put to sleep by Medea (*Fab.* 22; *Argo.* 4.145f) or by Jason (*Met.* 7.149f), or is killed by Medea (Eur. *Med.* 480f) or by Jason (Serv. *ad Georg.* 2.140); of a SPRING OR GROTTO, is killed by Cadmus because it has slain several of his men (*Met.* 3.28f; *Fab.* 178; *Lib.* 3.4.1; Eur. *Phoen.* 657f), and its teeth are extracted and given to Cadmus and Aeëtes by Athena (*Argo.* 3.1175f).

The dragon Python gives out prophecies (*Fab.* 140); pursues Leto, who is rescued by Aquilo (the North Wind) (*Fab.* 53, 140); is killed by the arrows of Apollo (*H. to Ap.* 300f, 355f; *Argo.* 2.705f; *Met.* 1.438f; *Lib.* 1.4.1), to whom a wolf brings laurel to betoken his great victory (Serv. *ad Aen.* 4.377).

Leads ANTINOË and other refugees to a river where they are to settle (Paus. 8.8.4, 8.8.5).

Swallows MENESTRATUS, who, to get rid of the destructive monster, has clad himself in hook-studded armor (Paus. 9.26.5). (See also "Sea monster," above.)

DRAUGHTS

(See **Game.**)

DRAWING

(See **Painter; Picture.**)

DRINKING

(See also **Vessel, Cup; Wineskin.**)

From cupped hands. ARTAXERXES accepts the water in a poor man's hands and rewards the donor with a golden cup (Plut. 48.5). DIOGENES, watching a child drink from his hands, throws away his cup (Diog. Laërt. 6.2.37).

From spring or pool. The ARGONAUTS, as they carry their ship across Libya, stop to drink in the Garden of the Hesperides (*Argo.* 4.1450f). DEME-TER tries to drink but is prevented by rustics who muddy the water, for which they are turned into frogs (Serv. *ad Georg.* 1.378; Ovid tells a similar story about Leto and her babies, *Met.* 6.346f). HERACLES drinks from a spring he has created by stamping his foot in the Garden of the Hesperides (*Argo.* 4.1436f). PICUS and FAUNUS, Satyr-like demigods, are trapped by Numa as they drink (Plut. 4.15). Blind TEIRESIAS drinks and dies (*Lib.* 3.7.3).

DRUM

Attribute of Cybele (Rhea) and her votaries; Juno; Muses; Ops; Satyrs.

DYING FIGURE

(See also **Bed; Blood; Corpse; Fighting; Killing; Sleeping Figure; Suicide; Wounded Figure.**)

Held by another. ADONIS, after being slashed by a boar, by Aphrodite (*Met.* 10.719f). ANTONY, after stabbing himself, by Cleopatra (Plut. 44.77). DARIUS, whom traitors have attacked, by Alexander (Ps.-Cal. 196f). DEÏANEIRA, after stabbing herself, by Hyllus (Soph. *Trach.* 923f). DIDO, on her funeral pyre, by her sister Anna (*Aen.* 4.685f). GLAUCE, after being set afire by a poisoned robe that has been brought as a gift by Medea's children, by her father Creon, who is then similarly consumed (Eur. *Med.* 1168f). HIPPOLYTUS dies in Theseus' arms as Artemis explains his innocence of the accusation contained in Phaedra's letter (Eur. *Hipp.* 1431f). PROCRIS, after being accidentally wounded by her husband Cephalus while hunting, dies in his arms (*Met.* 7.845f).

Under other circumstances. HIPPOLYTUS is carried to his father Theseus and Artemis (Eur. *Hipp.* 1342f). MYRENE's bridegroom dies of grief when she is changed into a tree (Serv. *ad Aen.* 3.23). Aged OEDIPUS, summoned by a divine voice to his death, is attended by Theseus alone as his daughters lament apart (Soph. *Oed. Col.* 1594f). Huge TALOS dies when his blood drains from his ankle because of Medea's magic (*Lib.* 1.9.26; *Argo.* 4.1677f).

EAGLE

(See **Bird.**)

EARS

Pointed: attribute of Fauni; Pan; Satyrs (q.v.); Sileni; Silenus. Of an ass: Ignorantia. Midas acquires the ears of an ass when he judges Pan's music superior to Apollo's (*Met.* 11.174; *Fab.*191).

Licked by snakes (see **Snake** [Performing kindly acts]).

Cleaning of TEIRESIAS' ears by Athena gives him the ability to understand birds (*Lib.* 3.6.7).

EATING

In the epics, the taking of food is such a commonplace theme that one instance can hardly be distinguished from another. Accordingly, such scenes are not indexed unless they have some particular feature or purpose.

Of babies. CRONUS swallows his offspring, vomiting them forth later (*Lib.* 1.1.5; Hes. *Theog.* 459f; *Fasti* 4.197f). PROETUS' DAUGHTERS devour their babies when driven mad by Dionysus (*Lib.* 2.2.2).

Of men and women. The LAESTRYGONIANS (*Od.* 10.116f, 10.124f; *Met.* 14.235), the Cyclops POLYPHEMUS (*Od.* 9.287f; *Aen.* 3.622f), and the monster SCYLLA (*Od.* 12.245f) seize and devour Odysseus' men. ZEUS swallows his wife Metis, who is pregnant with Athena (*Lib.* 1.3.6; Hes. *Theog.* 929 e–t. In *Theog.* 888f he stuffs her into his belly.).

Of served human flesh. CLYMENUS is served by his daughter Harpalyce the baby that resulted from his rape of her, for which he kills her (*Fab.* 206). ERYSICHTHON, insatiable and tormented by the hag Fames, finally eats himself (*Met.* 8.875f). The GODS dine on Pelops, whom Tantalus serves to them; Demeter, having eaten his shoulder, replaces it with one of ivory when he is restored to life (*Ep.* 2.3 and n. 3, Loeb edn.; *Met.* 6.406f; *Fab.* 83). HARPAGUS dines on the flesh of his son at a a banquet given by King Astyages (Herod. 1.119). POLYTECHNUS is served his son by Aëdon and Chelidonis, the daughters whom he has wronged (Ant. Lib. 11). TEREUS is served his son Itys by his wife Procne to avenge his rape of her sister Philomela; all three become birds (*Met.* 6.647; *Lib.* 3.14.8; *Fab.* 45). THYESTES eats his sons, who are served to him by his brother Atreus; he vomits when their heads are shown to him (Aes. *Agam.* 1.590f; *Fab.* 88; *Ep.* 2.13; Sen. *Thy.* 851f). ZEUS, in disguise, is served human flesh by Lycaon (or by his sons); reacting with violence, he turns Lycaon into a wolf (*Met.* 1.226f; *Poet. Astr.* 2.4; *Lib.* 3.8.1; *Fab.* 176).

Of an ox. The DIOSCURI, IDAS, and LYNCEUS quarter and devour one of a herd they have stolen (*Lib.* 3.11.2). HERACLES and LEPREUS consume a whole ox apiece, after which they quarrel (Paus. 5.5.4).

Of other things. CRONUS swallows a stone wrapped in baby clothes, believing it to be baby Zeus (Hes. *Theog.* 485f; *Lib.* 1.1.7; *Fab.* 139). ERYSICHTHON, driven by the winged hag Fames, gorges himself on a vast table of food (*Met.* 8.814f). ODYSSEUS' men eat lotus and have to be dragged back to their ships and bound (*Od.* 9.91f). PERSEPHONE eats the pomegranate seeds that Hades gives her; because Ascalaphus sees this and tells of it, he becomes an owl (*H. to Dem.* 370f, 411f; *Lib.* 1.5.3; *Met.* 5.534f). PORCIA swallows a hot coal to kill herself when she learns of Brutus' death (Plut. 46.53). TYDEUS eats the brain from the head of Melanippus (*Lib.* 3.6.8).

Made impossible. IXION and PEIRITHOÜS are prevented from eating the banquet before them by a torch-wielding Fury (*Aen.* 6.601f). MIDAS' food turns to gold at his touch (*Met.* 11.106f; *Fab.* 191). TANTALUS reaches in vain for the fruit hanging nearby (*Met.* 4.457f; *Ep.* 2.1; *Fab.* 82; *Od.* 11.588f).

Hospitality offered to strangers. ODYSSEUS is entertained by Nausicaä and her maids (*Od.* 6.246f); by Alcinoüs and Arete (*Od.* 7.175f); by Calypso in her cave (*Od.* 5.192f); in the guise of a beggar, by the swineherd Eumaeus (*Od.* 14.74f, 14.418f, 15.310f, 16.49f). Odysseus and his men are entertained by Circe (*Od.* 10.467f, 12.29f), who changes all but Odysseus into pigs (*Od.* 10.233f) or into a variety of animals (*Met.* 14.273f). ZEUS and HERMES, in disguise, are entertained by the aged couple Philemon and Baucis (*Met.* 8.626f); with POSEIDON also, by Hyrieus (*Fasti* 5.499f) and by Oenopion (Serv. *ad Aen.* 1.535).

Feasting on the shore. The ARGONAUTS, before their departure (*Argo.* 1.450f). ODYSSEUS and his men feast on game by their ships (*Od.* 9.161f); while he sleeps, his men cook and eat some of the forbidden cattle of Helius (*Od.* 12.353f). TROJANS feast on the deer shot by Aeneas (*Aen.* 1.174f, 1.210f); they finish a meal by devouring the flat loaves that have served as plates (*Aen.* 7.107f; cf. 3.255f, 3.394f, where this meal is foretold).

Formal banquets. ALCINOÜS entertains Odysseus, who tells his story after the bard Demodocus has sung (*Od.* 8.499f, 9.1f, 13.24f). CATO THE

YOUNGER dines and discourses with friends before his suicide (Plut. 36.67). CEPHEUS celebrates the marriage of Perseus and Andromeda with a feast at which Perseus recounts his adventures and Phineus demands the bride for himself (*Met.* 4.762f, 5.1f). CLEOPATRA entertains Caesar (Suet. *Caes.* 52.1) and Antony (Plut. 44.26–27). King DARIUS entertains a herald dressed as Ammon (Alexander), who flees when recognized (Ps.-Cal. 177f). DIDO gives an elaborate banquet for Aeneas and the Trojans, at which the bard Iopas sings and Aeneas tells his story (*Aen.* 1.697f). PENELOPE's SUITORS pass the time in feasting and carousing (*Od.* 1.109f, 1.144f, 17.356f, 18 pass., 20.247f). Old and blind, PHINEUS entertains the Argonauts and tells them of dangers to come (*Argo.* 2.301, 2.490f).

A choice. PROMETHEUS sets two piles of ox meat before Zeus; one pile consists of bones concealed under a layer of choice pieces, the other of rich pieces hidden under entrails. ZEUS must choose his portion (Hes. *Theog.* 535f).

EAVESDROPPING

(See also **Spying.**)

AJAX and ODYSSEUS overhear Trojan girls talking on the wall above their hiding place (*Ilias Mikra* 3, in Schol. on Aristophanes, *Knights* 1056).

VINDICIUS overhears a plot to restore Tarquin (Plut. 6.4; Livy 2.4).

ECLIPSE

Occurs as PELOPIDAS prepares to march against the tyrant Alexander of Pherae; it portends his own death (Plut. 15.31); as ROMULUS starts to build Rome's wall (Plut. 2.12), and as he is being taken to heaven; a storm also is in progress (Plut. 2.27); as XERXES prepares to march against Greece (Herod. 7.37).

EGG

Produced by NEMESIS, who is pregnant by Zeus (*Poet. Astr.* 2.8), is placed in Leda's lap by Hermes (or a shepherd), and gives birth to Helen (*Poet. Astr.* 2.8; *Lib.* 3.10.7).

One or two eggs produce Helen, Clytemnestra, Polydeuces, and Castor (*Lib.* 3.10.7, n. 7, Loeb edn.).

Conveyed to shore by fish in the Euphrates River, is warmed by doves and gives birth to Aphrodite (*Fab.* 197).

ELEPHANT

Attribute of India; the Indian Dionysus.

Ridden by Dionysus in triumph in India (Diod. Sic. 4.3.1).

Used in battle against Alexander by DARIUS at Arbela (Gaugamela) (Arrian 3.11.6) and by huge King POROS in India (Arrian 5.16.4; Plut. 33.60; Ps.-Cal. 216, in which account they flee from statues Alexander has heated); Poros dismounts to surrender to Alexander (Arrian 5.19.1); against Persian cavalry by the ETHIOPIANS (*Aeth.* 9); against the Romans by HANNIBAL (Plut. 16.12, 16.26) and by PYRRHUS (Plut. 21.20, 21.21, 21.25).

Given to or captured by ALEXANDER in India and added to his army (Arrian 4.22.6, 4.30.7f, 6.15.6).

Rafted across the Rhone by Hannibal (Livy 21.28).

Cross the Alps in HANNIBAL's army (Livy 21.34f).

Suddenly exposed behind a curtain fails to intimidate Fabricius as he confers with Pyrrhus (Plut. 21.20).

EMBASSY

(See **Speaker**.)

EMERALD

Attribute of Melpomene.

ENGINE

Siege engines and artillery of the Greeks and Romans consisted of the battering ram (*aries*), assault tower on wheels (*helopolis, turris*), assault shelter (*vinea, testudo*), and various missile-shooting devices (*tormentum, ballista, catapulta, scorpio, onager*). They were prominent in such actions as Alexander's siege of Tyre (Plut. 33.24; Arrian 2.23.1f), Demetrius Poliorcetes' assaults on Salamis (Cyprus) and Rhodes (Diod. Sic. 20.48 and 20.91), Archimedes' defense of Syracuse (Plut. 16.15, 16.16), and Caesar's sieges of Avaricum (Caesar *B.G.* 7.25) and Massilia (Caesar *B.C.* 2.2).

ENVOY

(See **Speaker**.)

ERINYES

(See **Furies.**)

EROS, EROTES

Attribute of Aphrodite.

ERUPTION

(See **Volcano.**)

EUMENIDES

(See **Furies.**)

EYE

Evil eye: attribute of the Telchines, whom Zeus exiled to the sea (*Met.* 7.365f).

One eye: attribute of Arimaspian horsemen (see **Horseman**); the Cyclopes (q.v.). A single eye is shared in turn by the Graeae (Phorcides), the three (or two, *Met.* 4.772) daughters of Phorcys; Perseus snatches it as it is being passed, in order to compel their cooperation (*Lib.* 2.4.2; *Poet. Astr.* 2.12).

Three eyes: attribute of Zeus (Paus. 2.24.5, 2.45.2, 8.46.2).

Many eyes: attribute of Argus. ARGUS kills a bull and wears its hide (*Lib.* 2.1.2); kills a cattle-stealing Satyr (*Lib.* 2.1.2); is set by Hera to guard a heifer (Io) (*Fab.* 145; *Met.* 1.622f); follows a heifer (Io) (Aes. *Prom.* 679.f); is put to sleep by Hermes' music and wand (*Met.* 1.676f); is beheaded or killed with a rock by Hermes (*Met.* 1.715f; *Fab.* 145; *Lib.* 2.1.3); Argus' eyes are transferred by Hera to her peacock's tail (*Met.* 1.722f).

Blind in one eye: attribute of Antigonus; Hannibal; Philip; Sertorius; Zaleucus and his son (see below, "Blinding").

Blinding of ANCHISES by Zeus with a thunderbolt because he boasted of his amour with Aphrodite (Serv. *ad Aen.* 2.648); of BRYAS in his sleep, by the young virgin he has raped (Paus. 2.20.1); of the shepherd DAPHNIS, by Nomia because of his unfaithfulness to her; she also turns him to stone (Serv. *ad Ecl.* 5.20, 8.68); of DARDANUS in his sleep by Artemisia, who then leaps into the sea (Photius, p. 153a); of the Giant EPHIALTES by the arrows of

Apollo and Heracles (*Lib.* 1.6.2); of ERYMANTHUS, because he sees Aphrodite bathing (Ptolem. Heph. 1.306); of LYCURGUS of Sparta, one of whose eyes is knocked out by Alcander, after which they become friends (Plut. 3.11); of LYCURGUS of Thrace by Zeus for chasing Dionysus (*Il.* 6.139f); of MELANIPPE by her father Desmontes, because she had two sons by Poseidon (*Fab.* 186); of METOPE by her father Echetus, with nails; he makes her work a mill (*Argo.* 4.1093f); of OEDIPUS by his own hand, after finding Jocasta hanged (Soph. *Oed. Tyr.* 1273f; *Lib.* 3.5.9; *Fab.* 67), or by others (fragment of Eur. *Oedipus,* see Rose, p. 206); of ORION in a drunken sleep, by Oenopion because he seduced Merope (*Lib.* 1.4.3; *Poet. Astr.* 2.4.3); of PHINEUS by Aquilo, who sends the Harpies to torment him (Serv. *ad Aen.* 3.209), or by Zeus for revealing his sacred intentions (*Argo.* 2.178f; *Fab.* 19); of PHINEUS' SONS by their father (*Fab.* 19; *Lib.* 3.15.3) or by their stepmother (Soph. *Ant.* 973f; Serv. *ad Aen.* 3.209); of PHOENIX by his father Amyntor, for seducing his concubine (*Lib.* 3.13.8; fragment of Eur. *Phoenix,* see Rose, p. 207); of King POLYMESTOR by Hecuba, for killing her son (Eur. *Hec.* 1035f, 1149f; *Met.* 13.558f), or by Polydorus and Ilione (*Fab.* 109); of the Cyclops POLYPHEMUS by Odysseus et al. with a stake (*Od.* 9.382f; *Aen.* 3.634f); of TEIRESIAS by Athena, because he saw her and Chariclo bathing (*Lib.* 3.6.7; Callimachus, *Baths of Pallas* 57f), or by the gods for revealing their secrets (*Lib.* 3.6.7), or by Hera for siding with Zeus in a dispute (*Lib.* 3.6.7; *Fab.* 75; *Met.* 3.333f); of the bard THAMYRIS by the Muses for belittling their music (Eur. *Rhes.* 921f); of ZALEUCUS in one eye, in order to halve the full penalty of blindness assessed against his son for adultery (Val. Max. 6.5b.3).

Blind in both eyes. (Blindness may be indicated pictorially by the absence of pupils, by drawing eyes as slits, or by providing a guide or staff.) Old APPIUS CLAUDIUS persuades the senate to reject the peace offered by Pyrrhus' envoy (Plut. 21.19). The bard DEMODOCUS sings at Alcinoüs' banquet for Odysseus (*Od.* 8.62f). MELANIPPE, imprisoned by Desmontes, has her sight restored by her lover Poseidon (*Fab.* 186). OEDIPUS appears before Theban elders (Soph. *Oed. Tyr.* 1298f); parts from his daughters and King Creon (Soph. *Oed. Tyr.* 1478f); is imprisoned by his sons Polyneices and Eteocles (Eur. *Phoen.* 63f); is led from Thebes by Antigone, leaving the bodies of his wife and sons (Eur. *Phoen.* 1708f); is brought to a sacred place, marked by a statue of a horseman, where he encounters a stranger, city elders, and his daughter Ismene (Soph. *Oed. Col.* 1f); is welcomed by King Theseus of Athens (Soph. *Oed. Col.* 549f); tries to help Antigone, who has been seized by some guards (Soph. *Oed. Col.* 826f); is rejoined by Antigone and Ismene when Theseus has them freed (Soph. *Oed. Col.* 1095f); rejects reconciliation with Polyneices (Soph. *Oed. Col.* 1252f); summoned by a god, he comes to the place where he is to die; there he bids farewell to his daughters and, attended by Theseus alone, waits for death to take him (Soph. *Oed. Col.* 1594f). ORION carries as a guide a Cyclops (Serv. *ad Aen.* 10.763) or a boy (*Lib.* 1.4.3); he is carried by Celadion to Helius to be healed (*Poet. Astr.* 2.4). PHINEUS welcomes the Argonauts (*Argo.* 2.194f). TEIRESIAS is consulted by Liriope, who is carrying her baby (*Met.* 3.346f); is led by a boy to Oedipus (Soph. *Oed. Tyr.* 300f) and to Creon (Soph. *Ant.* 988f); and by his daughter, to Creon (Eur. *Phoen.* 834f); dressed as a Bacchant, he meets old Cadmus (Eur. *Bacch.* 170f); his ghost is evoked from Hades by Odysseus (*Od.* 11.90f).

FABULOUS BEINGS AND CREATURES

Individually described (see **Monster**).

Described only as various and terrifying, are encountered in the underworld by AENEAS and the Sibyl (*Aen.* 6.282f); by ALEXANDER (Ps.-Cal. 209, 224, 258).

FACE

(See also **Head; Mask.**)

Two faces: attribute of Janus. Janus detects the nymph Crane (Carna) attempting to steal away behind him (*Fasti* 6.107f). Three faces: attribute of Hecate. Four faces: an Etruscan deity associated with Janus (Serv. *ad Aen.* 7.607).

Covered by the hands (see **Hand**).

ARTEMIS and her nymphs conceal their identities from the river god Alpheius by covering their faces with mud (Paus. 6.22.9).

FAGOT

(See **Stick.**)

FALLING

(See also **Chasm; Leaping.**)

In most cases by accident or forced by another.

From a ship (see **Ship**).

From the sky or other height. BELLEROPHON falls from the winged horse Pegasus when a fly stings it (Pind. *Isth.* 7.44; Schol. on Pind. *Ol.* 13.130; *Poet. Astr.* 2.18). DEMOPHON falls onto his sword when his running horse stumbles (*Ep.* 6.16). ELPENOR, a comrade of Odysseus', while tipsy and half awake, walks off the roof of Circe's palace (*Od.* 10.552f, 11.62f). HELLE falls from the Golden Ram carrying her and Phrixus, into the Hellespont (*Lib.* 1.9.1; *Fab.* 3). ICARUS, when his wings melt, falls into the sea (*Met.* 8.227f) or onto an island (Arrian 7.20.5). PHAËTHON, his body ablaze from Zeus' thunderbolt, falls from Phoebus' (Helius') chariot into a river (*Met.* 2.311f; *Fab.* 152, 154) or onto the treasury of Merops, setting it afire (fragment of Eur. *Phaëthon,* see Rose, p. 201).

After being thrown or pushed. Baby ASTYANAX is taken from Andromache and hurled from the wall of Troy by Odysseus (Serv. *ad Aen.* 3.489) or by Neoptolemus (*Ilias Mikra* 14, in Schol. *ad Lycophrona* 1268). ATE is thrown from Olympus by Zeus (*Il.* 19.125f), along with a statue of Athena (the Palladium) (*Lib.* 3.12.3). CHELONE and her little hut, by Hermes, into a river where she becomes a tortoise (Serv. *ad Aen.* 1.505). HEPHAESTUS, from Olympus by Zeus; he falls to Lemnos; the women there minister to him (*Il.* 1.590f; *Lib.* 1.3.5); and by Hera into the sea, where Thetis and Eurynome look after him (*H. to Ap.* 316f; *Il.* 18.394f). IPHITUS, from the walls of Tiryns, by Heracles in a fit of madness (Soph. *Trach.* 269f; *Lib.* 2.6.2). LICHAS, by Heracles into the sea for bringing the poisoned robe that is destroying him (Soph. *Trach.* 777f; *Lib.* 2.7.7; *Fab.* 36); Lichas becomes a rock in the sea (*Met.* 9.216f). LYCAON's corpse, into a river by Achilles (*Il.* 21.120f). MARCUS MANLIUS, from the Capitoline after being convicted of sedition (Plut. 8.36). MYRTILUS, a charioteer, into the sea by Pelops, for trying to rape his bride; he curses the house of Pelops before he drowns (*Ep.* 2.8; *Fab.* 84). PERDIX (Talos), from a roof, by his uncle and teacher Daedalus, who is jealous of his invention of the saw (*Fab.* 39), or from the Acropolis; Athena catches him and turns him into a partridge (*Met.* 8.244f; *Lib.* 3.15.8). PERIMELE, into the sea by her father, where the river god Acheloüs receives her (*Met.* 8.593f). POLYDORUS' corpse, into the sea by Polymestor (*Met.* 13.435f). SCIRON is kicked or flung down from a cliff into the sea by Theseus (*Ep.* 1.3; *Fab.* 38; Plut. 1.10). A negligent SENTRY, from the Capitoline Hill (Plut. 8.27; Livy 5.47). SIDE, by Hera to the underworld because she rivaled her in beauty (*Lib.* 1.4.3). SINIS is catapulted into the sea by a bent tree released by Theseus (Plut. 1.8; *Lib.* 3.16.2; *Met.* 7.440f). STHENEBOEA is pushed off Pegasus into the sea by Bellerophon (fragment of Eur. *Stheneboea,* see Powell, p. 131f). The evil-eyed TELCHINES are thrown into the sea by Zeus (*Met.* 7.365f). THESEUS is pushed by Lycomedes from a cliff (Plut. 1.35) or into an abyss (*Ep.* 1.24).

To the ground. AJAX OÏLEUS is made to slip and fall during a footrace by Athena, allowing Odysseus to win (*Il.* 23.773f; cf. Nisus, who trips another to let Euryalus win, *Aen.* 5.315f). BRUTUS pretends to trip as he leaves a temple with the sons of Tarquin so that he may be the first to kiss his mother, i.e., Earth, the mother of all (Livy 1.56; *Fasti* 2.717f).

FASCES

(See also **Stick.**)

Attribute of Justitia; a Lictor (q.v.).

FATES

Three stately or hag-like women named Clotho, Lachesis, and Atropos, who are habitually engaged in carding, spinning, and cutting the thread of some mortal's life. They were known as the Moirai or Parcae.

With clubs kill two GIANTS (*Lib.* 1.6.2).

Tell ALTHAEA that her baby Meleager will die when a stick burning on the hearth is consumed; Althaea then extinguishes the stick (*Lib.* 1.8.2; *Met.* 8.451f).

Grant that ALCESTIS may die in place of her husband Admetus (*Lib.* 1.9.15).

FAUN

(See **Satyr.**)

FAWN

(See also **Deer.**)

Carried and then dropped by an eagle, is interpreted to be an encouraging response by Zeus to Agamemnon's plea for help against Hector (*Il.* 8.245f).

FAWN SKIN

(See **Skin, of Animal.**)

FEAST

(See **Eating.**)

FEATHER

Falling from one of the Stymphalian birds, wounds Oïleus aboard the *Argo* (*Argo.* 2.1033f).

Used as arrows by the Stymphalian birds in their attack on the Argonauts (*Argo.* 2.1033f; *Fab.* 20).

FEMALE FIGURE

(See **Human Figure.**)

FIGHTING

(See also **Centaur; Chariot; Killing; Warrior; Weapon.**)

Included here are the more noteworthy clashes that occur in battle and single combats between armed warriors, in which the weapons used are not specified in the source cited. Great battles and assaults are not indexed because they are almost indistinguishable from one another. Murders of defenseless persons by weapons or means unspecified are under **Killing.**

ZEUS FIGHTING GIANTS

Involving deities. CRONUS and the TITANS fight Ammon, and against Dionysus, Athena, and the Amazons (Diod. Sic. 3.71.2f). DIONYSUS, Ammon, and Zeus fight the Titans (Diod. Sic. 3.73.7–8). OLYMPIANS fight the Titans (Hes. *Theog.* 629f) and repel the assault on Olympus of the Giants, whom they hurl into Tartarus (*Fab.* 150), and of gigantic Otus and Ephialtes (*Lib.* 1.7.4; *Aen.* 6.582f). OLYMPIANS and the "HUNDRED-

HANDED" (Cottus, Briareüs, Gyes) fight the Titans (Hes. *Theog.* 664f). OLYMPIANS and HERACLES fight the Giants (*Lib.* 1.6.1–2; Diod. Sic. 4.21.6). POSEIDON, Anubis, Athena, Aphrodite, Ares, the Furies, Eris, Enyo, and Apollo take sides at the naval battle of Actium (*Aen.* 8.698f). ZEUS, Hera, Poseidon, and Athena assist the Greek assault on Troy (*Aen.* 2.608f).

One against one. ACHILLES kills Briseïs' husband and takes her captive (*Il.* 19.291f); black Memnon, son of Eos (*Ep.* 5.3); and Tenes, who has attacked him for seducing his sister (Plut. *Quaestiones Graecae* 28); he fights the river Scamander, by which he is forced to flee (*Il.* 21.234f). APOLLO fights Idas for Marpessa's hand; Zeus parts them and gives Marpessa her choice (*Lib.* 1.7.9). ARES, after routing Odysseus, is attacked by Athena (*Ep.* 7.34 n. 7, Loeb edn.). ATHENA slays a Gorgon during the battle between gods and Giants (Eur. *Ion* 986f). CASTOR kills Lynceus, who is trying to recover his promised bride from him, and is killed by Lynceus' brother Idas (*Fab.* 80). The brothers ETEOCLES and POLYNEICES kill each other at one of the gates of Thebes (*Lib.* 3.6.3) even though their mother Jocasta tries to intervene (Sen. *Phoen.* 511f). HERACLES fights and kills Lepreus, after being bested by him in a bull-eating contest (Paus. 5.5.4); King Amyntor, who tries to block his passage (*Lib.* 2.7.7); Coronus, resulting in the rout of the Lapiths; and Cycnus, son of Ares and Pelopia (*Lib.* 2.7.7), and the sons of Chrysaor, one at a time (Diod. Sic. 4.18.2); Heracles wounds Ares and fights Hades to bring back Alcestis from the underworld (*Lib.* 1.9.15, 2.7.3); his fight with Cycnus, son of Ares and Pyrene, refereed by Ares, is halted by a thunderbolt (*Lib.* 2.5.11). Three HORATII take on three Curiatii individually; two Horatii fall and the third runs away in order to separate the Curiatii and deal with them one by one (Livy 1.25). POLYDEUCES kills Idas to avenge the slaying of his brother Castor (*Fab.* 80). ROMULUS kills the king of the Caenenses (Serv. *ad Aen.* 6.859) and Acron (Plut. 2.16). TELEGONUS kills Odysseus, not knowing he is his father (*Telegony* 1, in Proclus). A Gallic champion (UNNAMED) is defeated by the Roman FABIUS AMBUSTUS (Plut. 4.13); by MARCELLUS (Serv. *ad Aen.* 6.855); by TORQUATUS' SON (Serv. *ad Aen.* 6.824).

One against two or more. CORIOLANUS defends a fallen warrior (Plut. 12.3). HECTOR, emboldened by Zeus, advances on Ajax and the Greek host to burn their ships (*Il.* 15.694f). HERACLES fights the Minyans (*Lib.* 2.4.11), Hippocoön and his sons (Paus. 3.15.9), and the Amazons, killing Hippolyte (*Fab.* 30; *Lib.* 2.5.9). MARCELLUS rescues his brother, who is surrounded by Carthaginians (Plut. 16.2). NEOPTOLEMUS defends himself at Apollo's altar against Orestes et al. (Eur. *Andro.* 1118f). PATROCLUS fights Trojans; he is stunned by a blow of Apollo's hand, wounded in the back by Euphorbus, and killed by Hector (*Il.* 16.805f). SOCRATES comes to the aid of wounded Alcibiades (Plut. 11.7). TURNUS, alone in the Trojan camp, fights his way to the river and escapes by swimming (*Aen.* 9.731f).

Two against one. Old ODYSSEUS and his son Telemachus fight Telegonus, his son by Circe; Odysseus falls (*Fab.* 127).

Two against two. The DIOSCURI fight with Idas and Lynceus over cattle (*Lib.* 3.11.2). SARPEDON and GLAUCUS breach the Greek wall and are met by the two Ajaxes (*Il.* 12.307f). THEANO's TWINS attack, at their mother's instigation, the foundling twins she had earlier adopted and passed off as her own; but they are overcome when the foundlings' father, Poseidon, comes to help his sons (*Fab.* 186).

Three against many. ALEXANDER and two of his soldiers are surrounded in an enemy town; all are wounded but are rescued when the Macedonians break in (Plut. 33.63).

Battle halted by women. SABINE WIVES of Romans stop the battle between their husbands and their fathers and brothers (Livy 1.13; *Fasti* 3.215f).

FINGER

Held to the lips: attribute of Harpocrates (Sigalion, Horus). At the lips of a head only: a genius.

ORESTES, hounded by black Furies, bites off a finger, at which the Furies turn white and his madness leaves him (Paus. 8.34.2–3).

FINS

Replacing hands: attribute of Decreto; Eurynome; the Telchines.

FIRE

(See also **Altar; Coal; Forge; Hearth; Light; Pyre; Spark; Star; Suicide; Torch; Volcano.**)

Ship afire (see **Ship**). Fire-breathing (see **Giant; Monster**).

On an altar: attribute of Concordia; Fides; Hestia. On a hearth: Hestia; Vesta. On the ground: the Parcae (Fates).

Stolen and given to man by PROMETHEUS, in a hollow stalk (Aes. *Prom.* 109f, 254f; Hes. *W. & D.* 50f, *Theog.* 561f; *Lib.* 1.7.1; *Fab.* 144); by means of a torch that he ignites at Helius' chariot (Serv. *ad Ecl.* 6.42); after he has taken it from Hephaestus' forge (Plato, *Protagoras* 321, C–E).

Invented by the metal-working DACTYLI (Diod. Sic. 5.64); by HERMES for the purpose of cooking a cow he has stolen (*H. to Her.* 105f); by PHORONEUS (Paus. 2.19.5).

Sacred. The Vestal AEMILIA relights Vesta's eternal fire by placing a part of her robe in the embers (Val. Max. 1.1.7). EUCHIDAS runs from Plataea to fetch unpolluted fire from Delphi and runs back again, after which he expires (Plut. 17.20). A mirror is used to rekindle Delphi's fire from the sun's rays (Plut. 4.9).

On the head. Attribute of the Dioscuri. It appears on the head of AUGUSTUS, as represented on the shield of Aeneas (*Aen.* 8.678f); of HERSILIA, Romulus' wife, as Iris conducts her to heaven (*Met.* 14.840f); of the boy IÜLUS (Ascanius), arouses Aeneas to rescue his family et al. from burning Troy (*Aen.* 2.682f); of LAVINIA, as she stands at an altar with her father (*Aen.* 7.71f); of the sleeping boy SERVIUS; Queen Tanaquil stops Tarquin from extinguishing it (Livy 1.39; Serv. *ad Aen.* 2.683). (See also **Rays.**)

On the body of ACHILLES as, wearing Athena's aegis, he terrifies the Trojans with a battle cry (*Il.* 18.203f); of a BOY, is caused by bitumen and is extinguished before Alexander's eyes (Plut. 33.35); of a GIRL who conceives Caeculus when a spark from the hearth lands in her lap (Serv. *ad Aen.* 7.678); of GLAUCE (Creüsa), who is burned to death by a poisoned robe and crown sent by Medea, as is Creon when he tries to help her (Eur. *Med.* 1186f; *Lib.* 1.9.28), as is Jason also (*Fab.* 25); of HECUBA, dreaming that she is giving birth to a firebrand (i.e., Paris) (*Aen.* 7.319f; Cic. *de Div.* 1.21.42); of HERACLES, when he puts on a robe poisoned with the blood of Nessus (*Met.* 9.159f; *Lib.* 2.7.7; *Fab.* 36); of the Giant MIMAS, whom Hephaestus has drenched with molten metal (*Lib.* 1.6.2); of OLYMPIAS, dreaming that she is on fire from a thunderbolt (Plut. 33.2).

Thrown into fire. King CISSEUS, by Archelaüs (*Fab.* 219). DEÏONEUS, by Ixion (Pind. *Pyth.* 2.39). STRANGERS, by the Taurians (*Ep.* 6.26).

Leaping into fire. ADRASTUS and HIPPONOÜS, as instructed by Apollo's oracle (*Fab.* 242). BROTEAS, maddened by Artemis (*Ep.* 2.2). EMPEDOCLES, into the crater of Etna (Diog. Laërt. 8.2.11). HASDRUBAL's wife, after throwing in first the bodies of her sons (Appian 8.131). (See also **Pyre.**)

Placed or held in fire. A BABY (see **Baby**). CHARICLEIA, condemned to be burned alive, is unharmed (*Aeth.* 8; cf. *Aeth.* 10, where she and Theagenes suffer trial by fire to prove their chastity). CROESUS, being burned alive by Cyrus, is saved by a downpour sent by Apollo (Herod. 1.86–87) or by Zeus (Bacchylides 3.23f). MUCIUS holds his hand in a brazier before Lars Porsena to demonstrate Roman courage (Livy 2.12; Plut. 6.17).

Stick placed in. One of the FATES, who are visiting Althaea and her baby Meleager, places in the fire a stick that represents the baby's life.

Althaea snatches it out and puts it away, but years later ends her son's life by burning it up (*Met.* 8.451f; *Lib.* 1.8.2; *Fab.* 171, 174; Aes. *Choëph.* 603f).

Earth afire. From PHAËTHON's attempt to drive his father's sun-chariot (*Met.* 2.210f); from ZEUS' thunderbolts during the battle with the Titans (Hes. *Theog.* 689f) and his fight with Typhoeus (Hes. *Theog.* 857f).

City afire. ROME, as the Gauls massacre the inhabitants (Plut. 8.22; Livy 5.41); as Nero sings of the destruction of Troy (Tac. *An.* 15.38–39). THEBES, in which Alexander meets Timocleia and her children (Plut. 33.12). TROY, during its destruction by the Greeks (*Aen.* 2.304f; cf. Eur. *Troad.* 1260f, where Talthybius et al. set the fire after the women have been captured), during which Aphrodite tells Aeneas he must leave (*Aen.* 2.590f), taking his family and other refugees (*Aen.* 2.707), and from which Antenor and his family escape with the connivance of Menelaüs (Serv. *ad Aen.* 1.242).

Building afire. ALCIBIADES, escaping from a burning building, is killed by Persian arrows (Plut. 11.39). ALEXANDER sets fire to Eumenes' tent to make him reveal the amount of his treasure (Plut. 30.2); he and Thaïs set fire to the palace at Persepolis during wild revelry (Plut. 33.38). DIONYSUS burns Pentheus' palace and Semele's tomb (Eur. *Bacch.* 594f). The GREEKS burn their camp before leaving Troy (*Od.* 8.499f; *Ep.* 5.15). PHAËTHON, his body ablaze, falls from the sun-chariot onto the treasury of the king of Ethiopia, setting it on fire (fragment of Eur. *Phaëthon,* see Rose, p. 201). PHYLEGYAS sets fire to a shrine of Apollo, because he has violated his daughter Coronis (Serv. *ad Aen.* 6.618). TURNUS fires the Trojans' camp (*Aen.* 9.530f). VESTA's temple catches fire, from which Metellus rescues her statue (*Fasti* 6.437f). ZEUS burns the palace of Lycaon and turns him into a wolf (*Met.* 1.230f); the palace of Tullus Hostilius, who perishes therein (Livy 1.31).

Bridge afire. The Romans destroy the Sabines' bridge over the Anio by floating burning timbers down on it (Livy 1.37).

Volcanic, or river of fire. Fire emerges from the earth to thwart an attack on Rome (*Met.* 14.785f); from the place where Heracles has buried Cacus (*Aen.* 8.251f). AENEAS and the Sibyl come to the fiery river Phlegethon (*Aen.* 6.548f). ALEXANDER comes to a fiery spring or pool (Plut. 33.35). DAMON and PHINTIAS rescue their aged parents from Etna (*Fab.* 254; in Paus. 10.28.2 they are named the Dutiful Men of Catana; in Val. Max. 5.4.4 their names are Amphinomus and Anapias). HEPHAESTUS, in the form of fire, overcomes water (the river god Scamander) that is about to engulf Achilles (*Il.* 21.342f); he sends fire, at Caeculus' request, to surround a crowd, convincing them that Caeculus is his son (Serv. *ad Aen.* 7.678). Two-faced JANUS repels the Sabines from Rome with a stream of fiery water (*Fasti* 1.267f).

As a portent. An arrow shot by ACESTES bursts into flame, presaging some (unspecified) future event (*Aen.* 5.522f). Fire appears in the sky, signifying the gods' displeasure with Rome (Livy 3.6.10), and blazes from an offering as Themistocles takes the auspices before the battle of Salamis (Plut. 7.13).

A transformation of HEPHAESTUS (see "Volcanic . . .," above); of PROTEUS, as he tries to escape from the grasp of Aristaeus (*Georg.* 4.409) and Menelaüs (*Od.* 4.454); of THETIS as she tries to escape from the arms of Peleus (*Lib.* 3.13.5); of ZEUS, as he abducts and seduces Aegina (*Fab.* 52; *Lib.* 3.12.6).

FIREBRAND

(See **Fire; Light; Stick; Torch.**)

FISH

(See also **Fishing.**)

Attribute of Aphrodite. Fish-tailed: Decreto; Eurynome; Glaucus (see **Fishing**); Nereïds; Scylla; Triton; Tritons. (See also the creature to which the tail is attached; **Monster; Sea Deity.**)

A transformation of APHRODITE, to escape from the monster Typhoeus, as other gods assume other shapes (*Met.* 5.331); of NEMESIS, as she tries to escape from Zeus (*Cypria* 8, in Athenaeus 8.334B).

Changed into. SCYLLA, after jumping overboard from Minos' ship, becomes a fish and is ever pursued by a sea eagle (Nisus) (*Fab.* 198).

Are enchanted by ORPHEUS' lyre (*Argo.* 1.569f).

Is given to POLYCRATES by a fisherman. When it is cut open, the ring Polycrates had thrown into the sea is found within (Herod. 3.42).

FISHING

(See also **Net.**)

ANTONY and CLEOPATRA amuse themselves catching fish (Plut. 44.29).

ERYSICHTHON'S DAUGHTER, sold as a slave by her father, eludes her master when Poseidon turns her into a fisherman (*Met.* 8.852f).

GLAUCUS catches fish that nibble grass and escape back to the sea; when he eats the same grass, he becomes a sea god with a fish's tail instead of legs (*Met.* 13.930f).

MENELAÜS' crewmen catch fish when supplies run short (*Od.* 4.363f).

PALAMEDES is drowned by Odysseus and Diomedes while he is fishing (Paus. 10.31.1).

FIST

(See also **Hand.**)

Attribute of Furor.

FLAG

(See **Standard.**)

FLAYING

(See also **Skin, of Man.**)

APOLLO flays the Satyr Marsyas after their music contest (*Met.* 6.382f; *Lib.* 1.4.2; *Fab.*165).

ATHENA flays the Giant Pallas and carries his skin as a shield (*Lib.* 1.6.2).

CAMBYSES has an unjust judge flayed and his skin used to make the seat of the throne from which the man's son thereafter passes judgment (Herod. 5.25; Val. Max. 6.36.3).

FLEECE

(See also **Ram; Sheep.**)

The GOLDEN FLEECE is placed in a tree by Phrixus (*Argo.* 2.1145f; *Lib.* 1.9.1), where it is guarded by a dragon (*Argo.* 2.404f), and from which Jason takes it after he or Medea puts the dragon to sleep (*Argo.* 4.123f; *Met.* 7.149f; *Lib.* 1.9.23). It is worn by Jason (*Argo.* 4.162f), covers his and Medea's bridal bed (*Argo.* 4.1141f), and is presented by Jason to Pelias (*Lib.* 1.9.27).

With the gift of a snowy fleece, PAN wins Selene's favors (*Georg.* 3.391f).

FLIGHT

(See also **Captive; Chariot; Flying; Horseman; Running; Ship.**)

Ending in metamorphosis. ARETHUSA, fleeing the river god Alpheius, escapes into mist and turns into water (*Met.* 5.600f). ASTERIA, from Zeus, leaps into the sea and becomes a quail (*Lib.* 1.4.1). CASTALIA, from Apollo, leaps into a well and becomes a spring (Schol. on Statius, *Thebaïd* 1.697). COMBE, from her sons, becomes a bird (*Met.* 7.382f). CORONIS, from Poseidon, is turned into a crow by Athena (*Met.* 2.569f). DAPHNE, from Apollo, is changed by Peneus into a laurel tree (*Met.* 1.502f). LOTIS, fleeing from Priapus, turns into water-lotus flowers (*Met.* 9.346f). NEMESIS, from Zeus, turns into a goose and her pursuer into a swan (*Lib.* 3.10.7; cf. *Cypria* 8, in Athenaeus 8.334B, where she becomes a fish or other creature). PHILOMELA and PROCNE, from axe-wielding Tereus; all become birds (*Met.* 6.666f; *Lib.* 3.14.8; *Fab.* 45). SMYRNA (Myrrha), from her sword-wielding father Cinyras, becomes a tree (*Met.* 10.474f; *Lib.* 3.14.4; *Fab.* 58). SYRINX, from Pan, is turned into reeds, from which Pan makes his pipes (*Met.* 1.705).

Ending in capture. APEMOSYNE, fleeing from Hermes, trips and falls (*Lib.* 3.2.1). AURA, from Dionysus, is moved by Aphrodite to yield (Nonnus 260). BRITOMARTIS, from Minos, is caught in a net (Paus. 2.30.3). CHLORIS, from winged Zephyrus (*Fasti* 5.201f). IO, from Zeus, is hindered by a cloud (*Met.* 1.588f).

Ending in escape. ATHENA flees from amorous Hephaestus (*Lib.* 3.14.6). HELEN, from a tattered stranger (Menelaüs) to the tomb of Proteus (Eur. *Hel.* 541f). HYPSIPYLE, from the women of Lemnos (*Fab.* 15). LETO, carrying her twins, from Hera (*Met.* 6.337f). MEDEA, from her home by moonlight to join the Argonauts (*Argo.* 4.35f) and from Corinth, after killing her sons (*Fab.* 25); after poisoning Creon and abandoning her sons (Schol. on Eur. *Medea* 273). PROCRIS, from her deceitful husband Cephalus (*Met.* 7.743f). PROETUS' DAUGHTERS, made mad by Dionysus or Hera, from Melampus et al. (*Lib.* 2.2.2). RHOEO'S SISTERS, startled from sleep when pigs overturn some wine jars, run to the sea and leap in (Diod. Sic. 5.62.3). SCYLLA, from the sea god Glaucus (*Met.* 13.908f).

Ending in death from a snake bite. For EURYDICE, fleeing from Aristaeus (*Georg.* 4.453f; Serv. *ad Georg.* 4.317); for HESPERIA, fleeing from Aesacus (*Met.* 11.767f).

Of men and women. DIONYSUS and MAENADS flee from Lycurgus, who is wielding an ox-goad; Dionysus dives into the sea (*Il.* 6.130f). PARIS and HELEN (*Fab.* 92; in *Cypria* 1, recorded in Proclus, the escape is by ship).

Of men from women. HIPPOLYTUS flees, from Phaedra (*Ep.*1.18). NARCISSUS, from Echo (*Met.* 3.390f). PERSEUS, after beheading Medusa, is borne on his winged sandals away from her pursuing sisters (Hes. *Sh. Her.* 228f). A young SUITOR for Atalanta's hand; in a race against her, he is overtaken and killed (*Lib.* 3.9.2).

Of men from others. AENEAS runs from Achilles, abandoning his cattle (*Il.* 20.89f, 20.188f). CREON, from his son Haemon, who wants to kill him because he caused Antigone to hang herself (Soph. *Ant.* 1231f). DOLON, a Trojan spy clad in a wolfskin, from Diomedes and Odysseus (*Il.* 10.351f). PHOENIX escapes from his friends and kinfolk who try to prevent his leaving home because of his father's enmity (*Il.* 9.472f).

From battle or combat. ACHILLES runs from the river Scamander (*Il.* 21.234f). AENEAS' PHANTOM, from Turnus; Hera has sent it to lure Turnus onto a ship, out of Aeneas' reach (*Aen.* 10.636f). APOLLO, in the likeness of Agenor, from Achilles, seeking to draw him out of battle (*Il.* 21.599f). EURYALUS, from Rutulian horsemen when he is detected during a night scouting mission (*Aen.* 9.371f). HECTOR, from Diomedes; after being stunned by Diomedes' spear; he runs to his chariot and escapes (*Il.* 11.357f); from Achilles, around the walls of Troy (*Il.* 22.136f). The single survivor of the three HORATII, from the three Curiatii, in order to separate them and deal with them one by one (Livy 1.25). IDAEUS, from Diomedes; Hephaestus wraps him in mist (*Il.* 5.20f). ODYSSEUS, from Hector, abandoning Nestor and leaving it to Diomedes to rescue the old man (*Il.* 8.87f). POLITES, from Pyrrhus (Neoptolemus), by whom he is killed before Priam and Hecuba's eyes (*Aen.* 2.529f). TELEPHUS, from Achilles; he becomes entangled in a vine and is wounded (*Ep.* 3.17). TURNUS, outnumbered in the Trojan camp, escapes by running to the Tiber and diving in (*Aen.* 9.816f); he runs from Aeneas when his sword breaks (*Aen.* 12.742f). TURNUS' SOLDIERS flee when Aeneas approaches (*Aen.* 12.462f).

Of a group. AENEAS and other survivors flee from burning Troy (*Aen.* 2.796f). ANTENOR and his family, from Troy with the connivance of Menelaüs (Serv. *ad Aen.* 1.242). Baby PYRRHUS, in the care of several attendants, from a troop of soldiers; held up by a river, they cross on a raft (Plut. 21.2). VESTALS, from Rome and the invading Gauls, transporting their temple's sacred objects in L. Albinus' wagon (Livy 5.40).

FLOOD

(See also **River; Sea; Water.**)

In a flood, fish are taken among treetops, and dolphins and Nereïds visit the abodes of men (*Met.* 1.293f).

Personified. ACHELOÜS sweeps away several nymphs, who become islands (*Met.* 8.583f). SCAMANDER, protesting against Achilles' fouling his waters with Trojan corpses, attacks him, nearly drowns him, and forces him to flee (*Il.* 21.211f). (See also **River God; Sea Deity.**)

Sent by deities. DIONYSUS sends rain that causes the river Boar to flood and destroy the city of Libethra, fulfilling a prophecy (Paus. 9.30.5). POSEI-DON sends a flood to punish Laomedon for refusing to pay his promised wage for building Troy's wall (*Met.* 11.205f). ZEUS sends a flood to extinguish the fire on earth (*Fab.* 152) and to wipe out evil man (*Lib.* 1.7.2), in which he is aided by Poseidon (*Met.* 1.276f); he sends a flood to destroy the wall before the Greek camp at Troy, with Apollo and Poseidon helping (*Il.* 12.17f).

Survivors of flood. Old CERAMBUS is rescued by winged nymphs (*Met.* 7.354f). DEUCALION and PYRRHA land on Parnassus (*Met.* 1.316f) or Etna (*Fab.* 153). PHILEMON and BAUCIS are installed by Zeus and Hermes as custodians of a temple above flood waters, in time becoming oak trees (*Met.* 8.693f).

FLOWER

(See also **Crown; Garland; Herb; Wreath.**)

Attribute of Aurora; Chloris; Flora; Graces; Horae (seasons). Lotus: Horus (on his head); Isis (also holding a sistrum, q.v.). Pomegranate (tulip-like): Spes (holding it in one hand, her robe in the other). Poppy: Aphrodite; Bonus Eventus; Copia; Demeter (in her hand). Rose: Aphrodite; Eros. Scattered: Comus. Floral garment: Flora; Jupiter. Floral wreath: Flora; Juno.

Held in the hand. CHLORIS (Flora) touches Hera's breast with a rare flower, causing her to conceive Ares (*Fasti* 5.255f). ODYSSEUS wards off Circe's magic with the flowering herb moly and his sword (*Met.* 14.291f; *Od.* 10.287f).

Formed from a body or its blood. ADONIS' blood is made to put forth anemones by Aphrodite (*Met.* 10.731f). AJAX's blood turns into hyacinths after he kills himself (*Met.* 13.394f). Lovelorn CLYTIE, as she gazes at her beloved Sun, turns into heliotrope (*Met.* 4.256f). CROCUS becomes a flower after he is accidentally killed by Hermes' discus (Serv. *ad Georg.* 4.182); or after he dies of love for the nymph Smilax, who also becomes a flower (*Met.* 4.283). HYACINTHUS, killed by a discus thrown by Boreas, who is angry because Apollo has won the boy from him, turns into a flower (Serv. *ad Ecl.* 3.13), or is killed accidentally by Apollo's own discus, whereupon his blood becomes a purple flower (*Met.* 10.209f). LOTIS, fleeing from Priapus, turns into water-lotus flowers (*Met.* 9.346f). NARCISSUS, dying of love for his own reflection, becomes a yellow and white flower (*Met.* 3.502f).

Being picked. DRYOPE picks water-lotus flowers (the transformation of the nymph Lotis) for her baby; the flowers drip blood; she is changed into a tree (*Met.* 9.342f). EUROPA picks flowers with which to adorn a bull (Zeus) (*Met.* 2.850f). PERSEPHONE, intent on gathering flowers, falls into Hades' hands (*H. to Dem.* 2.8f).

Heads of flowers are flicked off by Tarquin with a stick, in silent response to an envoy's question (Livy 1.54; *Fasti* 2.705f).

FLUTE

(See also **Musical Instruments; Pipes.**)

A FLUTE PLAYER AND A WINE POURER

Consists usually of two pipes, less often of one.

Attribute of Bacchants; Corybantes; Eumolpus (*Ep.* 3.24); Euterpe; Olen; Shepherds (q.v.).

Invented by ARDELOS (Paus. 2.31.4) or ATHENA (Pind. *Pyth.* 19f).

Held or played by ATHENA, before the gods; she throws it away when Hera and Aphrodite make fun of her or when, in a reflection, she sees her cheeks distorted as she plays (*Fasti* 6.697f; *Lib.* 1.4.2; *Fab.* 165); by GIRLS, as Lysander has the Athenian fleet burned and the Long Walls razed (Plut. 23.15); by ISMENIAS, as Alexander destroys Thebes (Ps.-Cal. 132); by LAR-

NIA, a courtesan, at a banquet for Demetrius (Plut. 43.16, 43.27); by MAR-SYAS, a Satyr; he learns to play Athena's discarded flute and competes against Apollo's lyre (*Met.* 6.384f; *Lib.* 1.4.3); by a SIREN as Odysseus' ship passes by; another sings, and a third plays a lyre (*Ep.* 7.18–19).

FLY

(See also **Bees.**)

Stinging. A fly stings a cow (Io), causing her to flee (*Lib.* 2.1.3; Aes. *Prom.* 561f, 671f). A swarm attacks HERACLES while he sacrifices at Olympia (Paus. 5.14.1). HERACLES' COWS scatter when stung by flies (*Lib.* 2.5.10). PEGASUS is stung by a fly, causing Bellerophon to fall to earth (Pind. *Isth.* 7.44; *Poet Astr.* 2.18; Schol on Pind. *Ol.* 13.130).

FLYING

(See also **Ascension; Falling; Leaping.**)

Wings (q.v.) are attributes of most figures represented as flying. However, deities who have no wings transport themselves through the air at will and with such frequency that such scenes are distinguishable only by the presence of other iconographic elements.

FOAL

(See also **Horse.**)

Offered to CRONUS by Rhea to be swallowed in place of baby Poseidon (Serv. *ad Georg.* 1.12; Paus. 8.8.2).

FOOD

(See **Eating.**)

FOOT

(See also **Boot; Crippled Man; Kicking; Sandal; Shoe.**)

Winged feet (see **Wings**).
Both bound: attribute of Saturn.

One bare. JASON, having lost a sandal (q.v.), appears before Pelias (*Argo.* 1.5f; *Lib.* 1.9.16).

Both lamed. Baby OEDIPUS is crippled for life when his feet are pierced or cruelly bound before he is exposed (*Lib.* 3.5.7; Soph. *Oed. Tyr.* 1349f).

One lamed. PHILOCTETES suffers from a putrid wound that does not heal (Soph. *Phil.* 220f, 542f, 975f, 1220f; *Ep.* 3.27).

Being washed. As EURYCLEIA washes the foot of a beggar (Odysseus), she recognizes from a scar that he is her long-absent master (*Od.* 19.386f).

FOOTSTOOL

(See **Throwing.**)

FORGE

(See also **Tools.**)

Attribute of the Cyclopes. They make thunderbolts for Zeus, a chariot for Ares, an aegis-breastplate for Athena (*Met.* 8.424f; *Argo.* 1.730f), and assist Hephaestus with the arms for Aeneas (*Aen.* 8.443f).

Attribute of the Dactyli, discoverers of fire and metalworking (Diod. Sic. 5.64).

Attribute of Hephaestus and his workshop, where he is visited by his wife APHRODITE, who asks for arms for Aeneas, which he and the Cyclopes produce (*Aen.* 8.387f); where ATHENA comes asking for arms and he tries to seduce her (*Lib.* 3.14.6); where, at EOS' request, he makes arms for Memnon (Serv. *ad Aen.* 1.751; *Aen.* 8.384); where HELIUS informs him of Aphrodite's faithlessness and he fashions a golden net with which to catch her and Ares *in flagrante delicto* (*Met.* 4.171f; *Od.* 8.266f); from which PROMETHEUS steals fire (Plato, *Protagoras* 321 C–E); where THETIS comes asking for arms for Achilles; Aphrodite makes her welcome, and Hephaestus sets to work (*Il.* 18.369f).

FOX

(See also **Dog; Wolf.**)

Symbol of the city of Messene (*Lib.* 2.8.5).

Procris, Cephalus, Amphitryon, et al. hunt the huge TEUMESSIAN FOX; the dog Laelaps chases it until Zeus turns both to stone (*Met.* 7.763f; *Lib.* 2.4.7).

FROG

A toad is a symbol of Argos (*Lib.* 2.8.5).

Rustics are turned into frogs when they muddy water about to be drunk by DEMETER, while searching for Persephone (Serv. *ad Georg.* 1.378); by LETO, in flight from Hera with her babies (*Met.* 6.343f).

Presented to DARIUS, along with a bird, a mouse, and five arrows, by a Scythian herald (Herod. 4.131).

FRUITS

(See also **Cornucopia; Eating.**)

Attribute of the Horae; Pomona; Priapus. In the hand: Asclepius. In the folds of a robe: Apheliotes; Zephyrus.

Recede from the grasp of TANTALUS (*Od.* 11.588f; *Met.* 4.457f; *Ep.* 2.1; *Fab.* 82).

Produced from inedible things when touched by ANIUS' DAUGHTERS (*Met.* 13.652f).

FUNERAL

(See **Burial; Corpse; Tomb.**)

FURIES

(See also **Harpies.**)

In Aeschylus they are Gorgon-like women, robed in black, wreathed with snakes, and with eyes dripping blood. They are also represented as solemn women in black with snakes in their hair, and snakes or torches in their hands. Euripides and later writers give them wings. They were called Erinyes and Eumenides collectively.

Birth of, from the blood of Ouranos (Hes. *Theog.* 176f; *Lib.* 1.2.4).

In the garb of. POLYXOS' slaves take Helen away and hang her (Paus. 3.19.10).

Are awakened from sleep by the ghost of CLYTEMNESTRA, as Orestes, stained with her blood, seeks to be purified by Apollo (Aes. *Eumen.* 39f);

they discover Orestes clinging to Athena's statue in supplication (Aes. *Eumen.* 235f, 397f).

Receive the daughters of Pandareos from the Harpies (Paus. 10.30.1).

Appear before HERA in the underworld (*Met.* 4.447f); at the wedding of PROCNE and TEREUS, along with an owl (*Met.* 6.430f).

Act as accusers at the trial of ORESTES, whom Apollo defends before Athena, acting as judge (Aes. *Eumen.* 245f, 336f; Eur. *Iph. Taur.* 961f; *Ep.* 6.25); they are appeased by Athena and Peitho after Orestes' acquittal (Aes. *Eumen.* 794f).

Hounded by Furies. ALCMAEON, for killing his mother (*Fab.* 73). CATILINE, hanging fom a cliff in Hades (*Aen.* 8.668f). ORESTES, for the murder of Clytemnestra (and Aegisthus) (Aes. *Choëph.* 1048f; *Fab.* 119; Eur. *Iph. Taur.* 931f; *Ep.* 6.25); Electra tries to calm him (Eur. *Orest.* 253f, 401f); they make him attack cattle (Eur. *Iph. Taur.* 280f) and bite off one of his fingers (Paus. 8.34.3). THESEUS and PEIRITHOÜS, in the underworld, until rescued by Heracles (*Fab.* 79).

FURIES HOUNDING ORESTES

Hounded by a single Fury. ALCMAEON, for matricide (*Lib.* 3.7.5). AMATA, by Allecto, who places a snake at her breast (*Aen.* 7.341f). A COW (Io), at the instigation of Hera (*Met.* 7.124f). HERACLES, by Lyssa, causing him to slay his wife and children (Eur. *Her.* 815f). INO and ATHAMAS, at whom Tisiphone, sent by Hera, hurls snakes (*Met.* 4.481f). PEIRITHOÜS and IXION are prevented from eating by a torch-brandishing Fury (*Aen.* 6.601f).

PELOPS' descendants, by Megaera, who has sent the ghost of Tantalus to effect her curse on his house (Sen. *Thy.* 29f). SINNERS in the underworld are lashed by Tisiphone (*Aen.* 6.570f). TURNUS, asleep, has a torch thrown at him by Allecto (*Aen.* 7.446f); he is assailed and terrified by an owl (a Fury) just before his fight to the death with Aeneas (*Aen.* 12.861f).

One Fury puts a stop to the nymph JUTURNA's assistance to her brother Turnus, at which she returns to her pool (*Aen.* 12.869f).

GAME

(See also **Lots.**)

Dice: attribute of the Charites.

Dice rolled or tossed by Alcibiades' friends in a roadway; Alcibiades lies in front of a wagon to prevent interruption of the game (Plut. 11.2); by Eros and Ganymede (*Argo.* 3.114f); by Heracles and the keeper of his temple (Plut. 2.5); by Palamedes and Thersites (Paus. 10.31.1); by Patroclus and Clysonymus, who is killed by the former when they quarrel (*Il.* 23.87f; *Lib.* 3.13.8).

Draughts (checkers) is played by the two Ajaxes, and watched by Protesilaüs and Palamedes (Eur. *Iph. Aul.* 192f); is played by Penelope's suitors (*Od.* 1.106f).

See also the various events (e.g., **Boxing; Running**); weapons and gear (e.g., **Spear; Chariot**).

Athletic contests in honor of Anchises (*Aen.* 5.104f); of Archemorus, held at Nemea by the "Seven Against Thebes" (*Lib.* 3.6.4); of Patroclus (*Il.* 23.257f).

GARLAND

(See also **Flower; Vine; Wreath.**)

Used as a chain to bind Silenus as he entertains the company with a song (*Ecl.* 6.16f).

GARMENT

(See also **Belt; Skin; Trousers; Veil.**)

The literary sources give so little particular information about the style of garments worn, and artistic representation is so varied, following the fashion of the period, that only in a few instances may we attribute to a god or mortal a particular form of dress.

ATTRIBUTE

Short, covering the left shoulder only (*exomis*): attribute of Charon; Hephaestus; Virtus (with right breast bare); working men. Knee-length, caught up at the waist: Artemis; a huntress. A tunic or shawl, decorated with a Gorgon's face and having a fringe of tassels or snakes: Athena (see **Aegis**). Of "watery" appearance: personifications of the ocean or rivers (e.g., Nile, *Aen.* 8.711f). Forming a hood: Telesphorus; (saffron) Aurora; (black) Nyx. Decorated with stars: Isis; Jupiter; Nox. Of flowers: Flora; Jupiter.

ROBE OR MANTLE

Unwoven or unraveled (see **Loom; Thread**).

Presented to or placed upon ARSINOË, by Alcmaeon, along with a necklace (q.v.)(*Lib.* 3.7.5); ARTAYNTA, by Xerxes reluctantly (Herod. 9.109); ATHENA's statue, by the Trojan women (*Il.* 6.297f; *Aen.* 1.479f); DARIUS, before he becomes king, by the Greek Syloson (Herod. 3.139); DEÏANEIRA, by the dying Centaur Nessus (*Met.* 9.132); GLAUCE (Creüsa), Creon's daughter and Jason's bride, by Medea or her children; when she puts it on, it poisons her or burns her to death (Eur. *Med.* 1156f; *Lib.* 1.9.28; *Fab.* 25); HARMONIA, by Athena and Hephaestus (*Fab.* 148) or by Cadmus, together with a necklace, at her wedding (*Lib.* 3.4.2); HERACLES, by Lichas; it poisons him when he puts it on (Soph. *Trach.* 755f); LICHAS, by Deïaneira (Soph. *Trach.* 600f); PROCNE, by an old woman who received it from Philomela (*Met.* 6.578f); the SHRINE OF DELPHI (Apollo's statue or altar?) by Alcmaeon's sons, together with a necklace (*Lib.* 3.7.7); XERXES, by his wife Amestris (Herod. 9.109).

Poisoned or on fire. Consumes GLAUCE (Creüsa) and those who touch her; i.e., Creon (*Lib.* 1.9.28; Eur. *Med.* 1186f) or both Creon and Jason (*Fab.* 25). Torments HERACLES into hurling its donor into the sea and seeking death for himself (Soph. *Trach.* 755f; *Lib.* 2.7.7; *Met.* 9.152f; *Fab.* 25).

Enfolds AGAMEMNON, hindering his defense when Clytemnestra (and Aegisthus) attack him (Aes. *Agam.* 1381f, *Eumen.* 633f; *Ep.* 6.23; Sen. *Agam.* 936f).

Displayed. ANTONY holds up to the Roman people the robe Caesar was wearing when he was killed (Plut. 44.14). ORESTES, after killing Clytemnestra and Aegisthus, displays to the palace serving-women the robe in which Agamemnon was entangled when he was killed (Aes. *Choëph.* 980f).

At work on a robe. PHILOMELA, because she cannot speak, weaves scenes of her misfortunes to inform her sister Procne of them (*Lib.* 3.14.8; *Met.* 6.576f). (See also **Loom.**)

Unraveled by PENELOPE, who has promised to marry one of her importunate suitors when she has finished weaving it (*Od.* 19.137); by TARCHE-

TIUS (or his agent) to prevent his imprisoned daughter and her maid from ever finishing their weaving (Plut. 2.2).

A cause of strife, is recovered, together with a necklace, by the sons of PHEGEUS, after they kill Alcmaeon, and is subsequently retaken by Alcmaeon's sons when they kill their father's murderers (*Lib.* 3.7.5, 3.7.6).

Found. PYRAMUS comes upon the robe dropped by Thisbe when she fled from a lioness and which the beast has mangled (*Met.* 4.101f).

Used as a sail by DAEDALUS to escape from Crete (Serv. *ad Aen.* 6.14).

Covers a corpse. ALEXANDER covers the body of Darius (Plut. 33.43). ORESTES reveals the body of Clytemnestra to Aegisthus (Soph. *Elec.* 1466f).

CLOTHING

Baby garments, shown to King CERCYON by shepherds, prove to him that the baby they have found is his daughter's (*Fab.* 187); conceal a stone that Rhea is giving Cronus to swallow in the place of baby Zeus (Hes. *Theog.* 485f; *Lib.* 1.1.7; *Fab.* 139).

Invented by MELUS, the first man to shear a sheep (Serv. *ad Ecl.* 8.37).

Of a girl is stripped from LEUCIPPUS by Daphne et al., who wish every member of their group to join in their bathing; finding him to be a man, they kill him (Paus. 8.20.2).

Royal regalia. ALEXANDER bestows the trappings of kingship on the gardener Abdolonimus (Q. Curt. 4.1).

Spread on the ground before CATO by his soldiers to honor their departing commander (Plut. 36.12).

GATE

(See also **Door.**)

One of horn and one of ivory provide passage from Hades for dreams true and false, respectively (*Od.* 19.562f; *Aen.* 6.894f).

Each of the seven gates of Thebes has a champion to defend it against the Argive warrior assigned to attack it (Aes. *Seven* 375f; Eur. *Phoen.* 1090f).

GAUL

(See **Barbarian.**)

GENITALS

(See also **Blood; Phallus.**)

Enlarged: attribute of Priapus.

Cut off. Hermaphroditic AGDISTIS' male organs are cut off by the gods (Paus. 7.17.5). ATTIS castrates himself (*Fasti* 4.233f; Cat. 63.1f). CRONUS castrates his father Ouranos (Hes. *Theog.* 162f; *Lib.* 1.1.4).

GENIUS

In Roman religion a genius was a spirit, personifying an individual's personality that watched over him. Families, states, places, houses, and institutions also had their genii. When a genius makes itself visible, it appears in the form of a snake. In Greece such a spirit, called daimon, personified a man's genius, lot, or fortune.

GENIUS OF A PLACE

GHOST

(See **Phantom.**)

GIANT

(See also **Monster** for gigantic figures that have more than human characteristics; **Fighting,** for the activities of the race of Giants and Titans.)

Rock-hurling (see **Ship**). Man-eating (see **Eating**). One-eyed (see **Cyclops**). Many-headed and -handed (see **Head**). Snake-legged and -headed (see these entries).

Mountain-climbing. OTUS and EPHIALTES pile Mt. Pelion on Ossa to attack the gods of Olympus and are slain by Apollo (*Fab.* 28; *Od.* 11.315f; *Lib.* 1.7.4; *Aen.* 6.582f).

Fire-breathing. CACUS is strangled in his cave by Heracles, whose cattle he has stolen (*Aen.* 8.259f); or he is clubbed to death (*Fasti* 1.575f; Livy 1.7).

Female. The Laestrygonian queen takes three of Odysseus' men to her cannibal husband, who seizes one to eat. (*Od.* 10.112f).

Tormented by snakes or vultures, TITYOS lies in the underworld, as punishment for trying to rape Leto (*Fab.* 55; *Od.* 11.576f; *Lib.* 1.4.1).

Wild Giants are encountered by ALEXANDER (Ps.-Cal. 209).

GIFT

(See **Garment; Ring; Vessel.**)

GIRDLE

(See **Belt.**)

GIRL

(See also **Boy; Children; Human Figure.**)

IPHIGENEIA is taken from Clytemnestra by Odysseus and Diomedes and brought to Agamemnon (*Fab.* 98).

NAUSICAÄ et al. encounter shipwrecked Odysseus on the beach (*Od.* 6.127f).

Dressed as a girl. ACHILLES, among the daughters of Lycomedes, selects a weapon from among the trinkets offered by Odysseus, revealing thereby his male identity (*Met.* 13.162f; *Fab.* 96); seizes a weapon when a trumpet blows; is brought by Thetis to Lycomedes (*Lib.* 3.13.8). DIONYSUS is brought to Ino and Athamas by Hermes (*Lib.* 3.4.3).

Seven Athenian girls and seven boys are delivered to Minos or to his ship as reparation for his son's death (Plut. 1.17).

White-skinned CHARICLEIA is conspicuous among the members of her dark Ethiopian family (*Aeth.* 10).

GLOBE

(See also **Ball.**)

Attribute of Aeternitas; Anubis; Bacchus; Ceres; Cybele; Fortuna (placing it aside); Honos (standing in armor upon it); Lachesis (pointing at it with a staff); a Muse; Nemesis; Phoebus; Providentia; Salus (with it at her feet); Tyche (with it on her head); Urania; Venus. Winged: Fortuna; Volupia. Symbol of the sky (q.v.).

GOAD

(See also **Staff.**)

Used by LUSSA to drive Heracles mad and to kill his wife and sons (Eur. *Her.* 815f); by LYCURGUS to drive Dionysus and Maenads from his kingdom; Dionysus leaps into the sea (*Il.* 6.130f).

GOAT

Attribute of Aphrodite Epitragia (Plut. 1.18); Apollo; Bacchus; Copia; Fidius; Hera Aigophagos [Goat-eater] (Paus. 3.15.9); Mercury; Priapus.

Suckling a baby (see **Baby**).

In this form, DIONYSUS is brought to the nymphs of Nysa by Hermes (*Lib.* 3.4.3; Diod. Sic. 3.66.3); attempts to escape from the monster Typhoeus (*Met.* 5.329); HERMES seduces Penelope, of which union Pan is born (Serv. *ad Aen.* 2.44).

Leads ARCHELAÜS to the place where he founds Aegeae (*Fab.* 219).

Drag brush to raise dust, a stratagem of Alexander's (Ps.-Cal. 173).

Are killed for food by shipwrecked GREEKS, who find them in a cave containing a statue of Dionysus (Paus. 2.23.1); by ODYSSEUS' MEN (*Od.* 9.156f).

Is substituted by DIONYSUS for a boy about to be sacrificed (Paus. 9.8.1).

GOAT-FISH

In this form, PAN jumps into a river to escape the monster Typhoeus (*Poet. Astr.* 2.28).

GOAT-HEADED

Attribute of Pan.

GOAT-HORNED

(See **Horn.**)

GOAT-LEGGED

(See **Satyr.**)

GOAT'S HEAD

Forming a helmet: attribute of Juno.

Emerging from the back of a hybrid creature or forming one of the three heads of a creature (see **Chimaera**).

GOATSKIN

(See **Skin, of Animal.**)

GOD

(See also **River God; Sea Deity.**)

Most incidents in which a divinity appears will be found elsewhere, under a more particular head.

Gods in council: *Il.* 1.533f, 4.1f, 7.443f, 8.1f, 8.442f, 15.14f, 15.149f, 20.4f, 24.31f; *Od.* 5.1f; *Aen.* 10.1f.

As a deus ex machina. APOLLO appears to Theseus, Adrastus, and Theban matrons (Eur. *Suppl.* 1183f); with Helen, he appears to Orestes, Pylades, Menelaüs, Electra, Hermione, and women of Argos (Eur. *Orest.* 1625f). ARTEMIS appears to Theseus and dying Hippolytus (Eur. *Hipp.* 1284f). ATHENA appears to King Thoas and temple maidens (Eur. *Iph. Taur.* 1435f), to Ion and his mother Creüsa (Eur. *Ion* 1549f), and to Furies and women of Athens (Aes. *Eumen.* 778f). DIONYSUS appears to Cadmus, Agave, and Bacchants after Pentheus' dismemberment (Eur. *Bacch.,* frags. of lacuna at 1329). The DIOSCURI appear to Orestes, Electra, and peasant women, standing by the corpses of Clytemnestra and Aegisthus (Eur. *Elec.* 1233f), and to Theoclymenus, on the point of stabbing his servant, and to women captives (Eur. *Hel.* 1642f). HERACLES appears to Philoctetes and Neoptolemus as they leave a cave (Soph. *Phil.* 1408f), and to Alcmene and Philoctetes (Sen. *Her. Oet.* 2048f). HERMES appears to Prometheus, who is in chains, and daughters of Oceanus (Aes. *Prom.* 941f). A MUSE, holding the body of Rhesus, appears to Hector and soldiers (Eur. *Rhes.* 885f). THETIS appears to Peleus and women of Phthia (Eur. *Andro.* 1226f).

Gods and mortals. APHRODITE, after talking with Aeneas and Achates in the guise of a huntress, resumes her divine form and disappears (*Aen.* 1.402f); persuades Aeneas not to kill Helen, who has taken asylum at an altar

(*Aen.* 2.588f). ATHENA speaks to Odysseus beside his ship (*Il.* 2.166f); as a herald she stands by him as he speaks in council (*Il.* 2.279f); as a shepherd she awakens him from sleep (*Od.* 13.221f); as Mentes she is welcomed by Telemachus to the hall where his mother's suitors are feasting (*Od.* 1.103f); and as Mentor she speaks to him as he prays by the shore (*Od.* 2.262f) or lies awake (*Od.* 15.9f). EGERIA counsels the priest-king Numa at nocturnal meetings in her grove (Livy 1.19, 1.21). RHEA is sent by Zeus to plead with Demeter to restore earth's fertility (*H. to Dem.* 441f). The deified ROMULUS appears in splendor to Julius Proculus (Plut. 1.28; Livy 1.16). THETIS tells Achilles to give Hector's body to Priam (*Il.* 24.120f); she tells Peleus to get the Argonauts to resume their journey (*Argo.* 4.852f). (For activities of HERMES and IRIS, see **Wings.**)

GOLD

Shower of. (ZEUS) visits Danaë in her prison and begets Perseus (*Met.* 4.610f; *Lib.* 2.4.1; *Fab.* 63); he visits Alcmene and begets Heracles (Pind. *Isth.* 7.5.7).

Golden touch. MIDAS, with a touch, turns various objects (including food and drink) into gold, by the power of Dionysus (*Met.* 11.106f; *Fab.* 191).

Buried and uncovered. ODYSSEUS betrays Palamedes by burying gold in his tent (or at its former site) and by later revealing it to Agamemnon as proof of Palamedes' treason (*Fab.* 105; *Ep.* 3.8).

Offered as a bribe. FABRICIUS refuses a Samnite bribe (Serv. *ad Aen.* 8.444) and one from Pyrrhus (Plut. 21.20). PHOCION rejects bribes offered by Alexander's agents (Plut. 35.18) by Harpalus (Plut. 20) and by Menyllus (Plut. 29). POLYMNESTOR accepts a bribe to forward the Greeks' aim to extirpate the house of Priam by killing Polydorus; by mistake he kills his own son (*Fab.* 109; cf. *Aen.* 3.49f, where he kills Polydorus for his gold).

GOOSE

(See **Bird.**)

GORGON

(See also **Aegis; Monster.**)

Frightful, snake-haired and tusked woman, often winged.
GORGONS flank the omphalos (q.v.) in Apollo's temple at Delphi (Eur. *Ion* 224).

A GORGON fights with ATHENA during the battle between gods and Giants (Eur. *Ion* 986f).

A phantom GORGON in the underworld is threatened by Heracles with his sword, as Meleager watches (*Lib.* 2.5.12).

MEDUSA is beheaded by Perseus, who is equipped with winged sandals; the winged horse Pegasus is born from her trunk as Perseus flies off with her head, pursued by her sisters (*Lib.* 2.4.2–3; Paus. 5.18.5; Hes. *Sh. Her.* 216f). MEDUSA'S HEAD, when displayed by Perseus with his face averted, turns to stone certain of his enemies (*Lib.* 2.4.3; *Fab.* 64; *Met.* 5.180f, 5.236f), especially Phineus (*Met.* 5.230f) and Polydectes (*Met.* 5.242f); it also turns living plants into coral (*Met.* 4.740f) and Atlas into a mountain (*Met.* 4.655f; Serv. *ad Aen.* 4.246); it is given by Perseus to Athena (*Lib.* 2.4.3), who appears with it at her breast to Iodama, thus turning her to stone (Paus. 9.34.1).

HEAD OF A GORGON

GRACES

Personifications of grace and beauty, usually three in number. They were called Charites or Gratiae collectively; their names were Aglaia, Euphrosyne, and Thalia.

Attribute of, or attendants of: Aphrodite; Apollo; Dionysus; Eros; Hera; Hermes; Horae; Jupiter; the Muses (q.v.).

GRAIN

(See also **Corn Ears.**)

Attribute of Demeter.

GRAPES

(See also **Vine.**)

Attribute of Dionysus.
In the form of a bunch of grapes, DIONYSUS impregnates Erigone (*Met.* 6.125).

GRASSHOPPER

Aged TITHONUS is turned into a grasshopper by Eos (Schol. *ad Il.* 11.1).

GRAVE

(See also **Burial; Tomb.**)

Graves may be marked by columns, pillars, stelae, *heroöns,* and shrines.

GRIEVING

(See also **Castaway; Corpse; Parting; Suppliant; Tears.**)

Resulting in metamorphosis (see **Bird; Star; Tree; Water**).
CAESAR weeps as he reads of Alexander's achievements at an early age, because his own ambition is still unfulfilled (Plut. 34.12).
HERACLITUS is described as the "Weeping Philosopher" (Arrian 8.13).
On the shore. ACHILLES, because of his humiliation by Agamemnon and the loss of Briseïs; Thetis consoles him (*Il.* 1.348f); because of the death of Patroclus; Thetis and other Nereïds console him (*Il.* 18.65f, 24.11f). ARIADNE, when she is deserted by Theseus (Cat. 64.52f; *Met.* 8.175f); by Dionysus (*Fasti* 3.469f). ODYSSEUS, because Calypso will not let him leave her island (*Od.* 4.555f, 5.81f, 5.151f, 7.259f). PHYLLIS, after she is deserted by Demophon (*Heroïdes* 2.127f; *Fab.* 59). SAPPHO is weeping for her lover Phaon, when a Naiad appears (*Heroïdes* 15.157f).
At a tomb or shrine. CINYRAS mourns for his daughters on the temple steps into which they have been transformed (*Met.* 6.98f). CLYMENE and her daughters mourn Phaëthon at his tomb (*Met.* 2.338f; *Argo.* 4.596f; *Fab.* 154).

GRIFFIN

A lion with the head and wings of an eagle.

Attribute of Apollo (perhaps seated on it); Nemesis. With a wheel: Minerva.

SARCOPHAGUS WITH GRIFFINS

One attacks AURA with a snake whip (Nonnus 48.458f).

Several fight the one-eyed Arimaspian horsemen, who are stealing their gold (Herod. 3.116).

GUIDE

For a blind man (see **Eye**).

Hermes acting as guide (see **Underworld**).

GUINEA HEN

(See **Bird.**)

GULL

(See **Bird.**)

HAG

(See **Old Woman.**)

HAIR

(See also **Head; Seaweed; Snake-haired; Water.**)

Ablaze (see **Fire**). On the body (see **Centaur**).

"Watery": attribute of Jupiter Pluvius; river and sea deities. Woolly: Colchians (Herod. 2.104); Egyptians; Ethiopians. Cut short, signifies mourning and servitude.

Combed by POLYPHEMUS, a Cyclops, with a rake, in an effort to win the favor of Galatea (*Met.* 13.764); by SPARTAN SOLDIERS, before the battle at Thermopylae (Herod. 7.208).

Being cut. DIONYSUS' curls are cut off by Pentheus (Eur. *Bacch.* 492f). ROMAN WOMEN contribute their hair to make ropes for missile-hurling engines (Serv. *ad Aen.* 1.720).

A lock cut or dedicated by ACHILLES, who cuts a lock from his head to put in the hands of dead Patroclus (*Il.* 23.141f); by BERENICE from her own head, to be dedicated to her husband's safe return (Cat. 66.33f; *Poet. Astr.* 2.24); by COMAETHO, from the head of her father Pterolaüs, thereby killing him (*Lib.* 2.4.5, 7); by ELECTRA and CHRYSOTHEMIS, to offer to Agamemnon's spirit (Soph. *Elec.* 448f); by GREEK WARRIORS, to place on Patroclus' corpse (*Il.* 23.135f); by MEDEA, to leave as a memento for her mother as she leaves her home (*Argo.* 4.27f); by SCYLLA, from the head of her father Nisus, which kills him (*Lib.* 3.15.7–8; *Met.* 8.85f; Aes. *Choëph.* 6.8f; *Fab.* 198); she gives it to Minos, who rejects it in horror (*Met.* 8.94f); by TECMESSA, from her dead husband Ajax, for their son (Soph. *Ajax* 1171f); by THESEUS, from his own head, to dedicate it to Apollo at Delphi (Plut. 1.5).

HAIRNET

Attribute of Amphitrite (she may also have a crab claw on her forehead).

HALCYON

(See **Bird.**)

HAMMER

(See also **Forge.**)

Attribute of Hephaestus.

Wielded by HEPHAESTUS to nail Prometheus to a cliff or rock, as Might and Violence look on (Aes. *Prom.* 64f); by PROCRUSTES to lengthen a guest to fit the length of his bed (*Ep.* 1.4).

HAND

(See also **Boxing; Fist.**)

Held in fire (see **Fire**).

Open: attribute of Justitia. Clasped hands: Fides. Grasping the throat: Invidia. Two hands on each wrist: Apollo (symbolic of power and prudence). Snake-fingered: the monster Typhoeus (see **Snake-headed**).

Held over the mouth. ODYSSEUS, inside the Trojan horse, stops Anticlus from answering Helen, who is calling to the warriors within (*Od.* 4.287f; *Ep.* 5.19).

Used to deliver a blow. ACHILLES kills Thersites for belittling Penthesileia, the Amazon he has just killed (Quint. Smy. 1.750f); for gouging out her eye (Schol. *ad Lycophrona* 999). APOLLO shoves Patroclus away from the walls of Troy (*Il.* 16.698f) and stuns him with a blow on his back as he slaughters Trojans (*Il.* 16.789f). ATHENA fells Aphrodite when she tries to help fallen Ares (*Il.* 21.422f).

Cut off. HERMES' hand is cut off in his sleep by the sons of Choricus, because he has seduced their sister Palaestra (Serv. *ad Aen.* 7.138). MINYAN ENVOYS' hands, ears, and noses are cut off by Heracles (*Lib.* 2.4.11; Diod. Sic. 4.10.3).

HANGING

(See also **Suicide; Swinging.**)

Means of suicide employed by ALTHAEA and ALCYONE (Cleopatra) when their son and husband Meleager dies (*Lib.* 1.8.3; *Met.* 8.526f; *Fab.* 174); by AMATA, because of the imminent fall of her city to the Trojans (*Aen.* 12.593f); by ANTIGONE, in her tomb; she is found by Creon with her betrothed Haemon, also dead by his own hand (Soph. *Ant.* 1100f, 1219f); by ANTIGONE, daughter of Eurytion, when she is told, falsely, that Peleus is unfaithful (*Lib.* 3.13.3); by ARACHNE, after losing a weaving contest to

Athena; she becomes a spider (*Met.* 6.134f); by ARIADNE, after Theseus sails away (Plut. 1.20; but see **Ship** [Deserting a lover]); by CLEITE, when her husband Cyzicus is killed (*Argo.* 1.1063f); by DEÏANEIRA, after Heracles is poisoned by the robe she has sent him (*Lib.* 2.7.7); by ERIGONE, after she finds the body of her father Icarius, to which her dog has led her (*Lib.* 3.14.7; *Fab.* 130); by IPHIS, at hard-hearted Anaxarete's door (*Met.* 14.737f); by JOCASTA, after learning that her husband Oedipus is also her son; Oedipus discovers her body (Soph. *Oed. Tyr.* 1263f; *Lib.* 3.5.9; *Od.* 11.278f); by LEDA, shamed by her daughter Helen's elopement with Paris (Eur. *Hel.* 136); by MAIDENS who, under the influence of Dionysus, are following Erigone's example (*Fab.* 130); by MYRRHA, but she is thwarted by her nurse (*Met.* 10.378f); by OENONE, upon finding her husband Paris dead (*Lib.* 3.12.6); by PELEIA and MELUS, because of the death of Adonis; they are turned into a dove and an apple by Aphrodite (Serv. *ad Ecl.* 8.37); by PHAEDRA, because her love is not returned by Hippolytus (Eur. *Hipp.* 776f; *Ep.* 1.19; *Fab.* 47); by PHYLLIS, whom Demophon has abandoned; she becomes a tree (*Ep.* 6.17; *Fab.* 59, 243; Serv. *ad Ecl.* 5.10); by THEMISTO, after killing her own sons, thinking they were those of her rival Ino (*Fab.* 1).

Means of execution. Of AGIS IV of Sparta, by treacherous Leonidas and Amphares, who allow his grandmother and mother to see his body, after which they hang both women (Plut. 39.20); of HELEN, by Polyxo's slaves, who are dressed as Furies (Paus. 3.19.10); of the goatherd MELANTHIUS and several faithless serving women after Odysseus' return, by his son Telemachus and loyal Eumaeus and Philoetius (*Od.* 22.187f, 22.465f).

As punishment. CATILINE, from a cliff in Hades, where he is tormented by Furies (*Aen.* 8.668f). HERA, from Olympus with weights attached to her feet, by Zeus (*Il.* 15.18f; *Lib.* 1.3.5, 2.7.1; cf. *Fab.* 166, where it is Hephaestus who hangs her up; but for the usual tale of his punishment of his mother, see **Seated Figure**). MARSYAS, a Satyr who lost a music contest to Apollo, is hung in a tree and flayed (*Lib.* 1.4.2; *Fab.* 135).

Corpses wrapped in oxhides hang in trees (in Colchis this is the manner of disposing of the dead); JASON et al. pass through this unusual necropolis (*Argo.* 3.200f).

HARE

Attribute of Eros; Venus.

Is cut open; inside Cyrus finds a letter (Herod. 1.123–4).

Born of a mare, portends disaster for Xerxes' host (Herod. 7.57).

HARP

Attribute of Venus.

HARPIES

Harpies ("Snatchers") in Homer and Hesiod personify storm winds, to whom mysterious disappearances were attributed. Originally birds with the heads of fair maidens, they later became foul, predatory creatures.

Carry off the daughters of Pandareus (*Od.* 20.66f; Paus. 10.30.1).

Snatch food from AENEAS and his followers and are repelled with weapons after which the Harpy Celaeno prophesies hardship to come (*Aen.* 3.210f); from blind PHINEUS and are chased away by the winged sons of Boreas, who pursue until Iris stops them (*Argo.* 2.184f, 2.262f, 2.426f).

A HARPY

HAT

(See also **Basket; Crown; Helmet.**)

Broad-brimmed with a flat crown, perhaps with ties (petasus): attribute of Caracalla (imitating Alexander); Hermes; Macedonian kings (with upturned brim); Triptolemus. Conical and brimless (pileus): artisans (especially Daedalus and Hephaestus); the Dioscuri; Flamines (with an ornament on the apex); Libertas; mariners, especially Charon and Odysseus; Salii.

Brimless, with a high crown folded forward (Phrygian cap): Aeneas (affecting Carthaginian dress, *Aen.* 4.215f); Attis; Ganymede; Fortuna; Libertas; Mithras; Ops; Paris; Pelops. Ram's horn cap: Ammon. Toque-like: Telesphorus

Turban. Worn by MIDAS to conceal his ass's ears (*Met.* 11.180f).

Of an unspecified shape is blown overboard from ALEXANDER's head and retrieved by a sailor who is punished for putting it on (Arrian 7.22.2f); is snatched from the head of LUCUMO by an eagle and then replaced (Livy 1.34); is given to PERSEUS by nymphs to make him invisible (*Lib.* 2.4.2).

HAWK

(See **Bird.**)

HEAD

(See also **Beheading; Bust; Face; Mask.**)

With horns (see **Horn**). With two or more faces (see **Face**). Of an animal or monster (see particular species of animal, e.g., **Bird, Snake;** also see **Animal Head** and **Monster**).

With a finger at its lips: attribute of a genius.

On a pillar or other base. HERMAE, which are monuments of about the height of a man, bearing the head of Hermes (later of other deities), are common markers of boundaries. They are also objects of worship and serve many other functions. PRAXIDICE is represented by her head only.

On the ground may represent the birth of an autochthonous deity (e.g., Aphrodite, Diod. Sic. 5.5), the emerging shade of someone dead, or a stage in the growth of warriors from the dragon's teeth sown by Cadmus, Aeëtes, or Jason, and of men and women from stones thrown by Deucalion and Pyrrha (see **Bust; Stone; Warrior**).

Displayed, carried, or mistreated. The head of AGAMEDES is being carried by Trophonius when suddenly he falls into a chasm (Paus. 9.37.3); heads of ATALANTA's SUITORS decorate the stadium where she outran them in races for her hand (*Fab.* 185); head of CICERO is brought to Antony, exposed on the Rostra and abused by Fulvia (Dio 47.8.3–4); of CRASSUS, along with his hand, is presented to Hyrodes, the Parthian king (Plut. 28.32); of CYRUS THE ELDER is placed in a blood-filled vessel before Queen Tomyris (Herod. 1.214; Val. Max. 9.106.1); of CYRUS THE YOUNGER is shown by Artaxerxes to his soldiers in order to rally them (Plut. 48.13); of an ENEMY is shown to Alexander by Ariston, who is rewarded with a cup (Plut. 33.39);

of EURYSTHEUS is given to Alcmene, who sticks pins in the eyes (*Lib.* 2.8.1); of GAIUS GRACCHUS is weighed by his murderers (Plut. 40.17); heads of HIPPODAMEIA'S SUITORS adorn the palace of her father Oenomaüs, who had caught and killed them in chariot chases (*Ep.* 2.5; *Fab.* 84); head of IMBRIUS is thrown at Hector's feet by Ajax Oïleus (*Il.* 13.201f); of ITYS is hurled by Philomela at his father Tereus as he is unwittingly eating the boy's flesh (*Met.* 6.656f); heads of the two MAGI, usurpers of the throne of Persia, are shown to the people by Darius et al. (Herod. 3.79); head of MEDUSA (see **Gorgon**); of MELANIPPUS is given to Tydeus, who splits it and eats the brain (*Lib.* 3.6.8); heads of NISUS and EURYALUS are shown on spears to the latter's mother and the Trojans inside their fort (*Aen.* 9.465f); head of ORPHEUS is attacked by a snake until Apollo drives it away (*Met.* 11.50f); it floats down the Hebrus River (*Georg.* 4.523f); of PENTHEUS is carried on the thyrsus of the Maenad Agave, who has herself with other crazed women torn him apart (Eur. *Bacch.* 1197f); when Agave comes to her senses, she recognizes it as her son's head (Eur. *Bacch.* 1276f); of POMPEY is brought to Caesar, who turns away and weeps (Plut. 32.80, 34.48); of PYRRHUS is brought to Alcyoneus by Antigonus and thrown at his feet (Plut. 21.34); heads of THYESTES' SONS are brought to their father on a platter as he unknowingly eats their flesh (Sen. *Thy.* 1074f; *Fab.* 88); head of VARUS is sent to Augustus (Velleius Paterculus 2.119); heads of the VICTIMS of Cacus decorate his cave (*Aen.* 8.195f; *Fasti* 1.557f); of WARRIORS killed by Aeneas hang on his chariot (*Aen.* 12.509f).

Used to roof or build a temple by ANTAEUS (Pind. *Isth.* 4.52[87]f); by CYCNUS (Schol. on Pind. *Ol.* 2.82[149]; *Lib.* 2.7.7, n. 1, Loeb edn.).

Buried. The heads of the bridegrooms of the daughters of Danaüs are buried by their brides (*Lib.* 2.1.5).

Bald-headed. Attribute of Argippaeans of Scythia, both men and women (Herod. 4.23); Satyrs (q.v.); Silenus; Venus Calva, who, after restoring the hair of Roman women that they contributed to make bowstrings, is honored by a statue (Serv. *ad Aen.* 1.720). ARISTAGORAS reads the message written on a slave's scalp after his hair is shaved off (Herod. 5.35).

Two-headed. EURYTUS and CTEATUS (the Moliones or Actoriones) are twins with a single body, two heads, four arms, and four legs, or two men joined. They defeat Nestor in a chariot race (*Il.* 23.638f) and are killed by Heracles (*Lib.* 2.7.2).

Three-headed. Attribute of the triple deity Hecate-Artemis-Selene; Saturn. GERYON is shot by Heracles for his cattle (Hes. *Theog.* 289f).

Four-headed. Attribute of the Dii Quadrivii, who are honored by busts on pillars at crossroads.

Many-headed. BRIAREÜS (Aegaeon), COTTUS and GYES, each of whom is also equipped with many arms (Apollodorus calls them "the Hundred-handed"); they aid the gods against the Titans (Hes. *Theog.* 147f, 664f; *Lib.* 1.1.1), guard the Titans' prison (Hes. *Theog.* 734f; *Lib.* 1.2.1), and are imprisoned by Ouranos (Hes. *Theog.* 150f, 617f). BRIAREÜS (Aegaeon) is brought to Olympus by Thetis to quell a revolt against Zeus (*Il.* 1.396f; *Aen.* 10.565f). SCYLLA, equipped with six long necks with fanged heads, snatches sailors from Odysseus' passing ship (*Od.* 12.89f, 12.244f).

HEADBAND

(See also **Crown.**)

Attribute of Demeter; Hera; poets; priests; priestesses (especially Vesta); prophets.

HEADGEAR

(See **Basket; Crown; Hat; Helmet.**)

HEARTH

(See also **Fire; Stick.**)

Attribute of Hestia; Vesta.
PENELOPE sits at the hearth with a beggar whom she does not recognize as her husband Odysseus (*Od.* 19.53f).
PHOCION'S WIFE buries his bones by the hearth (Plut. 35 ad fin.).

HEIFER

(See **Cow.**)

HELMET

(See also **Arms and Armor.**)

Attribute of Aphrodite Victrix; Apollo Amyclaeus; Ares; Athena; Bellona; Honos; Pericles; Roma (who is usually seated); Victoria; Virtus (with one foot placed on it and her right breast bare). Egg-shaped: the Dioscuri. In the form of a goat's head: Juno. Goat-horned: Hera; Pyrrhus (Plut. 21.11). Chimaera-crested: Turnus (*Aen.* 7.785f). Horned: Agamemnon (*Il.* 11.41f).

Boar's head helmet is stolen by AUTOLYCUS and given to Odysseus by Meriones (*Il.* 10.255f).

A magic helmet (Hades'?) is lent to Perseus to make him invisible to Medusa (*Poet. Astr.* 2.12; Hes. *Sh. Her.* 227).

Comes off. DARDANUS loses his helmet in a battle and fights to recover it (Serv. *ad Aen.* 3.170). Because HECTOR's helmet frightens his baby son as Hector is leaving Andromache for battle, he takes it off (*Il.* 6.466f). PARIS' helmet comes off in Menelaüs' hand as he is dragging Paris along; Aphrodite causes the chin strap to break and whisks Paris away to safety; Menelaüs hurls the helmet away (*Il.* 3.369f). PATROCLUS' helmet falls off when Apollo strikes him on the back with his hand (*Il.* 16.793).

Used as a container in which ALEXANDER is offered water, which he refuses because there is none for his men (Plut. 33.42), or which he pours on the ground (Arrian 6.26.2); from which JASON sows the dragon's teeth that become armed men (*Met.* 7.121f; *Argo.* 3.1354f; see also **Sowing** or **Warrior** for accounts that do not mention a helmet); from which lots are cast or drawn, see **Lots.**

HELMSMAN

(See **Ship.**)

HERALD

(See **Speaker.**)

HERB

(See also **Branch; Flower.**)

A bunch of sacred herbs (*sagmina*) is carried by Fetiales and Roman ambassadors to make them inviolable.

MENTHE is turned into mint by Persephone (*Met.* 10.728f).

Magic herbs. MEDEA gives Jason magic herbs that will aid him in trials to come (*Met.* 7.98f). ODYSSEUS is given moly by Hermes; with it he counters Circe's magic when she tries to turn him into a pig (*Od.* 10.302f; *Met.*

14.291). POLYIDUS, observing a snake revive its dead mate with an herb, uses the same to restore the boy Glaucus to life (*Lib.* 1.3.1; a similar story about Moire and Tylus is found in Nonnus 25.451f).

HERDSMAN

(See **Cattle; Sheep; Shepherd.**)

HERON

(See **Bird.**)

HIDE

(See **Skin.**)

HIPPOPOTAMUS

Attribute of Typhon (Typhoeus).

HITTING

(See **Boxing; Fist; Hand.**)

HOE

(See also **Shovel.**)

Attribute of Aristaeus.

Used as a weapon by CELER to kill Remus when he scornfully jumps over Rome's wall, which Romulus is building (*Fasti* 4.841f, where the tool [*rutrum*] used may also be taken to mean a shovel; Plut. 2.10 mentions no weapon and suggests that Romulus may have struck the blow himself); by HERACLES to kill Sylaeus in his vineyard (Diod. Sic. 4.31.7).

HOOD

(See **Garment, Robe.**)

HOOK

Attribute of Voluptas.

HOOPOE

(See **Bird.**)

HORN

(See also **Animal; Cornucopia; Hat; Head; Helmet.**)

Horns on the head, varying in size from rudimentary to full: attribute of Ceres; Jupiter; river gods (q.v.). Goat horns: Aegerocerus; Faun, Pan, and Satyrs (q.v.). Ram or bull horns: Dionysus. Cow horns: Io-Isis. Horn used for drinking: Pan; Silenus. Crescent-shaped: Io-Isis, who also wears a crown of grain when she appears to Telethusa et al. (*Met.* 9.684f). Horns extending from the shoulders: Lunus. Sometimes horns indicate metamorphosis into a horned animal (see the particular species).

Horned. ACIS emerges from a spring (*Met.* 13.890f); CIPUS sees horns on his head in his reflection in a pool (*Met.* 15.565f); placing a wreath to hide them, he addresses an assembly (*Met.* 15.590f); WOMEN of Amathus sacrifice their guests (*Met.* 10.220f) and are turned into bulls (*Met.* 10.235f); women of Cos wear horns at the departure of Heracles and his band (*Met.* 7.363f).

Broken from the head of a goat, is used by AMALTHEIA to supply food for baby Zeus (*Fasti* 5.115f); of a bull (the river god Acheloüs) by HERACLES, becomes a horn of plenty (*Met.* 9.85f; *Fab.* 31).

Being blown. Attribute of Triton. The Fury ALLECTO from a rooftop arouses Latins and Trojans to war with a curved horn (*Aen.* 7.511f). (See also **Conch; Trumpet.**)

HORSE

(See also **Bridle; Chariot; Horseman; Wagon.**)

Attribute of Epona (seated, with her hand on its head); Poseidon. Suckling a baby (See **Baby**).

Brought forth by POSEIDON from the earth with a blow of his trident, as Athena produces an olive tree (*Georg.* 1.12f; Serv. *ad Aen.* 7.128).

Born. Swift ARION is born of a Fury (Demeter) and Poseidon (*Lib.* 3.6.8). (See also "Winged," below.)

Changed into a horse. CRONUS, in order to seduce the Oceanid Philyra, becomes a horse (*Fab.* 138; *Met.* 6.126); caught in bed with Philyra by Rhea, he turns into a stallion to escape (*Argo.* 2.1232f; cf. Serv. *ad Georg.*

3.93, which records that Philyra also becomes a horse; the Centaur Cheiron is her offspring); DEMETER, trying to evade the lust of Poseidon, who becomes a stallion (Paus. 8.25.5); MELANIPPE, to escape her searching father Cheiron; she later becomes a constellation (*Poet. Astr.* 2.18); OCYRHOË, after prophesying baby Asclepius' healing powers and her father Cheiron's death (*Met.* 2.642f); ODYSSEUS by Athena (Serv. *ad Aen.* 2.44); ZEUS, to seduce Dia, wife of Ixion, whose offspring is a Centaur (Serv. *ad Aen.* 8.293).

Giving birth to a hare portends disaster to Xerxes' fleet (Herod. 7.57).

Picture of one, drawn on the door of Antenor's house in Troy, protects it from sacking by the Greeks (Serv. *ad Aen.* 2.15).

Given or taken. AEMILIUS PAULUS, wounded at Cannae, refuses the offer of a horse on which to escape (Plut. 10.16; Livy 22.49). HERACLES takes the man-eating mares of Diomedes the Thracian and brings them to Eurystheus (*Lib.* 2.5.8). King LATINUS gives the Trojans many splendid horses (*Aen.* 7.274f). ODYSSEUS and DIOMEDES, with Athena's aid, takes Rhesus' horses after slaughtering him and his men while they sleep (Eur. *Rhes.* 595f, 756f; *Il.* 10.498f). Tuscan King PORSENNA gives the Roman girl Cloelia a fine horse out of respect for her courage (Plut. 6.19; Diod. Sic. 4.15.3). POSEIDON gives Peleus two immortal horses at his wedding to Thetis (*Lib.* 3.13.5). (See also **Foal.**)

In or near water. AENEAS and his Trojans from their ships spy four horses on shore, a portent of war to come (*Aen.* 3.537f). ALEXANDER's horse leaps with him into a river and swims to safety (Ps.-Cal. 184). ARGONAUTS are astounded to see one of Poseidon's horses emerge from the sea near their stranded ship (*Argo.* 4.1368f). CLOELIA on horseback leads her fellow hostages, who swim after her, from Porsenna's camp across the Tiber to Rome (Plut. 6.19).

Talking. XANTHUS, one of Achilles' chariot team, prophesies his master's death to him (*Il.* 19.405f).

Weeping. ACHILLES' horses weep when Patroclus is killed and refuse to be driven away until Zeus intervenes (*Il.* 17.426f); they weep at Achilles' corpse (Quint. Smy. 3.742f).

Neighing. DARIUS' horse neighs at a mare tethered by design near him as he rides with colleagues; this occurrence fulfills an oracle and wins him Persia's throne (Herod. 3.85, 3.86).

Being led. DARIUS' attention is caught by a beautiful woman leading a horse while carrying a jar on her head and twirling a spindle, which she does to attract his notice and to win his favor for her brothers (Herod. 5.12).

Being killed. HERACLES kills Diomedes' man-eaters (*Fab.* 30). (See also **Altar, Animal Sacrifice.**)

Killing. ANTHUS is torn to pieces by the horses of his father and is transformed into a bird (Ant. Lib. 7). DIOMEDES the Thracian is thrown by Heracles to his own horses and is devoured (Diod. Sic. 4.15.3). GLAUCUS is devoured by his horses after losing a chariot race to Iolaüs (*Fab.* 255, 273.12). LYCURGUS is destroyed by horses through the agency of Dionysus (*Lib.* 3.5.1).

Wooden (The Trojan Horse). EPEIUS constructs it and GREEK HEROES climb into it (*Ep.* 5.14; *Aen.* 2.13f); it is struck by Laocoön's spear (*Aen.* 2.50f) and is dragged into Troy (*Ep.* 5.16; *Aen.* 2.234f). HELEN calls to the warriors within (*Ep.* 5.19; *Od.* 4.277f). SINON releases them (*Ep.* 520; *Aen.* 2.257f; *Od.* 8.514f). Several WARRIORS, fleeing from Trojan defenders, climb back into it (*Aen.* 2.399f).

Winged (Pegasus). Attribute of Apollo. He is born from the blood or body of Medusa (*Met.* 4.785f; *Lib.* 2.4.2); he creates a spring with a blow of his hoof (*Met.* 5.254f). ATHENA bridles him for Bellerophon (Paus. 2.4.1). BELLEROPHON rides him against the Amazons (*Lib.* 2.3.2), the Chimaera (q.v.) (Hes. *Theog.* 325f; *Lib.* 2.3.1; Eur. *Ion* 201f; *Fab.* 57), and the Solymi (*Lib.* 2.3.2; Homer too, in *Il.* 6.178f, records these trials but does not mention Pegasus); he falls off to his death (*Poet. Astr.* 2.18) or to injury, when Pegasus is stung by a gadfly (Pind. *Isth.* 7.44; Schol. on Pind. *Ol.* 13.130). STHENE-BOEA is pushed off to her death by Bellerophon, whose death she had tried to contrive (fragment of Eur. *Stheneboea*, see Powell p. 131f). [Some artists have represented Perseus astride Pegasus when he rescues Andromeda (see **Dragon**), perhaps because they associate the two since Pegasus was born from Medusa's blood after Perseus killed her, or perhaps because Hesiod describes Perseus as a horseman (*hippota*) at *Sh. Her.* 216.]

One-eyed horse or mule is ridden or driven by OXYLUS, a circumstance that results in his becoming guide of a naval force of Dorians (*Lib.* 2.8.3; Paus. 5.3.5–6).

Of the sea, with hind quarters of a marine creature (Hippocamp): attribute of Amphitrite; Aphrodite; Poseidon; Sea Deities. With the head of a ram rather than of a horse: attribute of Palaemon.

HORSEMAN

(See also **Horse; Hunter; Huntress; Warrior.**)

A male nude, carrying a banner and fleeing Fate: attribute of Fortuna.

ALEXANDER, while still a boy, tames and rides Bucephalus (Plut. 33.6; Ps.-Cal. 48); mounted, receives the surrender of huge King Poros after he dismounts from his elephant (Arrian 5.19.1f); rides into camp from a boat to receive a wild welcome from his soldiers, who believed him dead (Arrian 6.13.1f).

MARCUS CURTIUS rides into a chasm in the Forum (Livy 7.6; Val. Max. 5.6.2).

METTUS CURTIUS rides into a swamp to escape pursuit (Livy 1.12; Plut. 2.18).

ODYSSEUS and DIOMEDES ride off on Rhesus' horses after slaughtering him and his men in their sleep (*Il.* 10.513f).

Twin horsemen. The Dioscuri (Castor and Polydeuces) are frequently represented on horseback. They bring the news of a Roman victory to the people (Plut. 12.3).

In battle. ALEXANDER leads the attack on the defenders of Darius' chariot (Plut. 33.33). BERENICE rallies Ptolemy's warriors (*Poet. Astr.* 2.24). CAMILLA and her troop engage the Trojans (*Aen.* 7.803f, 11.597f); she is killed by Arruns' spear (*Aen.* 11.799f). CAMILLUS, though wounded, leads the rout of the Aequians and Volscians (Plut. 8.2). The DIOSCURI aid the Romans at Lake Regillus (Plut. 12.3). M. VALERIUS is killed trying to catch fleeing Tarquin (Livy. 2.19). MASISTIUS, the Persian cavalry commander, is overwhelmed by Aristides' hoplites in a skirmish before the Battle of Plataea (Plut. 17.14). MINOS, splendidly accoutred, attracts the admiration of Scylla as he leads the attack on her father's city (*Met.* 8.24f). P. DECIUS MUS charges and breaks the enemy's infantry line, thereby causing its rout by the Romans (Livy 8.9).

One-eyed Arimaspians fight Griffins (q.v.) for gold (Herod. 3.116).

In single combat, ACHILLES overcomes Penthesileia (Quint. Smy. 1.536f); BRUTUS and ARRUNS fall together (Plut. 6.9; Livy 2.6); MARCELLUS unhorses and slays the Gallic king (Plut. 16.7); POMPEY kills a Celtic champion (Plut. 32.7); Q. FABIUS defeats a Gallic champion (Plut. 8.17).

In flight. ADRASTUS is saved from the Thebans by his divine horse Arion (*Lib.* 3.6.8). ALEXANDER rides into a river to escape from some Persians (Ps.-Cal. 182). The DIOSCURI, carrying off Phoebe and Hilaira, escape from the girls' suitors (*Fab.* 80; in this account and in the one that follows about the rescue of Pyrrhus, horses are not mentioned but may be assumed as being the appropriate means of flight). Baby PYRRHUS' attendants flee from pursuing soldiers to a river which they cross by raft (Plut. 21.2).

Falling off. DEMOPHON falls off onto his sword when his horse stumbles (*Ep.* 6.17). FLAMINIUS is thrown by his horse as he prepares to lead his army against Hannibal (Plut. 10.3; Livy 22.3).

Cavalry. ASCANIUS' troop of boys performs maneuvers at the games honoring Anchises (*Aen.* 5.533f). PALLAS and his troop are sent off with Aeneas by Evander to aid the Trojan cause (*Aen.* 8.552f). RUTULIANS capture and murder Euryalus, then kill Nisus who is trying to rescue him (*Aen.* 9.367f).

HORSE'S HEAD

Attribute of Carthage; Demeter. By a cave: Ceres. On a female form or statue: Demeter. Symbol of a mortal's journey into death.

Exhumed, shows DIDO where Hera intends her to build Carthage (*Aen.* 1.443f; Serv. ad loc.).

HOUSE

ATHENA builds a house that Momus finds fault with, as he does with Prometheus' man and Zeus' bull, for which he is expelled from Olympus (Aesop 100).

PROMETHEUS is the first to instruct man in building houses (Aes. *Prom.* 448f).

HUMAN FIGURE

Since nearly every scene contains a human figure, it is not itself a distinguishing feature. Identification of a scene must therefore rest on other evidence, such as something palpable. Lacking this, it may be that a human activity (e.g., **Eating, Seduction,** etc.) or human condition (e.g., **Captive, Old Woman, Beggar,** etc.) depicted in the scene may indicate where it can be identified. For a human figure having some animal characteristic, see that particular animal and also **Monster.**

SMALL-SCALE   (See also **Baby; Eating.**)

Such figures may be the symbol of a soul, representations of household gods (Lares and Penates) or the Keres, who, when they appear in the form of tiny gnat-like beings, personify diseases.

Figures held in the hand: the GRACES (q.v.) may be represented in the hand of their chief patron, Apollo (Paus. 9.35.1); NIKE (winged and holding

ZEUS HOLDING NIKE, SYMBOL OF VICTORY

a wreath, symbol of victory) may appear in the hand of Athena, a conqueror, or Zeus.

The following events can only be taken figuratively, forcing the artist who depicts them to ignore the incongruity or to adopt the convention of scale that avoids it.

ATHENA is born full-grown from the head of Zeus (Hes. *Theog.* 924f; *Lib.* 1.3.6).

DIONYSUS is sewn into Zeus' thigh and later born from it (*Lib.* 3.4.3).

HEPHAESTUS is born from Hera's thigh (Serv. *ad Aen.* 8.454).

HERA, Hestia, Poseidon, Hades, and Demeter are vomited up by Cronus (*Lib.* 1.1.5, 1.2.1; Hes. *Theog.* 494f).

METIS, wife of Zeus, when about to give birth to Athena, is put by her husband into his belly (Hes. *Theog.* 888f, id. 929 e–t, Loeb edn.).

BOTH MALE AND FEMALE   AGDISTIS springs from the seed of Zeus; the male organs are cut off by the gods (Paus. 7.17.5).

HERMAPHRODITUS is formed from the union of the bodies of a son of Hermes and the nymph Salmacis (*Met.* 4.372f).

HUNTER

Of game (see the animal being hunted).

Incidents involving hunters. ACTAEON happens upon Artemis and her nymphs bathing, for which she sprinkles him with water and turns him into a stag that his own dogs attack (*Met.* 3.143f). ADONIS is seduced by Aphrodite, as they rest from hunting (*Met.* 10.519f). AENEAS and DIDO, leading an elaborate hunting party, take refuge from a storm in a cave (*Aen.* 4.120f). ATHAMAS is driven mad by Hera and kills his sons with arrows (*Fab.* 5). CEPHALUS rejects the advances of Eos because he is faithful to Procris; disguised as a stranger, Eos gives him gifts with which to test his wife's chastity (*Fab.* 189); as he and Procris hunt, he hurls his spear into a thicket at a sound he thinks is made by game and hits Procris, who dies in his arms (*Met.* 7.840f; *Lib.* 3.15.1). EPAPHUS' death while hunting is contrived by jealous Hera (*Fab.* 150). HIPPOLYTUS hunts with and does honor to Artemis, to the neglect of the worship due to Aphrodite (Eur. *Hipp.* 10f, 58f); he hunts with friends (Sen. *Phaed.* 1f) and repels Phaedra's importunities (Sen. *Phaed.* 618f). MELANIPPE'S TWINS by Poseidon are waylaid while hunting by Theano's sons, but with their father's aid the twins kill their attackers (*Fab.* 186). NARCISSUS is stealthily tracked by the nymph Echo, who gives back the words he calls to his companions; he flees when she tries to embrace him (*Met.* 3.370f). ORION, for attempting to seduce Artemis, is killed by her arrows, or by a scorpion (Serv. *ad Aen.* 1.535; *Poet. Astr.* 2.26); he is put to sleep by Satyrs and blinded by Oenopion (Serv. *ad Aen.* 10.763). THEOCLYMENUS discovers Helen and Menelaüs at the tomb of Proteus (Eur. *Hel.* 1165f).

HUNTRESS

Attempted seduction of AMYMONE, by a Satyr, whom Poseidon drives off (*Fab.* 169); ARTEMIS, by Orion (see **Hunter**), or by Otus and Ephialtes, who become diverted by the deer sent by Apollo (*Fab.* 28).

Seduction of AMYMONE, by Poseidon, after driving off a Satyr (*Fab.* 169); CALLISTO, by Zeus, masquerading as Artemis (*Met.* 2.419f); CRANE, by two-faced Janus, who is able to detect her attempt to steal away behind his back (*Fasti* 6.107f).

Transformed. ARGE, boasting of her speed while running down a stag, is turned into a doe by Helius (*Fab.* 205). CALLISTO, into a bear by Hera, after her pregnancy has caused Artemis to drive her away (*Met.* 2.477f). CHIONE, into a constellation by Zeus and Hermes (Serv. *ad Aen.* 4.250). SYRINX, into reeds as she runs from Pan (*Met.* 1.689f).

Slain. HARPALYCE, by herdsmen protecting their cattle (*Fab.* 193). HIPPOLYTE, accidentally by Penthesileia, who was aiming at a deer (*Ep.* 5.1 and n. 4, Loeb edn.). PROCRIS, accidentally by her husband Cephalus (*Met.* 7.745f, 7.840f; *Lib.* 3.15.1).

Other incidents. APHRODITE, as a huntress, converses with Aeneas and Achates (*Aen.* 1.314f). ARTEMIS taunts Aura, pregnant by Dionysus (Nonnus 48.749f). ATALANTA receives the skin of the Calydonian Boar from Meleager (*Met.* 8.428f). CHARICLEIA discovers Theagenes wounded among other wounded and dead in a fight on the seashore (*Aeth.* 1).

HYBRID CREATURES
(See **Animal; Monster.**)

IBIS

(See **Bird.**)

ICICLE

Attribute of Boreas.

INSCRIPTION

(See also **Writing.**)

On a tree. PARIS carves the name of his love Oenone (*Heroïdes* 5.21f).

On a shield. AENEAS hangs a shield, bearing an inscription recording his visit, on a temple of Apollo at Actium (*Aen.* 3.286f).

On a copper plate that a spring has spewed forth, tells ALEXANDER that Persia will fall to Greece (Plut. 33.17).

On a tomb is read by ALEXANDER, who has added to it the plea that Cyrus' tomb not be further molested (Plut. 33.69).

ISLAND

(See also **Rock.**)

Formed from a clod of earth thrown from the *Argo,* is named Calliste (later Thera) (*Argo.* 4.1755f); from nymphs who have been swept away when Acheloüs floods in anger (*Met.* 8.583f); from Perimele, whom her father has thrown into the Acheloüs (*Met.* 8.590f); from a quail (q.v., for the metamorphosis of Asteria), carries Asteria's sister Leto to Delos, or is itself the place where Leto gives birth to Artemis and Apollo (see **Baby** [Birth of]) (*Lib.* 1.4.1; *Fab.* 53; cf. Serv. *ad Aen.* 3.73, where Zeus forms this floating island from a stone); from a ship of the Phaeacians by Poseidon, after it has delivered Odysseus to Ithaca (*Od.* 13.159f).

Submerges under Alexander and his men, who have mistaken a whale for an island (Ps.-Cal. 224).

IVY

(See **Vine; Wreath.**)

JAR

(See **Vessel.**)

JAY

(See **Bird.**)

JEWELRY

(See also **Necklace; Ring.**)

Attribute of Fortuna.

Contributed by Roman women to make a golden gift to Apollo as promised by Camillus (Plut. 8.8; Livy 5.25).

JUDGE

(See also **Trial.**)

King ALCINOÜS decides, on Arete's evidence, that Medea belongs to Jason, and rejects the Colchians' demand for her return (*Argo.* 4.1174f; *Fab.* 23).

King ASTYAGES discovers that the slave boy before him, accused by a noble Mede and his son, is his own grandson Cyrus (Herod. 1.115).

ATHENA absolves Orestes, who is accused by the Furies and defended by Apollo, from the retribution demanded for killing his mother (Aes. *Eumen.* 734f; Eur. *Iph. Taur.* 961f; cf. *Ep.* 6.25, which records that Tyndareüs or Erigone may be his accusers).

BRUTUS condemns his traitorous sons to flogging and execution (Plut. 6.6).

CAMILLUS presides at the trial of Marcus Manlius, accused of subversion, which is held on the Capitoline Hill, ironically the scene of Manlius' heroic rout of the invading Gauls (Plut. 8.36).

Young HERACLES is faced with the choice between two lovely women, one representing a life of noble deeds, the other a life of pleasure (Xen. *Mem.*

2.1.21; cf. Cic. *de Off.* 1.32, where Heracles has to choose between the roads of virtue and pleasure. See also **Allegorical Figures**).

MINOS assigns by lot the newly dead to their places in the underworld (*Aen.* 6.431f) while Rhadamanthus, attended by the Fury Tisiphone, assigns punishments to unrepentant sinners (*Aen.* 6.566f).

NERO condemns his wife Octavia to prison so that he may be free to marry Poppaea (Tac. *An.* 14.60f).

The shepherd PARIS considers the bribes offered by Hera and Athena, but awards the golden apple to Aphrodite (*Fab.* 92; *Ep.* 3.2).

SISAMNES is flayed by Cambyses because he accepted a bribe, and his skin is used for the seat of a throne; Otanes replaces his father as judge and is told by Cambyses to be ever mindful of what he sits upon (Herod. 5.25; Val. Max. 6.36.3).

SP. CASSIUS' FATHER orders his ex-consul son to be scourged and executed for trying to buy his way to power (Livy 2.41; Livy also records here that Cassius may have been judged by the quaestors Fabius and Valerus).

TORQUATUS orders his son to be beheaded or clubbed to death for accepting against orders a Gaul's challenge to single combat (Serv. *ad Aen.* 6.824; Val. Max. 2.7.6, 6.9.1).

King TULLUS HOSTILIUS of Rome condemns the traitorous Alban leader Mettius Fufetius, whose unarmed troops are surrounded by armed Romans, to be tied to two chariots and torn apart (Livy 1.28).

ZEUS gives Marpessa her choice of suitors; she picks Idas over Apollo (*Lib.* 1.7.9); he arbitrates the claims of Aphrodite and Persephone for Adonis (*Lib.* 3.14.4; in *Poet. Astr.* 2.7 Calliope is named as the judge).

JUMPING

(See **Leaping.**)

KEY

Attribute of Amor; the custodian of a shrine; Diana; Ge (Gaea); Hades; Hecate; Janus; Portunus. A bunch of keys: Aeacus.

KICKING

ALTHAEMENES kicks Apemosyne to death, not believing her claim that it was Apollo who seduced her (*Lib.* 3.2.1).

CAMBYSES kicks or otherwise assaults his pregnant wife (Herod. 3.32).

The goatherd MELANTHEUS kicks a beggar (Odysseus) (*Od.* 17.233f).

NERO kicks pregnant Poppaea (Tac. *An.* 16.6; Suet. *Nero* 35).

SCIRON kicks passersby from a cliff into the sea (Plut. 1.10), one of whom is devoured by a turtle (*Ep.* 1.2).

THESEUS gives Sciron a taste of his own medicine (*Ep.* 1.3; *Fab.* 38).

KILLING

(See also **Altar; Dismembering; Flaying; Hair; Suppliant;** and the weapon employed.)

Here may be found murders, assassinations, and other killings by a weapon or means not specified in the source cited. Killings in battle, single combat, or fair fight will be found under **Fighting** or the weapon employed.

BY ONE MAN

Of other men. By ACHILLES of Thersites for mocking his grief at Penthesileia's death (*Ep.* 5.1) or for mutilating her corpse (Schol. *ad Lycophrona* 999); by AEGISTHUS of Agamemnon (*Od.* 3.194f, 3.303f) at an altar (Soph. *Elec.* 270); by AMPHITRYON of Electryon, in a quarrel over cattle (Hes. *Sh. Her.* llf); by ARES of Halirrhothius, for trying to rape Euryte (*Lib.* 3.14.4); by ATREUS of his own son, thinking him to be his brother's son (*Fab.* 86); by EVANDER of his father Echemus at the instigation of his mother (Serv. *ad Aen.* 8.51); by HERACLES of Phylas, for violating the sanctuary of Delphi (Diod. Sic. 4.37), of the plowman Theiodamas (*Argo.* 1.1213f), of King Lycus, who is threatening his wife Megara and their children (Eur. *Her.*

749f; *Fab.* 22; Sen. *Her. Fur.* 964f), of King Laogoras and his children, at a banquet (*Lib.* 2.7.7), of the oxherd Eurytion and his dog Orthos (Hes. *Theog.* 293f), of Zetes and Calaïs, the winged sons of the North Wind, for their part in the *Argo*'s leaving him behind while he was looking for Hylas (*Argo.* 1.1298f), of the sons of Actor, whom he ambushed (Paus. 5.2.1), of Iole's father Eurytus et al., for rejecting his claim to her (Serv. *ad Aen.* 8.291; *Fab.* 35), of the father and brothers of Periclymenus, whom Poseidon saves by turning him into an eagle (*Fab.* 10); by HYMENAEUS of sleeping pirates, for abducting his beloved and other maidens (Serv. *ad Aen.* 4.99); by MELEAGER of his uncles, for protesting his awarding the Calydonian Boar's hide to Atalanta (*Fab.* 174); by MENELAÜS of Deïphobus, in order to recover Helen (*Ep.* 5.22); by OEDIPUS of King Laius, during an altercation at a crossroads over the right of way (*Fab.* 67; *Lib.* 3.5.3; Soph. *Oed. Tyr.* 1398f; Eur. *Phoen.* 37f); by ORESTES of Aegisthus (*Od.* 3.196f, 3.305f), of Aletes, whose sister Erigone is saved from the same fate by Artemis (*Fab.* 122), of Neoptolemus, in the temple at Delphi (*Fab.* 123; *Ep.* 6.14; Eur. *Andro.* 1114f); by PATROCLUS of Clitonymus, over a game of dice (*Il.* 23.87f; *Lib.* 3.13.8); by POLYMNESTOR of Polydorus, for his gold (Eur. *Hec.* 4f; *Aen.* 3.53f), of his son Deïpylus, whom he mistakes for Polydorus (*Fab.* 109); by TYDEUS of the sons of Cadmus, who have ambushed him (*Il.* 4.391f).

Of women. By AEOLUS of his daughter Canace, for incest with her brother (*Fab.* 238); by ALCMAEON of his mother Eriphyle for her part in his father's death (*Lib.* 3.7.5); by CERCYON of his unmarried daughter Alope, whom he has imprisoned for bearing a child (*Fab.* 187); by HAEMON of his wife Antigone, when Heracles fails to persuade King Creon to pardon her for disobeying his command; Haemon kills himself also (*Fab.* 72); by LYCURGUS of his wife and child when he is made mad by Dionysus (*Fab.* 132).

Of a man and a woman. By ORESTES of Aegisthus and his mother Clytemnestra, for killing his father Agamemnon (*Ep.* 6.25). (See also the entry for Orestes under the heading that follows.)

BY TWO, OR ONE WITH AN ACCOMPLICE

Of a single victim. By AEGISTHUS and CLYTEMNESTRA of Agamemnon, while he dines (*Od.* 11.405f) or while he is in the bath or entangled in his clothing (*Ep.* 6.23; Aes. *Agam.* 1345, but elsewhere in the play Aegisthus is not involved in the deed; Sen. *Agam.* 936f; see also **Axe**); by AMPHION and ZETHUS of King Lycus, for mistreating their mother Antiope (*Lib.* 3.5.5; cf. *Fab.* 8, where Hermes intervenes to save Lycus); by DEÏPHOBUS and PARIS of Achilles, who has come seeking to marry Polyxena (*Fab.* 110; cf. Dares 34, where Achilles is ambushed in Apollo's shrine and Antilochus is also killed); by HARMODIUS and ARISTOGEITON of the Athenian tyrant Hipparchus (or his brother) (Thucy. 6.54–9; Paus. 1.8.5, 1.29.15); by MENELAÜS and ODYSSEUS of sleeping Deïphobus; Helen admits them after removing Deïphobus' sword (*Aen.* 6.520f); by ORESTES and PYLADES of Clytemnestra (Soph. *Elec.* 1403f; Aes. *Choëph.* 930f), instigated by Apollo (Eur. *Orest.* 27f), and of Aegisthus (Aes. *Choëph.* 870f; see also **Altar; Knife; Sword**); by PHEGEUS' SONS of Alcmaeon, in an ambush, for dealing falsely with their father (*Lib.* 3.7.5); by TELAMON and PELEUS of Phocus (*Argo.* 1.92).

BY SEVERAL MEN

Of a single victim. By jealous ATHLETES of Minos' son Androgeüs, who has defeated them in athletic games (*Lib.* 3.15.7); by CARACALLA and SOLDIERS of his brother Geta, who dies in their mother's arms (Dio 78.2); by DORIAN SOLDIERS of Codrus, an early king of Athens who dresses himself as a servant and provokes them to kill him in order to fulfill a prophecy that Athens will not fall to invaders if its king dies (Val. Max. ext. 1); by ROMULUS, REMUS, et al. of Amulius, who has usurped the throne of Alba Longa (Plut. 2.8); by intoxicated SHEPHERDS of Icarius, who has given them the wine (*Lib.* 3.14.7); by TARQUIN's ADHERENTS of Servius Tullius, king of Rome, to clear their master's way to the throne (Livy 1.48); by THEBE's BROTHERS of the sleeping tyrant Alexander of Pherae, as Thebe holds the lamp and urges them on (Plut. 15.35); by VOLSCIAN CONSPIRATORS of Coriolanus, a Roman exile, in a political power struggle; his corpse is honored by the Volscian people (Plut. 12.39).

BY WOMEN

Of a variety of victims. By CLYTEMNESTRA of Agamemnon while he prepares for a bath and is entangled in a robe (Aes. *Agam.* 1107f, 1125f, 1379f; Aes. *Eumen.* 633f; Eur. *Orest.* 25f; see also **Axe**); of Cassandra (Aes. *Agam.* 1313f), as dying Agamemnon tries to help her (*Od.* 11.421f); by COCALUS' DAUGHTERS of King Minos at the instigation of Daedalus (*Fab.* 44); by DANAÜS' DAUGHTERS of their bridegrooms; Hypermnestra alone spares her husband (*Fab.* 168; see also **Knife**); by LEMNIAN WOMEN of all the men on their island (*Argo.* 1.609f; *Lib.* 1.9.17); by MEDEA of her children, to punish Jason for taking another wife (*Lib.* 1.9.28; *Fab.* 25; Eur. *Med.* 1271f); by PELIAS' DAUGHTERS of their aged father, before cooking his body under Medea's direction to rejuvenate him (*Fab.* 24; *Lib.* 1.9.27); by ROXANE (or by her order) of Statira (Barsine), Alexander's other wife, and her sister, out of jealousy (Plut. 33.77); by THEMISTO of her babies, believing them to be Ino's (*Fab.* 1, 4); by TYRO of her sons, because of a prophecy that they would kill her father (*Fab.* 60); by angry WOMEN of old Melissa, from whose body bees emerge (Serv. *ad Aen.* 1.430). (See also **Warrior, Female**.)

KING

Most scenes in which kings appear will be found under more specific headings. See particularly **Judge; Officer; Old Man; Warrior.**

CREON rejects the intercession on behalf of condemned Antigone of his son Haemon (Soph. *Ant.* 683f) and of Heracles (*Fab.* 72); he gives his daughter Megara to Heracles (*Fab.* 72).

CROESUS displays his wealth to an unimpressed Solon (Herod. 1.30).

Ethiopian HYDASPES and his queen recognize their white-skinned daughter Charicleia (*Aeth.* 10).

LATINUS welcomes Aeneas and his followers to Italy (*Aen.* 7.192f).

MIDAS receives the "golden touch" from Dionysus (*Fab.* 191; *Met.* 11.100f).

MINOS' lust for Eriboea, one of the group of girls and boys comprising Athens' annual tribute to the Minotaur, is thwarted by Theseus (*Poet. Astr.* 2.5; Bacchylides 16); he rejects the vital lock of hair that Scylla has cut from her father's head, hoping to win Minos' favor (*Met.* 8.90f).

Egyptian PROTEUS sends Paris away and keeps Helen, her servants, and her treasure for Menelaüs to recover (Herod. 2.115).

Indian TAXILES confers with Alexander (Plut. 33.59).

XERXES receives Spartan heralds who refuse to make obeisance (Herod. 7.136); he shows off his army to some Greek spies, then frees them to report its vast numbers (Herod. 7.146).

KINGFISHER

(See **Bird, Halcyon.**)

KISS

(See also **Seduction.**)

Given by APOLLO to Cassandra causes her true prophecies thereafter to be disbelieved (Serv. *ad Aen.* 2.247); by BRUTUS to the earth, which act is his interpretation of an oracle given to him and two other men that the first to kiss his mother shall rule (Livy 1.56; *Fasti* 2.717f); by CALLINES and other officers to Alexander to show their devotion (Arrian 7.11.5f); by DEMETER, who is in the form of an old woman, to a sick child; this cures the child (*Fasti* 4.538f); by DOLIUS, an old retainer, to Odysseus on his return (*Od.* 24.386f);

by PYGMALION to the ivory maiden he has fashioned; this brings her to life (*Met.* 10.280f).

KNIFE

(See also **Dismembering; Fighting; Flaying; Killing; Suicide; Sword.**)

Although a knife is not always mentioned in the sources below, this instrument seems the most appropriate to the action in each scene.

Used to cut out a tongue (see **Tongue**). Used in sacrificial rites (see **Altar**).

Used to commit suicide. ALTHAEA drives a dagger to her heart after burning the brand on which Meleager's life depends (*Met.* 8.531f). ARRIA stabs herself and then holds the dagger out to her husband Paetus (Pliny the Younger 3.16). CALLIRHOË, in grief, cuts her throat by a spring after Coresus has taken his own life at the altar instead of sacrificing her (Paus. 7.21.1). LAODAMIA stabs herself when Hermes takes her husband Protesilaüs back to Hades (*Ep.* 3.30). LUCRETIA stabs herself after telling her husband, father, and Brutus of being raped by Tarquin (Livy 1.58; *Fasti* 2.831f). MENOECUS cuts his throat at Thebes' gate, making the sacrifice that will save his city (*Lib.* 3.6.7). THEANO stabs herself when her sons' bodies are brought to her (*Fab.* 186). One THEBAN MAIDEN cuts her throat and a second stabs herself with a shuttle to avert a plague (*Met.* 13.692f).

Used by women. DANAÜS' DAUGHTERS, excepting Hypermnestra, kill their sleeping bridegrooms (*Lib.* 2.1.5). DAPHNE et al. strip the clothes from the sole member of their band who is reluctant to bathe with them; discovering a man, they kill him with knives and spears (Paus. 8.20.4). ELECTRA with a knife and Orestes kill their mother Clytemnestra (Eur. *Elec.* 1142f). HECUBA et al. blind Polymestor and kill his sons, with Agamemnon's connivance (Eur. *Hec.* 1035f, 1149f). MEDEA cuts old Aeson's throat and replaces his blood with a rejuvenating brew (*Met.* 7.285f). PROCNE kills and cuts up her son Itys, preparatory to cooking his flesh; Philomela helps her (*Met.* 6.640f). WOMEN (young men dressed as women) are substituted by Alexander II for the women invited to dine with insolent Persian ambassadors, whom they stab to death (Herod. 5.20).

Used by men. ALEXANDER kills several Persians at their campfire (Plut. 33.24). ATTIS castrates himself (*Fasti* 4.233f). CASCA strikes Caesar in the neck, whereupon others attack him, some with swords (Suet. *Caes.* 82; Plut. 34.71). GYGES kills King Candaules in his sleep with a dagger the queen hands to him (Herod. 1.12). MUCIUS kills an attendant beside Porsenna instead of the king himself (Livy 2.12; Plut. 6.17). The augur NAVIUS, challenged by Tarquin, cuts a whetstone in two (Livy 1.36). ORESTES, attended by Pylades, assists Aegisthus in the sacrifice of a bull and kills him with the same knife (Eur. *Elec.* 815f). PARIS carves Oenone's name (or a verse) in the bark of a tree (*Heroïdes* 5.21); in Apollo's temple he stabs Achilles, who is being embraced by Deïphobus (Dictys 4.11). PAUSANIAS, awakened when Cleonice overturns a lampstand, and fearing assassination, stabs her to death (Plut. 25.6). VERGINIUS kills his daughter to save her from the lust of the decemvir Appius Claudius (Livy 3.48).

Held up to incite vengeance by BRUTUS for the rape and suicide of Lucretia (*Fasti* 2.831f) and by her husband as well (Livy 1.59); by VERGINIUS for the death of his daughter Verginia (Livy 3.50).

Stuck in a tree by IPHICLUS and removed by Melampus, who scrapes rust from it into a cup for Iphiclus to drink (*Lib.* 1.9.12).

Being buried, seals the oath sworn by Adrastus to Theseus never to attack Thebes again (Eur. *Suppl.* 1205f).

KNOT

ALEXANDER cuts the Gordian knot that is tied on a chariot pole (Plut. 33.18; Arrian 2.3.1).

LADDER

(See also **Climbing.**)

Attribute of Aphrodite; Eros.

Used to scale a wall by ALEXANDER, leading the assault on an Indian fortress (Plut. 33.63); by ARATUS, leading his men into Sicyon, despite the warning given by barking dogs (Plut. 47.5–8), into Acrocorinth (Plut. 47.21), and in the assault on Argos, from which he is repulsed (Plut. 47.27); by CAPANEUS at Thebes; Zeus hits him with a thunderbolt (Eur. *Suppl.* 497f, *Phoen.* 1175; *Lib.* 3.6.7); by PYRRHUS, who is the first to enter Eryx (Plut. 21.22).

LAKE

(See **Water.**)

LAMB

(See **Sheep.**)

LAMP, LANTERN

(See **Light; Torch.**)

LAUGHING

An old crone in bridal dress, ANNA PERENNA, reveals her face and laughs at Ares, who believed it was Athena he was on the point of seducing (*Fasti* 3.677f).

DEMETER, temporarily diverted from her grief at losing Persephone, laughs at Iambe's jokes (*H. to Dem.* 200f).

DEMOCRITUS earns the title "The Laughing Philosopher" (Aelian 4.20, 4.29).

OLYMPIAN GODS laugh at Hephaestus as he hobbles about serving wine (*Il.* 1.586f).

LAUREL

(See **Branch; Wreath.**)

LEAPING

(See also **Chasm; Falling; Flight.**)

From a ship (see **Ship.**) In competition or for exercise (see **Weights**).

Into the sea. AEGEUS (*Fab.* 43; see "From a height," below). AESACUS, after Hesperia dies from snakebite; he becomes a cormorant (*Met.* 11.783f). ALCYONE, to join her lost husband Ceÿx; they are reunited as halcyons nesting on the sea (*Met.* 11.731f; *Fab.* 65). AURA, after dismembering one of her twin babies in a fit of madness (Nonnus 48.848f). CECROPS' DAUGHTERS, when driven mad by Athena (*Fab.* 166). DIONYSUS, as he and several Maenads run from Lycurgus (*Il.* 6.130f). ENALUS and his beloved, to escape being sacrificed; dolphins save them (Plut. *Moralia* 163c, 984e). INO with her baby; they become sea deities and are followed by other women who become birds (*Met.* 4.525f). SCYLLA, to escape from Nisus; she becomes a fish and her pursuer an osprey (*Fab.* 198). The SIRENS, after their singing fails to lure Odysseus into their power because he has been lashed to his ship's mast (*Fab.* 141).

Into a river. HORATIUS, after holding at bay the Tuscan attackers until the bridge is cut, dives into the Tiber and swims back to Rome (Plut. 6.16; Livy 2.10). TURNUS, alone in the Trojan camp on the Tiber, fights his way to the water and swims to safety (*Aen.* 9.816f).

A CONTESTANT USING WEIGHTS IN THE BROAD JUMP

From a height. AEGEUS, from the Acropolis when he sees a black sail on Theseus' ship (Paus. 1.22.5; *Ep.* 1.10). CECROPS' DAUGHTERS, from the Acropolis when Athena drives them mad (*Lib.* 3.14.6; Paus. 1.18.2). DAE-DALION, from a cliff in his grief for Chione; Apollo turns him into a hawk (*Met.* 11.339f; *Fab.* 200). HERO, from a tower, when she sees Leander's body on the shore below (Serv. *ad Georg.* 3.258). MELIBOEA, from a roof; unharmed, she steps aboard a ship that has no crew (Serv. *ad Aen.* 1.720). MENOECUS, from Thebes' wall, making the sacrifice that will alleviate the famine the city is suffering (*Fab.* 67). PREXASPES, from a tower, after urging the Persian crowd below to revolt against the usurping Magi (Herod. 3.75). PYRENEUS leaps from a wall trying to catch the Muses, who have put on wings to escape (*Met.* 5.291f). The SPHINX, when Oedipus solves her riddle (*Lib.* 3.5.8). TIMAGORAS, from the Acropolis when he is spurned by the boy Meles, who in remorse also leaps to his death (Paus. 1.30.1).

Into fire. EMPEDOCLES, into the crater of Etna (Diog. Laërt. 8.2.11). HASDRUBAL'S WIFE, into the flames of Carthage (Livy 51, epitome). (See also **Pyre.**)

Over a wall. REMUS scornfully leaps over the wall Romulus has started to build for Rome, and is killed by him (Plut. 2.10; Livy 1.7) or by Celer (*Fasti* 4.841f).

LEG

Wooden: attribute of Pluto.

LEOPARD

(See also **Lion; Panther; Tiger.**)

Attribute of Cybele; Dionysus.

A form assumed by PROTEUS in an effort to escape from Menelaüs' grasp (*Od.* 4.457); by THETIS to escape from Peleus (*Met.* 11.245).

A camel-headed lion or leopard is a Camelopard (see **Lion**).

LEOPARD SKIN

(See **Skin, of Animal.**)

LETTER

(See also **Book; Writing.**)

Usually in the form of a scroll, tablet, or sheet.

Attribute of Calliope; Clio; Clotho; Fides.

AGAMEMNON gives a letter for Clytemnestra to an old messenger; Menelaüs intercepts and reads it, which causes him to quarrel with his brother (Eur. *Iph. Aul.* 96f).

ALEXANDER reads a letter from Darius that an embassy has delivered along with a ball, a thong, and a chest of gold; he has them bound but later released (Ps.-Cal. 103–106); ill in bed, he drinks a cup of medicine as his trusted physician reads the letter Alexander has received and read warning him that his physician will try to poison him (Plut. 33.19; Ps.-Cal. 155f; Arrian 2.4.8).

BELLEROPHON delivers a letter from King Proetus to King Iobates requesting him to execute the bearer, who allegedly has molested Proetus' wife (*Lib.* 2.3.1; *Fab.* 57; *Il.* 6.167).

BYBLIS drops a letter expressing her passion for her brother; he picks it up, reads it, and hurls it to the ground (*Met.* 9.522f).

CYRUS finds a letter from Harpagus in the body of a hare that a hunter has brought (Herod. 1.123–4).

IPHIGENEIA reads a letter to the two captives before her; the contents reveal that one is her brother Orestes (Eur. *Iph. Taur.* 760f).

ODYSSEUS drops a letter accusing Palamedes of being a traitor (or places it in a dead soldier's hand); Agamemnon reads it (*Ep.* 3.8; *Fab.* 105).

PALAMEDES, marooned on an island, sets adrift a wooden tablet with a message that he hopes will reach his brother (fragment of Eur. *Palamedes,* see Rose, p. 206).

PHAEDRA, after she has hanged herself, is found by Theseus with a letter in her hand that falsely accuses his son Hippolytus of raping her (Eur. *Hipp.* 808f; *Fab.* 47).

LICTOR

(See also **Axe; Beheading; Whip.**)

An official attendant of a high Roman magistrate who carries fasces (a bundle of sticks bound about an axe) as the symbol of office.

Arrests tyrannical APPIUS CLAUDIUS (Livy 3.56).

A LICTOR CARRYING FASCES

In excessive number cow the Roman populace for APPIUS CLAUDIUS (Livy 3.36).

Compels old FABIUS MAXIMUS to dismount to show respect for the office of his son, a consul (Plut. 10.24; Livy 24.44).

Attempts to arrest PUBLIUS VOLERO and LAETORIUS; in each case a mob resists (Livy 2.55, 2.57).

LIGHT

(See also **Fire; Rays; Torch.**)

Illumination produced by beacon, candle, lamp, lantern, thunderbolt, or torch.

Providing illumination. ATHENA lights the empty banquet hall to help a beggar (Odysseus) and Telemachus to remove arms from it before the suitors return (*Od.* 19.33f). CINYRAS discovers that the lover in his bed is his daughter Myrrha (*Met.* 10.471f). CLEONICE overturns a lamp, awakening Pausanias, who stabs her, thinking her an assassin (Plut. 25.6). PSYCHE discovers that her secret lover is Eros (Apuleius 8). A SERVANT lights Penelope and Odysseus to their bed (*Od.* 23.289f). THEBE holds the lamp while her brothers kill the tyrant Alexander in his bed (Plut. 15.35). In a cave (see **Cave**).

Beacon or signal warns CLYTEMNESTRA of Agamemnon's return (Aes. *Agam.* 21f, 281f); held by HELEN, summons the Greek ships from Tenedos (*Aen.* 6.518f; Serv. *ad Aen.* 2.256); in HERO's tower guides Leander as he swims to her (*Heroides* 15.57f); set by NAUPLIUS, lures ships to destruction (*Fab.* 116; *Lib.* 2.1.5); set in a tree by PHILOTIS, summons Romans to the massacre of the invading Latins in their sleep (Plut. 2.29, 8.33); set by SINON, summons the Greek fleet from Tenedos (*Ilias Mikra* 2, in Schol. *ad Lycophrona* 344).

Casts a shadow. BOUTADES traces the silhouette of her beloved (*Nat. Hist.* 35.151).

Supernatural brilliance. ZEUS appears in all his splendor to Semele, who catches fire; baby Dionysus is snatched from her burning body (*Met.* 3.305f; Eur. *Bacch.* 88f; *Lib.* 3.4.3; *Fab.* 167, 179).

LIGHTNING

(See **Thunderbolt**.)

LION

(See also **Leopard; Panther; Tiger.**)

Attribute of Juno; Lucina; Rhea (enthroned between two lions or drawn in her chariot by them). Symbol of Delos.

With the head of a woman, man, ram, or falcon, sometimes winged (see **Monster; Sphinx**).

With an eagle's head and wings (see **Griffin**).

With the head of a camel, called Camelopard, is presented to the Ethiopian king (*Aeth.* 10).

A transformation of ATALANTA and HIPPOMENES, who are assigned to pulling Rhea's chariot (*Met.* 10.698f; *Fab.* 185); of DIONYSUS, which frightens the sailors on his ship into jumping overboard; they turn into dolphins (*H. to Dion.* 44f); of PERICLYMENUS, during his fight with Heracles (*Lib.* 1.9.9); of PROTEUS, in an attempt to escape from the grasp of Aristaeus (*Georg.* 4.408) or Menelaüs (*Od.* 4.456).

Hunted and killed. ALCATHOÜS kills the lion of Cithaeron and wins the daughter of Megareus (Paus. 1.41.4). ALEXANDER kills a huge lion during a hunt (Plut. 33.40). HERACLES vainly shoots arrows at the Nemean Lion; he drives it into a cave with his club, chokes it to death, and carries it to Eurystheus (*Lib.* 2.5.1; *Fab.* 30; Theocritus 25); he kills the lion of Cithaeron and wears its skin, with its head forming a helmet (*Lib.* 2.4.10; cf. *Fab.* 30, which records that the Nemean Lion provided this garment).

Attacks and kills HYAS; his sisters die of grief (*Fasti* 5.173f; *Fab.* 192); MILO, whose hands have been caught in a cleft in a tree (Val. Max. 9.12b.9).

Frightens THISBE, who flees to a cave, dropping her cloak, which the beast mangles (*Met.* 4.96f).

Yoked with a boar by ADMETUS to the chariot in which he carries off Alcestis (*Fab.* 50, 51).

Lion and boar characterize the manner in which Tydeus and Polyneices fight each other; Adrastus feels that this marks them as the ones destined by an oracle to become his daughters' husbands (Eur. *Suppl.* 140f; cf. *Fab.* 69, 70, where the two are identified by the boar and lion skins that they wear).

LION SKIN

(See **Skin, of Animal.**)

LITTER

(See also **Bed.**)

On which someone is carried. ALCESTIS, about to die, is carried by Admetus et al. (Eur. *Alc.* 233f, 606f). Wounded ANTONY is hoisted to Cleopatra's chamber (Plut. 44.77). Dying HERACLES is carried to his son Hyllus (Soph. *Trach.* 965) and to a pyre (Soph. *Trach.* 1255f). Ill T. LATINIUS is taken into the senate house, where he speaks and is cured (Livy 2.36). MELAMPUS is carried by jailors from his prison, which then collapses (Schol. *ad Od.* 11.287).

LIZARD

(See also **Dragon.**)

The boy ABAS is changed into a lizard when sprinkled with water by Demeter (*Met.* 5.453f).

LOAF OF BREAD

(See also **Stone.**)

PISTOR et al. throw down loaves on Gauls besieging the Capitoline to imply that food is plentiful for the defenders (*Fasti* 6.349f).

LOOM

(See also **Garment, Robe.**)

Invented by Athena.

Being plied by AËDON in competition with Polytechnus, who is making a chair, to see who can finish first (Ant. Lib. 11); by ANDROMACHE at the moment she hears the lamentation caused by Hector's death (*Il.* 22.437f); by ARACHNE and an old woman (Athena) in competition; Arachne loses and is changed into a spider (*Met.* 6.11f); by CALYPSO, when Hermes visits her (*Od.* 5.55f) and when Odysseus et al. arrive (*Od.* 10.252f); by HELEN when Laodice (Iris) comes to bring her to identify for Priam the Greek heroes (*Il.* 3.125f); by MINYAS' DAUGHTERS; as they weave and spin instead of joining Bacchic revelry, they are turned into bats, their handiwork into vines (*Met.* 4.389f); by PENELOPE, weaving a robe that she unravels at night (*Od.* 2.94f, 19.137f, 24.138f); by PHILOMELA, weaving in pictures the tale of her misfortunes, of which she cannot speak because her tongue has been cut out (*Met.* 6.576f); by TARCHETIUS' DAUGHTER, who is in chains; what she and her maid weave, a servant unravels at night (Plut. 2.2).

LOTS

(See also **Game; Voting.**)

Attribute of the Thriae, who cast them into an urn as they prophesy.

Cast or picked from a vessel by APOLLO, as he teaches Hermes the art of pebble divination (*Lib.* 3.10.2); by seven ARGIVE CAPTAINS, to determine which gate of Thebes each one is to attack (Aes. *Seven* 376f); by HECTOR and ODYSSEUS, to decide whether Paris or Menelaüs is to throw his spear first (*Il.* 3.314f); by the HERACLEIDAE, for their respective realms (*Lib.* 2.8.4); by MINOS, as he assigns souls to their places in the underworld (*Aen.* 6.431f); by NESTOR, to decide which Greek hero is to face Hector; Ajax recognizes the lot that falls out as his (*Il.* 7.181f); by THESEUS and PEIRITHOÜS, for possession of Helen (Plut. 1.31); by TYRRHENUS and LYDUS, to determine which of them is to emigrate from Lydia to form a colony elsewhere (Serv. *ad Aen.* 1.67, 2.781); by ZEUS, POSEIDON, and HADES, to allot to them their respective realms (*Il.* 15.190; *Lib.* 1.2.1).

LOTUS

(See **Flower.**)

LOVERS

(See **Seduction.**)

LYNX

Attribute of Dionysus.

LYNCUS is changed into a lynx by Demeter as he is in the act of killing sleeping Triptolemus (*Met.* 5.657f).

LYNX SKIN

(See **Skin, of Animal.**)

LYRE

(See also **Musical Instruments.**)

Attribute of Apollo; Bacchus; Cupid; Erato; Orpheus and bards generally; Paris; Priapus; Terpsichore.

ACHILLES is playing his lyre when Ajax and Odysseus come to talk to him (*Il.* 9.185f).

ALEXANDER plays at a party and is chided by his father for his skill, because he considers it an unsuitable accomplishment for one born to higher things (Plut. 9.2).

AMPHION's playing charms stones into forming a wall, while his brother Zethus has to work to perform the same task (*Argo.* 1.735f; *Lib.* 3.5.5).

APOLLO, holding his lyre upside down, competes with the Satyr Marsyas, who plays pipes (*Lib.* 1.4.3; Diod. Sic. 3.59.2–5; see also **Flaying**); he competes with pipe-playing Pan before Tmolus (forest personified) and Midas, who acquires ass's ears for disagreeing with Tmolus' judgment that Apollo is the winner (*Met.* 11.155f); he competes with Linus and kills him (Paus. 2.29.3); he sings his grief for Hyacinthus (*Met.* 10.205f).

ARION charms animals with his singing (*Fasti* 2.79f); he escapes from murderous sailors by leaping from the ship to the back of a dolphin that his music has attracted (*Fasti* 2.95f; Herod. 1.24; *Fab.* 194); he emerges from the dolphin's tomb to confront the sailors, who have reported his death (*Fab.* 194; see also **Cross**).

CALLIOPE represents the Muses when they are challenged to a singing contest by the daughters of Pierus (*Met.* 5.337).

DEMODOCUS sings at a feast for Odysseus and accompanies the dancers (*Od.* 8.62f, 8.256f, 8.477f).

HERACLES is taught to play it by Atlas (Serv. *ad Aen.* 1.74) and by Linus, whom he strikes with it (*Lib.* 2.4.9).

HERMES invents the lyre by stretching strings on a framework he has attached to a tortoiseshell (*H. to Her.* 24f; *Lib.* 3.10.2); he trades it to Apollo for some cattle (*Lib.* 3.10.2); he charms Apollo with it and trades it for a beautiful whip (*H. to Her.* 418f, 496f).

IOPAS, pupil of Atlas, entertains Dido, Aeneas, et al. at a banquet (*Aen.* 1.740f).

MUSAEUS encounters Aeneas and the Sibyl in the underworld (*Aen.* 6.666f).

NERO sings about the fall of Troy as Rome burns (Tac. *An.* 15.39).

ORPHEUS attracts wild animals to him with his music (*Met.* 10.86f); he moves stones and trees with it (*Lib.* 1.3.2; *Argo.* 1.26f); singing to the Argonauts, he stops a quarrel (*Argo.* 1.494f), attracts fish (*Argo.* 1.569f), celebrates a victory (*Argo.* 2.155f), and drowns out the Sirens' song (*Argo.* 4.903); he charms Persephone and other denizens of the underworld (*Met.* 10.11f; *Georg.* 4.464f); leading his beloved Eurydice from Hades, he loses her when he turns to look at her (*Lib.* 1.3.2; *Met.* 10.48f), but later rejoins her (*Met.* 10.61f); he is torn to pieces by Maenads (*Lib.* 1.3.2; *Met.* 11.1f) or killed by drunken Thracians, whom their women have incited to it, or by Zeus' thunderbolt, or by his own hand (Paus. 9.30.3).

PHEMIUS sings for Penelope's wooers as they feast, causing her to weep (*Od.* 1.153f, 1.325f); he begs Odysseus for his life (*Od.* 22.339f).

PIERUS' DAUGHTERS, who claim musical talent superior to the Muses, are changed into magpies when the best of them is judged inferior to Calliope (*Met.* 5.315f, 5.669f).

POLYPHEMUS, a Cyclops, sings to the nymph Galatea (Theocritus 11; cf. *Met.* 13.780f, where the instrument is a "pipe with a hundred reeds").

SILENUS sings to two youths and a maid after they free him from his floral chains (*Ecl.* 6.13f).

One SIREN plays a lyre, another a flute, and a third sings as Odysseus' ship passes by (*Ep.* 7.18–19).

THAMYRIS competes with the Muses; defeated, he is made blind and his talent taken from him (his lyre broken?) (*Lib.* 1.3.3).

MAD WOMEN

(See also **Leaping; Maenads.**)

Fleeing to the woods. LATIN WOMEN, inflamed by Amata with hostility to the Trojans, carry off Aeneas' intended bride (*Aen.* 7.346f); confronting Latinus, they demand war (*Aen.* 7.580f). PROETUS' DAUGHTERS are driven mad by Hera; they are cured when Artemis intercedes for them (Bacchylides 43f; Serv. *ad Ecl.* 6.48), or are cured by Melampus after he rounds them up (*Lib.* 2.2.2).

MAENADS

(See also **Mad Women.**)

Female followers of Dionysus, they are frequently represented dancing and carousing with Satyrs (q.v.), wearing animal skins, and carrying staffs (thyrsi, q.v.), and timbrels or flutes. Sometimes they have snakes for hair (Eur. *Bacch.* 104).

In a frenzied state. They seize and tear Orpheus apart as he sings (*Lib.* 1.3.2) or kill him with farm tools (*Met.* 11.lf); seize and dismember cattle (Eur. *Bacch.* 735f); rout armed men with their thyrsi and fronds of ivy (Eur. *Bacch.* 758f).

In flight with their patron DIONYSUS from Lycurgus (*Il.* 6.130f).

Disguised as Maenads. Aged CADMUS and TEIRESIAS confer with Pentheus (not so disguised) (Eur. *Bacch.* 170f). PENTHEUS is placed by Dionysus in a tree from which he spies on their rites; detected, he is pelted with stones, torn from his perch, and dismembered (Eur. *Bacch.* 1050f; *Lib.* 3.5.2). PROCNE rescues her imprisoned sister Philomela, who is similarly disguised (*Met.* 6.527f). SOLDIERS help Dionysus capture Nysus (*Fab.* 131).

MAGPIE

(See **Bird.**)

A MAENAD, WEARING AN ANIMAL SKIN, CARRIES A
THYRSUS AND LYNX (OR PANTHER)

MAN

(See **Human Figure.**)

MASK

Attribute of Momus; a Muse; Satyrs. Comic: Thalia. Tragic: Melpomene.
    Of DIONYSUS is suspended in vineyards to ensure the gods' favor (*Georg.*
2.388f).

Of a DOG's HEAD is worn by worshippers of Isis.

Of SILENUS is sometimes applied to a vessel used for casting lots.

MESSENGER

(See **Speaker.**)

MILL

Being turned by METOPE, who has been blinded by her cruel father Echetus for taking a lover; she is being further punished by being made to grind grains of bronze (*Argo.* 4.1093f); by a WOMAN performing her daily chore when Zeus thunders from a cloudless sky, upon which she utters in Odysseus' hearing a wish that her mistress' suitors depart; both occurrences answer auspiciously a prayer Odysseus has made to Zeus (*Od.* 20.98f).

MIRROR

(See also **Toilette.**)

At SOCRATES' suggestion, a pupil studies his reflection in order to direct his life according to what he sees (Diog. Laërt. 2.5.33).

Used to kindle fire. ARCHIMEDES ignites Roman ships that are attacking Syracuse (Galen, *de Temperamentis* 3.2). Sacred fire is relighted at Delphi (Plut. 4.9).

MISSILE

(See **Arrow; Discus; Loaf of Bread; Spear; Stone; Throwing.**)

MIST

(See also **Phantom; Rain; Whirlwind.**)

Attribute of Discordia. Enveloping the body: Lucina.

Concealing flight, rescue, or arrival. APHRODITE rescues Paris from Menelaüs' onslaught (*Il.* 3.383f) and hides Aeneas and Achates from sight as they enter Carthage (*Aen.* 1.411f, 1.516f). APOLLO rescues Hector from Achilles (*Il.* 20.443f) and also Agenor (*Il.* 21.590f). ARTEMIS carries Iphigeneia from the altar, where Agamemnon is about to sacrifice her, and substitutes a deer (Eur. *Iph. Aul.* 1540f; *Met.* 12.29f; *Fab.* 98). ATHENA provides the mist in which Arethusa evades the river god Alpheius; Arethusa is transformed into a stream (*Met.* 5.621f); Athena casts a mist around Odysseus; then, in the form of a water carrier, she guides him into the city of the Phaeacians (*Od.* 7.14f). DIONYSUS rescues Ino and her son from execution (*Fab.* 2). HEPHAESTUS rescues Idaeus from Diomedes (*Il.* 5.20f). HERA conceals Jason's arrival at Aeëtes' palace (*Argo.* 3.210f) and her own approach to Semele, before assuming the guise of Semele's old nurse (*Met.* 3.273f). POSEIDON rescues Aeneas from Achilles (*Il.* 20.318f; *Aen.* 5.803f); the twin Moliones from Nestor (*Il.* 11.750f).

Conceals the lovemaking of BOREAS and OREITHYIA (*Argo.* 1.216f); of ZEUS and HERA (*Il.* 14.342f); of ZEUS and IO, whom he turns into a heifer in an attempt to deceive Hera (*Met.* 1.588f).

Resembling Hera is embraced by ENDYMION, for which Zeus hurls him to Hades (fragment of Hes. *Eoiai* 260); by IXION, from which union is born a Centaur (*Fab.* 62; *Ep.* 1.20).

Carries HERACLES from his pyre to heaven (*Lib.* 2.7.7).

Emerging from a box, envelops PSYCHE; Eos rescues her (Apuleius 9).

MONKEY

Attribute of Vulcan.

The thievish CERCOPES are changed into monkeys by Zeus (*Met.* 14.91f).

MONSTER

(See also **Allegorical Figures; Dragon; Fabulous Beings and Creatures; Snake.**)

PART HUMAN, MALE

BRIAREÜS (Aegaeon), COTTUS, GYES each have a hundred arms and fifty heads. (See **Arm; Head.**)

CACUS is gigantic and fire-breathing. (See **Giant.**)

CENTAURS are simply hairy savages in the earliest accounts, later becoming men to the feet with a horse's body and hind legs attached, and finally men to the waist merging with the body and four legs of a horse. (See **Centaur.**)

CYCLOPES (notably Polyphemus) are one-eyed Giants. (See **Cyclops.**)

EURYTUS and CTEATUS (Moliones or Actoriones) are twins with a single body, two heads, four arms, and four legs, or two men joined. (See **Twins.**)

GERYON is a man with three heads, or he is three men joined (Pausanias). He is also more vaguely described as triple-bodied (Aeschylus and Euripides). Sometimes he is represented as winged. (See **Head.**)

The GIANTS (i.e., the race of Gigantes born from the blood of Ouranos) are fearsome, huge, snake-legged beings. (See **Fighting.** For six-armed Giants [unnamed], see **Arm.**)

JANUS has two faces. (See **Face.**)

The MINOTAUR is a man with the head of a bull. (See **Bull.**)

PAN, PANES, FAUNUS, FAUNI are goat-legged and horned sylvan creatures. (See **Satyr.**)

SATYRS and SILENI have pug noses, pointed ears, often little horns, and a goat's or horse's tail. Older Satyrs were called Sileni. The acquisition by Satyrs of goat legs and larger horns resulted from confusion with Panes and Fauni. (See **Satyr.**)

The SPHINX (Egyptian) has a human head, not distinctly male or female, on a wingless and recumbent lion's body. (See **Sphinx.**)

TELCHINES have fins in place of hands. (See **Dog; Flood; Wolf.**)

TRITON, NEREÜS, GLAUCUS are sea deities with a fish's tail in place of legs. (See **Fish; Sea Deity.**)

TYPHOEUS (Typhon, Typhaon) is a monster with a hundred snake-heads and snakes for fingers and for legs. According to Apollodorus, he is winged and breathes fire. (See **Snake-headed.**)

PART HUMAN, FEMALE

DELPHYNE is a dragon of which half is a maiden. (See **Dragon.**)

ECHIDNA is a cannibalistic monster, half beautiful woman, half snake. (See **Snake-legged.**)

The FURIES (Erinyes, Eumenides) are terrible, snake-haired, winged, avenging deities, but not always represented with all of their attributes. Sometimes they appear as stately women with torches or snakes in their hands and snakes in their hair. (See **Furies.**)

The GORGONS (notably Medusa) are fearsome, snake-haired, tusked, and frequently winged. (See **Gorgon.**)

The HARPIES are winged women with birds' feet or birds with a woman's head. (See **Harpies.**)

HECATE is sometimes described as having three bodies or three heads, each of a different animal. She is also described as having six arms. (See **Head.**)

The KERES (Ceres) are fanged and taloned personifications of the inevitability of death. (See **Corpse** [Dragged].)

SCYLLA is a nymph whose waist is encircled with the heads of dogs and whose lower body is that of a fish or snake, or whose legs are those of several dogs. (See **Dog's Head**). She is also described as having six long necks, each with a terrible head. (See **Head.**)

The SIRENS are women with birds' feet or birds with a woman's head. (See **Sirens.**)

The SPHINX (Greek) has the head and breasts of a woman, the body of a winged lion, and sometimes a serpent's tail. It may be represented in any position, even in flight, but is usually seated. (See **Sphinx.**)

HYBRID CREATURES

These may also be an artistic convention representing the successive transformations of such deities as Proteus, Thetis, Metis, Nereüs, Acheloüs, and Periclymenus into various beasts.

A CAMELOPARD is a lion or leopard with the head of a camel. (See **Lion.**)

CERBERUS is a three-headed dog, sometimes with a mane and tail of snakes. Hesiod ascribes fifty heads to it. (See **Dog.**)

The CHIMAERA is a monster with the heads of a lion, a goat, and a serpent, or having a lion's head and forelegs, a goat's body, and a serpent's tail for hindquarters. The goat element of the latter creature may be represented by a goat's head grafted onto its back. (See **Chimaera.**)

FAMA is a fanciful, winged monster personifying Rumor; it has many eyes, ears, and tongues. (See **Wings, Affixed to Creatures.**)

A GRIFFIN has a lion's body and the head and wings of an eagle. (See **Griffin.**)

A HIPPOCAMP is a seagoing horse with a fish's tail for hindquarters. (See **Horse.**)

A HIPPOCAMP

The HYDRA is a reptilian monster with nine heads on long necks. (See **Dragon.**)

ORTHOS is Geryon's two-headed dog. (See **Dog.**)

PEGASUS is a winged horse. (See **Horse.**)

The SPHINX (Egyptian) may have a human head—not distinctly male or female—or the head of a ram or falcon on its wingless, lion's body. It is always lying down. (See also **Part Human, Female,** above, and **Sphinx.**)

(Unnamed) ram-headed horse. (See **Horse.**)

(Unnamed) sea monster. (See **Dragon.**)

NOT DESCRIBED

CAMPE is the jailer of the Cyclopes and is slain by Zeus (*Lib.* 1.2.1) or by Dionysus (Diod. Sic. 3.72.3).

CHRYSAOR springs from Medusa's severed neck along with Pegasus (Hes. *Theog.* 281).

MOON

(See also **Crescent.**)

Crescent-shaped: attribute of Artemis; Selene.

MOUSE

Attribute of Apollo Smintheus.

Chased by the child GLAUCUS, who falls into a jar of honey (*Lib.* 3.3.1); by the monster TYPHON (this mouse is the Egyptian deity BUTO, who has transformed herself in her effort to escape) (Ant. Lib. 28).

Given to DARIUS by a Scythian herald, along with a bird, a frog, and five arrows (Herod. 4.131).

Mice eat the bowstrings of SCAMANDER's sleeping followers, indicating that they are to settle where they are (the Troad) (Serv. *ad Aen.* 3.108).

MOUTH

(See also **Spitting; Tongue.**)

Gagged: attribute of Angerona (Anguish).

Inside the Trojan Horse, ODYSSEUS puts his hand over Anticlus' mouth to keep him from answering Helen, who is outside (*Od.* 4.287f).

MUD

ARTEMIS and her nymphs smear it on their faces to conceal their identities from the river god Alpheius (Paus. 6.22.9).

MULE

(See **Horse.**)

MURDER

(See **Killing;** or the weapon or means employed.)

MUSES

(See also **Lyre; Musical Instruments.**)

They are stately goddesses of song and prophecy, originally three in number. Later accounts mention four, seven, and eight until Hesiod settles on nine and gives them their familiar names: Calliope, Clio, Erato, Euterpe, Melpomene, Polymnia, Terpsichore, Thaleia, and Urania. They are frequently attendants of Apollo.

In singing defeat PIERUS' DAUGHTERS, who become magpies (*Met.* 5.300f); the SIRENS, whom they strip of their feathers (Paus. 9.34.2); THAMYRIS, whom they make blind (Eur. *Rhes.* 921f; *Lib.* 1.3.3; *Il.* 2.594f).

MUSHROOMS

Transformed into men, who found Corinth (*Met.* 7.392f).

MUSICAL INSTRUMENTS

(See also **Conch; Cymbals; Drum; Flute; Lyre; Pipes.**)

These may be represented in a contemporary rather than classical form (e.g., the lyre as violin or mandolin), or another instrument substituted for the one mentioned in a source. When the source does not refer to the instrument used by a singer, it is assumed to be a lyre.

Attribute of the Charites; Corybantes; a Muse (excepting Clio and Urania).

MYRTLE

(See **Branch; Wreath.**)

NAIL

Attribute of Fortuna.

NECKLACE

(See also **Jewelry.**)

Presented. A precious necklace, made by Hephaestus, and a robe are given to Harmonia by CADMUS at their wedding, at which the gods are present. Their descendant Polyneices gives the necklace to Eriphyle (she actually receives the robe from another hand). Her son Alcmaeon gives them to Arsinoë, his first wife, whose father Phegeus returns them to Alcmaeon. He in turn gives them to his second wife, Callirrhoë. The sons of Phegeus and of Callirrhoë by Alcmaeon fight for possession of the precious objects; the latter two are victorious and present them to the shrine at Delphi (*Lib.* 3.4.2, 3.6.2, 3.7.2, 3.7.5–7).

Taken from a cradle by ION convinces him that he is the son of Creüsa, who is watching him (Eur. *Ion* 1431f).

NEGRO

(See **Dark Skin.**)

NEST

(See **Bird: Halcyon, Sparrow.**)

NET

(See also **Fishing; Hairnet.**)

Caught in a net. APHRODITE and ARES are trapped in bed by Hephaestus, to the amusement of other gods (*Od.* 8.272f; *Met.* 4.171f; *Fab.* 148). BRITOMARTIS (Dicte), a huntress nymph, as she runs from Minos; she is rescued by Artemis (Paus. 2.30.3; Serv. *ad Aen.* 3.171). HARPALYCE, a sylvan maiden with a kid she has stolen; she is killed by the shepherds of the flock

(Serv. *ad Aen.* 1.317). Two Satyrs, PICUS and his son FAUNUS; they assume fearful shapes as they try to escape (Plut. 4.15).

A large bone (the shoulder of Pelops) is dredged from the sea by a fisherman (Paus. 5.13.5).

NIGHTINGALE

(See **Bird.**)

NOSE

Retroussé (pug): attribute of Satyrs; Sileni; Silenus.

HERACLES cuts off the noses of heralds from Orchomenos (Paus. 9.25.4).

NUDE FIGURE

(See also **Bathing; Breast; Seduction; Statue; Toilette.**)

Five MAIDENS are selected for their various perfections by the painter Zeuxis to serve as models for an ideal figure (*Nat. Hist.* 35.64).

PHRYNE disrobes before the Areopagus and wins acquittal from the charge against her (Quint. *Inst.* 2.15.9; Athenaeus 13.590e).

RHODOPE in her chamber is spied on by Gyges, with the connivance of her husband Candaules (Herod. 1.8f).

NUMERAL

The number four is sacred to Hermes, seven to Apollo.

NURSE

(See **Baby; Breast; Old Woman.**)

NYMPH

(See **Human Figure.**)

OAR

(See also **Ship.**)

Attribute of Misenus.

Planted by Odysseus on Elpenor's tomb (*Od.* 12.11f).

Carried by Odysseus as he wanders afar, until he meets a man who, living far from boats and the sea, takes it for a winnowing fan; at that, Odysseus plants it in the ground and performs a sacrifice (*Od.* 23.266f; this meeting is one that Teiresias prophesies will occur in the future).

Broken by Heracles while rowing the *Argo* (*Argo.* 1.1164f).

OFFICER

(See also **Warrior.**)

Here are scenes in which an officer is prominent but no more precise identification of the event is offered. The distinction between *officer* and *warrior* is based on the milieu in which each performs. The former is a historical person of high rank in an organized military force, the latter a legendary hero for whom fighting is a way of life.

Alexander pardons Timoclea, who has killed the Macedonian soldier who raped her (Plut. 38.12), and also pardons a Persian in Macedonian armor, who has tried to assassinate him (Ps.-Cal. 162); he rejects the offer of a Persian satrap to serve under him (Ps.-Cal. 163); he bestows the insignia of kingship on the gardener Abdolonimus (Q. Curt. 4.1); he visits Darius' captive queen and her family (Q. Curt. 3.12; cf. Plut. 33.21, which records that he sent Leonatus in his place); he confers with the Indian potentate Taxiles (Plut. 33.59) and with his officers, who are suggesting a night attack on Darius' host (Plut. 33.31); he accepts the surrender of a huge Indian, King Poros (Arrian 5.19.1).

Caesar meets Cleopatra, who has had herself carried past the guard, rolled in a rug (Plut. 34.54); he has the Roman public treasury forced open in spite of Metellus' remonstrance that he does not have the right to do so (Plut. 34.41); he forms a pact with Pompey and Crassus at Luca (Plut. 32.51).

CAMILLUS is wildly welcomed by the populace after ridding Rome of the Gauls (Plut. 8.30).

CORIOLANUS, at the head of an army, is met outside Rome by his wife, mother, and sons, who induce him to abandon the assault on his native city (Livy 2.40).

CYRUS magnanimously restores captive Pantheia to her husband Abradatas, who had been allied against him (Xen. *Cyro.* 6.1.45f).

FABIUS puts a valued soldier, who has been absent without leave, under the orders of his ladylove, to keep him under control (Plut. 10.20).

FABRICIUS scrupulously rejects a gift of gold from Pyrrhus (Plut. 21.20).

FLAVIOLEIUS is the first officer in Fabius' army to take an oath to conquer or die (Livy 2.46).

HANNIBAL, Gisco, et al. study the Roman army before the battle at Cannae (Plut. 10.15).

MARCELLUS presents a war-horse to the soldier Bantius as a reward for the scars he earned at Cannae (Plut. 16.10).

OCTAVIAN forms a pact with Antony and Lepidus (Plut. 44.17); he calls on Cleopatra while she is still mourning for Antony (Plut. 44.83).

SCIPIO restores to her father a beautiful captive, who is being offered to him for his pleasure (Polybius 10.19.3f).

TULLUS HOSTILIUS and the Alban commander Mettius Fufetius confer and decide to have their champions settle the issue of the war (Livy 1.23).

OLD MAN

(See also **Beggar; Phantom; Priest; Speaker.**)

Personification of Hiems (wintry appearance); river gods (q.v.; bearded, "watery" appearance); Silenus (bald, jovial); Silvanus (cheerful); Tempus (with spade, staff, or crutch); Thanatos (winged, leaning on a staff).

Treating with invading Gauls (see **Barbarian**).

As teacher, guide, or friend. ARISTOTLE instructs Alexander (Plut. 33.7; Ps.-Cal. 37). BUTES (Apollo) addresses young Ascanius (*Aen.* 9.638f). EVANDER shows Aeneas the future site of Rome (*Aen.* 8.306f); he sends Pallas with a troop to accompany Aeneas to war (*Aen.* 8.560f). INDIAN PHILOSOPHERS converse with Alexander (Plut. 33.64). MENTOR (Athena) advises Telemachus and accompanies him on the voyage to Pylos (*Od.* 2.267f, 2.405f, 3.29f); she stands with Odysseus and Telemachus as the suitors prepare to attack (*Od.* 22.205f). NESTOR gives his son advice before a chariot race (*Il.* 23.301f) and he (actually Oneiros, i.e., "Dream," in his likeness) appears to sleeping Agamemnon (*Il.* 2.5f). A PERSIAN ENVOY is offered a chair by Alexander (Plut. 33.58). PHOENIX rears baby Achilles and instructs him in his youth (*Il.* 9.442f, 9.485f). PLATO's argument enrages Dionysius, tyrant of Syracuse, whom he is trying to instruct in statecraft (Plut. 45.5). A SERVANT saves young Orestes from a blow of Aegisthus' fist (Eur. *Elec.* 16f). SOCRATES censures his pupil Alcibiades for unseemly behavior (Plut. 11.6); in prison, he discourses with friends before he is put to death by poison (Diog. Laërt. 2.5.42). SOLON disparages King Croesus' conviction that wealth provides the greatest happiness (Herod. 1.30).

Being visited. ANCHISES welcomes Aeneas and the Sibyl to Elysium and conducts them through it (*Aen.* 6.679f). ANIUS, priest of Apollo at Delos, welcomes Aeneas and the Trojan ships (*Aen.* 3.79f; *Met.* 13.632f). ANTENOR receives Odysseus and Menelaüs, who have come to Troy to negotiate Helen's return (*Il.* 3.205f), and speaks in favor of it (*Il.* 7.348f). DIOGENES, sitting in the sun by a barrel, asks his visitors (Alexander et al.) not to cast their shadows on him (Plut. 33.14; Arrian 7.2.1). DOLIUS, an old retainer, kisses Odysseus' hand on his return (*Od.* 24.386f). EVANDER welcomes Heracles to Pallanteum (Livy 1.7). LAËRTES, laboring in his vineyard, is embraced by his son Odysseus (*Od.* 24.315f). NESTOR and his son Peisistratus welcome strangers, Telemachus and Mentor (Athena), to their board (*Od.* 3.31f). NUMA mollifies the wrath of Zeus, who has been brought unwillingly to earth by the charms of Picus and Faunus (Plut. 4.15).

With a woman. MYCON, wasting away in prison, is breast-fed by his daughter Pero (Val. Max. 5.46.1). NUMA is instructed in matters spiritual and divine by the nymph Egeria (Plut. 4.4). PRIAM is told by Helen, as they stand on Troy's battlements, the identities of Greek warriors (*Il.* 3.162f). THESTOR and LEUCIPPE are about to slay Queen Theonoë when they discover her to be his long-lost daughter and her sister; Thestor had previously been sent to kill a priest in his cell who turned out to be his daughter Leucippe (*Fab.* 190). TITHONUS, immortal but not ageless, is put away by his ever-youthful consort Eos in a chamber, where he shrivels to eternity (*H. to Aph.* 233f). TROJAN ELDERS cannot help admiring Helen's beauty, even though she is the cause of Troy's woes (*Il.* 3.146f). XENOCRATES' moral probity is tested by the seductive courtesan Phryne (Laïs) (Val. Max. 4.3 ext. 3).

Rallying warriors. CAMILLUS stems the flight of Roman soldiers and leads them to victory (Plut. 8.37). POSEIDON assumes the form of an old man to reassure Agamemnon and to arouse the faltering Greeks with a war cry (*Il.* 14.135f).

In the garb of Maenads (q.v.). CADMUS and blind TEIRESIAS are accosted by Pentheus (Eur. *Bacch.* 248f).

Being rejuvenated. AESON, after his throat is cut by Medea and his blood replaced by her magic brew, is restored to youth (*Met.* 7.285f; cf. the unsuccessful attempt of PELIAS' DAUGHTERS to rejuvenate their father in the same way, *Met.* 7.331f).

Hurled down the steps of the Curia, King SERVIUS TULLIUS is dethroned by the usurper Tarquin before their respective adherents (Livy 1.48).

OLD WOMAN

(See also **Allegorical Figures; Phantom; Priestess.**)

In charge of a baby (see **Baby**).

The blind PHORCYDES share a single eye that Perseus steals as it is being passed from one to another (*Lib.* 2.4.2).

In this form, ALLECTO appears to sleeping Turnus (*Aen.* 7.415f); APHRODITE conducts Helen from the battlements of Troy to Paris' bedchamber (*Il.* 3.383f); APOLLO approaches sleeping Chione and seduces her (*Met.* 11.309f); ATHENA visits Arachne at her loom (*Met.* 6.26f); DEMETER sits by a well to which the daughters of Keleos have come to draw water (*H. to Dem.* 98f); she is found grieving by a rustic and his daughter and taken to their cottage (*Fasti* 4.503f), where she cures a sick child with a kiss (*Fasti* 4.538f); HERA is carried across a stream by Jason (*Argo.* 3.66f; *Fab.* 13, 22) and visits Semele, her rival for Zeus' love, in order to eliminate her (*Met.* 3.273f); IRIS, as Beroë, incites the Trojan women to put an end to their wandering by setting fire to their ships (*Aen.* 5.618f); VERTUMNUS presses his suit to the nymph Pomona so eloquently that, when he resumes his natural form, he wins her (*Met.* 14.654f).

Leads MYRRHA to her father's bed as an owl cries (*Met.* 10.452f); THEAGENES to Princess Arsace, who has conceived a passion for him (*Aeth.* 7).

Performs various services. MYRRHA'S NURSE stops her from hanging herself (*Met.* 10.378f). PHAEDRA'S NURSE comforts her lovesick mistress (Eur. *Hipp.* 176f) and is cursed by Hippolytus when she discloses Phaedra's love for him (Eur. *Hipp.* 565f). PHILOMELA'S SERVANT takes the robe in which Philomela has woven pictures of her misfortunes to her sister Procne (*Met.* 6.579f).

Dressed as a young bride, ANNA PERENNA laughs in Ares' face when he lifts her veil to kiss her and finds a crone rather than Athena (*Fasti* 3.677f).

Filthy and emaciated, personifies FAMES (Hunger), who is sent by Demeter to infect Erysichthon with insatiable hunger by embracing him

(*Met.* 8.814f); INVIDIA (Envy), who at Athena's direction infects Aglauros by touching her breast (*Met.* 2.760f).

OMPHALOS

An egg-shaped and ornamented stone that marks the center of the world at Delphi. It may have a wreath on it and be flanked by Gorgons (Eur. *Ion* 224).

APOLLO SEATED ON THE OMPHALOS

ORATOR

(See **Speaker.**)

OSPREY

(See **Bird.**)

OWL

(See **Bird.**)

OX-GOAD

(See **Staff.**)

PADDLEWHEEL

(See **Shell.**)

PAINTER

(See also **Picture.**)

APELLES paints Alexander holding a thunderbolt (*Nat. Hist*. 35.92) and Alexander's mistress Pancaspe (Campaspe) (*Nat. Hist*. 35.86); he tells Alexander that his learned discourse about art is amusing to the studio assistants (*Nat. Hist*. 35.85); he is told by a shoemaker that he has a detail wrong in a picture (*Nat. Hist*. 35.85); he draws one line and Protogenes draws another in a test of their draftsmanship (*Nat. Hist*. 35.82).

BOUTADES' DAUGHTER traces the outline of her lover's shadow on a wall (*Nat. Hist*. 35.151).

PARRHASIOS' painting of a curtain deludes Zeuxis into trying to open it (*Nat. Hist*. 35.65).

ZEUXIS inspects naked maidens and selects five for their various perfections to be models for an ideal figure (*Nat. Hist*. 35.64); his painting of a bunch of grapes attracts birds (*Nat. Hist*. 35.65).

PANPIPES

(See **Pipes.**)

PANTHER

(See also **Leopard; Lion; Tiger.**)

Attribute of Amor; Diana. Sometimes with wings: Dionysus.

Adopts one baby after its twin has been devoured by their mad mother Aura (Nonnus 48.910).

Several devour LYCURGUS, who has been thrown to them by Dionysus (*Fab*. 132).

PANTHER SKIN

(See **Skin, of Animal.**)

PARASOL

Held by HERACLES to shield his mistress Omphale from the sun (*Fasti* 2.311f).

PARTING

(See also **Captive; Grieving; Ship; Suppliant.**)

Of AENEAS from an angry and distraught Dido (*Aen.* 4.388f); of CORIOLANUS from his wife and mother after he yields to their plea that he give up his intention to take Rome (Plut. 12.36); of EURYDICE from Orpheus when she is unwillingly drawn back to Hades because he looks back at her while leading her to the upper world (*Met.* 10.56f; *Georg.* 4.491f); of GAIUS GRACCHUS from his wife and child as he sets off to face his enemies (Plut. 40.15); of HECTOR from Andromache and baby Astyanax as he returns to battle (*Il.* 6.405f); of JASON from his aged parents before the departure of the *Argo* (*Argo.* 1.260f), and from Hypsipyle, his lover on Lemnos (*Argo.* 1.886f); of NEOPTOLEMUS from Deïdameia and aged Lycomedes, to follow Odysseus and Diomedes to war (Quint. Smy. 7.750f); of PALLAS from his old father Evander before setting off to war with Aeneas (*Aen.* 8.560f); of REGULUS from his wife, sons, and the Roman senate, to return to Carthage and prison or death, because he had given his word (Hor. *Odes* 3.5f; Livy *Epitome* of Bk. 18).

PARTRIDGE

(See **Bird.**)

PATH

(See **Road.**)

PEACOCK

(See **Bird.**)

PEBBLE

(See **Game; Lots.**)

PEEPING

(See **Spying.**)

PELICAN

(See **Bird.**)

PERSONIFICATION

(See **Allegorical Figures; River; River God; Sea Deity; Water.**)

PHALLUS

(See also **Genitals.**)

Symbol of fertility; also, having apotropaic properties, it is associated with the worship of Demeter, Hermes, Pan, and especially Dionysus.

Attribute of Horus; Mutunus; Priapus.

PHANTOM

Included here are likenesses of other persons, apparitions, ghosts, and shades, but not mortal likenesses assumed by divinities. For phantoms in the underworld, including Elysium or other paradise, see **Underworld.**

BRUTUS' evil genius, of terrible and unnatural form, comes to him in his tent to tell them they will meet at Philippi (Plut. 46.36).

Appearing in a dream. The Fury ALLECTO, to Turnus, to make him fight the Trojans (*Aen.* 7.445f). Deified HERACLES, to Myscelus, ordering him to emigrate (*Met.* 15.19f). HERMES (Ammon), to Alexander, telling him to assume his (the god's) dress and be his own messenger to Darius (Ps.-Cal. 174). An image of IPHTHIME, created and sent by Athena, to Penelope to reassure her that Telemachus will return (*Od.* 4.796f). ISIS, with other Egyptian deities and a snake, to Telethusa to tell her not to destroy the child she is about to bear (*Met.* 9.686f). ONEIROS (Dream) in the form of old Nestor, to Agamemnon, telling him to attack the Trojans (*Il.* 2.5f). PENATES (household gods), to Aeneas, telling him not to remain in Crete (*Aen.* 3.147f). The river god TIBERINUS, to Aeneas, telling him to go to Evander for help (*Aen.* 8.26f).

Of the dead appears to the sleeping. ANCHISES tells Aeneas to visit him in the underworld (*Aen.* 5.722f). CEŸX (actually Morpheus) tells Alcyone that he has drowned (*Met.* 11.650f). CLYTEMNESTRA, her wounds showing, comes to arouse the Furies against Orestes (Aes. *Eumen.* 94f). DIDO (actually Lavinia, who has counterfeited Dido's appearance and fatal wound) tells her sister Anna to flee from Aeneas' palace (*Fasti* 3.639f). HECTOR, his wounds visible, tells Aeneas to leave Troy to found a new city (*Aen.* 2.270f) and appears to Andromache (Sen. *Tro.* 493f). PATROCLUS, to Achilles asleep on the shore, asking him to bury him (*Il.* 23.65f). SYCHAEUS, with his wounds showing, to his wife Dido, telling her that he has been murdered and that she must flee (*Aen.* 1.353f).

Of the dead appears to the living. ACHILLES halts the departure of the Greeks, demanding the sacrifice of Polyxena (Eur. *Hec.* 36f; *Fab.* 110) and warns Agamemnon of the fate awaiting him (*Nostoi* 1). CREÜSA tells Aeneas to stop searching for her and to resume the flight from Troy (*Aen.* 2.771f). DARIUS appears from his tomb to his wife et al. (Aes. *Pers.* 580f). ELPENOR, heroines, and heroes emerge from the underworld to converse with Odysseus (*Od.* 11.51f and pass.). GHOSTS from Hades appear to Creon (Sen. *Oed.* 584f). POLYDORUS incites his mother to avenge his murder (Eur. *Hec.* 30f). ROMULUS descends from heaven to tell Julius Proculus to assure the Romans of their future greatness (Livy 1.16; *Fasti* 2.499f). STHENELUS emerges from his tomb in full panoply to see the *Argo* sail by (*Argo.* 2.915f).

Substitutes for a real figure. A phantom of AENEAS, created by Apollo, encourages the Trojan warriors (*Il.* 5.499f, 5.514f) and one created by Hera flees from Turnus and lures him aboard a ship (*Aen.* 10.636f); of DIONYSUS, made by himself (Bromius), is attacked by Pentheus, whose palace then collapses (Eur. *Bacch.* 629f); of HELEN, created by Hera, sails with Paris to Troy (Eur. *Hel.* 31f, 582f; *Ep.* 3.5); of HERA, created by Zeus out of mist, is seduced by Ixion, and a Centaur is born from it (*Ep.* 1.20; *Fab.* 62).

PICTURE

(See also **Painter.**)

AENEAS, examining the pictures (reliefs?) on the doors of a temple, is joined by Achates and Deïphobe (*Aen.* 6.14f).

AENEAS and ACHATES inspect the pictures (reliefs?) on the wall or platform of a newly built temple in Carthage (*Aen.* 1.450f).

ALEXANDER is shown his portrait by Candace of Ethiopia (Ps.-Cal. 240).

PERSINNA, Queen of Ethiopia, at the moment of intercourse with her husband, the Ethiopian king, sees a picture of white-skinned Andromeda on the wall, which causes her daughter Charicleia to be born white (*Aeth.* 2,4); this picture is subsequently compared with the girl Charicleia and establishes her as the daughter of Persinna (*Aeth.* 10).

PHAËTHON, approaching the palace of Helius (Phoebus), inspects the pictures on the doors (*Met.* 2.1f).

The PICTURE of a horse on the door of Antenor's house in Troy serves to protect it from molestation by the Greeks (Serv. *ad Aen.* 2.15).

PIG

(See also **Altar, Animal Sacrifice; Boar.**)

Attribute of a swineherd, especially EUMAEUS, who welcomes a beggar (Odysseus) (*Od.* 14.29f) and also Telemachus (*Od.* 16.12f); he cooks a pig for the beggar (*Od.* 14.55f, 14.418f).

Men are turned into pigs by CIRCE with her wand (*Od.* 10.237f); she feeds them (*Od.* 10.241f) and, at Odysseus' behest, restores their human form (*Od.* 10.388f).

A sow with her litter marks the future site of new Troy (Alba Longa) (*Aen.* 3.389f, 8.42f, 8.81f); is examined by the seers Mopsus and Calchas, trying to predict the number of her unborn litter (*Ep.* 6.4); called Phaea, is killed by Theseus (*Ep.* 1.1).

Pigs overturn wine jars, which awakens RHOEO's SISTERS and causes their flight into the sea (Diod. Sic. 5.62.3).

PILLAR

(See also **Stele; Tomb; Vessel, Funerary Urn.**)

A pillar may be used to represent a tomb, shrine, or building.

Two pillars. Attribute of Heracles. ATLAS holds the pillars that separate earth and sky (*Od.* 1.52f). DARIUS erects a pair on the shores of the Bosporus (Herod. 4.87). Two or more pillars are erected by DIONYSUS in India, according to what is considered an interpolation in *Lib.* 3.5.2. HERA-

CLES erects two, marking the limits of Libya and Europe (*Lib.* 2.5.10); they are visited by Alexander (Ps.-Cal. 258).

Tied to a pillar. OTUS and EPHIALTES are tied with snakes in the underworld; an owl perches above (*Fab.* 28).

Silver columns support the entrance to the abode of STYX (Hes. *Theog.* 775f).

PINE CONE

Hand-held: attribute of Asclepius. On the tip of a staff (thyrsus, q.v.): Dionysus; Maenads (q.v.).

PIPES

(See also **Flute.**)

An instrument consisting of a set of flutes bound together, also called a Panpipe (syrinx).

Attribute of Faunus; Hermes; Pan; Silvanus.

CALAMUS' pipes turn back into their original reeds (calami) as he grieves for drowned Carpos (Serv. *ad Ecl.* 5.48).

HERMES constructs a Panpipe as he guards Apollo's cattle; he trades it to Apollo for a golden wand and knowledge of pebble divination (*Lib.* 3.10.2); he pipes to sleep hundred-eyed Argus, who is guarding a cow (Io) (*Met.* 1.676f).

PAN makes pipes out of the reeds into which the nymph Syrinx has been transformed (*Met.* 1.711f); he teaches the boy Daphnis to play (Serv. *ad Ecl.* 5.20); he competes with Apollo, playing a lyre, before Tmolus (forest personified); Midas, who disagrees with Tmolus' judgment in favor of Apollo, acquires ass's ears as a result (*Met.* 11.155f).

POLYPHEMUS plays and sings of his love for Galatea, who hears him as she rests in Acis' arms (*Met.* 13.782f).

PIT

(See also **Burial; Chasm; Well.**)

ODYSSEUS digs a pit, from which emerge the shades of dead heroines and heroes to converse with him (*Od.* 10.516f, 11.25f).

PERSIAN HERALDS are thrown into a pit at Athens and at Sparta (Herod. 7.133).

PITCHER

(See **Vessel.**)

PLOW

Attribute of Neptune.

Its invention is falsely claimed by MYRMEX, whom Athena turns into an ant (*Fab.* 52; Serv. *ad Aen.* 4.402).

Plowing is performed by CADMUS, at Athena's command, after he kills a dragon (*Met.* 3.101f; *Lib.* 3.4.1; Eur. *Phoen.* 657f); by CINCINNATUS, when he is interrupted by a deputation asking him to assume the dictatorship (Livy 3.26; Cic. *de Sen.* 16.56); by DIONYSUS (or under his instruction), when he first conceived the idea of attaching oxen to a plow (Diod. Sic. 3.64.1); by EROS (Moschus, *Epigram* 7); by GORDIUS with oxen on which an eagle alights (Justin 11.7.5); by JASON behind fire-breathing bulls (*Argo.* 3.1320f; *Met.* 7.115f; cf. *Argo.* 3.409f, in which Aeëtes describes having accomplished the same task); by ODYSSEUS behind a horse and an ox, feigning madness; to call his bluff, Palamedes lays his baby son Telemachus in the way (*Fab.* 95); by ROMULUS behind a bull and a cow, to mark the boundary of Rome (Plut. 2.11; *Fasti* 4.825f); by TARCHON (Tyrrhenus), when he observes a clod of earth change into a man (Tages) (*Met.* 15.552f); by THEIODAMAS, when Heracles comes and demands his ox (*Argo.* 1.1213f).

POLE

(See also **Staff; Stake.**)

Used by HERACLES to carry the two Cercopes suspended head down (*Lib.* 2.6.3, n. 3, Loeb edn.).

POMEGRANATE

(See also **Eating; Flower.**)

Attribute of Juno; Proserpina; Victoria.

POOL

(See **Water.**)

POPPY

(See **Flower.**)

PRAYING

(See **Altar; Suppliant.**)

PRIEST

(See also **Altar; Old Man; Temple.**)

CALCHAS, holding a cup, is told by a seer that he will die before he drinks; convulsed by the absurdity, he chokes to death (Serv. *ad Ecl.* 6.72).

CHRYSES' plea for the return of his daughter Chryseïs is rejected by Agamemnon; he prays to Apollo to punish Agamemnon and the Greeks (*Il.* 1.14f).

HELENUS, when threatened by Odysseus, reveals how Troy may be taken (*Aethiopis,* in Proclus, 2); with Andromache, he welcomes Aeneas and the refugee Trojans (*Aen.* 3.344f).

LATINUS, lying on fleeces, consults oracular Faunus (*Aen.* 7.92).

LEUCIPPE, in priest's garb, is searching for her long-lost sister Theonoë, whom she fails to recognize when she is captured and imprisoned by that sister; her identity becomes known through the agency of old Thestor, her father, who has also been searching for Theonoë (*Fab.* 190). (See also **Captive, Women; Old Man.**)

NUMA meets the nymph Egeria by night in a grove to receive instruction regarding religious observances (Livy 1.19, 1.21).

PANTHUS, leading his grandchild and carrying sacred objects, comes to Aeneas' house while Troy burns (*Aen.* 2.318f).

PRIESTESS

(See also **Altar; Old Woman; Temple.**)

The Fury ALLECTO, in the guise of an aged priestess, appears to sleeping Turnus (*Aen.* 7.415f).

CHARICLEIA crowns Theagenes after he wins a footrace (*Aeth.* 4).

HERSE and other lovely young priestesses are watched by Hermes as they move in procession to a temple (*Met.* 2.711f).

IPHIGENEIA faces Orestes and Pylades, who have been captured and brought before her (Eur. *Iph. Taur.* 468f); she reveals to them the contents of a letter proving to Orestes that she is his sister (Eur. *Iph. Taur.* 725f); holding a statue, she meets King Thoas at her temple (Eur. *Iph. Taur.* 1156f) and leads a procession to a ship in which she escapes with Orestes and Pylades from Thoas' soldiers (Eur. *Iph. Taur.* 1345f).

MEDEA prepares magic ointment (*Argo.* 3.858f), which she presents to Jason (*Argo.* 3.956f); by uttering incantations from the *Argo,* she causes huge Talos to bleed to death (*Argo.* 4.1659f); she invokes the powers of darkness and concocts a magic brew (*Met.* 7.179f, 7.240f), which she injects into old Aeson's veins to rejuvenate him after having cut his throat to draw off his blood (*Met.* 7.287f); she cuts the throat of an old ram and cooks it in a cauldron, from which a lamb jumps out, as Pelias' daughters look on (*Met.* 7.312f; *Fab.* 24); she supervises the daughters' attempt to do the same for their old father and finishes the job when their hands falter (*Met.* 7.312f).

MYRENE recognizes the pirates who once abducted her and has them arrested (Serv. *ad Aen.* 3.23).

The PYTHIAN PRIESTESS produces the cradle in which she found Ion when he was a baby and gives it to him, as Creüsa watches from an altar (Eur. *Ion* 1337f); the PYTHIA whom Alexander has come to consult is dragged by him to the temple when she proves reluctant to prophesy (Plut. 33.14).

The SIBYL of Cumae is visited in her cave by Aeneas (*Aen.* 3.443f, 6.42f; *Met.* 14.129) and leads him to the underworld, where he meets Dido, Anchises, et al. (*Aen.* 6.262f).

PROCESSION

To a shrine or altar (see **Priestess** [Herse]). To a ship (see **Priestess** [Iphigeneia]).

Triumphal and Dionysiac scenes are not indexed because they are commonplace and more tableau than act or event.

PROW

Of a ship, including its ram, is an attribute of Saturn.

PRUNING HOOK

(See **Sickle.**)

PURSE

(See **Bag; Gold.**)

PURSUIT

(See **Flight; Running.**)

PYGMY

Pygmies battle cranes (*Il.* 3.3f).

PYRE

(See also **Ascension; Fire; Tomb.**)

For a hero in torment. HERACLES' pyre is built and set afire by Philoctetes, to whom in gratitude he gives his bow and arrows; Heracles rises from it to heaven (*Fab.* 36, 102; *Met.* 9.229f; Sen. *Her. Oet.* 1744f, 1835f; cf. Soph. *Trach.* 1264f, where his son Hyllus lights the fire, and *Lib.* 2.7.7, where Poeas provides this service).

For the corpse of ACHILLES is surrounded by heroes and deities paying him tribute (*Od.* 24.784f); of CAESAR, who is mourned by the people of Rome (Plut. 34.74, 44.14); of CHIONE, daughter of Daedalion, who has to be restrained from leaping into the flames (*Met.* 11.332f); of CORONIS, from whose body Hermes snatches baby Asclepius (*Met.* 2.619f; Paus. 2.26.5); of DIDO, the flames of which are visible to Aeneas' departing ship (*Aen.* 5.1f);

DIDO ON HER FUNERAL PYRE

of ELPENOR is built by Odysseus et al. (*Od.* 12.8f); of ETEOCLES, to which Antigone adds Polyneices' body, for which she is arrested (*Fab.* 72); of MEMNON, from which birds rise, then fall back into the flames (*Met.* 13.600f); of PATROCLUS, on which Achilles sacrifices Trojan captives; Iris brings Boreas and Zephyrus to make it burn (*Il.* 23.127f); of POLYXENA, to which Agamemnon lets Hecuba add Polydorus' body (Eur. *Hec.* 572f, 895f); of POMPEY (headless) is built and fired by Philip and an old veteran of his army (Plut. 32.80).

Place or means of suicide. ADRASTUS and HIPPONOÜS obey Apollo's order to leap into a pyre (*Fab.* 242). CALAMUS, an old and sick philosopher, burns himself to death after taking leave of Alexander et al. (Plut. 33.69). DIDO kills herself with Aeneas' sword, on top of the pyre she has had built (*Aen.* 4.494f; *Met.* 14.80f). EVADNE leaps into Capaneus' pyre (Eur. *Suppl.* 1014f; *Lib.* 3.7.1). LAODAMIA leaps into the flames in which Adrastus is burning the statue of her husband Protesilaüs (*Fab.* 104). OENONE leaps into Paris' burning pyre (Quint. Smy. 10.456f).

Reincarnation. Two youths, the CORONI, emerge from the pyre of Orion's daughters (*Met.* 13.692f).

Extinguished. CROESUS et al. are about to be burned alive when Cyrus relents and orders the fire quenched; his men fail to do this, but Apollo answers Croesus' prayer with heavy rain (Herod. 1.86–87; according to Bacchylides 3.33f, Zeus sends the rain).

QUAIL

(See **Bird.**)

QUARRELING

(See **Fighting; Killing.**)

QUEEN

The following scenes cannot appropriately be placed under more particular headings.

DIDO negotiates with Africans for land on which to build Carthage (*Aen.* 1.365f); encircles with strips of hide tied together an area on which to build Carthage (Serv. *ad Aen.* 1.367); supervises the building of the city (*Aen.* 1.503f); receives Trojan refugees (*Aen.* 1.509f); welcomes Aeneas and

IRIS, WITH CADUCEUS, CARRYING A CHILD

Achates (*Aen.* 1.588f); receives gifts from the boy Ascanius (Eros) et al. (*Aen.* 1.697f); shows Aeneas her city (*Aen.* 4.74f); charges Aeneas with perfidy (*Aen.* 4.304f, 4.364f).

QUIVER

(See also **Hunter; Huntress.**)

Attribute of Apollo; Artemis; Eros; Minerva; Narcissus; Venus.

RABBIT

(See **Hare.**)

RAFT

(See also **Boat; Ship.**)

ALEXANDER is transported by raft across the Hydaspes River at night in a storm (Plut. 33.60).

HERACLES' statue is towed on a raft by a rope made of women's hair (Paus. 7.5.3).

ODYSSEUS builds a raft on which he leaves Calypso's isle (*Od.* 5.262f, 7.264f) and is caught in a storm sent by Poseidon (*Od.* 5.291f, 7.270f); he improvises a raft out of timbers of his ship, which a thunderbolt has shattered, and is carried on it into the whirlpool of Charybdis, which swallows it, leaving Odysseus hanging from a tree until the raft reappears and he can drop back onto it (*Od.* 12.422f).

Baby PYRRHUS and his attendants are carried over a river, out of reach of pursuing soldiers (Plut. 21.2).

RAIN

(See also **Mist; Rainbow; Snow; Storm.**)

Puts out fire. CROESUS et al., about to be burned alive by Cyrus, are saved by a downpour sent by Apollo (Herod. 1.86–87) or by Zeus (Bacchylides 3.33f). TROJAN SHIPS, which the women have set afire while their men are watching cavalry maneuvers, are saved by Zeus (*Aen.* 5.693f).

Of gold (Zeus) showers down on ALCMENE (Pind. *Isth.* 7.5–7); on DANAË (*Fab.* 63; *Met.* 4.610f, 6.113f; *Lib.* 2.4.1).

Bloody rain is sent by ZEUS to portend war (*Il.* 11.52f); the death of his own son Sarpedon (*Il.* 16.459f); Caesar's murder (*Met.* 15.788f).

RAINBOW

Attribute or personification of Iris, who descends on its path to the Trojan women by their ships and assumes the form of old Beroë (*Aen.* 5.604f). (See also **Wings** [Iris].)

RAKE

Used by PolyPHEMUS to comb his hair (*Met.* 13.764f); by SILENUS to clean out Polyphemus' cave (Eur. *Cycl.* 29f).

RAM

(See also **Altar; Fleece; Sheep; Shepherd** .)

Attribute of Ammon; Aphrodite; Eros.

Battering ram (see **Engine**).

In this form, PAN seduces Theophane (a sheep), of which a golden-fleeced ram is the result (*Fab.* 188), and also Bisaltis (*Met.* 6.117f); ZEUS escapes from the monster Typhoeus (*Met.* 5.327f).

Carries ODYSSEUS, tied or clinging underneath it, out of Polyphemus' cave (*Od.* 9.425f); PHRIXUS and HELLE off at the moment they are to be sacrificed; as they fly over the Hellespont, Helle falls off (*Fasti* 3.857f; *Argo.* 2.1145f; *Lib.* 1.9.1; *Fab.* 3).

Killed or sacrificed. A black ram by AENEAS as the Sibyl offers a black heifer before they enter the underworld (*Aen.* 6.243f); a ram by AJAX, who beheads one and whips another in a fit of madness (Soph. *Ajax* 232f); by MEDEA, who cooks it in a cauldron; a live lamb leaps out to the amazement of Pelias' daughters (*Fab.* 24; *Met.* 7.312f; *Lib.* 1.9.27); by ODYSSEUS, beside a pit from which ghosts are to emerge (*Od.* 11.23f); by PHRIXUS (this is the Golden Ram that brought him to Colchis and whose fleece is sought by Jason; citations as above under "Carries").

Finds water in a desert for DIONYSUS (*Fab.* 133); for HERACLES et al. (Serv. *ad Aen.* 4.196).

RAM'S HEAD

On a male figure represents Ammon.

On a recumbent lion (see **Sphinx** [Egyptian]).

On a horse whose hindquarters are those of a sea creature, represents PALAEMON.

PHRIXUS, ON THE GOLDEN RAM, REACHES FOR HELLE

Mask is put on by ZEUS (Ammon) when Heracles insists on seeing him (Herod. 2.42).

RAM'S HORN

Attribute of Ammon.

RAM'S SKIN

(See **Fleece.**)

RAPE

(See **Seduction.**)

RATTLE

(See **Sistrum.**)

RAVEN

(See **Bird, Crow.**)

RAYS

(See also **Fire; Light; Sun.**)

Attribute of Helius; Hera; Phoebus-Apollo.

PHOEBUS-APOLLO, enthroned in radiance amid his retinue, greets his son Phaëthon (*Met.* 2.19f).

READING

(See **Book; Letter.**)

REAPING HOOK

(See **Sickle.**)

REED

DEMOSTHENES bites the reed he uses for writing and dies from the poison in it, thereby avoiding arrest (Plut. 41.29).

Changed into reeds. CALAMUS' pipes, as he grieves for drowned Carpos (Serv. *ad Ecl.* 5.48); the nymph SYRINX, when her pursuer Pan is about to catch her (*Met.* 1.705f).

Rustling reeds betray the fact that MIDAS has ass's ears concealed under his turban (*Met.* 11.182f).

REVELRY

(See **Drinking; Eating.**)

RIBBON

(See also **Headband.**)

On the feet: attribute of Saturn.

RING

Thrown into the sea by MINOS from his ship; Theseus dives in to retrieve it (Bacchylides 16.52; Paus. 1.17.3; *Poet. Astr.* 2.5); by POLYCRATES from his ship, in payment for his good fortune (Herod. 3.41).

Given or received. The priest CALASIRIS offers to Nausicles the ring that he has taken from the altar fire, as ransom for Charicleia (*Aeth.* 5). IASEUS gives a ring from his finger to Phocus as a token of friendship (Paus. 10.30.2). POLYCRATES gets his ring back when it is found in a fish (Herod. 3.42). THESEUS recovers Minos' ring from Thetis or Amphitrite in their abode in the sea, along with a wreath, and returns it to Minos (*Poet. Astr.* 2.5; Paus. 1.17.3).

Worn by Prometheus as a symbol of eternal imprisonment (*Poet. Astr.* 2.15).

RITE

(See **Altar.**)

RIVER

(See also **Boat; Flood; Raft; River God; Ship; Swimming; Water.**)

As a barrier. CAESAR temporarily halts his army at the Rubicon, the crossing of which will constitute a declaration of war; then he has a trumpeter sound the advance (Plut. 34.37; Suet. *Caes.* 1.32). JASON carries an old woman (Hera) across a stream (*Fab.* 13, 22; *Argo.* 3.66f). MOEROS, delayed by a river, arrives barely in time to save his friend Seluntius from being crucified in his place (*Fab.* 2.5.7; cf. the Damon and Pythias story in Cic. *de Off.* 3.10, *Tusc.* 5.22).

Blocked by ACHILLES, who fills the Scamander with the bodies of Trojans, causing it to rise in anger (*Il.* 21.218f; see also **River God**); by HERACLES, who piles stones in the Strymon to make it unnavigable (*Lib.* 2.5.10) and who diverts two streams into the stables or ox-pens of Augeas (*Fab.* 30; *Lib.* 2.5.5).

RIVER GOD

(See also **Horn; Sea Deity; Seduction; Water.**)

Sometimes this deity may be identified by horns on his head, by a "watery" beard and garment, or by an urn out of which water pours.

With horns. ACHELOÜS sweeps away several Echinadian nymphs, who become islands (*Met.* 8.583f); wrestling with Heracles for the hand of Deïaneira, he has one of his horns torn off (*Met.* 9.82f; Soph. *Trach.* 9f, 499f; *Lib.* 2.7.5). ACIS emerges from the stream flowing out of his burial place (*Met.* 13.885f). NUMICIUS helps Aphrodite wash Aeneas' corpse (*Met.* 14.602f).

Horns not specified. CRIMISUS (Crinisus), in the form of a dog (or bear), mates with Egesta (Serv. *ad Aen.* 4.30). CYRENE is visited by her son Aristaeus (*Georg.* 4.357f). ENIPEUS (Poseidon) seduces Tyro (*Lib.* 1.9.8) and Iphimedeia (*Met.* 6.116). SCAMANDER tries to drown Achilles and pursues him when he flees; they fight, with Athena and Poseidon standing by; Scamander (Water) is overcome by Hephaestus (Fire) (*Il.* 21.233f).

ROAD

At a fork in the way, HERACLES is faced with a choice between the road to virtue and the road to pleasure (Cic. *de Off.* 1.32; cf. Hes. *W. & D.* 288f, where Hesiod points out to his brother Perses that he has a similar choice to make).

ROBE

(See **Garment.**)

ROCK

(See also **Island; Statue; Stone.**)

In the sea. AJAX OÏLEUS swims from his foundered ship to a rock, which Poseidon then demolishes with his trident (*Od.* 4.499f; *Ep.* 6.6); he is impaled on a sharp rock by Athena after she has destroyed his ship with a bolt (*Aen.* 1.42f). LICHAS, after Heracles flings him into the sea, becomes a rock with the shape of a man (*Met.* 9.223f). MENOETES clambers onto a rock after being thrown overboard (*Aen.* 5.176f). The PHAEACIAN ship that has taken Odysseus back to Ithaca is turned into a ship-like rock by Poseidon (*Od.* 13.159f).

ROPE

(See also **Bonds; Hanging; Knot.**)

Supporting a swing (see **Swinging**).

Attached to a statue, ship or raft. AENEAS cuts his ship's mooring cable in his haste to leave Carthage (*Aen.* 4.579f). ARTEMIS' statue is connected with the besieged city of Ephesus by a rope that symbolizes the protection she is giving the city (Herod. 1.26). CLAUDIA by herself tows a ship with Cybele's statue aboard, thus proving her chastity (*Fasti* 4.297f). HERACLES' statue is towed on a raft with a rope made of women's hair (Paus. 7.5.3). TENNES, ashore, cuts the rope that moors Cycnus' ship to a rock or a tree at Tenedos (Paus. 10.14.2).

Made by Roman women from their hair for use in missile-throwing engines (Serv. *ad Aen.* 1.720).

Eaten by a donkey as fast as Oknos plaits it (Paus. 10.29.2).

ROSE

(See **Flower.**)

ROWING

(See **Boat; Oar; Ship.**)

RUDDER

Attribute of Fates (q.v.); Fortuna; Glaucus; Oceanus; Salus; Triton; Tyche.

RUG

CLEOPATRA gains admission to Caesar's presence by having herself carried in rolled up in a rug (Plut. 34.54).

RUINS

ALEXANDER visits Troy (Plut. 33.15).

Old GAIUS MARIUS sits among the ruins of Carthage (Plut. 22.40).

RUNNING

(See also **Flight.**)

EUCHIDAS runs to Delphi and back to Plataea with unpolluted fire; he dies of exhaustion (Plut. 17.20).

PHEIDIPPIDES (Philippides) runs from Athens to Sparta with news of the Persian landing at Marathon, and he runs back; on the way he is accosted by Pan (Herod. 6.105–6; Paus. 1.28.4).

In a race. ACHILLES, in full armor, keeps pace with a four-horse chariot (Eur. *Iph. Aul.* 206f). ATALANTA outruns a suitor whose life is therewith forfeit (*Met.* 10.575f); she overtakes and kills a suitor herself (*Fab.* 185); she is defeated by Hippomenes (Meilanion) because she stops to pick up the golden apples he throws off to the side (*Met.* 10.652f; *Fab.* 185; *Lib.* 3.9.2). EPEIOS wins the race for his father's throne (Paus. 5.1.4). EURYALUS wins when his friend Nisus, as he falls, trips Salius (*Aen.* 5.315f). ODYSSEUS wins when Ajax Oïleus is caused by Athena to slip on some bull's entrails (*Il.* 23.757f). SUITORS race for the daughters of Danaüs (Pind. *Pyth.* 9.193f). THEAGENES in full armor wins and receives a prize from Charicleia (*Aeth.* 4).

Over water is an accomplishment of EUPHEMUS, the world's fastest human (*Argo.* 1.179f; *Fab.* 14).

SACK

(See **Bag; Bundle; Wineskin.**)

SACRIFICING

(See **Altar.**)

SAIL

(See also **Boat; Raft; Ship.**)

Attribute of Fortuna (riding on a swan); Galatea.

Invented by DAEDALUS to enable him and Icarus to escape from Minos' galleys in their small boats (Paus. 9.11.3).

SANDAL

Winged (see **Wings**).

Stolen by an eagle. APHRODITE's, while she is bathing, is given by the eagle to Hermes, who holds it hostage until she yields to his passion (*Poet. Astr.* 2.16). RHODOPIS', while she is bathing, is given to Psammetichus, who puts it on her foot (Aelian 13.33).

Wearing only one, having lost the other while carrying an old woman (Hera) across a stream, JASON appears before Pelias (*Argo.* 1.5f; *Lib.* 1.9.15; *Fab.* 12, 13).

Concealed by AEGEUS, who places a pair of sandals with a sword under a stone, to be found later by Theseus (*Lib.* 3.15.7, 3.16.1).

SARCOPHAGUS

(See also **Burial; Chest; Tomb.**)

AJAX, alone of Greek heroes, is buried in a coffin rather than being cremated (*Ep.* 5.7).

ALCMENE's body is removed by Hermes and a stone substituted (Pherecydes, in *Frag. Hist. Graec.* 1.82).

ALEXANDER's sarcophagus is viewed by Augustus (Suet. *Aug.* 18).

Two sarcophagi are carried in NUMA's funeral procession, one for his body, one for his books; when the former is washed open by a flood, it is found empty (Plut. 4.22).

SATYR

Male woodland spirit with one or more animal characteristics, e.g., horse or goat tail, pointed ears, pug nose, horns (budding or goat-like), goat legs. Satyrs' older counterparts, bald and bearded, were the Sileni, so called after Silenus, Dionysus' companion. Satyrs' acquisition of goat legs resulted from identification with Panes and Fauni.

AEGIPAN and Hermes restore the tendons to the limbs of Zeus (*Lib.* 1.6.3).

FAUNUS, as an oracular divinity, is consulted by Latinus, who is lying on fleeces (*Aen.* 7.92f).

PAN meets the runner-messenger Pheidippides (Philippides) on the road to Sparta (Paus. 1.28.4; Herod. 6.105–6).

A SATYR steals some cattle and is killed by many-eyed Argus (*Lib.* 2.1.2).

SATYRS are sent by Apollo to look for his stolen cattle (Soph. *Ich.*, see Rose, p. 171).

SATYR DRINKING

SATYRS put Orion to sleep and Oenopion blinds him (Serv. *ad Aen.* 10.736).

SILENUS, fighting with Dionysus against the Giants, spears Enceladus (Eur. *Cycl.* 5f); he and his crew row in search of kidnapped Dionysus (Eur. *Cycl.* 10f); he is offered wine by Odysseus (Eur. *Cycl.* 151f).

A baby. PAN, with all his goat-like characteristics formed, is born to Penelope after her seduction by Hermes in the shape of a goat; at the sight of him, Odysseus takes to his heels (Serv. *ad Aen.* 2.44; cf. Serv. *ad Georg.* 1.16, where Penelope's suitors are named the sires, and *H. to Pan* 35f, where Dryopes' daughter is the mother and the one who flees at the sight of him); Hermes shows his son to the gods, who are charmed by him (*H. to Pan* 40f).

And a woman. FAUNUS steals to the bed of sleeping Omphale, only to discover that it is Heracles in Omphale's clothing that he has to deal with (*Fasti* 2.332f). PAN, pursuing Syrinx, grasps only the reeds into which she is transformed, and out of which he constructs a Panpipe (*Met.* 1.698f); he wins Selene with the gift of a fleece (or by assuming the form of a ram?) (*Georg.* 3.391f); he finds Demeter in a cave, grieving for Persephone (Paus. 8.42.3). A SATYR (Zeus) seduces Antiope (*Met.* 6.110; *Lib.* 3.5.5; *Fab.* 8). A Satyr asleep is wounded by the huntress Amymone; he tries to rape her but is driven off by Poseidon, who succeeds where the Satyr failed (*Lib.* 2.1.4; *Fab.* 169, 169A). Satyrs are disturbed by a strange sound that (as the nymph Cyllene explains) is being made by Hermes, playing on his newly invented lyre (Soph. *Ich.*, see Rose, p. 171).

Making music. MARSYAS finds Athena's discarded flute and challenges Apollo, who defeats him even though he plays with his lyre upside down; Marsyas is flayed for his presumption (*Fab.* 165; *Met.* 6.382f; *Lib.* 1.4.2; Paus. 1.24.1). PAN teaches Daphnis to play the pipes (Serv. *ad Ecl.* 5.20) and competes on his pipes against Apollo's lyre before Tmolus (forest personified), as judge, and Midas, who acquires ass's ears when he disagrees with Tmolus' judgment in favor of Apollo (*Met.* 11.153f).

Captive or enslaved. FAUNUS and his father Picus (whose symbol or manifestation is a woodpecker) are tied up by Numa while they sleep and are compelled to call down the king of the gods from heaven (*Fasti* 3.299f; cf. Plut. 4.15, which describes both as Satyrs and records that they were caught in a net from which they tried to escape by changing their shapes). SILENUS is brought in floral chains to King Midas amid revelry (*Met.* 11.90f). SILENUS and SILENI tend herds and perform menial tasks for the Cyclops Polyphemus (Eur. *Cycl.* 22f); SILENI receive Odysseus et al. when they come ashore and again at Polyphemus' cave (Eur. *Cycl.* 85f).

SAUCER

(See **Vessel, Cup.**)

SAW

Invented by DAEDALUS' NEPHEW, whom Daedalus throws from a roof out of jealousy (*Fab.* 39), or from the Acropolis (*Met.* 8.244f; *Lib.* 3.15.8).
Used by PROCRUSTES to trim a guest to fit his bed (*Ep.* 1.4).

SCALES

Attribute of Atropos; Iustitia; Kairos (with wings on feet and shoulders); Themis (often with a cornucopia).

Used. BRENNUS adds his sword to the weights measuring the gold Rome is to pay to the Gauls, at which juncture CAMILLUS arrives, removes the gold, and orders the Gauls to depart (Plut. 8.28–29; Livy 5.48–49). OPIMIUS weighs the head of C. Gracchus to calculate the reward owed for his murder (Plut. 40.17). ZEUS weighs the fates of the Greeks and Trojans battling on the plain below Mt. Ida (*Il.* 8.68f); of Achilles and Memnon (Pind. *Ol.* 2.148, *Nem.* 3.110, 6.83); of Achilles and Hector (*Il.* 22.209f); of Aeneas and Turnus (*Aen.* 12.725f).

SCEPTRE

(See also **Caduceus; Staff; Stick.**)

An unreliable attribute, since it is no more than a symbol of authority or precedence and may from time to time be carried by any deity, king, queen, herald, seer, judge, or speaker in council (qq.v.). The most prominent sceptred divinities and royalty are Zeus, Hera, Rhea, Demeter, Hestia, Pluto, Persephone, Oceanus, Triptolemus, and Agamemnon.

Used as a weapon by HADES to strike the water nymph Cyane, when she tries to block his way to the underworld as he carries off Persephone (*Met.* 5.420f); by ODYSSEUS to beat cowardly Greek warriors (*Il.* 2.198f; *Met.* 13.216f) and ugly, hunchbacked Thersites for speaking insolently to Agamemnon (*Il.* 2.265f).

Sprouting branches is held by AGAMEMNON when he appears in a dream to Clytemnestra (Soph. *Elec.* 416f).

Presented, together with a crown, by ALEXANDER to Abdolonimus (a lowly gardener but of royal blood), making him king of Sidon (Q. Curt. 4.1);

by NINUS to his queen Semiramis, who forthwith orders his execution (Diod. Sic. 2.2; Val. Max. 7.1).

SCISSORS

Attribute of Atropos.

SCORPION

Attribute of the Horae (Seasons); Mithras.

Bites and kills ORION when he intercepts its attack on Leto (*Fasti* 5.541f); because he tried to violate Artemis (*Lib.* 1.4.5, n.2, Loeb edn.); because he offended Gaea (*Poet. Astr.* 2.26).

SCROLL

(See also **Book; Box; Letter; Writing.**)

Attribute of Calliope; Clio; Clotho; Fides.

Scrolls falling from the sky portend Hannibal's invasion of Italy (Plut. 10.2).

SCULPTOR

(See **Statue.**)

SCYTHE

(See also **Sickle.**)

Attribute of Saturnus.

HERACLES takes Daphnis' place in a reaping contest to save him from defeat and the loss of his beloved Pimplea (Serv. *ad Ecl.* 8.68).

SEA

(See also **Castaway; Falling; Leaping; Ship; Swimming; Water.**)

CRONUS throws Ouranos' genitals into the sea, producing the sea foam from which Aphrodite is formed (Hes. *Theog.* 188f; *Met.* 4.536f).

EUPHEMUS, the world's fastest human, can run over the sea (*Argo.* 1.179f; *Fab.* 14).

ORION walks on the sea (*Lib.* 1.4.3) or through it (*Aen.* 10.763f).

SEA ANIMAL

(See **Dragon; Horse** [Of the sea]; **Snake.**)

SEA DEITY

A sea deity's characteristics and attributes are variable but indicate that the sea is their element. Triton and Tritons usually, Glaucus frequently, are represented as having fish tails. For the most part, they may be found elsewhere under more pertinent headings. The names of the important sea deities, other than those listed below, are Amphitrite, Glaucus, Nereus, Nereus' daughters (Nereïds), Palaemon, Poseidon, Proteus, and Thetis.

TRITON WITH HIS RUDDER AND CONCH

EIDOTHEA converses with Menelaüs while his men are trying to catch fish (*Od.* 4.363f).

GALATEA rejects the jealous Cyclops Polyphemus in favor of Acis (*Met.* 13.738f).

LEUCOTHEA (Ino) provides Odysseus with a veil to keep him afloat after his raft breaks up (*Od.* 5.333f).

OCEANUS, carried by a bird of some sort, visits Prometheus (Aes. *Prom.* 285f).

TRITON attacks some bathers, who are saved when Dionysus fights him off; Triton is lured ashore by a bowl of wine and beheaded by the men whose cattle he has stolen (Paus. 9.20.4).

SEA FOAM

Attribute of Aphrodite.

Formed from the genitals of Ouranos, which Cronus has thrown into the sea, gives birth to Aphrodite (Hes. *Theog.* 188f; *Met.* 4.536f).

SEAL, SEA LION

Attribute of Proteus.

Emerging from the sea, terrifies HIPPOLYTUS' horses (Serv. *ad Aen.* 6.445, 7.761).

Changing into a seal, PSAMATHE tries to avoid the advances of Aeacus (*Lib.* 3.12.6).

Concealed in seal skins provided by Eidothea, MENELAÜS et al. wait for Proteus and his herd of seals to come from the sea; when he does, they seize him (*Od.* 4.435f).

SEA MONSTER

(See **Dragon; Snake.**)

SEASHORE

(See also **Castaway; Corpse; Grieving; Ship; Swimming.**)

NAUSICAÄ and her companions are playing ball on the shore when Odysseus approaches, holding a branch to cover his nakedness (*Od.* 6.127f).

SEATED FIGURE

(See also **Altar; Chair; Throne.**)

ALEXANDER sits on the throne of Darius (Plut. 33.37).

EILEITHYIA, sitting with legs crossed and fingers laced, delays Alcmene's delivery of Heracles (*Met.* 9.292f).

HERA is held fast by invisible cords on a throne built by Hephaestus (*Fab.* 166; Serv. *ad Aen.* 8.454); Dionysus brings Hephaestus to Olympus to release her (Paus. 1.20.2).

OLYMPIAS, on a birthing stool, is delivered of Alexander while Nectanebos explains the constellations (Ps.-Cal. 25).

PENELOPE and a beggar (Odysseus) sit by the fire (*Od.* 19.53f, 19.100f); she sits before the beggar and Telemachus (*Od.* 23.85f, 23.164f).

A STRANGER in royal regalia sits on Alexander's throne while he is playing ball with friends (Plut. 33.73).

TARQUIN, after assembling the senate, seats himself in the seat of old King Servius Tullius, who confronts him angrily (Livy 1.48).

THESEUS and PEIRITHOÜS are bound by snakes to the Seat of Forgetfulness in the underworld (*Ep.* 1.24).

A YOUNG MAN is made by Cambyses to sit as judge on a chair covered with his father's skin (Herod. 5.25; Val. Max. 6.36.3).

SEAWEED

As hair: attribute of Nereus; Oceanus; Phorcys; Proteus; Triton.

SEDUCTION

(See also **Bed; Captive; Flight; Sleeping Figure.**)

Since pictorial distinctions between courting, lovemaking (licit or illicit), seduction weakly resisted, rape, and incest are unreliable, any scene that appears to reveal sexual interest or to be leading to sexual activity of some kind may be found under this single, imprecise euphemism.

When there is neither distinctiveness nor pictorial interest in the act of seduction and it has been recorded only for a genealogical purpose, it will not be included here. For the names of nearly all of those with whom the gods and heroes casually consorted, consult a classical dictionary, the indexes to Apollodorus and Hesiod in the Loeb editions, and the Preface to Hyginus' *Fabulae.*

BY A GOD

Seduced by Apollo. CHIONE, who is also visited during the same night by Hermes (*Fab.* 200). CREÜSA, in a cave below the Acropolis (Eur. *Ion* 8f). In the form of a wolf, he seduces the huntress CYRENE (Serv. *ad Aen.* 4.377); of a shepherd, ISSE (*Met.* 6.124); of a snake, DRYOPE (Ant. Lib. 32); of an old woman, LEUCOTHOË; interrupting her at her spinning, he wins her confidence, then resumes his divine form (*Met.* 4.229; cf. *Met.* 11.309f, where he works the same stratagem on Chione).

By Ares. ALTHAEA, who is also visited by Oeneus on the same night (*Fab.* 171). APHRODITE, observed by Helius; the lovers are later trapped in bed by Hephaestus' golden net, to the amusement of the other gods (*Od.* 8.266f; *Met.* 4.171f; *Fab.* 148f). Sleeping RHEA SILVIA (Ilia) (*Fasti* 3.11f; Plut. 2.4; Livy 1.4).

By Dionysus. AURA, after Aphrodite stops her from running away from him (Nonnus 48.260) or when Dionysus drugs her wine (Nonnus 48.599f). In the form of a bunch of grapes, he makes ERIGONE pregnant (*Met.* 6.125).

By Hermes. APEMOSYNE, after she falls as she tries to run away from him (*Lib.* 3.2.1). APHRODITE, when she comes to retrieve her sandal (*Poet. Astr.* 2.16). CHIONE, after he puts her to sleep with his wand (*Met.* 11.307f). HERSE, after he turns to stone her jealous sister Aglauros because she has been keeping him from Herse's chamber (*Met.* 2.819f). LARA, while he is leading her to the underworld (*Fasti* 2.599f). POLYMELE, whom he has seen dancing with Artemis and other maidens (*Il.* 16.181f). In the form of a goat, he seduces PENELOPE; Pan is the result (Serv. *ad Aen.* 2.44).

By Poseidon. AETHRA, after Aegeus has already lain with her (*Lib.* 3.15.7); AMYMONE, a water nymph, after he drives off a lustful Satyr (*Fab.* 169, 170; *Lib.* 2.1.4). CAENIS, while she is walking alone on the seashore, after which he grants her wish to become a man (*Met.* 12.195f). A FURY (Demeter), the offspring of which union is the horse Arion (*Lib.* 3.6.8). MEDUSA, a beautiful nymph, before Athena's statue in her shrine, whereupon the goddess turns Medusa's hair into snakes (*Met.* 4.798f). In the form of a horse, he seduces DEMETER (*Met.* 6.118); of a bird, MEDUSA (*Met.* 6.119); of a dolphin, MELANTHO (*Met.* 6.120); of a ram, THEOPHANE (a sheep) (*Fab.* 188); of a river god, sleeping TYRO (*Met.* 6.133; *Lib.* 1.9.8; *Od.* 11.235f).

By Zeus. ALCMENE; during the same night her husband Amphitryon also comes to her (Hes. *Sh. Her.* 30f). The huntress CALLISTO, whom jealous Hera then turns into a bear (*Fab.* 177). IO, after he thwarts her escape by enveloping her in mist; at Hera's approach, he changes her into a heifer (*Met.* 1.588f; *Fab.* 145). MAIA, in a cave, while Hera is asleep (*H. to Her.* 5f). METIS, even though she assumes various shapes in an effort to escape (*Lib.* 1.3.6; Hes. *Theog.* 886f). In the form of fire, he seduces AEGINA (*Lib.* 3.12.6; *Fab.* 52; *Met.* 6.113); of her husband Amphitryon, ALCMENE (*Lib.* 2.4.8; *Fab.* 29); of a Satyr, ANTIOPE (*Met.* 6.110); of Artemis, the huntress CALLISTO (*Met.* 2.425f); of a shower of gold, DANAË, in her prison (*Fab.* 63; *Met.* 4.610f, 6.113; *Lib.* 2.4. See also Pind. *Isth.* 7.5–7, where in similar form he visits Alcmene); of a snake, DEOIDA (*Met.* 6.114); of a cuckoo, HERA, during a storm (Paus. 2.17.4, 2.36.2; Schol. on Theocritus 15.64); of a swan, LEDA (*Lib.* 3.10.7; *Fab.* 76) and NEMESIS (*Poet. Astr.* 2.8; cf. *Lib.* 3.10.7, where Nemesis has the form of a goose); of a shepherd, MNEMOSYNE (*Met.* 6.114).

By others. ACHELOÜS, a river god, seduces Perimele (*Met.* 8.592f); AMMON, Amaltheia (Diod. Sic. 3.68.1–2); BOREAS, as mist, Oreithyia (*Argo.* 1.216f); the river god CEPHISUS, Liriope (*Met.* 3.342f); CRIMISSUS, as a dog or bear, Egesta (Serv. *ad Aen.* 1.550); CRONUS, Philyra; detected by Rhea, he runs away in the form of a horse (*Argo.* 2.1232f; cf. *Fab.* 138, where he effects the seduction in the form of a horse); two-faced JANUS, Crane (Carna), who is unable to steal away undetected from one who can see behind him as well as before (*Fasti* 6.107f); NILUS (the Nile), Callirrhoë, an Oceanid (Serv. *ad Aen.* 4.250); PAN, Selene, whose favors he wins with the gift of a fleece (*Georg.* 3.391f); the river STRYMON, the Muse Euterpe (*Lib.* 1.3.3; Eur. *Rhes.* 351f, 919f); VERTUMNUS, Pomona, after he, in the form of an elderly woman, has persuaded her of his virtues (*Met.* 14.643f); ZEPHYRUS, Chloris (Flora), after a chase (*Fasti* 5.201f).

BY A MORTAL MALE

ACHILLES, dressed as a girl, seduces Deïdameia (*Lib.* 3.13.8); ADONIS, aided by Aphrodite, Erinome (Serv. *ad Ecl.* 10.18); AMPHITRYON, his wife Alcmene, after she has already been visited by Zeus (Hes. *Sh. Her.* 30f); the shepherd ANCHISES, Aphrodite (*Lib.* 3.12.2); the shepherd ATTIS, Sagaritis, a tree nymph, thereby breaking his oath of chastity (*Fasti* 4.221f); IASION, Demeter in a plowed field, for which he is killed by a thunderbolt (Hes. *Theog.* 969; *Lib.* 3.12.2; *Od.* 5.125f); IXION, a cloud resembling Hera (*Fab.* 62; *Ep.* 1.20); MINOS, Procris, winning her with the gift of a dog and a spear (*Lib.* 3.15.1); women (unnamed), who are attacked by snakes or wild animals emerging from Minos' body (Ant. Lib. 41; *Lib.* 3.15.1); the Egyptian sorcerer NECTANEBOS, Olympias, on whom he begets Alexander (Ps.-Cal. 13); ORION, Merope, for which her father Oenopion blinds him (*Lib.* 1.4.3); PARIS, Helen, after Aphrodite leads her to his bed (*Il.* 3.437f), and on the island of Cranaë (*Il.* 3.442f); PELEUS, Thetis, after grasping her while she is asleep and holding her fast through various transformations (*Met.* 11.235f); PHOENIX, his father's concubine, at his mother's instigation (*Il.* 9.449f; *Lib.* 3.13.8); PTELEON, Procris, with the gift of a gold crown (*Lib.* 3.15.1); a THESSALIAN YOUTH, Coronis, even though she is loved by Apollo; a white bird watches the pair (*Met.* 2.598f); THYESTES, Aërope, in her sleep; he makes off with the prized golden fleece or lamb of her husband Atreus (Eur. *Elec.* 717f). (See also **By a God,** above.)

Marriage, consummated in a cave, of AENEAS and DIDO (*Aen.* 4.123f, 4.165f); of HIPPOMENES and ATALANTA (*Met.* 10.689f); of JASON and MEDEA (*Argo.* 4.1128f; *Fab.* 23).

Rape by CLYMENUS of his daughter Harpalyce (*Fab.* 206); by EPOPEUS of his daughter Nyctimene (*Fab.* 204); by a MACEDONIAN SOLDIER of Timoclea (Plut. 33.12); by POLYTECHNUS of his wife's sister Chelidonis (Ant. Lib. 11); by SEXTUS TARQUINIUS of Lucretia, whom he threatens with his sword (Livy 1.58; *Fasti* 2.792f); by SISYPHUS of his niece Tyro (*Fab.* 60); by TEREUS of Philomela, after which he cuts out her tongue (*Met.* 6.519f, 6.555f; *Lib.* 3.14.8; *Fab.* 45); by THYESTES of Pelopia while she is washing a garment; he does not know that she is his daughter (*Ep.* 2.14; *Fab.* 87, 88).

Seduction evaded by women. Old ANNA PERENNA, dressed as a bride, mocks Ares when he lifts her veil, expecting to find Athena (*Fasti* 3.677f). ARTEMIS repels Orion with an arrow (*Fab.* 195). ATHENA fights off Hephaestus; his seed produces a snake (*Poet. Astr.* 2.13), a baby (*Lib.* 3.14.6), or a baby with snakes for legs (*Fab.* 116). CASSANDRA rejects Apollo's advances (*Fab.* 93). DEMETER is rescued from Iasion when he is hit by a thunderbolt (*Lib.* 3.12.1). EURYTE is rescued from Halirrhothius by Ares (*Lib.* 3.14.2). HERA is rescued from the Giant Porphyrion by Zeus' bolt and Heracles' arrow (*Lib.* 1.6.2). HIPPODAMEIA fights off the charioteer Myrtilus when Pelops leaves her to fetch water (*Ep.* 2.8). LETO is saved from the Giant Tityos by Zeus' bolt and the arrows of Artemis and Apollo (*Fab.* 55). LOTIS, awakened by Silenus' braying ass, repels Priapus, who has stolen upon her (*Fasti* 1.415f; cf. *Fasti* 6.319f, where Vesta is the object of Priapus' lust). OLYMPIAS is rescued from Pausanias by Alexander (Ps.-Cal. 68). SINOPE thwarts the lust of Zeus and Apollo by demanding inviolable virginity as the boon they have promised to her (*Argo.* 2.949f). The YOUNG MAIDEN who becomes the Cumaean Sibyl rejects Apollo's advances despite the gifts offered (*Met.* 14.130f).

BY A MORTAL OR DIVINE FEMALE

APHRODITE seduces the hunter Adonis (*Met.* 10.554f), the herdsman Anchises (*H. to Aph.* 53f), Ares (q.v. above), and Hephaestus, to get him to make armor for Aeneas (*Aen.* 8.370f). EOS carries off Tithonus to be her lover (*H. to Aph.* 218f). HERA, wearing Aphrodite's magic belt, beguiles Zeus; their lovemaking is concealed in a golden mist (*Il.* 14.292f, 14.342f). MYRRHA's (Smyrna's) passion for her father is abetted by her nurse, who leads her to his bed even though an owl warns of the dire result (*Met.* 10.452f; *Fab.* 58; *Lib.* 3.14.4). NYCTIMENE invades her father's bed and is changed into an owl (*Met.* 2.589f). The nymph PEGAE, smitten by the beauty of Hylas, who has come for water, draws him into her pool (*Argo.* 1.1221f).

PROCRIS, disguised as a hunter, lures her estranged husband Cephalus to his bedroom with the promise of a hunting dog and spear; she reveals herself to him and they are reconciled (*Fab.* 189). The nymph SALMACIS embraces Hermaphroditus like a snake in or beside her pool until their bodies become one (*Met.* 4.317f). SELENE makes love to eternally sleeping Endymion (*Lib.* 1.7.5; *Argo.* 4.57f; Cic. *Tusc.* 1.38). A WOMAN (Echidna?), who from the buttocks downward is a snake, seduces Heracles by promising to return his mares (Herod. 4.9).

Seduction vainly attempted by EOS, of the hunter Cephalus (*Fab.* 189); by PHAEDRA, of her stepson Hippolytus, whereupon she informs her husband Theseus that his son has raped her (*Met.* 15.500f; *Fab.* 47; cf. Eur. *Hipp.* 565f, in which Phaedra hangs herself when her passion for Hippolytus is revealed to him and she falsely accuses him to Theseus in a letter found in her hand); [after a similar rebuff, ANTEIA, or Stheneboea, according to *Lib.* 2.3.1, falsely accuses Bellerophon to Proetus (*Il.* 6.160f); DEMODICE (Biadice) accuses Phrixus to Cretheus (*Poet. Astr.* 2.20); and PHILONOME accuses Tenes to Cycnus (*Ep.* 3.24)]; by PHRYNE of the philosopher Xenocrates (Val. Max. 4.3 ext. 3).

SERPENT

(See **Dragon; Monster; Snake.**)

SHADE

(See **Phantom; Underworld.**)

SHEEP

(See also **Altar; Ram; Shepherd; Shepherdess.**)

Black: attribute of Pluto.

A lamb comes from the vessel in which MEDEA has cooked an old ram (*Lib.* 1.9.27).

A golden-fleeced lamb is stolen from its mother by Pan and presented to ATREUS (Eur. *Elec.* 699f); he strangles it and places it in a box; his wife Aërope gives the box to his brother Thyestes, who produces it before the people to prove his claim to the throne of Mycenae (*Ep.* 2.11).

Changed into a sheep. Poseidon changes THEOPHANE into a ewe, himself into a ram, and the local people into cattle to deceive the suitors who are searching for Theophane (*Fab.* 188).

Are sheared by MELUS, the first man to use wool for garments (Serv. *ad Ecl.* 8.37).

Are slaughtered by mad AJAX (*Fab.* 107).

Are tended by POLYPHEMUS and his dog; are targets of apples thrown by Galatea (Theocritus 6).

Carry ODYSSEUS and his men suspended beneath them from the cave of Polyphemus (*Od.* 9.425f).

Drag brush to raise dust to allow ALEXANDER's MEN to escape from an enemy force (Ps.-Cal. 173).

SHELL

As a seagoing vessel: attribute of Aphrodite. Equipped with paddle wheels: Amphitrite; Galatea; Venus. Drawn by Hippocampi: Amphitrite; Poseidon.

Used as a musical instrument (see **Conch**).

SHEPHERD

(See also **Sheep.**)

APOLLO, in the guise of a shepherd, seduces Isse (*Met.* 6.124).

ARISTAEUS is put in charge of the Muses' flock (*Argo.* 2.511f).

ATTIS, disguised as a shepherd, seduces Sagaritis (*Fasti* 4.221f).

DAPHNIS is turned to stone by a jealous nymph (*Met.* 4.276f).

HESIOD is given a laurel staff and the power of song by the Muses (Hes. *Theog.* 22f).

PARIS considers the bribes offered by Athena and Hera for the golden apple, but then awards it to Aphrodite (*Fab.* 92; *Ep.* 3.2).

SHEPHERDESS

CYRENE is carried off by Apollo (*Argo.* 2.500f).

SHIELD

(See also **Aegis; Arms and Armor; Fighting; Warrior.**)

Attribute of Aphrodite Victrix; Apollo; Furor; Mars; Victoria. Round, with a Gorgon's face on it: Athena. With thunderbolt device: Juno.

With identifying device. Such decoration is common but seldom recorded by poets. Therefore it is infrequently a clue to the identity of the bearer. Apollodorus mentions that a boar and a lion device identifies the shields of Polyneices and Tydeus, respectively (*Lib.* 3.6.1). The devices of the Seven Against Thebes are given as follows by Aeschylus and Euripides:

Warriors' names	Aeschylus (*Seven* 377f)	Euripides (*Phoen.* 1105f)
Adrastus	(not in Aeschylus)	snakes
Amphiaraüs	(no device)	(no device)
Capaneus	man carrying fire	a Giant
Eteoclus	man on a ladder	(not in Euripides)
Hippomedon	fiery monster	many-eyed Argus
Parthenopaeus	Sphinx and her victim	Atalanta and boar
Polyneices	Dike and a warrior	horses
Tydeus	moon and stars	lion skin and torch

Elaborately decorated. Is made by Hephaestus for ACHILLES and presented to him by Thetis (*Il.* 18.478f); for AENEAS, presented by Aphrodite (*Aen.* 8.626f); for HERACLES (Hes. *Sh. Her.* 139f).

Providing shelter. The ARGONAUTS huddle beneath their shields when the Stymphalian birds attack (*Argo.* 2.1082f). Fallen ODYSSEUS is protected by Ajax's shield (*Met.* 13.73f).

Being struck by the ARGONAUTS in order to drown out ill-omened noise as they sacrifice to Rhea (*Argo.* 1.1132f), to stir up the Stymphalian birds (*Argo.* 2.1080), and to scare them away (*Fab.* 20); by the CURETES to drown out the cries of baby Zeus (*Lib.* 1.1.7; *Fab.* 139).

Thrown by invading SABINES on the girl Tarpeia in ironic payment for admitting them to the Roman citadel (Plut. 2.17; Livy 1.11; *Met.* 14.776f).

Causing flight. The sight of the terrible shield of ABAS is enough to make warriors flee (Serv. *ad Aen.* 3.286).

Used to signal from a ship by AENEAS as he returns with reinforcements to the Trojan camp (*Aen.* 10.260f); by LYSANDER to start the naval battle of Aegospotami (Plut. 23.11).

Affixed to a pillar. AENEAS has great Abas' shield displayed, with an appropriate inscription (*Aen.* 3.286f).

Seized by a girl. ACHILLES, dressed as a girl (see **Girl**).

Made of the skin of the Giant Pallas is used by ATHENA in the fight between gods and Giants (*Lib.* 1.6.2).

In the sky. One falls from the sky before NUMA, portending Rome's greatness (Plut. 2.13; *Fasti* 3.371f; *Aen.* 8.664 and Serv. ad loc.).

Used as sleds by the CIMBRI to slide down Alpine slopes (Plut. 22.23).

SHIP

(See also **Boat; Castaway; Oar; Raft; Sail.**)

Since we are seldom told whether a ship is under sail or is being rowed, we must assume it may be either. The prow and ram of a ship are an attribute of Saturn.

BEING BUILT	ATHENA, builder of the first ship (*Fab.* 168), supervises Argus, builder of the *Argo,* and fits a speaking plank into it (*Argo.* 1.18f, 1.111f; *Lib.* 1.9.16). A ship is built to carry CYBELE's statue to Rome (*Fasti* 4.273f). DANAÜS builds a ship in which to escape from Egypt with his fifty daughters (*Lib.* 2.1.4). PROMETHEUS teaches man to build ships (Aes. *Prom.* 467f). TROJAN SUR-VIVORS build ships to carry them to a new home (*Aen.* 3.5f).
BEACHED, MOORED, STRANDED	ACHILLES sits beside his ships weeping for Patroclus and is consoled by Thetis and other Nereïds (*Il.* 18.65f; cf. *Il.* 1.349, where ships are not mentioned). APOLLO leaps aboard the Cretan vessel that has brought him to Krisa and enrolls the crew as custodians of his shrine (*H. to Ap.* 448f). ARCHIMEDES launches a ship by means of pulleys (Plut. 16.14). The ARGONAUTS, playing games on the beach by their ship, are visited by Thetis (*Argo.* 4.852f); they carry the *Argo* across the Libyan desert when it becomes stranded (*Argo.* 4.1235f) and arrive at the tree of the Hesperides after Heracles has left with its apples (*Argo.* 4.1396). CHARICLEIA finds dead and wounded sailors, one of them Theagenes, on a beach by their ships, as Ethiopian pirates approach (*Aeth.* 1). The GREEK FLEET is beached at Troy, and its protecting wall is assaulted by Hector et al. (*Il.* 7.433f, 14.27, 15.405, 15.704f, 16.114f; see also **Wall**).
DEPARTING	AENEAS and the refugee Trojans depart from Antandros (*Aen.* 3.5f); from Delos (*Aen.* 3.124); from Thrace (*Aen.* 3.169f); from Crete (*Aen.* 3.190f); from the Harpies (q.v. and *Aen.* 3.266f); from Actium (*Aen.* 3.289); from Buthrotum (*Aen.* 3.472f); from Etna (*Aen.* 3.666f); from Carthage (see "In flight," below); from Sicily (*Aen.* 1.34, 5.770f); from Cumae (*Aen.* 7.5f). ASCLEPIUS, in the form of a snake, leads his devotees aboard a ship (*Met.* 15.685f). The GREEKS sail away from Troy, only to hide behind Tenedos (*Aen.* 2.24f). SILENUS et al. row off to search for Dionysus (Eur. *Cycl.* 10f).

Preparation for. AGAMEMNON, as he is about to sail from Troy, is visited by the ghost of Achilles (*Nostoi* 1). ALEXANDER pours a libation from the bow before leaving India (Arrian 6.3.1). DANAÜS' DAUGHTERS are stopped by King Pelasgus from obeying a herald's order to return with him to Egypt (Aes. *Suppl.* 835f). MENELAÜS prepares to leave Troy for home with Helen et al. (Paus. 10.25.2). PARIS makes off with Helen, who takes much of her property with her (*Ep.* 3.3). The PHAEACIANS load the ship that will carry Odysseus home (*Od.* 8.34f; 13.70f). PIRATES, after loading Hera's statue aboard, find that their ship refuses to move (Athenaeus 15). TELE-MACHUS et al. load a ship under Mentor's (Athena's) direction before going in search of Odysseus (*Od.* 2.405f); while he is sacrificing before setting off for home, he is joined by fugitive Theoclymenus, whom he takes aboard (*Od.* 15.222f).

With farewells. AENEAS et al. take leave of Helenus and Andromache, now a priestess, as they set off to Italy (*Aen.* 3.472f) and of King Acestes and those Trojans who elect to stay behind in Sicily (*Aen.* 5.765f). CEŸX leaves his grief-stricken wife Alcyone (*Met.* 11.457f). HIPPOTES sends his daughter away from Troy to save her from being sacrificed to a sea monster (Serv. *ad Aen.* 1.550). JASON AND THE ARGONAUTS, to the acclaim of gods and fami-lies, launch the *Argo* and set off under oar before hoisting sail (*Argo.* 1.363f, 1.524f); they leave the women of Lemnos grieving at their departure (*Argo.* 2.878f). ODYSSEUS et al. take leave of Circe after receiving her gift of a ram and a ewe (*Od.* 10.569f, 11.1f). PHILOMELA takes ship with Tereus, leaving her aged father (*Met.* 6.504f).

Deserting a lover. AENEAS fails to slip out of Carthage undetected and leaves Dido distraught at his faithlessness (*Aen.* 4.584f); he sees the flames of her pyre from the sea (*Aen.* 5.1f). THESEUS sails away while Ariadne sleeps (*Fab.* 43; Cat. 64.122f) or is carried to sea by a squall while pregnant Ariadne is ashore in the care of local women (Plut. 1.20).

In flight. DAEDALUS and ICARUS escape in small sailboats from Minos' galleys (Paus. 9.11.3). DANAÜS flees from Egypt with his fifty daughters (*Lib.* 2.1.4). DIDO and her followers escape from Tyre and her evil brother Pygmalion (*Aen.* 1.360f). JASON AND THE ARGONAUTS escape Aeëtes' efforts to detain them and are pursued by him (*Argo.* 4.206), but they get away when Aeëtes stops to retrieve pieces of his son's body that his daughter Medea has thrown overboard (*Lib.* 1.9.24). MENELAÜS et al. escape from Egypt with Helen by overcoming the ship's crew, whom they have tricked into taking them aboard (Eur. *Hel.* 1526f). ODYSSEUS' fleet, after a battle on shore, escapes from the Cicones (*Od.* 9.60f). ORESTES, PYLADES, and IPHIGENEIA, who carries a statue of Artemis, forcibly commandeer a galley and escape from Tauris (Eur. *Iph. Taur.* 1345f; cf. *Fab.* 120, which does not mention a fight). PARIS and HELEN flee by night (*Cypria* 1, in Proclus). THESEUS et al. escape from Crete with Ariadne (*Met.* 8.174f). TROJAN SHIPS put to sea in haste when Polyphemus and other Cyclopes appear (*Aen.* 3.666f). (See also **Under Attack,** below.)

With captives. ANTIOPE, Queen of the Amazons, is lured aboard and carried off by Theseus (Plut. 1.26). ARIADNE is taken away from Theseus by Dionysus and a large force (Paus. 10.29.2). Young DIONYSUS is carried off by pirates (*H. to Dion.* 6f; *Lib.* 3.5.3; *Met.* 3.605f). EUROPA is carried off by Greek sailors (Herod. 1.2). HELEN elopes with Paris (*Ep.* 3.3). Io et al., attracted by the wares of Phoenician traders, are carried off by them (Herod. 1.1). MEDEA is carried off by Greek sailors (Herod. 1.2). ODYSSEUS' CREW-MEN, who have eaten lotus ashore, have to be dragged back aboard (*Od.* 9.98f). THESEUS and other Athenian boys and girls are carried off, as tribute to Crete (*Ep.* 1.7), by Minos himself (Plut. 1.17).

Without a crew. MELIBOEA goes aboard a ship that carries her to her lover Alexis (Serv. *ad Aen.* 1.720). TROJAN SHIPS launch themselves from the beach to escape fire, and become water nymphs (*Aen.* 9.117f; *Met.* 14.546f). TURNUS chases a phantom of Aeneas aboard a ship that Hera then sends to sea (*Aen.* 10.636f).

ARRIVING

ADMETE brings a statue of Hera to Samos (Athenaeus 15). AENEAS leads seven of his ships to shelter in Libya, where the crews refresh themselves on the beach (*Aen.* 1.170f); he leads the Trojan refugees to Delos and a welcome by the aged priest Anius (*Aen.* 3.78f); to the city of Buthrotum and a welcome from Andromache and Helenus (*Aen.* 3.293f); to their landfall in Italy, where they see four horses near a shrine (*Aen.* 3.531f); to the shore below Etna, where they find a man Odysseus left behind in his hurried departure (*Aen.* 3.570f); to Sicily and a welcome by Acestes, who wears a bearskin (*Aen.* 5.35f); to Cumae, where they leap ashore (*Aen.* 6.5f); and to the Tiber, where they feast ashore (*Aen.* 7.25f). AGRIPPINA, carrying the ashes of Germanicus, lands at Brundisium with his children, to the welcome of a huge crowd (Tac. *An.* 3.1). ALEXANDER rides ashore and is welcomed by his soldiers, who had believed him dead (Arrian 6.13.1). APOLLO leaps ashore to his shrine at Krisa (*H. to Ap.* 440f). The ARGONAUTS are met at the beach of Lemnos by armed women, who later bring gifts and welcome them ashore (*Argo.* 1.633f, 1.842f); they rescue the shipwrecked sons of Phrixus (*Argo.* 2.1102f). ASCLEPIUS, in the form of a serpent, disembarks at Rome and resumes divine form (*Met.* 15.736f). BRUTUS kisses the earth on disembarking, in order to fulfill his interpretation of an oracle (Serv. *ad Aen.* 3.96). CLEOPATRA, in sumptuous style, comes to meet Anthony in the Cydnus River (Plut. 44.26). An EGYPTIAN HERALD arrives to demand the return of the daughters of Danaüs (Aes. *Suppl.* 712f). The GREEK FLEET gathers at Aulis (Eur. *Iph. Aul.* 231f); it returns by night from Tenedos to Troy when summoned by a signal light (*Aen.* 2.254f). ODYSSEUS returns the girl Chryseïs to her father, a priest of Apollo (*Il.* 1.438f); he and his men find shelter and rest at Circe's island (*Od.* 10.140f, 12.1f) and at Trinacria (*Od.* 12.304f); he is carried while asleep by a Phaeacian ship to Ithaca and laid on the sand, with his presents set beneath an olive tree (*Od.* 13.116f). ORESTES and PYLADES wade ashore at Tauris and are made prisoners by herdsmen (Eur. *Iph. Taur.* 240f). PARIS and HELEN (perhaps only her phantom) arrive at Troy (*Ep.* 3.3.5; Eur. *Hel.* 31f, 582); are driven by a storm to the temple of Heracles in Egypt (Herod. 2.113). POMPEY lands at Mytilene where he finds his grief-stricken wife Cornelia (Plut. 32.74); he is murdered while being ferried to the shore of Egypt, as Cornelia watches from the ship that brought them (Plut. 32.79). PROTESILAÜS is the first Greek to leap ashore at Troy and to be killed (*Il.* 2.701f). THEOPHANE's SUITORS land to rescue her from Poseidon; she becomes a ewe, he a ram, and the suitors wolves (*Fab.* 188). THESEUS returns home in a ship with a black sail; on seeing it, his father leaps to his death (Plut. 1.22; *Ep.* 1.10; *Fab.* 43).

PASSING THE SHORE OR A HAZARD

AENEAS' two galleys are rowed up the Tiber to Pallanteum, where he is welcomed by Evander, after having been challenged by Pallas (*Aen.* 8.86f); they return to the Trojan camp as Aeneas signals with his shield (*Aen.* 10.290f). The ARGO passes the Centaur Cheiron, who wades into the water to wave as his wife holds up the baby Achilles for Peleus to see (*Argo.* 1.553f); it passes the ghost of Sthenelus standing by his tomb in full armor (*Argo.* 2.915f); it passes between the Clashing Rocks, preceded by a dove and helped with a push by Athena (*Argo.* 2.317f, 2.555f; *Fab.* 19; *Lib.* 1.9.22); it is rowed into a river where the Golden Fleece hangs (*Argo.* 2.1264f); it delivers Jason to the field where he is to harness fire-breathing bulls (*Argo.* 3.1278f); it is guided and lifted past Scylla and Charybdis by Nereïds (*Argo.* 4.930f); it is directed to the proper course by Hera's shout from a crag (*Argo.* 4.604f); it is saved from the giant Talos when Medea, by incantation, causes him to bleed to death (*Argo.* 4.1638f). CARMENTIS, from a ship, points out the future site of Rome to her son Evander (*Fasti* 1.499f). CHARICLEIA, dressed as Artemis, shoots from a ship at pirates fighting on shore (*Aeth.* 5). CLAUDIA tows free from a sandbank a ship carrying a statue of Cybele, thereby proving her chastity (*Fasti* 4.297f). ODYSSEUS, tied to the mast, is carried past the Sirens (*Od.* 12.177f); six of his men are plucked from the ship by the monster Scylla (*Od.* 12.244f). SERGESTUS, during a boat race, steers too close to the turning mark, shatters his oars, and runs aground (*Aen.* 5.202f).

ODYSSEUS PASSING THE SIRENS

UNDER ATTACK

Stones are hurled at ACHILLES' ship by Tenes to prevent his landing (*Ep.* 3.26); at the *Argo* by gigantic, brazen Talos (*Argo.* 4.1638f; *Lib.* 1.9.26); at the GREEK ARMADA by the Trojans (*Ep.* 3.29); at HERACLES' ship by the people of Cos (*Lib.* 2.7.1); at ODYSSEUS' departing ships by the Laestrygonians (*Od.* 10.121f; *Met.* 14.239f); and at his single remaining vessel by Polyphemus (*Od.* 9.436f, 9.480f).

AFIRE OR THREATENED BY FIRE

CALETOR is about to fire Ajax's ship when Ajax kills him (*Il.* 15.419f). HECTOR calls for fire as he grasps a Greek ship (*Il.* 15.704f). LYSANDER has the Athenian ships burned to the music of flute girls (Plut. 23.15). TROJANS fire a Greek ship when Ajax retreats (*Il.* 16.122f). TROJAN WOMEN set fire to their Greek captors' ships (*Ep.* 6.15c) and to their own ships when incited by Iris in the form of one of their number; Zeus sends rain to quench it when Aeneas appeals to him (*Aen.* 5.618f). TURNUS et al. are about to fire beached Trojan ships when they miraculously launch themselves and become sea nymphs (*Aen.* 9.69f; *Met.* 14.530f). TYRIANS, by means of a fire ship, destroy Alexander's assault tower (Arrian 2.19.1f).

AT SEA

ACHATES is the first of Aeneas' crew to sight Italy, upon which Anchises pours a libation to the gods (*Aen.* 3.521f). APOLLO shoots the helmsman of Menelaüs' ship (*Od.* 3.278f); in the form of a dolphin, he leaps aboard a Cretan ship that carries him to Krisa (*H. to Ap.* 397f). ARION attracts dolphins with his lyre and singing to the ship whose crew is threatening him (Herod. 1.24). DAEDALUS, escaping from Crete with Icarus, spreads his robe to the wind as a sail (Serv. *ad Aen.* 6.14). DIONYSUS causes vines and ivy to entwine the pirate vessel on which he is being kidnapped (*H. to Dion.* 38f; *Lib.* 3.5.3; *Met.* 3.662f). HELIUS, with his horses, is nightly transported in a golden goblet or bowl from his setting to his rising (Pherecydes, quoted in Athenaeus 9.39); he lends his vessel to HERACLES to transport Geryon's cattle (*Lib.* 2.5.10; Hes. *Theog.* 289f). MEDEA throws pieces of her brother from the *Argo* to delay her father's pursuit (*Lib.* 1.9.24). MENELAÜS et al. slaughter their Egyptian crew and escape with Helen, under the protection of her brothers Castor and Polydeuces (Eur. *Hel.* 1590f, 1642f). PALINURUS steers during a night passage while Aeneas sleeps; Aeneas steers after Sleep pushes Palinurus overboard (*Aen.* 5.513f, 5.833f, 5.867f). The PHAEACIAN ship that has carried Odysseus home is turned into a craggy islet by Poseidon (*Od.* 13.161f).

FIGURES LEAPING OVERBOARD	***Leaping or diving.*** ARION leaps to the back of the dolphin he has summoned with his lyre to escape from a murderous crew (*Fasti* 2.95f; *Fab.* 194; *Poet. Astr.* 2.17). BUTES, attracted by the Sirens ashore, dives from the *Argo* to join them but is rescued by Aphrodite (*Lib.* 1.9.25; *Argo.* 4.912f; *Fab.* 14). HECUBA leaps from Odysseus' ship and is changed into a bitch (*Fab.* 111). SAILORS leap overboard to escape from the wild beasts created by Dionysus and become dolphins (*H. to Dion.* 44f; *Lib.* 3.5.3; *Met.* 3.666f). THESEUS dives to recover a ring thrown by Minos (Bacchylides 16.52f; *Poet. Astr.* 2.5).

Thrown or pushed. MENOETES, by Gyas because he has steered too wide of a turning mark (a rock) during a race; he swims to the rock (*Aen.* 5.172f). MYRTILUS, by Pelops for claiming his right to Pelops' bride for one night (Paus. 8.14.11). PALINURUS, by Sleep, during the night while Aeneas sleeps (*Aen.* 5.857f, 6.349f). PHRONIMA, by Themison to fulfill an oath; he pulls her out again (Herod. 4.154). SCYLLA, by Minos' order, because she acted treacherously (Paus. 2.34.7).

FIGURES IN WATER NEARBY	***Sea deities giving aid.*** CYMODOCEA, one of several Naiads near Aeneas' ship, addresses him and gives the vessel a helpful shove (*Aen.* 10.215f). NEREÏDS guide the *Argo* through the whirlpool of Charybdis (*Argo.* 4.930f). PORTUNUS pushes Cloanthus' ship, enabling him to beat Mnestheus in a boat race (*Aen.* 5.238f). TRITON tows the *Argo* to the open sea (*Argo.* 4.1602f); with Cymothoë, he frees Aeneas' ships from rocks and shoals (*Aen.* 1.142f). (See also **Storm-tossed,** below.)

At the surface nearby. GLAUCUS addresses the crew of the *Argo* (*Argo.* 1.1309f) and informs Menelaüs of Agamemnon's death (Eur. *Orest.* 359f). HERACLES walks on the surface of the sea away from his stranded ship (Sen. *Her. Fur.* 344f). SCYLLA swims after Minos' ship and clings to it; she is attacked by an osprey (her father Nisus) and becomes a bird herself (*Met.*

8.142f; cf. *Lib.* 3.15.8, in which Minos ties Scylla to his ship and drowns her). THESEUS returns to Minos' ship with a ring Minos has thrown into the sea and wearing a wreath given him by Thetis (Bacchylides 16.119f). THETIS, a sea deity, attracts the love of Peleus, one of the crew of the *Argo* (Cat. 64.16f).

STORM-TOSSED

In the tide rip/whirlpool of Charybdis, AENEAS' fleet survives by turning back (*Aen.* 3.561f); the *Argo* is guided through by Nereïds (*Argo.* 4.930f), and ODYSSEUS' ship, in steering wide of this danger, loses several men to the monster Scylla (*Od.* 12.234f; see also **Raft**).

At sea. AGRIPPINA's ship breaks up, but she survives by clinging to wreckage (Tac. *An.* 14.5–8; Suet. *Nero* 34). The *Argo* meets a huge wave (*Argo.* 2.169f, 2.579f) and survives a storm when Apollo, at Jason's prayer, guides it to a harbor (*Argo.* 4.1701f). CAESAR attempts a stormy passage in a small boat (Plut. 34.44). CEŸX's ship founders and he drowns (*Met.* 11.1180f). The GREEK FLEET, homeward bound, is shattered by a storm that Agamemnon's ship survives (Aes. *Agam.* 653f); the fleet is assailed by Athena's thunderbolts and Poseidon's waves (Eur. *Troad.* 77f; *Aen.* 3.42f; Sen. *Agam.* 506f). HERACLES is driven to Cos by a storm sent by Hera (*Il.* 14.252f). ODYSSEUS' ships are caught in a storm sent by Zeus (*Od.* 9.67f), as is his remaining ship when his men open the bag of winds given him by Aeolus (*Od.* 10.47f); this other ship is dismasted and breaks up when struck by Zeus' bolt; out of the wreckage Odysseus fashions a raft (q.v.) (*Od.* 12.450f). PARIS and HELEN are driven off course to Egypt (Herod. 2.113). PHRIXUS' SONS cling to wreckage when their ship breaks up and are washed ashore (*Argo.* 2.1102f). TROJAN SHIPS are caught in a storm sent by Hera; one founders and several are driven into rocks and shoals before Poseidon calms the sea (*Aen.* 1.81f); they all survive an earlier storm (*Aen.* 3.192f).

Aground. AJAX OÏLEUS' ship is hit by Athena's bolt and driven onto rocks (*Fab.* 116; *Aen.* 1.42f; *Ep.* 6.6); it is driven ashore by Poseidon (*Od.* 4.499f), who shatters the rock to which Ajax clings (Sen. *Agam.* 506f). ANNA, Dido's sister, is wrecked on the shore of Italy, where she meets Aeneas and Achates (*Fasti* 3.601f). The GREEKS, homeward bound, are lured onto rocks by Nauplius' false beacon; Nauplius himself suffers from a similar deception (*Ep.* 6.7.11; *Fab.* 116; cf. *Lib.* 2.1.5, which does not specify ships returning from Troy). MENELAÜS is wrecked on the coast of Africa, where subsequently he finds Helen (Eur. *Hel.* 408f). TROJAN VESSELS are driven onto rocks and shoals from which they are rescued by Triton and Cymothoë (*Aen.* 1.108f).

IN BATTLE

Amphibious operations. AENEAS and the Trojans force a beachhead against Turnus' forces (*Aen.* 10.287f). ALEXANDER storms Tyre from his ships

(Arrian 2.23.1; Plut. 33.63). CAESAR'S SOLDIERS wade ashore against resistance from the Britanni (Caesar *B.G.* 4.23f). PROTESILAÜS is the first of the vast Greek force to leap ashore at Troy and to be killed (*Il.* 2.700f).

Naval battles. The ATHENIAN FLEET is defeated by the Syracusans in the harbor of Syracuse (Thucy. 7.70) and by the Spartans at Aegospotami, a defeat forecast by the appearance of the stars of the Dioscuri above the Spartan commander's vessel (Plut. 23.11, 23.12). The GREEKS and PERSIANS fight two engagements in the strait off Artemisium (Herod. 8.11, 8.16) and a final one at Salamis, where the surrounded Greeks rout the Persians as Xerxes watches from the shore (Herod. 8.84f; Plut. 7.13; Aes. *Pers.* 385f). HANNIBAL, in command of Prusias' fleet, has jars filled with snakes lobbed into Eumenes' vessels (Nep. *Han.* 10, 11). OCTAVIAN (Augustus) defeats Antony at Actium, after Cleopatra withdraws her squadron (Plut. 44.66), in a battle in which various martial deities take part (*Aen.* 8.675f). The ROMANS under the command of Duilius compensate for their naval inexperience by installing on each vessel a spiked contraption that, when lowered, holds a Carthaginian ship fast and provides a gangway on which to board it (Polybius 1.22f; Frontinus, *Strategemata* 2.3.24).

SHIRT

(See **Garment.**)

SHOE

(See also **Boot; Sandal.**)

Low: attribute of comic actors.

SHOULDER

When the gods reassemble the dismembered body of PELOPS, who has been served to them to eat, Demeter replaces the shoulder she has eaten with one made of ivory (*Ep.* 2.3 and n. 3, Loeb edn.; *Met.* 6.406f; *Fab.* 83).

Crescent-like shoulders: attribute of Lunus.

SHOUTING

A war cry uttered by ACHILLES from a rampart stems the Trojan advance (*Il.* 18.217f); by ERIS, as she brandishes a "sign of war" (*teras pole-*

moio, conjectured to be a flag, rainbow, or thunderbolt), heartens the Greeks in defense of their ships (*Il.* 11.3f); by an OLD MAN (Poseidon) rallies the Greeks (*Il.* 14.135f); by STENTOR (Hera) rallies the Greeks (*Il.* 5.784f).

SHOVEL

(See also **Hoe.**)

Used as a weapon by CELER to kill Remus when he scornfully jumps over Rome's unfinished wall that Romulus is building (*Fasti* 4.841f).

ODYSSEUS secretly buries gold in Palamedes' tent and later reveals it to Agamemnon et al. as proof of Palamedes' treason (*Fab.* 107; *Ep.* 3.8; Serv. *ad Aen.* 2.81).

SHOWER

(See **Gold; Rain; Storm.**)

SHRINE

(See **Altar; Temple; Tomb.**)

SICKLE

(See also **Scythe.**)

Attribute of Ceres; Cronus; Horae (Seasons); Pomona; Priapus; Saturnus; Vertumnus.

Used as a tool or weapon by CRONUS to castrate Ouranos; Gaea provides it (Hes. *Theog.* 161f; *Lib.* 1.1.4; Paus. 7.23.4); by HERACLES to slay the Lernean Hydra (Eur. *Ion* 190f) and to win for Daphnis a reaping contest, after which he beheads his opponent and restores to Daphnis his beloved Pimplea (Serv. *ad Ecl.* 8.68); by HERMES to behead many-eyed Argus after putting him to sleep (*Met.* 1.715); by PERSEUS to behead Medusa and to slay the sea monster threatening Andromeda (*Met.* 4.665f; *Lib.* 2.4.2); by POLYPHEMUS to trim his hair (*Met.* 13.764f); by POMONA to prune trees (*Met.* 14.623f); by PRIAPUS to drive off thieves (*Met.* 14.640f); by ZEUS in his fight with the monster Typhoeus (*Lib.* 1.6.3).

PERSEUS WITH THE HEAD OF MEDUSA

SICK PERSON

(See **Bed; Corpse; Dying Figure; Sleeping Figure; Wounded Figure.**)

SILENI

(See **Satyr.**)

SINGING

(See **Flute; Lyre; Muses; Pipes; Sirens.**)

SIRENS

Winged women with the feet of birds, or birds with the heads of women. They were the daughters of Acheloüs and the companions of Persephone; they were given wings to aid their search for her (*Met.* 5.551f; *Argo.* 4.891f). Homer does not describe them as being part bird. With their singing, Sirens lure mariners ashore to devour them.

Are defeated in singing by the MUSES, who pluck their feathers to make crowns (Paus. 9.34.2).

Sing or play instruments as the *Argo* passes by with Orpheus, who is also making music; no one aboard hears them except Butes, who tries to swim to them until he is rescued by Aphrodite (*Argo.* 4.903f); as ODYSSEUS is rowed past, he is lashed to the mast by his crew, whose ears are stopped with wax (*Od.* 12.177f; *Ep.* 7.18).

Are surrounded by the bones of their victims (*Od.* 12.39f).

Dive into the sea after ODYSSEUS escapes (*Fab.* 141).

SISTRUM

A hand-held rattle.

Attribute of Isis and her devotees.

Shaken or held by HERACLES to scare off the Stymphalian birds (*Argo.* 2.1052f); by HYPSIPYLE as she sings to baby Opheltes (fragment of Eur. *Hypsipyle,* see Rose, p. 200); by ISIS as she grants Telthusa's prayer that her daughter Iphis may become a boy (*Met.* 9.773f).

SITTING

(See **Seated Figure.**)

SKIN

(See also **Dark Skin; Flaying; Human Figure.**)

OF MAN OR GIANT

ATHENA, after flaying the Giant Pallas, uses his skin to shield her body in the fight between gods and Giants (*Lib.* 1.6.2; see also **Aegis,** and "Lion," below).

CAMBYSES has a throne covered with the skin of a man whose son is made to sit on it in his capacity as judge (Herod. 5.25; Val. Max. 6.36.3).

HERMES makes a purse from the skin of Choricus (Serv. *ad Aen.* 7.138).

OF ANIMAL

Attribute of a Maenad.

Bear: worn by ACESTES when he welcomes Aeneas et al. to his kingdom in Sicily (*Aen.* 5.35f); by the Argonaut ANCAEUS, who also carries an axe (*Argo.* 1.168f). Conceals the tendons of ZEUS, which Typhon has placed in a cave guarded by the she-dragon Delphyne (*Lib.* 1.6.3).

ISIS HOLDING A SISTRUM

Boar: presented to ATALANTA by Meleager as the trophy of the Cale-
donian hunt and taken from her by two envious fellow hunters, whom Meleager promptly dispatches (*Met.* 8.428f; *Lib.* 1.8.2). Worn by TYDEUS when
he and Polyneices, in a lion skin, come before Adrastus, who takes them to
be the boar and lion his daughters are destined to marry (*Fab.* 69, 70).

Bull: cut into strips by DIDO to encircle the area granted to her for the
city of Carthage (Serv. *ad Aen.* 1.367). Being urinated on (see **Urinating**).

Deer: worn by ODYSSEUS, disguised as an aged beggar, as Athena sends
him on his way home (*Od.* 13.436).

Fawn: attribute of Dionysus and his votaries, especially Maenads (q.v.); Orpheus (Diod. Sic. 1.11.4). Worn by PENTHEUS when Dionysus dresses him as a Maenad (Eur. *Bacch.* 827f) and by old TEIRESIAS and CADMUS (Eur. *Bacch.* 175f).

Goat: attribute of Lupercus and his votaries; Zeus (as baby or boy). (See also **Aegis.**)

Leopard: hangs at the door of ANTENOR's house in Troy to mark it exempt from pillaging by the Greeks (Paus. 10.27.1). Worn by MENELAÜS (*Il.* 10.25f).

Lion: attribute of Heracles (see **Lion**). Worn by AENEAS in the flight from Troy (*Aen.* 2.722); by AENEAS' horse (*Aen.* 8.552, if one takes the relative clause here to refer to *exsortem* [*equum*] rather than to *Aeneae*); by AGAMEMNON (*Il.* 10.21f); by DIOMEDES (*Il.* 10.177f); by NISUS (*Aen.* 9.305f); by OMPHALE, symbolizing her enslavement of Heracles (*Lib.* 2.6.3); by POLYNEICES (see "Boar," above). Carried by CADMUS as a shield in his fight with a dragon (*Met.* 3.52, 3.81f). Wrapped around baby Ajax by HERACLES (*Lib.* 3.12.7, n. 2, Loeb edn.). Attacked with an axe by the boy THESEUS when Heracles lays it aside to dine with Pittheus (Paus. 1.27.8).

Lynx: attribute of Pan.

Ox (see "Bull," above).

Panther: attribute of Dionysus; Maenads; Sileni. Worn by EVANDER (*Aen.* 8.460); by PARIS when he challenges the Greeks to single combat (*Il.* 3.15f).

Ram or sheep (see **Fleece**).

Wolf: attribute of Romulus. Worn by the Trojan spy DOLON when he is captured by Odysseus and Diomedes (*Il.* 10.333f).

SKINNING

(See **Flaying.**)

SKULL

Attribute of Atropos.

SKY

Supported by ATLAS (Hes. *Theog.* 517f, 746f); by HERACLES while Atlas goes to fetch the apples of the Hesperides for him (*Lib.* 2.5.11).

SLEEPING FIGURE

(See also **Bed; Corpse; Crippled Man; Dying Figure; Falling; Phantom; Wounded Figure.**)

A boy asleep may represent Hypnos.

Visited by a goddess. ENDYMION, eternally asleep, deathless and age-less, is visited in his cave by his lover, the goddess Selene (*Lib.* 1.7.5; *Argo.* 4.57f; Cic. *Tusc.* 1.38.92).

Seduced. AEROPE, by Thyestes (Eur. *Elec.* 719f). ANTIOPE, by a Satyr (Zeus) (*Fab.* 6, 7). AURA, by Dionysus, who has drugged her (Nonnus 48.599f). CALLISTO, by Zeus disguised as Artemis (*Met.* 2.419f). CHIONE, by Hermes after he puts her to sleep with his wand (*Met.* 11.307f). RHEA SILVIA, by Ares (*Fasti* 3.11f). TYRO, by Poseidon in the form of the river god Enipeus (*Od.* 11.235f; *Lib.* 1.9.8; *Met.* 6.113).

Seduction of, thwarted. AMYMONE is saved from an amorous Satyr by Poseidon, who then takes her himself (*Fab.* 169A). LOTIS (Vesta) manages to escape from Priapus when the braying of Silenus' ass awakens her (*Fasti* 1.415f, 6.319f).

Put to sleep by a deity. PENELOPE'S SUITORS, by Athena (*Od.* 2.393f). ZEUS, by Hypnos, who has been sent by Hera to prevent his becoming aware of a storm she has sent against Heracles' ship (*Il.* 14.249f).

Killed or maimed. BRIAS is blinded by the young virgin he has raped (Paus. 2.20.1). DARDANUS is blinded by Artemisia, who then leaps into the sea (Ptolem. Heph. 190, p. 153a). DEÏPHOBUS is killed after Helen takes away his sword and opens the door to Menelaüs and Odysseus (*Aen.* 6.520f). EGYPTUS' SONS are murdered on their wedding night by their brides, the daughters of Danaüs (*Lib.* 2.1.5). HERMES' hand is cut off by the brothers of Palaestra, whom he has seduced (Serv. *ad Aen.* 7.138). NISUS dies when his daughter Scylla (Megara) cuts off the lock of his hair on which his life depends (*Met.* 8.85f; Aes. *Choëph.* 618f; *Lib.* 3.15.7). ORION, put to sleep by Satyrs, is blinded by Oenopion (Serv. *ad Aen.* 10.763). The PIRATES who have abducted some maidens are killed by Hymenaeus (Serv. *ad Aen.* 4.99). WARRIORS in their camp are slaughtered by Diomedes and Odysseus (*Il.* 10.482f); by Nisus and Euryalus (*Aen.* 9.324f).

Killing of, prevented. TELEPHON (Aepytus) is saved by an old man from the axe of Merope, who is ignorant that he is her son (*Fab.* 137). TRIP-TOLEMUS is saved from Lyncus when Demeter turns Lyncus into a lynx (*Met.* 5.657f).

While someone sleeps. A swallow flies above sleeping ALEXANDER and perches on his head until he awakens (Arrian 1.25.6). ARIADNE sleeps as Theseus sails away (*Met.* 8.175f; Cat. 64.52f). CLYTEMNESTRA dreams that branches grow from Agamemnon's sceptre (Soph. *Elec.* 416f). That CUPID is her lover is revealed to Psyche when she lights a lamp while he is sleeping (Apuleius 8). EVENIUS' sheep are killed by wolves while he sleeps (Herod. 9.93). FURIES lie asleep about Orestes, who is seated in Apollo's shrine holding a bloody sword in the presence of Apollo and Hermes (Aes. *Eumen.* 39f). GALATEA, created from ivory by Pygmalion, is awakened by his kiss (*Met.* 10.280f). HEPHAESTUS, stunned by his fall from Olympus, is found and ministered to by the women of Lemnos (*Il.* 1.590f). JASON is awakened by nymphs when the *Argo* becomes stranded in Libya (*Argo.* 4.1312f). ODYSSEUS sleeps while the Phaeacians transport him to Ithaca and place him ashore (*Od.* 13.73f). ORESTES is watched over by Electra et al. until he awakens (Eur. *Orest.* 35f, 132f, 211f). RHOEO's SISTERS are asleep when pigs break their wine jars and wake them up, causing them to run into the sea (Diod. Sic. 5.62.3). SMERDIS is discovered by his wife Phaedima to have no ears (Herod. 3.69).

SLING

Used in battle by BALAERIC islanders (Caesar *B.G.* 2.7); by MEZENTIUS (*Aen.* 9.586f).

SMALL-SCALE FIGURE

(See **Baby; Boy; Children; Girl; Human Figure; Wings.**)

SMOKE

(See also **Mist.**)

Emerging from a cornucopia: attribute of Somnium.
Smoke from the earth marks the place where Heracles has buried Cacus (*Aen.* 8.251f).

SNAKE

(See also **Dragon.**)

Since the sources do not make a clear distinction between *snake* and *dragon,* it is made herein subjectively on the basis of the visual impression made by the text.

ASCLEPIUS AND TELESPHORUS

Attribute of Apollo; Artemis; Asclepius; Athena; Bona Dea; Dionysus and his votaries; Furies; a genius; Hermes; Kairos. Drinking from a cup: Hygeia; Salus. Eating: a genius. With its tail in its mouth: Aeternitas; Salus; Saturnus; Sol. Ornamenting a crown: Persephone. Winged: Felicitas; Fortuna; Mercury; Minerva. Symbol of Erichthonius, the snake-god of Athens (Paus. 1.25.7).

Festooned with snakes, HECATE appears from Hades when Jason summons her (*Argo.* 3.1209f).

Two snakes coil themselves about the feet of ATHENA's statue in Troy (*Aen.* 2.225f); are strangled by baby HERACLES (*Lib.* 2.4.8); twine themselves on HERMES' staff with which he is stopping their fight (*Poet. Astr.* 2.7; see also **Caduceus**); are a symbol of death (*Aen.* 2.203, 7.450, 8.289, 8.697); attack LAOCOÖN and his sons (*Aen.* 2.199f; *Ep.* 5.18).

Snakes are created from the seed of HEPHAESTUS, trying unsuccessfully to seduce Athena (*Poet. Astr.* 2.13); from the hair of lovely MEDUSA because she boasts about it to Athena (Serv. *ad Aen.* 6.289) or because she has offended Athena by lying with Poseidon in her temple (*Met.* 4.790f); from the blood dripping from Medusa's severed head (*Met.* 6.4f).

Snakes bind OTUS and EPHIALTES to a pillar in the underworld (*Fab.* 28); THESEUS and PEIRITHOÜS to the Seat of Forgetfulness in the underworld (*Ep.* 1.24).

Guarding the Golden Fleece (*Argo.* 2.1208f) is put to sleep by Medea (*Argo.* 4.127f).

In a jar or chest are given by ATHENA to the daughters of Erechtheus (*Poet. Astr.* 2.13) and to Heracles (*Lib.* 2.7.3); are found by CECROPS' DAUGHTERS, along with baby Erichthonius (*Lib.* 3.14.6; *Met.* 2.553f); are lobbed by HANNIBAL from his ships into those of the enemy (Nep. *Han.* 10, 11). A "lock of Gorgon's hair" is given by HERACLES to Sterope to be used to rout any force invading Tegea (*Lib.* 2.7.3; Paus. 8.47.5).

Emerging from an ALTAR devours a bird and its eight nestlings, an omen of the years remaining in the Trojan War (*Il.* 2.308f; *Met.* 12.11f); from ANCHISES' tomb appears to Aeneas et al. and feeds on the offerings on the altars (*Aen.* 5.84f); snakes from MINOS' body attack the woman he is seducing (Ant. Lib. 41); snake from a pillar of TARQUIN's palace causes consternation (Livy 1.56).

Snakes are found in their bridal chamber by ADMETUS and ALCESTIS (*Lib.* 1.9.15); by TIBERIUS GRACCHUS and CORNELIA (Plut. 39.1; Val. Max. 4.6.1).

Carried or held by ATHENA, who has taken it from Medusa's head; she gives it to Cepheus (Paus. 8.47.5); by DRYOPE, frightens some nymphs (Ant. Lib. 32); by an EAGLE, which drops it, portending the Trojans' repulse from the Greek camp (*Il.* 12.200f); by a FURY (q.v.); by HERA, who drops it into a pool or well in order to poison the water (*Fab.* 52); by MEDEA and placed in Absyrtus' tomb (*Fab.* 26); by a RAVEN, which brings it to Apollo (*Fasti* 2.257f); by THETIS, with which she attacks Peleus (Paus. 5.18.5).

In the form of a snake, the river god ACHELOÜS wrestles with Heracles for the hand of Deïaneira (*Met.* 9.62f; Soph. *Trach.* 8f); APOLLO, in Dryope's lap, frightens off her companions and makes her pregnant (Ant. Lib. 32); ASCLEPIUS leads his followers from his shrine to a ship, from which he disembarks at Rome and resumes his divine form (*Met.* 15.669f); CADMUS is embraced by his wife Harmonia, who becomes similarly transformed (*Met.* 4.576f; *Fab.* 6; *Lib.* 3.5.4), and together they ride in an ox-cart followed by a horde of barbarians (Eur. *Bacch.* 1330f); NECTANEBOS, an Egyptian sorcerer and king, lies beside Olympias, making her pregnant with Alexander; he kisses her in Philip's presence and announces Alexander's divine parentage; he changes into an eagle and flies away (Ps.-Cal. 21; Plut. 33.2); PERICLYMENUS wrestles with Heracles (*Lib.* 1.9.9); PROTEUS tries to escape from the grasp of Aristaeus (*Georg.* 4.408) and Menelaüs (*Od.* 4.454f); SALMACIS (*ut serpens*, "like a snake") embraces and kisses Hermes' son in her pool until their bodies merge into one (Hermaphroditus) (*Met.* 4.356f); THETIS tries to escape from Peleus' grasp (Pind. *Nem.* 4.62f); ZEUS seduces Deoïda (*Met.* 6.114).

Performing kindly acts. A snake feeds and revives its mate, which has been killed by Damason (Nonnus 25.451f) or by Polyidus (*Lib.* 3.3.1; *Fab.* 136). Two snakes lead ALEXANDER et al. to Ammon's temple in the Libyan desert (Arrian 3.3.5). A snake prevents AUGE from killing Telephus, whom she does not realize is her son (*Fab.* 100). Snakes look after EVADNE's BABY by Apollo, which she has abandoned in a thicket (Pind. *Ol.* 6.35f), and baby ION, abandoned by Creüsa in a cave (Eur. *Ion* 17f). Snakes lick the ears of MELAMPUS, enabling him to understand birds (*Lib.* 1.9.11; cf. Schol. *ad Il.* 7.44, where it is recorded that Cassandra and Helenus receive their prophetic powers in a similar way).

Attacking women. AMATA is bitten by the snake a Fury has placed on her breast (*Aen.* 7.346f). CLEOPATRA kills herself by the bite of an asp after Antony has killed himself (Plut. 44.86). EURYDICE is bitten as she flees from Aristaeus (Serv. *ad Georg.* 4.317) or while she is picking flowers (*Met.* 10.8f). HESPERIA is bitten as she is running from Aesacus (*Met.* 11.775f). Snakes from the body of MINOS attack the woman he is seducing (Ant. Lib. 41).

Attacking men. AEPYTUS is fatally bitten while hunting (Paus. 8.4.7). Baby ARCHEMORUS (Opheltes) is killed when Hypsipyle lays him down for a moment on the ground (*Lib.* 3.6.4; Bacchylides 36(8).10f). LAOCOÖN and his sons are killed at the Trojan horse by two huge snakes from the sea (*Aen.* 2.199f; *Ep.* 5.18). The seer MOPSUS is fatally bitten when he steps on a snake (*Argo.* 4.1502f; *Fab.* 14). ORPHEUS' severed head is attacked, until Apollo drives the serpent off (*Met.* 11.50f). PHILOCTETES is bitten on the foot as he is cleaning an altar (*Ep.* 3.27; Soph. *Phil.* 263f, 1326f; *Il.* 2.721f; *Fab.* 102). Gigantic TITYOS is punished in Hades by a snake that feeds on his liver (*Fab.* 50).

Killed or attacked by the archer ALCO (Alcon) while it is coiled around his son (Serv. *ad Ecl.* 5.11); by CYCHREUS as it ravages Salamis (*Lib.* 3.12.7);

by gigantic DAMASEN, whom Moire has summoned, because it has killed Hermus (Nonnus 25.451f); by old GRACCHUS, who sacrifices the one that represents his own life in order that the one that represents his young wife's may live (Plut. 39.1); by HERACLES who, although still a baby, strangles the two sent by Hera (*Lib.* 2.4.8; *Fab.* 30; Theocritus 24) and kills one that is ravaging Omphale's domain (*Poet. Astr.* 2.14); by INVIDIA (Envy), who is eating one when Athena comes to her (*Met.* 2.768f); by PHORBAS, because snakes are depopulating the island of Ophiussa (*Poet. Astr.* 2.14); by the seer POLYIDUS as it is approaching the body of the child Glaucus (*Fab.* 136; *Lib.* 3.3.1); by TEIRESIAS, who turns into a woman when he strikes or tramples two that are copulating; when the incident is repeated, he reverts to his original sex (*Lib.* 3.6.7; *Fab.* 75; *Met.* 3.322f); by WARRIORS (The Seven Against Thebes), after it has killed baby Archemorus (*Fab.* 74; *Lib.* 3.6.4).

SNAKE-HAIRED

Attribute of Discordia (*Aen.* 6.280); a Fury (q.v.); a Gorgon (q.v.), especially Medusa; a Ker (Cer); Maenads (q.v.).

KERES drag dead and wounded warriors from battle (*Il.* 18.535f).

MEDUSA's lovely hair is turned into snakes when she compares Athena's hair unfavorably with her own (Serv. *ad Aen.* 6.289) or because she has offended Athena by lying with Poseidon in her temple (*Met.* 4.790f).

SNAKE-HEADED (Multiple)

Attribute of Hydra (see **Dragon**); Typhoeus (Typhaon, Typhon), a monstrous, fire-breathing creature who may also have snakes for fingers and legs, or have snakes sprouting from his shoulders. Cf. Scylla, whose six heads are on snake-like necks (see **Head**).

TYPHOEUS attacks the gods, some of whom escape by turning themselves into various animals. He captures Zeus and imprisons him in a cave guarded by a dragon. He is blasted by a thunderbolt and buried by Zeus beneath Etna (Hes. *Theog.* 820f, 853f; *Lib.* 1.6.3; *Met.* 5.325f; Aes. *Prom.* 356f; *Fab.* 152).

SNAKE-LEGGED OR -TAILED

(See also **Fish.**)

Attribute of Boreas (see **Wings**); Cecrops; Echidna (Hes. *Theog.* 295f); Enceladus; Erichthonius (see **Chest** [Containing people]; **Baby** [Birth of]);

SCYLLA GRASPING TWO OF ODYSSEUS' MEN

Giants (see **Fighting; Monster**); Scylla (in addition to her more common features, viz. her waist of dogs' heads and six long necks; see **Dog's Head**); Zephyrus (see **Wings**).

Woman-snake ECHIDNA is killed by many-eyed Argus (*Lib.* 2.1.2; cf. Herod. 4.9–10, where he tells about a woman-snake who took Heracles' mares while he slept and refused to give them up unless he lived with her for a time; this the hero did, fathering three sons; he gives her his bow on leaving. There are some who believe she is Echidna).

Man-snake ENCELADUS is blasted by Zeus and buried beneath Etna (*Aen.* 3.578f). (See also **Monster.**)

Baby-snake (see **Baby**).

A bull-snake creature is sacrificed by BRIAREÜS and its entrails carried to Zeus by a hawk (*Fasti* 3.799f).

SNOW

Is falling as a nymph gives birth to a baby sired by Poseidon, which he names CHIOS (Snowman) (Paus. 7.4.6).

Using shields as sleds, CIMBRI warriors slide down Alpine slopes (Plut. 22.23).

SOLDIER

(See **Officer; Warrior.**)

SOWING

Of grain by EROS (Moschus, *Epigram* 7); by TRIPTOLEMUS from a chariot drawn by flying dragons (*Met.* 5.642f; *Lib.* 1.5.2).

Of dragon's teeth from which armed men grow, by AEËTES (*Argo.* 3.409f); by CADMUS at Athena's command (Eur. *Phoen.* 657f; *Lib.* 3.4.1; *Met.* 3.101f); by JASON (*Argo.* 3.1335f; *Met.* 7.121f; *Lib.* 1.9.23; *Fab.* 22).

SPARK

(See also **Coal; Fire.**)

Lands in the lap of a girl sitting by the fire, from which CAECULUS is conceived (Serv. *ad Aen.* 7.678).

SPARROW

(See **Bird.**)

SPEAKER

(See also **Suppliant.**)

IN COUNCIL Councils of gods or chieftains in which a particular incident of interest occurs will be found elsewhere. Here are listed without detail passages that describe major councils, for the convenience of those whose interest is in rhetoric or in what was said.

Councils of gods: *Il.* 1.533f, 4.1f, 7.443f, 8.1f, 8.442f, 15.14f, 15.149f, 20.4f, 24.31f; *Od.* 5.1f; *Aen.* 10.1f.

Councils of Greek chieftains: *Il.* 1.54f, 1.247f, 2.53f, 2.336f, 7.123f, 7.323f, 9.9f, 10.194f, 14.27f, 19.40f.

Councils of Trojan chieftains: *Il.* 7.345f, 8.489f, 18.243f.

ADDRESSING AN ASSEMBLY Q. FABIUS, before the Carthaginian Senate, issues Rome's declaration of war with a shake of his toga (Livy 21.18).

REGULUS rejects the pleas of senators and his wife and sons that he not honor his word by returning to Carthage and death (Hor. *Odes* 3.5f; Livy, *Epitome* 18).

TELEMACHUS upbraids the carousing suitors of his mother for their outrageous behavior (*Od.* 2.35f).

In order to arouse it. Blind old APPIUS CLAUDIUS shames the Roman Senate into rejecting peace with Pyrrhus (Plut. 21.18–19). CAESAR, with Pompey and Crassus beside him, stirs the people into giving him armed support against his political enemies (Plut. 34.14). CAESO FABIUS stirs the martial spirit of his clan to follow him to war (Livy 2.49). (See also **Corpse** [Displayed].)

Seated Greek and Trojan armies are addressed by HECTOR, issuing Paris' challenge to Menelaüs to settle the war by single combat (*Il.* 3.75f) and challenging any Greek to single combat (*Il.* 7.54f); by MENELAÜS, rebuking the Greeks for their reluctance to accept Hector's challenge (*Il.* 7.94f).

A hostile mob is addressed by ACHILLES in an effort to prevent the sacrifice of Iphigeneia (Eur. *Iph. Aul.* 1345f); by CATO, who succeeds in quelling a riot (Plut. 36.44); by M. SERVILIUS, showing his wounds to the disaffected soldiers of Aemilius Paulus; he regains their allegiance to their general (Plut. 14.31).

AS ENVOY

ALEXANDER, dressed as Hermes or Ammon, acts as his own envoy to the court of Darius (Ps.-Cal. 174).

Old DRANCES leads an embassy of Latins to Aeneas to arrange a truce for burying the dead (*Aen.* 11.100f); he and Turnus confer with Latinus regarding continuation of the war (*Aen.* 11.302f).

ILIONEUS et al. are welcomed by Queen Dido, as Aeneas and Achates look on from concealment in a mist (*Aen.* 1.509f); are welcomed by King Latinus; they exchange gifts (*Aen.* 7.152f).

MELEAGER's father, sisters, and mother vainly beg him to join in the defense of their city, but his wife succeeds in moving him to action (*Il.* 9.573f).

ODYSSEUS alone (*Met.* 13.181f), with Talthybius (*Ep.* 3.22), or with Diomedes, dupes Clytemnestra into yielding Iphigeneia to be taken away to be Achilles' bride (*Fab.* 98); he and Menelaüs enter Troy to demand the return of Helen, to which Priam and Antenor are receptive but Paris is violently opposed (*Il.* 3.205f, 7.345f; Serv. *ad Aen.* 1.243; Herod. 2.118; *Met.* 13.196f; *Ep.* 3.28); he returns the girl Chryseïs to her old father, a priest of Apollo (*Il.* 1.440f); he, with Ajax and old Phoenix (or Diomedes in place of Phoenix; Dictys 2.48), try to persuade Achilles to rejoin the fight against Troy (*Il.* 9.182f); he and Phoenix persuade Lycomedes to allow Neoptolemus (Pyrrhus), his daughter's son by Achilles, to take his father's place in the war (*Ep.* 5.11).

An embassy from Darius presents demands to ALEXANDER, which he rejects (Ps.-Cal. 64–65); of Parthians confronts CRASSUS, and one of them laughs mockingly at him (Plut. 28.18); from Scythia delivers to DARIUS a bird, a mouse, a frog, and five arrows (Herod. 4.131); of Samnites tries to bribe with gold M. CURIUS DENTATUS as he is cooking a frugal meal (Plut. 18.2; Val. Max. 4.3–5); of barbaric Cimbri on horseback visit MARIUS to set a time for their battle (Plut. 22.25); from Sparta refuses to make obeisance to XERXES (Herod. 7.136); from Persia is thrown into pits at both Athens and Sparta (Herod. 7.133). (See also **Gold.**)

SPEAR

(See also **Corpse; Fighting; Killing; Sceptre; Staff; Suppliant; Warrior; Wounded Figure;** also other weapons appropriate to the action, since artists feel free to depart from tradition in such a detail.)

Attribute of Aphrodite (victorious); Apollo Amyclaeus; Ares; Artemis; Athena; Bendis (holding two spears); Comus (also with an inverted torch); Honos (also with a cornucopia); Juno; Penates; Vertumnus; Vesta; Victoria; Virtus (with one breast bare); Zeus.

THROWN OR WIELDED IN BATTLE

ACHILLES and Hector throw at each other and Hector is wounded (*Il.* 20.438f); Achilles thrusts at the mist in which Apollo has concealed Hector (*Il.* 20.441f); after they both miss, Athena retrieves Achilles' spear for him, enabling him to kill Hector, armed only with a sword (*Il.* 22.272f); he and Aeneas pierce one another's shield (*Il.* 20.259f); he kills the Amazon Penthesileia as they fight on horseback (Quint. Smy. 1.536f) and black Memnon, son of Eos (Quint. Smy. 2.395f); his spear hits Cygnus, who is invulnerable, with no effect; he therefore tries to strangle him (*Met.* 12.72f); he wounds Telephus (*Fab.* 101; *Ep.* 3.17); he is wounded on the arm by Asteropaeus, who throws two spears at once, one from each hand; his spear misses, and Asteropaeus is trying to recover it when Achilles stabs him with his sword (*Il.* 21.161f).

AENEAS and TURNUS, meeting in single combat, first throw their spears (*Aen.* 12.710f); after recovering his spear, Aeneas throws at Turnus, wounding him in the thigh (*Aen.* 12.923f).

AGENOR hits Achilles' armor and is rescued from him in a mist by Apollo (*Il.* 21.590f).

AJAX fights alone against the Trojans with several spears sticking in his shield (*Il.* 11.489f, 11.544f); his spear is severed by Hector's sword (*Il.* 16.114f); he and Diomedes fight to a draw at the games for Patroclus (*Il.* 23.811f).

ALEXANDER on horseback kills Persian officers at the Granicus River (Arrian 1.15.6).

ARES attacks Athena, who flattens him with a rock (*Il.* 21.391f); he hurls his spear at Diomedes in his chariot but the driver, Athena, turns it aside (*Il.* 5.846f); he throws at Heracles, but Athena turns the point aside (Hes. *Sh. Her.* 450f).

ARRUNS takes Camilla unawares and kills her as she rides past (*Aen.* 11.799f).

The BEBRYCES, after their king is killed in a boxing contest by Polydeuces, attack the Argonauts with spears and clubs (*Argo.* 2.98f).

DIOMEDES wounds Aphrodite as she carries Aeneas out of battle, causing her to drop him (*Il.* 5.330f); from his chariot, he wounds Ares (*Il.* 5.855f); he knocks down Hector, who is attacking him and Odysseus (*Il.* 11.349f).

ETEOCLES and POLYNEICES fight with spears until the spears break; each falls by the other's sword outside the walls of Thebes (Eur. *Phoen.* 1356f).

EUPHORBUS spears Patroclus in the back after Apollo has stunned him with a blow of his hand (*Il.* 16.805f).

HECTOR and AJAX each strike the other's shield, but Hector alone is wounded (*Il.* 7.244f); Hector hurls a spear, Ajax a stone (*Il.* 14.402f); they fight at the Greek ships (*Il.* 15.405f, 16.114f); Hector kills Patroclus, already wounded, with a thrust (*Il.* 16.818f).

HERACLES wounds Ares in a fight at Pylos (Hes. *Sh. Her.* 359f); he kills Cycnus and wounds Ares when the latter tries to avenge his son's death (Hes. *Sh. Her.* 416f, 459f).

Old LAËRTES, inspired by Athena, throws and fells Eupeithes, starting a general battle between Odysseus et al. and the avengers of the slain suitors (*Od.* 24.520f).

MENELAÜS and PARIS engage in single combat; each hurls his spear into the other's shield (*Il.* 3.340f).

NISUS hurls his spear at the Rutulian horsemen who have captured Euryalus (*Aen.* 9.410f).

ODYSSEUS fights alone against the Trojans and kills several (*Il.* 11.401f, 11.459f); he fights with Telemachus et al. against the avengers of the dead suitors until Athena stops them (*Od.* 24.526f).

PANDARUS aims at Turnus but Hera turns the spear aside (*Aen.* 9.743f).

PATROCLUS fells Sarpedon as Zeus and Hera watch; he pulls his spear from the corpse (*Il.* 16.477f).

PENELOPE's SUITORS attack Odysseus and Telemachus, who have the support of Mentor (Athena) (*Od.* 22.205f, 22.241f).

PERSEUS hurls back at Phineus the spear thrown at him but hits another man because Phineus dodges behind an altar (*Met.* 5.32f).

PHILOPOEMEN's thighs are pierced by a spear, which he breaks in order to continue fighting (Plut. 19.6; Paus 8.49).

POLYDEUCES attacks Lynceus, who has wounded Castor (*Fasti* 5.707f).

PYRRHUS fights the champion Pantauches with spear and sword (Plut. 21.7).

RUTULIAN WARRIORS hem in Helenor and Lycus; Helenor runs on their spears, allowing Lycus to escape (*Aen.* 9.549f).

SILENUS wounds Enceladus as he and Dionysus enter the battle between the gods and the Giants (Eur. *Cycl.* 5f).

TELEGONUS kills Odysseus, the father whom he has never seen, with his barbed spear in a fight over cattle (*Ep.* 7.36).

TELEMACHUS kills Amphinomus, who is attacking Odysseus (*Od.* 22.89f).

TEUTHIS wounds Athena in the thigh (Paus. 8.28.5).

TLEPOLEMUS and SARPEDON throw their spears simultaneously; the former is killed and the latter wounded in the thigh (*Il.* 5.663f).

USED FOR MURDER OR EXECUTION

ACHILLES kills Thersites for mutilating the corpse of Penthesileia (Schol. *ad Lycophrona* 999).

ALEXANDER slays Cleitus when they quarrel at a banquet (Plut. 33.51f; Arrian 4.8.1); he attacks Pausanias, who is trying to violate Olympias (Ps.-Cal. 68).

DAPHNE and her companions, preparing to bathe after a hunt, strip reluctant Leucippus, who is masquerading as a girl, and kill him when they find him to be a man (Paus. 20.4).

LAESTRYGONIANS spear and eat some of Odysseus' men (*Od.* 10.124f).

MELEAGER kills his uncles for objecting to his awarding the skin of the Calydonian Boar to Atalanta (*Met.* 8.431f; *Fab.* 174).

SEMIRAMIS orders the execution of her husband Ninus after tricking him into conferring absolute power on her (Diod. Sic. 2.20; Aelian 7.1).

SHEPHERDS attack Catreus when he steps ashore because the barking of dogs prevents their hearing his name (*Lib.* 3.2.2).

MISSES THE MARK

ADRASTUS hits Atys instead of a boar (Herod. 1.43–44).

CEPHALUS throws at a sound in a thicket and hits his wife Procris (*Met.* 7.840f; *Fab.* 189; *Lib.* 3.15.1).

OTUS and EPHIALTES aim at a deer sent between them by Apollo and kill each other (*Lib.* 1.7.4; *Fab.* 28).

PELEUS, aiming at the Calydonian Boar, hits Eurytion instead (*Lib.* 3.13.2).

PENTHESILEIA hits Hippolyte instead of the stag she has aimed at (*Ep.* 5.1, n. 4, Loeb edn.; Quint. Smy. 1.24f).

THROWN FOR VARIOUS PURPOSES

A spear thrown over a border or from a pillar signifies a Roman declaration of war (*Fasti* 6.205f; Livy 1.32).

An ATTENDANT of baby Pyrrhus, whose party is being pursued, throws a spear with a message tied to it across a river (Plut. 21.2).

METABUS, in flight from his enemies, hurls baby Camilla tied to a spear over a river and swims over himself (*Aen.* 11.522f).

PENELOPE'S SUITORS practice spear throwing (*Od.* 4.625f).

ROMULUS hurls a spear from the Aventine Hill to the Palatine, where it becomes a tree (Serv. *ad Aen.* 3.46).

The Rutulian augur TOLUMNIUS breaks a truce by throwing a spear into a crowd of Trojans, after he observes an eagle seize a swan (*Aen.* 12.257f).

BRANDISHED, HELD, OR GIVEN

ACHILLES grabs a spear and shield from among Odysseus' trinkets and sheds his girl's clothing when a trumpet sounds (*Fab.* 96); he scrapes rust from his spear's point onto Telephus' wound to cure it (*Ep.* 3.20; *Fab.* 101); his spear, having missed Hector, is handed back to him by Athena (*Il.* 22.275).

APHRODITE hands Aeneas his spear after freeing it from the ground (*Aen.* 12.786f).

CURETES clash their spears on their shields to keep Cronus from hearing the cries of baby Zeus (*Lib.* 1.1.7; *Fab.* 139).

LYCURGUS threatens fleeing Dionysus and Maenads with an ox-goad (*Il.* 6.130f).

PELEUS receives from the Centaur Cheiron a spear that Hephaestus and Athena have made (*Cypria* 5; Schol. *ad Il.* 16.143).

PROCRIS is given an unerring spear and an indefatigable hound by Artemis (*Fab.* 189) or by Minos, to win her favors (*Lib.* 3.15.1); she gives them to her husband Cephalus (*Met.* 7.753f; *Fab.* 189).

STUCK IN THE GROUND

Two spears in the ground, with a third lashed horizontally between them, form a yoke (q.v.) under which the Romans force defeated enemies to pass in token of submission, or are themselves so humbled (Caesar *B.G.* 1.7, 1.12).

AENEAS tugs vainly at his spear, which Faunus has caused to stick fast in an attempt to save Turnus from him (*Aen.* 12.786f).

ASTEROPAEUS is trying vainly to recover for himself Achilles' spear, when that warrior kills him with a sword (*Il.* 21.173f).

ROMULUS' spear, which he has stuck in the ground, sprouts leaves (*Met.* 15.560f).

SPHINX

(For a description, see **Monster.**)

EGYPTIAN Sphinxes usually are found lying in rows flanking the approach to a temple.

The GREEK Sphinx is a common ornament of tombs and thought to be a symbol of death. One is sent by some god to plague Thebes and to devour

Oedipus and the Sphinx

whatever youth cannot answer her riddle (Eur. *Phoen.* 805f, 1019f); her riddle is solved by Oedipus, whereupon she plunges to her death (*Lib.* 3.5.8; *Fab.* 67).

SPIDER

Arachne, after losing a weaving contest to Athena, hangs herself and is changed into a spider (*Met.* 6.134f).

SPINDLE

(See also **Distaff; Spinning.**)

Attribute of Athena and her statue, the Palladium; Clotho; Necessitas. Carried by Heracles in token of his subservience to Omphale (Sen. *Phaed.* 332f, *Her. Oet.* 371f; Lucian *Dial. Deo.* 15[13]).

SPINNING

(See also **Spindle.**)

Arachne is widely admired for her skill in spinning and weaving (*Met.* 6.5f).

LEUCOTHOË and her maidens are busily spinning when a woman (Apollo) appears and sends the others out while he, in his own form, seduces the girl (*Met.* 4.219f).

LUCRETIA is found dutifully at work by lamplight when she is visited by her husband and, among others, Tarquin, who conceives a passion for her (Livy 1.57).

MINYAS' DAUGHTERS spin while other women are enjoying a festival (*Met.* 4.31f).

A WOMAN, richly dressed, spins flax, carries a pitcher on her head, and leads a horse in order to attract King Darius' notice (Herod. 5.12).

SPITTING

APOLLO spits into the mouth of Cassandra, causing her true prophecies thereafter to be disbelieved (Serv. *ad Aen.* 2.247).

GLAUCUS spits into the mouth of Polyidus and loses the gift of prophecy (*Lib.* 3.3.1).

SPRING

(See **Water.**)

SPYING

(See also **Eavesdropping.**)

GYGES watches the wife of Candaules disrobe in her chamber, with the connivance of her husband (Herod. 1.10).

STAFF

(See also **Caduceus; Club; Pole; Sceptre; Spear; Stake; Stick; Trident; Wand.**)

Tipped with pine cone, leaves, or grape clusters (see **Thyrsus**).

Attribute of a blind man (see **Eye**); Constantia; a deity; judge (q.v.); king (q.v.); official; old man (q.v.); speaker (q.v.); Thanatos (an old man with wings). Sprouting leaves: Apollo; Bacchus; Fidius (see also **Spear** [Romulus]). Beribboned: a priest (q.v.). Shepherd's: Apollo; Hades; Pan; a shepherd (q.v.); Thaleia. With a bird on it: Fidius; Juno. Entwined with

AN AUGUR'S STAFF OR *lituus*

snakes: Asclepius. Being used to chastise someone: Dike (Paus. 5.18.2). Pointing at a globe: Lachesis; Urania. Bent, or ending in a coil (*lituus*): an augur.

An AUGUR holding a *lituus,* and with a hand on the head of Numa, seeks his confirmation as king (Livy 1.18).

ROMULUS' *lituus* is found among some debris (Plut. 8.32).

Presented by ATHENA to blind Teiresias (*Lib.* 3.6.7); by the MUSES to the shepherd Hesiod (Hes. *Theog.* 29f).

Used. DIONYSUS kills one of the Giants with his ivy-wreathed staff (Eur. *Ion* 215f). ECHETLAOS fights at Marathon armed with a plow handle (Paus. 1.32.4). HIPPOCOÖN'S SONS kill Oinos with staves for hitting their watchdog with a rock, at which Heracles attacks them (Paus. 3.15.4–5). King LAIUS strikes at Oedipus with an ox-goad and is killed by him with his staff (Soph. *Oed. Tyr.* 801f). LUSSA (Madness) drives Heracles mad with an ox-goad, causing him to kill his wife and sons (Eur. *Her.* 815f). POSEIDON, in the form of the seer Calchas, strikes the two Ajaxes to instill them with valor (*Il.* 13.43f). A ROMAN ENVOY communicates Rome's command by drawing a circle in the earth around him, putting an end to Antiochus Epiphanes' siege of Alexandria (Livy 45.12). TARQUIN lops off the heads of the tallest poppies in wordless response to the question of his son's messenger about consolidating their hold on the city of Gabii (Livy 1.54; *Fasti* 2.705f).

STAG

(See **Deer.**)

STAKE

(See also **Pole; Staff.**)

Sharpened, is used by ODYSSEUS to put out sleeping Polyphemus' eye (*Od.* 9.382f; *Aen.* 3.630f).

STANDARD

Military: attribute of Victoria.

MINUCIUS lays his standards at Fabius' feet in token of obedience (Plut. 10.13; Livy 22.30).

STANDARD BEARER

CAESAR turns around one who is retreating and makes him move toward the enemy, thereby rallying his soldiers (Plut. 34.57).

STAR

Five-pointed: attribute of Salus. Decorating a robe: Genius Bonus; Isis; Jupiter; Nox. On the head: Augustus (*Aen.* 8.681); Castor and Polydeuces (*Fab.* 14, 80). Symbol of Julius Caesar and the Julian house (*Ecl.* 9.47; Hor. *Odes* 1.12.47).

Decorate the crown that DIONYSUS presents to Ariadne; afterward the crown becomes a constellation (*Met.* 8.176f).

Comet or shooting star indicates to the ARGONAUTS their route (*Argo.* 4.294f); is seen by CAESAR to fall into Pompey's camp (Plut. 34.50); passes over burning TROY (*Aen.* 2.692f) and marks the direction of flight from it (*Aen.* 2.801).

Stars of CASTOR and POLYDEUCES appear over Lysander's ship before the battle of Aegospotami (Plut. 23.12).

Constellations are explained by the magician NECTANEBOS to Olympias as she gives birth to Alexander (Ps.-Cal. 25).

Turned into stars. HYAS' SISTERS (Hyades), as they weep for him after he has been killed by a boar or lion (*Fab.* 192).

STATUE

Formed when humans are turned to stone (see **Stone**).

Beneath ATHENA's statue, Pelopia hides the sword of her ravisher Thyestes (*Ep.* 2.14; *Fab.* 87, 88).

A mounted COLONUS stands near the spot where blind Oedipus, led by Antigone, encounters his other daughter, Ismene, et al. (Soph. *Oed. Col.* 58f).

Statues of DAMIA and AUXESIA resist efforts to drag them off with ropes (Herod. 5.85).

A DIONYSUS is given by Zeus to Hera (Eur. *Bacch.* 291f); is found by shipwrecked sailors in a cave where goats live (Paus. 2.23.1).

An EROS is given to Phryne by Praxiteles (Athenaeus 13.591a, b).

HERACLES throws a stone at his own statue (*Lib.* 2.6.3).

The PALLADIUM, at which Electra, daughter of Atlas, has taken refuge, is wrenched from her by Zeus, who hurls it from heaven together with Ate; it falls to earth at Ilus' humble abode, where a temple is built for it (*Lib.* 3.12.3); holding desperately to it, Cassandra is torn away by Ajax Oïleus (*Ep.* 5.22; *Iliupersis* 1).

PENATES appear to sleeping Aeneas, telling him to move on from Crete (*Aen.* 3.147f).

PROTESILAÜS' statue is burned by Acastus; his wife Laodameia throws herself into the flames (*Fab.* 104).

STATUETTES are hung in trees at Athens in penance for the deaths of Icarius and Erigone (*Fab.* 130).

XERXES' fallen statue is addressed by Alexander as if it were alive (Plut. 33.37).

Created by ARGUS, who fashions a Rhea on a rocky promontory (*Argo.* 1.1117f); by ATHENA, of her friend Pallas; known as the Palladium, it is a wooden figure 4½ feet tall, wearing an aegis and holding a spear and spindle (*Lib.* 3.12.3); by the Centaur CHEIRON, a likeness of Actaeon for his dogs, who killed their master after he was turned into a stag (*Lib.* 3.4.4); by DAEDALUS, who is the first to carve the human form (*Lib.* 3.15.8); LAODAMEIA, who makes a likeness of her husband Protesilaüs so that she may embrace it (*Ep.* 3.30); by ZEUS, ATHENA, and PROMETHEUS, who fashion a bull, a horse, and a man, respectively; with each Momus finds fault and as a result he is expelled from Olympus by Zeus (Aesop 100).

Created and brought to life. GALATEA, by Pygmalion, who awakens her with a kiss after Aphrodite has given her life (*Met.* 10.243f). MAN, by Prometheus out of earth and water (*Lib.* 1.7.1; *Fab.* 142; *Met.* 1.80f), or by Cura out of mud. Zeus gives him life, and Tellus (Earth) demands that he be given her name (*Fab.* 220). PANDORA, by Hephaestus with the help of Aphrodite, Athena, and Hermes (Hes. *W. & D.* 60f; Hes. *Theog.* 571f; *Fab.* 142).

Showing signs of life. Many figures of DEITIES weep, portending Caesar's murder (*Met.* 15.792f). A HERA, when touched by Camillus or addressed by a young man, nods her assent to being moved to Rome (Plut.

8.6; Livy 5.22). An ORPHEUS is observed by Alexander to be sweating (Ps.-Cal. 121). A PALLAS (the Palladium) perspires and gesticulates and her eyes blaze when taken from Troy to the Greek camp (according to a tale told by Sinon, *Aen.* 2.172f).

Transported by boat or raft. A CYBELE on its way to Rome is towed free of a sand bar in the Tiber by a woman named Claudia after men fail in the attempt; she thereby proves her chastity (*Fasti* 4.273f). A HERA, brought by Admete from Argos to Samos, is loaded on a ship to be returned home, but the vessel refuses to move (Athenaeus 15). A HERACLES is towed on a raft by a rope made of women's hair (Paus. 7.5.3). SOLDIERS made of earthenware instead of living ones are sent off to the Trojan War by Cinyras (*Ep.* 3.9).

Transported by ox-cart. A CYBELE rides into Rome, led by Claudia and other girls (*Fasti* 4.333f). A FEMALE STATUE in bridal garments riding with Zeus is detected by jealous Hera, who tears its clothes off and laughs at the deception (Paus. 9.3.1).

Moved or carried. An ARTEMIS is being carried by Iphigeneia when she meets King Thoas at her temple and leads a procession to a ship (Eur. *Iph. Taur.* 1156f, 1205f); it is carried off by Orestes and Pylades, led by Iphigeneia (*Ep.* 6.27) concealed in a bundle of sticks (Serv. *ad Aen.* 2.116). A DIONYSUS is brought in a chest to a place where human sacrifice is to be made; its arrival causes the ceremony to be halted (Paus. 7.19.3). A HERA is moved to Rome by a chosen group of youths (Livy 5.22). The PALLADIUM is stolen from Athena's shrine in Troy by Odysseus (Eur. *Rhes.* 501f); by Odysseus and Diomedes, with Helen's aid (*Ep.* 5.13; *Aen.* 2.163f; *Met.* 13.337f); as Diomedes is carrying the statue, Odysseus threatens him with his sword but is disarmed and prodded back to camp by Diomedes (Eust. *ad Il.* 10.53; *Ep.* 5.13, n. 2, Loeb edn.); Diomedes hands over the Palladium to Nautes rather than to Aeneas, who is engaged in sacrificing (Serv. *ad Aen.* 2.166, 3.407). SACRED IMAGES are being carried from burning Troy by Panthus, leading his grandchild as well, when he meets Aeneas (*Aen.* 2.318f). A VESTA is rescued from her burning temple by Metellus (*Fasti* 6.437f).

Being worshiped. A statue of bearded APHRODITE is worshiped on Cyprus by men dressed as women and women dressed as men (Serv. *ad Aen.* 2.632); of APOLLO is petitioned by Clytemnestra, as Electra and an old man watch (Soph. *Elec.* 637f); of ARTEMIS is honored with flowers by Hippolytus, while that of Aphrodite is ignored (Eur. *Hipp.* 72f, 1092f); of ATHENA is appealed to by Orestes, as the Furies appear (Aes. *Eumen.* 235f), and has a robe placed on her knees by Trojan women (*Il.* 6.87f, 6.271f, 6.297f; *Aen.* 1.479f); statues of the GODS of Thebes are prayed to by Eteocles and the women of Thebes (Aes. *Seven* 267f); statue of HESTIA is asked by Alcestis to care for her children after she dies (Eur. *Alc.* 162f); of LETO is being honored when Niobe tries to stop the ceremony (*Met.* 6.146f); of King NECTANEBOS is visited and embraced by Alexander (Ps.-Cal. 5, 96, 97); of RHEA is propitiated by the Argonauts with dancing and noisemaking (*Argo.* 1.1123f). (See also **Suppliant.**)

STELE

(See also **Pillar; Tomb.**)

The term properly refers to a grave marker consisting of an upright pillar or a tall tablet with a device on top. But it is loosely applied to other funeral monuments, such as a column, a relief carving of the deceased, or a flat, square stone.

STELAE

Overturned, LYNCEUS' stele is pushed over by Idas onto Castor, killing him (*Fab.* 80). ORPHEUS' monument is upset and his bones in an urn on top are exposed when a crowd presses up to hear a shepherd, who is sleeping beside it, sing Orpheus' songs (Paus. 9.30.5).

Almost hurled by IDAS at Castor when a thunderbolt hits Idas (Theocritus 22.137).

Two mark the mound of ZETES and CALAÏS, the sons of Boreas, whom Heracles has killed and buried (*Argo.* 1.1298f).

STICK

(See also **Club; Staff; Wand.**)

Attribute of Momus. Pointing at a globe: Lachesis; Urania. In a bundle: a lictor (q.v.); Mars.

Sticks conceal a statue of Artemis that Orestes and Pylades are carrying off (Serv. *ad Aen.* 2.116).

Containing fire. PROMETHEUS steals fire from the gods and brings it to man hidden in a hollow stalk (Hes. *W. & D.* 50f, *Theog.* 561f; *Lib.* 1.7.1; *Fab.* 141).

Removed from fire. ALTHAEA takes from the fire a stick that the Fates have brought, telling her that her baby Meleager will live only as long as it is not burned up; she places it in a chest for safekeeping until, years later, she throws it into a fire because Meleager has killed her brothers (*Fab.* 171, 174; *Met.* 8.452f).

STONE

(See also **Apple; Ball; Coal; Discus; Egg; Game; Globe; Island; Loaf of Bread; Lots; Rock; Statue; Wall; Weights.**)

Thrown at a ship (see **Ship, Under Attack**). Egg-shaped and decorated (see **Omphalos**).

Held in the hand: attribute of Zeus, who is sometimes shown holding flint (a symbol of fire) instead of a thunderbolt.

Humans turned to stone. AGLAUROS, when she tries to stop Hermes from entering her sister Herse's room (*Met.* 2.819f). ANAXARETE, while watching the funeral procession of Iphis who killed himself for love of her (*Met.* 14.753f). BATTUS, for revealing Hermes' theft of cattle after he had been bribed not to (*Met.* 2.705f). The shepherd DAPHNIS by the nymph Nomia, to whom he has been unfaithful (Serv. *ad Ecl.* 8.68). LETHAEA, for boasting of her beauty; also her husband Olenus, because he wants to share her punishment (*Met.* 10.68f). LICHAS, after being hurled into the sea by Heracles, who is being tormented by the poisoned robe Lichas has brought to him (*Met.* 9.211f). NIOBE, as she tries to save the last of her children from being shot by Artemis and Apollo (*Met.* 6.301f; *Il.* 24.614f; *Fab.* 9). The PROPOETIDES (prostitutes of Amathus), for denying the divinity of Aphrodite (*Met.* 10.238f). THEBAN WOMEN, by Hera, on the height from which Ino has just leaped into the sea (*Met.* 4.543f). A VICTIM of a glance at three-headed Cerberus (*Met.* 10.65f) or at the head of Medusa (see **Gorgon**).

Animals turned to stone. A FOX and the HOUND pursuing it, the one uncatchable, the other indefatigable, by Zeus (*Lib.* 2.4.7). A WOLF sent by

Psamathe to kill Peleus' cattle, after the sea nymph is persuaded by Thetis to end the slaughter (*Met.* 11.392f).

Stones become men and women when tossed behind them by DEUCA-LION and PYRRHA (*Met.* 1.398f; *Lib.* 1.7.2; *Fab.* 153).

In Hades a stone is laid upon ASCALAPHUS by Demeter for revealing that Persephone is not eligible to return to the upper world (*Lib.* 1.5.3); it is rolled off by Heracles (*Lib.* 2.5.12); is everlastingly rolled uphill by SISYPHUS (*Od.* 11.593f; *Lib.* 1.9.3; *Fab.* 60); hangs threateningly over TANTALUS (*Fab.* 82; *Ep.* 2.1).

Thrown by ATHENA at mad Heracles for killing his wife Megara and their sons (Eur. *Her.* 1001f); by an ATTENDANT of baby Pyrrhus across a stream, with a message attached (Plut. 21.2); by HERACLES at his own statue, thinking it alive and hostile (*Lib.* 2.6.3); by HERMES kills many-eyed Argus, the guardian of a cow (Io) (*Lib.* 2.1.3); by JASON at the armed men rising from the earth (*Argo.* 3.136f; *Met.* 7.139f; *Lib.* 1.9.23; *Fab.* 22); by PER-IERES kills Clymenus, king of the Minyans (*Lib.* 2.4.11); by the Cyclops POLYPHEMUS at Acis, whom he has surprised with Galatea (*Met.* 13.878f; Serv. *ad Ecl.* 7.37); by POLYPOETES, winner of the weight throw at the games for Patroclus (*Il.* 23.836f).

Thrown or about to be thrown in combat by AENEAS, as he faces Achilles (*Il.* 20.285f); he kills Murranus (*Aen.* 12.896f); by AJAX stuns Hec-tor, who is lifted up by Apollo as heralds stop the fight (*Il.* 7.244f), and who is rescued by Aeneas et al. (*Il.* 14.402f); topples Epicles from the wall of the Greek camp (*Il.* 12.378f); by the Giant ALCYONEUS crushes Heracles' men and chariots (Pind. *Nem.* 4.25); by DIOMEDES stuns Aeneas, who is rescued by Aphrodite (*Il.* 5.297f); by ETEOCLES breaks Polyneices' spear (Eur. *Phoen.* 1401f); by HECTOR hits Ajax' shield (*Il.* 7.244f); wounds the archer Telamon (*Il.* 8.320f) and smashes the gate of the Greek camp (*Il.* 12.445f); by HEPHAESTUS strikes down the Giant Mimas (the stones are actually pieces of red-hot metal) (*Lib.* 1.6.2); by HERACLES, routing the Ligurians (*Poet. Astr.* 2.6); by IDAS, who is killed by Zeus' thunderbolt as he is about to hurl a stele at Castor (Theocritus 22.137); by PATROCLUS, kills Hector's charioteer (*Il.* 16.733f); by PERICLYMENUS from the wall of Thebes kills Parthenopaeus (Eur. *Phoen.* 1153f); by a SPARTAN at the battle of Plataea kills the Persian general Mardonius (Plut. 17.19); by TURNUS misses Aeneas, whose spear in return finds its mark (*Aen.* 12.896f); by a WOMAN from a housetop knocks Pyrrhus from his horse (Plut. 21.34).

Stoned to death. The girls AUXESIA (Persephone) and DAMIA (Deme-ter?), during a political insurrection at Troezen (Paus. 2.32.2). EUMOLPUS, a flute player, by Cycnus because of his complicity in the false accusation made by Cycnus' wife against her stepson (*Ep.* 3.25). LYCIDAS, by his fellow councilors for advising the surrender of Athens to the Persians; his wife and children are similarly treated by women (Herod. 9.5). MEDEA'S CHILDREN, for being the bearers, albeit innocent, of the gifts that caused Glauce's horrible death (Paus. 2.3.6). ORPHEUS, by frenzied Maenads (*Met.* 11.10f). PALAMEDES, on Agamemnon's order through the machinations of Odysseus (*Ep.* 3.8); in a well, by Odysseus and Diomedes (Dictys 2.15; Serv. *ad Aen.* 2.81). POSTUMIUS, by his soldiers in anger at his arrogance (Livy 4.50).

A shower of stones falls on the Alban Mount, an omen reinforced by a voice from the sky demanding a return to piety (Livy 1.31); pours down Parnassus onto a Persian force to aid the Delphians and the two local heroes who have materialized (Herod. 8.37–39); is sent by ZEUS to supply Heracles with weapons to use against the Ligurians (*Poet. Astr.* 2.6; Strabo 4.1.7).

Are gathered by TELAMON to defend himself against Heracles, who approaches with drawn sword (*Lib.* 2.6.4).

Are moved by the music of AMPHION's lyre to form a wall, while his brother Zethus has to work to accomplish the same task (*Argo.* 1.735; *Lib.* 3.5.5); by the music of ORPHEUS' lyre (*Lib.* 1.3.2).

Is cut in two by NAVIUS in front of Tarquin, to prove the validity of augury (Livy 1.36).

Provides a hiding place. AEGEUS places a sword and sandals under a stone, to be found later by Theseus and Aethra (*Lib.* 3.15.7, 3.16.1; Plut. 1.6; *Fab.* 37).

Wrapped in baby clothes, is given by RHEA to Cronus to swallow instead of baby Zeus (Hes. *Theog.* 485f; *Fab.* 139; *Lib.* 1.1.7).

Placed in a coffin by HERMES, substituting it for Alcmene's body (Plut. 2.28; Pherecydes, *Frag. Hist. Graec.* 1.82).

Forms a seat for THESEUS and PEIRITHOÜS in Hades, to which they are stuck fast (Paus. 10.29.9).

STORK

(See **Bird.**)

STORM

At sea (see **Raft; Ship**).

Sent by ZEUS, harasses the Greek army (*Il.* 7.478f).

Breaks on DIDO and AENEAS during a hunt, forcing them to take refuge in a cave (*Aen.* 4.160f); on blind OEDIPUS, ANTIGONE, et al., which portends that Oedipus' end is near (Soph. *Oed. Col.* 1456f, 1604f).

During a storm. ALEXANDER leads his army across the Hydaspes River (Plut. 33.60). CRASSUS leads his army across the Zeugma amid portents of the disaster of Carrhae to come (Plut. 28.19). The DELPHIANS fight a Persian force, aided by two indigenous heroes and an avalanche of stones from Parnassus (Herod. 8.37–39). ROMULUS vanishes and an eclipse occurs (Plut. 2.27, 4.2; Livy 1.16).

STYLUS

Attribute of Apollo; Calliope.

DEMOSTHENES bites on the poisoned instrument that he uses for writing and dies, thereby avoiding arrest (Plut. 41.29).

SUICIDE

Included here are suicides of which the means employed is not given in the source cited. Others are to be found under the weapon used and under **Fire; Hanging; Leaping; Pyre; Snake; Vessel, Cup; Writing.** *Fab.* 242 and 243 contain a compilation of most of the suicides recorded in Hyginus' work.

APPIUS CLAUDIUS, in prison for his responsibility for the death of Verginia (Livy 3.57–58).

CANACE, when her incest with her brother is discovered by their father Aeolus (*Fab.* 243).

CHTHONIA's SISTERS, after she is sacrificed to Poseidon by her father Erechtheus (*Fab.* 46; *Lib.* 3.15.4).

DEÏANEIRA, after Heracles has himself burned to death to escape from the torture of a poisoned robe (*Fab.* 36).

STHENEBOEA, when she loses Bellerophon to her sister (*Fab.* 57).

THEMISTO, when she finds she has killed her own children instead of her rival Ino's (*Fab.* 1, 4).

SUN

(See also **Globe; Rays.**)

A disc with a face and rays: attribute of Phoebus-Apollo. Held in the hand, with the moon in the other: Aeternitas; a genius. On the breast: Virtus.

The Sun God is begged by LEUCOTHOË to save her from burial (*Met.* 4.237f); by PHAËTHON to allow him to drive the sun-chariot (*Met.* 2.19f).

SUNDIAL

Attribute of Atropos.

SUPPLIANT

(See also **Altar; Captive.**)

Warrior pleading with another. ADRASTUS, fallen from his chariot, begs for mercy; he is spared by Menelaüs but killed by Agamemnon (*Il.* 6.45f). CINNA begs for his life but is slain by a centurion (Plut. 32.5). Dying HECTOR pleads with Achilles to give his body to his people (*Il.* 22.333f). LEIODES begs Odysseus for mercy but is beheaded (*Od.* 22.310f). LYCAON pleads in vain with Achilles (*Il.* 21.67f), as does Tros (*Il.* 20.463f). MAGUS begs Aeneas in vain for his life (*Aen.* 10.521f). TURNUS, wounded and helpless, asks Aeneas, not for mercy, but to give his body to his father (*Aen.* 12.930f).

Man pleading with man. ACHAEMENIDES, left behind in the land of the Cyclopes by Odysseus, begs Aeneas to rescue him (*Aen.* 3.599f). The singer ISMENIAS kneels to Alexander (Ps.-Cal. 128). MUSICANUS, an Indian potentate bringing elephants and other gifts, prostrates himself before Alexander (Arrian 6.15.6). ODYSSEUS, disguised as a beggar, prays to Zeus who thunders from a clear sky, an omen that is interpreted by a woman working at a mill (*Od.* 20.97f). ORESTES begs Menelaüs to save him from execution (Eur. *Orest.* 379f) and Apollo to save him from the Furies (Eur. *Iph. Taur.* 970f). PELEUS, in exile, holds out an olive branch to Ceÿx as he asks for a home (*Met.* 11.279f). King PERSEUS cravenly prostrates himself before his conqueror Aemilius Paulus (Plut. 14.26). The musician PHEMIUS begs Odysseus for his life and is pardoned (*Od.* 22.340f). A PHRYGIAN SLAVE entreats Orestes not to kill him and is finally forgiven (Eur. *Orest.* 1505f). POMPEY prevents the desertion of his father's troops by pleading with them on his knees in the camp's gateway (Plut. 32.3). PRIAM, on Troy's wall, begs Hector to come back into the city and avoid Achilles (*Il.* 22.25f) and visits Achilles' quarters to ask for Hector's body (*Il.* 24.477f). THEMISTOCLES, holding in his arms the son of Admetus and lying before his hearth, begs his former adversary for sanctuary (Plut. 7.24).

Man pleading with woman. CEPHALUS begs Procris' forgiveness for doubting her faithfulness to him (*Met.* 7.748f). DIONYSUS, to escape from Lycurgus, asks Thetis for sanctuary in her cave in the sea (*Il.* 6.135f). ODYSSEUS, recognized by Helen in spite of his disguise when he is spying in Troy, begs Hecuba for his life (Eur. *Hec.* 240f); he begs Circe to let him leave her island (*Od.* 10.477f); pleading to be sent home, he embraces the knees of Arete (*Od.* 7.139f). ORESTES is praying to Athena's statue when the Furies find him (Aes. *Eumen.* 235f). Young PHAËTHON pleads with Clymene for proof that Phoebus-Apollo is his father (*Met.* 1.762f).

Woman pleading with man. AETHRA begs her son Theseus to help the bereaved mothers of the seven invaders of Thebes (Eur. *Suppl.* 283f). ARTEMIS weeps on Zeus' lap after being whacked with her own bow by Hera (*Il.* 21.505f). CIRCE pleads with Odysseus to spare her (*Od.* 10.323f). CLEO-PATRA throws herself at Octavian's feet after he captures Alexandria (Plut. 44.83). CLYTEMNESTRA begs Achilles to prevent the sacrifice of Iphigeneia (Eur. *Iph. Aul.* 899f) and prays to Apollo's statue for protection from the vengeance of Electra, who is threatening her (Soph. *Elec.* 637f). DAPHNE coaxes from her father, the river god Peneus, a promise that she may remain unwed (*Met.* 1.481f). DEMETER begs Zeus to bring Persephone back from Hades (*Met.* 5.512f). ELECTRA kneels to Orestes and Pylades by an altar (Eur. *Elec.* 220f). HECUBA entreats Odysseus to prevent Polyxena's sacrifice (Eur. *Hec.* 274f) and Agamemnon to help her avenge the murder of her son Polydorus, who lies before them (Eur. *Hec.* 752f). HERMIONE begs Orestes to save her from the wrath of her husband Neoptolemus (Eur. *Andro.* 884f). HYPSIPYLE begs Amphiaraüs to save her from Eurydice, who blames her for the death of her baby Opheltes (fragment of Eur. *Hypsipyle,* see Rose, p. 200). JOCASTA tries to stop the fight between her sons Eteocles and Polyneices (Sen. *Phoen.* 511f). MEDEA begs Jason to take her with him from Colchis (*Argo.* 4.80f), King Creon for mercy (Eur. *Med.* 271f), and King Aegeus for sanctuary (Eur. *Med.* 708f). MELEAGER'S WIFE beseeches her husband to take part in the defense of their city (*Il.* 9.590f). PHAEDRA'S NURSE begs Hippolytus to give in to her mistress' passion for him, as Phaedra herself listens (Eur. *Hipp.* 601f). SOPHONISBA begs the Numidian Masinissa to save her from the Romans (Livy 30.12). THETIS entreats Zeus to punish the Greeks for dishonoring her son Achilles (*Il.* 1.500f).

Woman pleading with woman. ALCESTIS prays to Hestia's statue, asking her to protect her children when she dies (Eur. *Alc.* 162f). APHRO-DITE, slightly wounded by Diomedes, comes to her mother Dione for comfort (*Il.* 5.370f). HELEN begs Theonoë not to reveal that the traveler present is Menelaüs (Eur. *Hel.* 894f). MEDEA begs Arete for protection from the Colchians who are demanding her surrender (*Argo.* 4.1011f). MELIBOEA (Chloris) and AMYCLAS pray to Leto's statue and consequently are the only two of Niobe's children spared by Apollo and Artemis (Paus. 2.21.10).

Suppliant woman with baby or child. ANDROMACHE, holding Astyanax, pleads with Odysseus for their lives; Astyanax is taken from her

(Eur. *Troad.* 740f). CALLISTO, holding her baby Arcas, beseeches Hera for mercy but is turned into a bear (*Met.* 2.476f). CHILONIS and her children try to reconcile her father with her husband (Plut. 37.18). CREÜSA, holding baby Iulus, begs Aeneas to rescue them from burning Troy (*Aen.* 2.673f). IPHI-GENEIA, holding her baby brother Orestes, begs her father Agamemnon not to sacrifice her (Eur. *Iph. Aul.* 1243f). Despite the pleas of his wife LICINIA and child, Gaius Gracchus sets off for the senate even though he risks a violent death (Plut. 40.15).

Two or more suppliants. AETHRA, Adrastus, and other women entreat Theseus to help them recover the bodies of their men slain at Thebes (Eur. *Suppl.* 88f). ALEXANDER's SOLDIERS beg him to lead them home (Plut. 33.62) and to restore them to his favor (Plut. 33.71). ANDROMACHE and Astyanax beg Menelaüs to spare them; old Peleus takes their part (Eur. *Andro.* 530f). CATO's son and servants beg him not to kill himself (Plut. 36.68). CORIOLANUS' wife, mother, children, et al. come out of Rome to beg him not to attack the city (Livy 2.40; Plut. 12.34–36). DANAÜS' daughters, in Eastern garb and bearing olive branches, ask King Pelasgus for asylum (Aes. *Suppl.* 234f). DARIUS' mother and wife, believing him dead, beg Leonatus not to kill them until their lord has been buried; admitted to Alexander's presence, they kneel first to Hephaestion by mistake and are then reassured by Alexander (Q. Curt. 3.12). Old IOLAÜS and the Heracleidae (Children of Heracles) beg Demophon for asylum from Eurystheus (Eur. *Heracleidae* 226f). IPHIS and Telethusa, clinging to Isis' (Io's) altar, pray that Iphis may be changed into a man (*Met.* 9.770f). MELEAGER's father, mother, et al. fail to move him to defend their city; his wife succeeds (*Il.* 9.573f). Blind OEDIPUS and Antigone ask Theseus to grant them an end to their wandering (*Lib.* 3.5.9). A PRIEST and young people of Thebes beg King Oedipus to alleviate the plague besetting their city (Soph. *Oed. Tyr.* 1f). REGULUS' wife and sons plead with him not to honor his parole by returning to Carthage (Hor. *Odes* 3.5f; Livy, *Epitome* 18). SOLDIERS beg Metellus to be allowed to serve under him (Plut. 16.13). Three YOUNG SONS of Thyestes beg their uncle Atreus in vain for their lives (*Ep.* 2.13).

SWALLOW

(See **Bird.**)

SWAN

(See **Bird.**)

SWIMMING

(See also **Falling; Flood; Leaping; Sea; Ship; Water.**)

To shore (see **Castaway**).

ALEXANDER takes a swim in the Cydnus River (Arrian 2.4.7).

CLOELIA leads the escape of the girls who are hostage to Porsena by swimming the Tiber (Livy 2.13).

HERACLES crosses the Strait of Messina, holding onto the horn of a bull (Diod. Sic. 4.22.6).

HORATIUS, after defending the bridge to Rome until it is cut behind him, dives in and swims to safety (Livy 2.10; Plut. 6.16).

LEANDER drowns while swimming the Hellespont toward Hero's beacon (*Heroïdes* 18.57f, 19.119f).

METABUS, held up in his escape from his enemies by a swollen stream, hurls his baby daughter Camilla across tied to his spear; he then swims across (*Aen.* 11.561f).

MYRTILUS drowns after cursing Pelops, who has thrown him into the sea (*Ep.* 2.8; *Fab.* 84).

NYMPHS are swept away by the river god Acheloüs and become islands (*Met.* 8.583f).

ODYSSEUS floats for days, supported by Ino's (Leucothea's) veil, after his raft breaks up (*Od.* 5.373f).

ORION is swimming when Artemis shoots him in the head because Apollo has challenged her to hit what she takes to be only a distant, dark object (*Poet. Astr.* 2.34).

PONTIUS COMINIUS swims the Tiber to carry a message to the Romans besieged on the Capitol (Plut. 8.25).

SARON swims out to sea after an escaping deer and drowns (Paus. 2.30.7).

TURNUS, trapped inside the Trojan camp on the Tiber, escapes by swimming (*Aen.* 9.815f).

SWINGING

ATHENIAN GIRLS in rope swings do penance for the death of Erigone. The act symbolizes the search for the bodies of Erigone and her father Icarius in another element, since they are not to be found on earth (Serv. *ad Georg.* 2.389; *Fab.* 130; *Poet. Astr.* 2.4).

SWORD

(See also **Beheading; Fighting; Killing; Knife; Sickle; Suicide; Suppliant; Wounded Figure.**)

Attribute of Aphrodite (victorious); Chrysaor; Corybantes; Demeter; Furor; Mars; Melpomene; Mithras; Nemesis; Virtus.

ACHILLES, in the act of drawing his sword against Agamemnon, thinks better of it when Athena touches his hair (*Il.* 1.193f).

With drawn sword AEGISTHUS advances to kill Thyestes, who recognizes the sword as the one he lost when he raped Pelopia (*Fab.* 88); ARGIVE ELDERS face armed Aegisthus and Clytemnestra before the bodies of Agamemnon and Cassandra (Aes. *Agam.* 1650f); AUGE, on the point of killing Telephus in their bridal chamber, is prevented by a huge snake (*Fab.* 100); CINYRAS pursues his incestuous daughter Myrrha, who is changed into a tree (*Met.* 10.472f); CNEMON bursts into his father and stepmother's bedroom (*Aeth.* 1); HAEMON threatens Creon when they find Antigone hanged (Soph. *Ant.* 1231f); HERACLES is instructed in swordplay by Castor (*Lib.* 2.4.9); he approaches Telemon, who is gathering stones with which to defend himself (*Lib.* 2.6.4); LYNCUS, about to stab sleeping Triptolemus, is changed into a lynx by Demeter (*Met.* 5.657f); MENELAÜS is about to kill Helen but drops his sword at the sight of her breasts (*Ilias Mikra* 13; Aristophanes, *Lysistrata* 155 and scholia ad loc.); he is prevented from killing her by Aphrodite (Quint. Smy. 13.385f), as is Aeneas (*Aen.* 2.588f); ODYSSEUS steals up behind Diomedes, who is carrying the Palladium, but he is disarmed, trussed up, and prodded back to camp by Diomedes' sword (Eust. *ad Il.* 10.531; *Ep.* 5.13, n. 2, Loeb edn.); holding protective moly also, Odysseus threatens Circe, who has turned his men into pigs (*Od.* 10.321f), and he prevents ghosts from the underworld from approaching him (*Od.* 11.48f); ORESTES, holding an olive branch as well as a bloody sword, sits in Apollo's shrine surrounded by sleeping Furies as Apollo and Hermes appear (Aes. *Eumen.* 39f); ORESTES and PYLADES are on the point of killing Helen when she is magically lifted out of reach (Eur. *Orest.* 1295f, 1455f); they take Aegisthus into his palace to kill him (Soph. *Elec.* 1491f) and threaten Hermione in order to force Menelaüs to let them escape with Electra (Eur. *Orest.* 1346f, 1567f); PENTHEUS attacks a phantom Dionysus as his palace collapses (Eur. *Bacch.* 629f); a PERSIAN in Macedonian armor is apprehended before he can kill Alexander, who releases him (Ps.-Cal. 162); POLYNEICES enters Thebes, where he finds his mother Jocasta with his brother and enemy Eteocles (Eur. *Phoen.* 263f); TARQUIN approaches Lucretia's bed (*Fasti* 2.792f; Livy 1.58); TELEPHUS is about to kill his bride Auge when the name she utters (that of

Heracles), in a call for help, reveals that she is also his mother (*Fab.* 100). TERENTIUS approaches and stabs the bed from which Pompey has stolen away (Plut. 32.3); THEOCLYMENUS threatens to kill a servant but is restrained by the Dioscuri (Eur. *Hel.* 1639f); old THESTOR is about to kill a priest (his daughter Leucippe disguised) when she recognizes him; they are on the point of killing Theonoë when they discover that she is their daughter and sister, respectively (*Fab.* 190).

Brandished by ARCHIDAMIA as she incites the Spartan elders to resist Pyrrhus (Plut. 21.27); by POSEIDON as he rallies the Greeks (*Il.* 14.361f).

Wielded in battle or fight by ACHILLES to attack Aeneas, who is armed with a huge stone (*Il.* 20.285f), to kill Memnon, son of Eos (Quint. Smy. 2.385f), to kill Tenes, who has tried to prevent his landing by throwing stones (*Ep.* 3.26), to kill Asteropaeus, who is vainly trying to free from the ground a spear with which to defend himself (*Il.* 21.173f), and to slaughter fleeing Trojans in the Scamander River (*Il.* 21.7f); by AENEAS and TURNUS in single combat; Turnus flees when his sword breaks until his sister Juturna, in the likeness of his charioteer Metiscus, brings him another; Aeneas kills him as he begs Aeneas to return his body to his father (*Aen.* 12.710f, 12.731f, 12.783f, 12.950f); by AGAMEMNON to kill Iphidamas and Coön (*Il.* 11.232f); by ALEXANDER, fighting alone inside an Indian stronghold until help arrives (Arrian 6.9.5–6), against Darius, who wounds him (Plut. 33.20), and against gigantic King Poros, whom he kills (Ps.-Cal. 219; cf. Arrian 5.19.1, where Poros surrenders to him: see **Elephant**); by CAESAR, fighting beside his soldiers in a battle in Gaul (Caesar *B.G.* 2.25.2); by the brothers ETEOCLES and POLYNEICES in their fight to the death (Eur. *Phoen.* 1219f, 1359f); by HECTOR to sever Ajax's spear (*Il.* 16.114f) and to face Achilles and his spear (*Il.* 22.273f); by the three HORATII, paired off against the Curiatii brothers; after two of the former fall, the third runs away until his three pursuers are spread out enough for him to kill singly (Livy 1.25); by HORATIUS COCLES, defending the bridge to Rome against an army, at first with two other Romans, then alone (Livy 2.10); by IDAS to kill Castor, who has interfered with the burial of his brother Lynceus (*Fab.* 80); by LYNCEUS to wound Castor, after which he is killed by Castor's brother Polydeuces (*Fasti* 5.708f); by MENELAÜS in single combat with Paris, on whose helmet his sword shatters (*Il.* 3.340f); by NEOPTOLEMUS to defend himself in Apollo's shrine when beset by Orestes and a crowd of Delphians (Eur. *Andro.* 1118f); by ODYSSEUS et al. in a fight with the suitors' avengers, until Athena stops it (*Od.* 24.526f); by PARIS et al. when they ambush Achilles and Antilochus in Apollo's shrine (Dares 34); by PENELOPE'S SUITORS as they are being shot down by Odysseus' arrows (*Od.* 22.79f); by PERSEUS, defending himself from Phineus' adherents (*Met.* 5.157f); by POLYDEUCES to kill Idas and recover Castor's body (*Fab.* 80); by PYRRHUS in single combat with Pantauchus, who is rescued by his men (Plut. 21.7), and with a challenger whom he cuts in two (Plut. 21.24); by TIMOLEON in defense of his wounded brother (Plut. 13.4); by TURNUS, alone inside the Trojan camp (*Aen.* 9.731f).

Put to the sword. ACHILLES by Paris, as he is being embraced by Deïphobus in Apollo's temple (Dictys 4.11). AEGISTHUS and CLYTEMNESTRA by Orestes (by Pylades also?) (Aes. *Choëph.* 870f). AEGYPTUS' SONS by their brides, the daughters of Danaüs (Aes. *Prom.* 859f). Old AESON by Medea, who cuts his throat and replaces his blood with a rejuvenating brew (*Met.* 7.285f). AGRIPPINA in her bed is stabbed and clubbed by Nero's soldiers (Tac. *An.* 14.5–8). APSYRTUS by Jason, after Medea lures her brother into an ambush (*Argo.* 4.452f). The tyrant ARCHIAS at a banquet, by Theban patriots dressed as women (Plut. 15.11). ARCHIMEDES by a Roman soldier as he is engaged in research or while he is carrying various instruments to show to Marcellus (Plut. 16.19; Livy 25.31). ATREUS by Aegisthus, with the sword with which his mother Pelopia has killed herself (*Fab.* 88). CAESAR by Casca, Brutus, et al. in the senate house (Plut. 34.71; Suet. *Caes.* 82; *Met.* 15.799f). The CHILDREN of Jason and Medea by their mother (Eur. *Med.* 1236f; *Met.* 7.394f). CLYTEMNESTRA by Orestes (Eur. *Elec.* 1165f, *Orest.* 819f). EURYALUS by one of the Rutulian horsemen who have captured him, as Nisus runs to his aid (*Aen.* 9.420f). HORATIUS' SISTER by Horatius himself because she mourns for her betrothed, whom her brother has just killed in heroic defense of Rome (Livy 1.26). The boy ITYLUS by his mother Aëdon, who has mistaken him for a child of her enemy Niobe (*Od.* 19.518f). Faithless MELANTHIUS by Telemachus and Eumaeus after they mutilate him (*Od.* 22.474f). PALINURUS by rustics as he climbs ashore from the sea (*Aen.* 6.358f). King PERSES by Medus, who gets the sword from Medea (*Fab.* 27). POLYDORUS by Polymnestor for his gold (*Met.* 13.435f). POLYXENA by a priest or by Neoptolemus at the tomb of Achilles (*Ep.* 5.23; Eur. *Hec.* 107f, 521f; *Met.* 13.441f). POMPEY by men aboard a vessel ferrying him to the shore of Africa from the galley where his wife is watching (Plut. 32.79). King PORSENA'S SECRETARY by Mucius, who mistakes him for the king (Plut. 6.17). SAILORS on an Egyptian boat by Menelaüs et al. in order to escape with Helen (Eur. *Hel.* 1590f). SERTORIUS by his soldiers at a banquet (Plut. 29.26). The traitor SP. MAELIUS by Servilius in front of Cincinnatus et al. (Livy 4.14). TIMOPHANES, tyrant of Corinth, by patriots, as his brother Timoleon stands aside weeping (Plut. 13.4). TURNUS by Aeneas as he pleads to be granted burial by his people (*Aen.* 12.887f). VERGINIA by her father to save her from the lust of tyrannical Appius Claudius (Livy 3.48). WARRIORS emerging from the earth, by Cadmus (Eur. *Phoen.* 657f), and by Jason (*Argo.* 3.1377f; cf. *Argo.* 3.409, where Aeëtes tells of accomplishing the same feat with his spear). Sleeping warriors by Diomedes and Odysseus, after which they lead off Rhesus' horses (Eur. *Rhes.* 595f, 756f; *Il.* 10.482f), and by Nisus and Euryalus (*Aen.* 9.324f).

Used for committing suicide by AJAX, who plants it in the ground and impales himself on it (*Ep.* 5.7; *Fab.* 107; Soph. *Ajax* 814f; *Met.* 13.386f; Pind. *Nem.* 7.24f); by AMPHINOME at Pelias' hearth, after she has cursed him for killing her husband and son (Diod. Sic. 4.50); by AMPHION, from grief at the slaughter of his and Niobe's children (*Met.* 6.271f); by CANACE, after her incest with her brother (*Fab.* 243; *Heroïdes* 11.119f); by CATO THE YOUNGER, who rejects aid from a physician (Plut. 36.70); by DEÏANEIRA, after unintentionally poisoning Heracles; she dies in Hyllus' arms (Soph. *Trach.* 923f); by DEMOPHON accidentally, when he falls from his horse onto his sword (*Ep.* 6.16); by DIDO, who uses Aeneas' sword as she lies on the pyre she has had built (*Aen.* 4.663f); by EURYDICE after she hears of her son Haemon's suicide (Soph. *Ant.* 1298f); by HAEMON, on finding that Antigone has hanged herself (Soph. *Ant.* 1231f); by the Centaur-maiden HYLONOME, who falls on the blade that has killed her lover (*Met.* 11.426f); by JOCASTA beside the bodies of her sons Eteocles and Polyneices (Eur. *Phoen.* 1455f) or in the presence of Oedipus, who has blinded himself (Sen. *Oed.* 1072f); by LAODAMEIA when Hermes takes her husband Protesilaüs off to Hades (*Ep.* 3.30); by LUCRETIA after she tells her husband and Junius Brutus of being raped by Tarquin (Serv. *ad Aen.* 6.818, 8.646); by M. ANTONY, by falling on it after his servant has set him an example (Plut. 44.77); by M. JUNIUS BRUTUS, who falls on it (or has it held by a friend) after his defeat at Philippi (Plut. 46.52); by MENOECEUS to save Thebes; he sacrifices himself on its wall (Eur. *Phoen.* 1008f, 1090f) or at one of its gates (*Lib.* 3.6.7); by OTHO, who falls on it, to the great distress of his servants and soldiers (Plut. 50 ad fin.); by PELOPIA after snatching from Aegisthus the sword that identifies him as her son and Thyestes as her ravisher (*Fab.* 88); by PHAEDRA, after confessing to Theseus that her accusation against Hippolytus is false (Sen. *Phaed.* 1255f); by PYRAMUS, on finding Thisbe's bloody robe (*Met.* 4.115f) and by THISBE on finding Pyramus dead (*Met.* 4.128f); by VARUS et al. after his army is ambushed and destroyed by the Germans (Dio 56.21).

Used for cutting or chopping by ALEXANDER on the Gordian knot (Plut. 33.18; Arrian 2.3.1); by CINYRAS on a tree (his daughter Myrrha), releasing baby Adonis from her womb (Serv. *ad Aen.* 5.72; see also **Boar; Tree**); by HALIRRHOTHIUS, son of Poseidon, on Athena's olive tree; the blade comes off and decapitates him (Serv. *ad Georg.* 1.18). (See also **Axe; Rope.**)

Presented by AJAX to his small son (Soph. *Ajax* 573f); to Ajax by Hector, who receives a belt in return (*Il.* 7.303f); to CANACE by one of her father's guards, who also conveys his order that she kill herself (*Heroïdes* 11.93f); to CATO THE YOUNGER, as he sits reading, by a young servant (Plut. 36.70); to HERACLES by Hermes (*Lib.* 2.4.11).

Shown to the Roman people by BRUTUS who, taking it from Lucretia's body, seeks to inflame them against the Tarquins (Serv. *ad Aen.* 6.818, 8.646); by VERGINIUS who, having just killed his daughter to save her from the lust of Appius Claudius, incites them to vengeance (Livy 3.48–50).

Placed in or taken from hiding. ACASTUS steals Peleus' sword while he sleeps and hides it in a pile of dung (*Lib.* 3.13.3). AEGEUS places his sword and sandals beneath a stone, where Theseus subsequently finds them with Aethra's help (Plut. 1.6; *Lib.* 3.15.7, 3.16.1; *Fab.* 37). PELOPIA secures the sword of her ravisher Thyestes and hides it beneath a statue of Athena (*Ep.* 2.14; *Fab.* 87, 88). TARQUIN has weapons concealed in the house of Turnus Herdonius to be found there as proof of his treachery (Livy 1.51).

Recognized as his own by AEGEUS when Theseus produces it at table to cut his meat, causing him to dash from Theseus' hand the cup of poison prepared by Medea (Plut. 1.12; *Ep.* 1.6); by THYESTES when he sees it in the hand of Aegisthus, who is coming to kill him (*Fab.* 88).

Thrown into the scales by the Gaul BRENNUS as Rome's tribute is being weighed (Livy 5.48; Plut. 8.28).

Falls from the hand of MENELAÜS when, on the point of killing Helen, he sees her bare breasts (*Ilias Mikra* 13; Aristophanes, *Lysistrata* 155 and Schol. ad loc.).

Suspended over the head of DAMOCLES at Dionysius' banquet (Cic. *Tusc.* 5.21).

Selected from among the trinkets that Odysseus offers to the daughters of Lycomedes, by ACHILLES, who is dressed as one of them (*Lib.* 3.13.8; *Fab.* 96; *Met.* 13.162f).

TABLE

(See also **Eating.**)

Overturned by T𝐇𝐘𝐄𝐒𝐓𝐄𝐒 when he learns that he has been served his own son's flesh by Atreus (Aes. *Agam.* 1590f); by Z𝐄𝐔𝐒 in the guise of a laborer, when he is served human flesh by Lycaon's sons, whom he blasts with thunderbolts; he also turns their father into a wolf (*Fab.* 176; *Lib.* 3.8.1; *Met.* 1.232f; *Poet. Astr.* 2.4).

TABLET

(See also **Book; Letter; Writing.**)

Attribute of Calliope (also holding a stylus).

TAIL

Attribute of Satyrs; Sileni (qq.v.).
Of a creature in place of legs (see **Snake-legged or -tailed**).

TAMBOURINE

(See **Drum.**)

TASSEL

The aegis (q.v.), usually worn by Athena, is often represented with a fringe of what appear to be tassels, rather than snakes, and is so described at *Il.* 2.447f.

TEARS

(See also **Grieving.**)

Attribute of Heraclitus, the "Weeping Philosopher" (Aelian 8.13).
Nymphs and others, weeping for M𝐀𝐑𝐒𝐘𝐀𝐒, create a stream (*Met.* 6.382f). Stone N𝐈𝐎𝐁𝐄 sheds tears for her children (*Met.* 6.306f).

TEMPLE

(See also **Altar.**)

Round: attribute of Vesta.

AENEAS inspects pictures on the doors of Apollo's temple at Cumae (*Aen.* 6.9f).

ALEXANDER visits the temple of Ammon at Siwa (Plut. 33.27).

CREÜSA meets a priest (her lost son Ion) at Apollo's temple at Delphi (Eur. *Ion* 237f), above which Athena appears to them et al. (Eur. *Ion* 1549f).

PHLEGYAS sets fire to a shrine of Apollo in retaliation for Apollo's seduction of his sister Coronis (Serv. *ad Aen.* 6.618).

TRIOPAS tears down Demeter's temple; for doing this, she sends a snake to torment him (*Poet. Astr.* 2.14).

With two portals. Temples of Janus have two doors facing in opposite directions. When they are closed, peace reigns (Plut. 4.20; Livy 1.19). AUGUSTUS closes the doors of Janus' temple in Rome, which was done but twice before (Suet. *Aug.* 22). HERA bursts open the doors of a temple in Lavinium (guarded by Janus) when King Latinus refuses to do so; this signifies that there will be war between Latins and Trojans (*Aen.* 7.607f).

Surrounded by flood waters. The hut of BAUCIS and PHILEMON is transformed into Zeus' temple; the old couple become its priests and are transformed into oaks when they die (*Met.* 8.700f). DEUCALION and PYRRHA pray at Themis' shrine when the flood recedes (*Met.* 1.371f).

THIMBLE

Attribute of the Graces.

THREAD

Attribute of the Moirai or Parcae (Fates, q.v.).

Given to THESEUS by Ariadne or Daedalus, enables him to retrace his steps after killing the Minotaur in the Labyrinth (*Ep.* 1.9; *Met.* 8.172f; *Fab.* 42).

Unraveled at night by PENELOPE from a shroud for Laërtes or a robe that she weaves by day (*Od.* 2.94f, 19.149f, 24.138f); by TARCHETIUS' servant from a web of cloth being woven by his daughter with the help of her maid; this prevents its completion, which would free her to marry (Plut. 2.2).

THRONE

(See also **Chair; Judge; Seated Figure.**)

Attribute of Rhea; deities in general; kings and others who wield power. Eagle throne: Jupiter. Lion throne: Astarte. Adorned with celestial bodies: Jupiter.

THROWING

(See also **Ball; Discus; Falling; Spear; Stone.**)

A BEGGAR (Odysseus) is the target of various missiles: a footstool, thrown by Antinoüs (*Od.* 17.409f, 17.462f) or by Eurymachus, which knocks a wine jar from a bearer's hand (*Od.* 18.394f); an ox's hoof thrown by Cte-sippus, which he dodges (*Od.* 20.299f).

THUNDERBOLT

(See also **Light; Storm; Torch.**)

Attribute of Anteros; Eris (if the conjecture is correct that *teras polemoio* [portent of war] at *Il.* 11.4 is a thunderbolt); Zeus (from whom come all thunderbolts unless it is indicated otherwise).

Forged by HEPHAESTUS and the Cyclopes (*Lib.* 1.2.1; *Aen.* 8.424f; *Georg.* 4.170f; *Argo.* 1.730f; Hes. *Theog.* 138f).

Sent as a sign. Thrown by APOLLO, it guides the *Argo* to a safe harbor (*Lib.* 1.9.26). It reveals baby ASCLEPIUS' divinity to a shepherd (Paus. 2.26.4). With other signs, it portends CAESAR's murder (*Met.* 15.787f). It promises empire to King NUMA and the Romans (*Fasti* 3.333f). Lightning and thunder herald the death of OEDIPUS to Antigone, Ismene, and Theseus (Soph. *Oed. Col.* 1448f). OLYMPIAS dreams that it kindles fire on her body (Plut. 33.2). It proves to THESEUS that Minos is a son of Zeus (Bacchylides 16; *Poet. Astr.* 2.5). Thunder is heard in a clear sky in answer to a beggar's (Odysseus') prayer; it is a sign that Zeus grants the wish expressed by a woman working at a mill (*Od.* 20.97f).

Halts the combat of DIOMEDES and HECTOR in their chariots (*Il.* 8.133f); of the DIOSCURI with Idas and Lynceus (*Fasti* 5.713f); of GREEKS and TROJANS (*Il.* 8.75f; 15.377); of HERACLES with APOLLO for possession of the Delphic tripod (*Lib.* 2.6.2); of ODYSSEUS et al. with the avengers of Penelope's suitors (*Od.* 24.539f).

ZEUS WITH ATTRIBUTES: EAGLE, AEGIS, AND THUN-
DERBOLT

Thwarts the attempted rape of DEMETER by Iasion (*Lib.* 3.12.1); of
HERA by the Giant Porphyrion (*Lib.* 1.6.2); of LETO by huge Tityos (*Fab.*
55).

Strikes ADONIS as he fights a boar (Ares) (Serv. *ad Ecl.* 10.18);
ANCHISES and cripples him, for revealing that he has been Aphrodite's lover
(*Aen.* 2.648f; *Fab.* 94; *H. to Aph.* 286f); the river god ASOPUS as he is chasing
Zeus, who is carrying off his daughter Aegina (*Lib.* 3.12.6); CAPANEUS as he
climbs an assault-ladder at Thebes (*Lib.* 3.6.7; *Fab.* 68; Eur. *Phoen.* 1176f,
Suppl. 497f); the Giant ENCELADUS, who is buried under Etna (*Aen.* 3.577f);
ERECHTHEUS, at Poseidon's request (*Fab.* 46); GAULS, who are attacking
Delphi during a storm (Paus. 10.23.3); IASION, after seducing Demeter in a
plowed field (*Od.* 5.125f); IDAS, who is about to hurl a stone at Castor (*Lib.*
3.11.2); LYCAON and his sons, for offering a guest (Zeus) human flesh; they
become wolves (*Lib.* 3.8.1; *Met.* 1.230f; *Fab.* 176); MENOETIUS, the son of a
Titan, sending him to Hades (Hes. *Theog.* 514f); PHAËTHON as he drives his
father's sun-chariot (*Met.* 2.311f); SALMONEUS, as he hurls torches from his
chariot in imitation of Zeus (*Fab.* 61; *Lib.* 1.9.7; *Aen.* 6.585f); SEMELE, who
has insisted that her lover Zeus appear to her in all his splendor (*Met.* 3.305f;

Lib. 3.4.3; *Fab.* 167; Eur. *Bacch.* 32f); the Titans in their battle with the three "Hundred-handed," setting the earth afire (Hes. *Theog.* 689f); the monster Typhoeus, who is buried under Etna (Hes. *Theog.* 836f; Aes. *Prom.* 356f; *Lib.* 1.6.3; *Argo.* 2.1211f).

Strikes the ship of Ajax Oïleus and impales him on a rock; the bolt is thrown by Athena (*Aen.* 1.40f; Sen. *Agam.* 579f; *Ep.* 6.6; cf. Eur. *Troad.*, where Athena's bolts and Poseidon's waves assail a fleet of homeward-bound Greek ships); of Odysseus, shattering it (*Od.* 7.248f).

Sets fire to the EARTH (see also "Strikes [Titans]," above); to the palace of Pentheus, from which Dionysus emerges to join his devotees (Eur. *Bacch.* 585f); to the palace of Tullus Hostilius because he performed a rite improperly (Livy 1.31).

Opens a chasm that swallows Amphiaraüs and his chariot (*Lib.* 3.6.8).

Is brandished by Alexander as Apelles paints his portrait (Plut. 33.4; *Nat. Hist.* 35.92).

THYRSUS

A staff carried by Dionysus and his followers, e.g., Maenads (q.v.), Satyrs (q.v.), and Sileni (q.v.). It is tipped with a pine cone or sometimes by vine leaves and grape clusters.

Used as a weapon by Bacchants to rout armed men (Eur. *Bacch.* 758f); by Dionysus to kill the Giant Eurytus (*Lib.* 1.6.2).

Dropped by Dionysus and Maenads as they flee from Lycurgus (*Il.* 6.130f).

Taken away by Pentheus from Dionysus (Eur. *Bacch.* 494f).

TIARA

(See **Crown.**)

TIGER

(See also **Panther.**)

Attribute of Dionysus.

Form assumed by Proteus to escape from the grasp of Aristaeus (*Georg.* 4.407); by Thetis in her struggle with Peleus (*Met.* 11.245).

TOAD

(See **Frog.**)

TOILETTE

APHRODITE is often shown at her toilette, a scene not related to any particular incident. She is usually attended by Graces and Erotes. On one occasion she is visited by Athena and Hera (*Argo.* 3.43f).

HERA adorns herself and borrows Aphrodite's magic girdle in order to beguile Zeus (*Il.* 14.153f).

SEMIRAMIS is interrupted at her toilette by the news and noise of rebellion (Val. Max. 9.3b.4).

TOMB

(See also **Altar; Burial; Pillar; Stele; Temple.**)

Visits paid to tombs. By ALEXANDER to Achilles' (Plut. 33.15; Arrian 1.12.1) and to Cyrus', which he finds already plundered (Plut. 33.69; Arrian 6.29.4); by AUGUSTUS to Alexander's (Suet. *Aug.* 18); by NEOPTOLEMUS to his father Achilles' (Quint. Smy. 9.43).

Encounters at tombs. HELEN is seeking asylum at the tomb of King Proteus from Theoclymenus when Teucer, who has been shipwrecked, appears (Eur. *Hel.* 68f); MENELAÜS, also a castaway, and, later a hunter, Theoclymenus, join her (Eur. *Hel.* 541f, 1165f). ORESTES and PYLADES are joined at Agamemnon's tomb by Electra (Aes. *Choëph.* 1f).

Ghosts appearing from their tombs. ACHILLES, to demand the sacrifice of Polyxena (*Fab.* 110). DARIUS, evoked by his queen Atossa (Aes. *Pers.* 606f). STHENELUS, in full armor, as the *Argo* sails by (*Argo.* 2.911f).

Sacrifice offered at a tomb. By AENEAS to Anchises before the games to be held in his honor (*Aen.* 5.77f). NEOPTOLEMUS sacrifices Polyxena to Achilles (Eur. *Hec.* 107f, 521f; *Ep.* 5.23; *Met.* 13.441f).

Various scenes. ACHILLES displays at Patroclus' tomb the prizes to be won at the funeral games (*Il.* 23.257f). ANDROMACHE tries to keep Odysseus et al. from razing Hector's tomb (Sen. *Tro.* 705f). BIRDS, which were once Memnon's comrades, grieve at his tomb (Serv. *ad Aen.* 1.751). CREON, coming to free Antigone who has been entombed alive, finds her hanged and Haemon, his son, also a suicide (Soph. *Ant.* 1100f). MEDEA places snakes in the tomb of her brother Apsyrtus (*Fab.* 26). Trees at PHYLLIS' tomb shed their leaves in grief (*Fab.* 59). THETIS at Achilles' tomb displays the prizes that the gods have donated, to be won at his games (*Od.* 24.87f).

TONGS

(See also **Tongue.**)

Attribute of Hephaestus.

TONGUE

Forcibly removed. PELEUS cuts the tongues from his hunting trophies to show to Acastus, as proof that he has killed more animals than Acastus (*Lib.* 3.13.3). TEREUS holds Philomela's tongue with tongs and cuts it out to prevent her from telling that he has raped her (*Met.* 6.555f; *Lib.* 3.14.8). ZEUS tears out Lara's tongue because she betrayed his affair with Juturna to Hera (*Fasti* 2.599f).

TOOLS

Attribute of Daedalus. Blacksmith tools: Hephaestus. (See **Anvil; Arms and Armor; Axe; Forge; Hammer**.)

ODYSSEUS uses axe, adze, auger, and hammer, which Calypso has on hand, to construct a raft (*Od.* 5.235f).

Farm tools are used by Thracians to kill Orpheus (*Met.* 11.34f). (See **Hoe; Rake; Scythe; Shovel; Sickle.**)

Drafting tools (see **Carpenter's Square; Compass**).

TORCH

(See also **Fire; Light; Thunderbolt; Wedding**.)

Attribute of Amor; Artemis (as Moon Goddess); Aurora; Bacchants; Bellona; Demeter; Eros Luseros; Furies (q.v.); Hecate; Hymen (see **Wedding**); Iacchus; Mithras; Phoebus Apollo; Phosphoros. Inverted: Comus; Hypnos; Thanatos. On the breast: Venus. Extinguished: Anteros; Pax.

HECUBA dreams she is giving birth to a burning brand (*Lib.* 3.12.5; cf. *Fab.* 91, which records that snakes issue from the flame).

Being extinguished. ALTHAEA quenches and puts away the brand the

Furies have placed in the fire on her hearth when they tell her that her baby Meleager will die when the brand is wholly consumed (*Met.* 8.451f; *Lib.* 1.8.2; *Fab.* 171, 174; Aes. *Choëph.* 603f).

Thrown by an OLD HAG (Allecto) at Turnus in his sleep to infect him with war-madness (*Aen.* 7.456f); by SALMONEUS from his chariot in imitation of Zeus, who punishes his presumption with a real bolt (*Fab.* 61; *Lib.* 1.9.7; *Aen.* 6.585f).

Used to set fire by BEROË (Iris) and other Trojan women to their own ships because they are tired of voyaging (*Aen.* 5.641f); by CALETOR to the ship of Ajax, who kills him (*Il.* 15.419f); by CORIOLANUS to the town of Corioli (Livy 2.33f); by PHILOCTETES to Heracles' pyre (*Fab.* 102; *Met.* 9.229f; Sen. *Her. Oet.* 1835f; cf. Soph. *Trach.* 1264f, where it is Hyllus who applies the torch); by THAÏS and ALEXANDER et al. to Persepolis after a lively party (Plut. 33.38); by TROJANS to a Greek ship when Ajax is driven from it by Hector (*Il.* 16.122f); by captive TROJAN WOMEN to their captors' ships (*Ep.* 6.15c); by TURNUS to the Trojans' ships, which Cybele rescues by setting them adrift and turning them into sea nymphs (*Aen.* 9.107f). (See also **Pyre.**)

Used as a weapon by CORYNAEUS to ignite the beard of Ebysus (*Aen.* 12.297f); by ELECTRA to threaten Iphigeneia at an altar, until Orestes intervenes (*Fab.* 122); by ETRUSCANS, who make a sally from their city against the attacking Romans (Livy 4.32); by a FURY in the underworld to keep Peirithoüs and Ixion from partaking of the banquet set before them (*Aen.* 6.601f); by HECATE to kill the Giant Clytius (*Lib.* 1.6.2).

In hand, ALEXANDER flees on horseback from pursuing Persians (Ps.-Cal. 182); CASSANDRA joins the captive Trojan women and the herald Talthybius (Eur. *Troad.* 298f); CHARICLEIA prepares to make sacrifice; she hands it to Theagenes (*Aeth.* 3); DEMETER searches the earth for her daughter Persephone (*Met.* 5.438f; *Lib.* 1.5.1; *H. to Dem.* 47f); EUCHIDAS runs from Delphi, bringing unpolluted fire to rekindle the sacred flame at Plataea; he dies of exhaustion (Plut. 17.20); THEONOË's ATTENDANTS accompany her to a meeting with Helen and Menelaüs, who beg her to help them escape from Egypt (Eur. *Hel.* 865f).

TORSO

Resting on the ground may represent a figure emerging from the earth, as may a head or a bust (see **Bust**).

GERYON (having three bodies to the waist) is killed by Heracles and his cattle taken (*Lib.* 2.5.10; *Fab.* 30).

TORTOISE

(See also **Turtle**.)

Attribute of Aphrodite; Hermes; Pan; Urania.

In this form, APOLLO rests in Dryope's lap; he turns himself into a snake in order to scare away her companions (Ant. Lib. 32).

Dropped by an eagle onto AESCHYLUS' bald pate (Val. Max. 9.12b.2).

Created when CHELONE and her hut are thrown into a river by Hermes (Serv. *ad Aen.* 1.505).

A tortoiseshell is made into a lyre by HERMES (*Lib.* 3.10.2; *H. to Her.* 24f).

TOWER

(See also **Falling; Leaping; Wall**.)

HERO leaps from her tower when she sees Leander's body on the shore below (Serv. *ad Georg.* 3.258).

SCYLLA watches a battle from her tower and falls in love with Minos, one of the enemy (*Met.* 8.17f).

TREASURE

(See **Gold; Vessel**.)

TREE

(See also **Branch; Vine**.)

Myrtle: attribute of Aphrodite. Laurel and palm: Apollo. Fir: Artemis. Olive: Athena. Palm: Hermes. Poplar: Heracles. Oak: Zeus.

Supporting figurines (see **Statue** [Statuettes]) or swings (see **Swinging**).

Coming into being. Hermaphroditic AGDISTIS' male organs, cut off by the gods, put forth an almond tree (Paus. 7.17.5). ATHENA creates the olive by striking the ground with her spear after Poseidon's trident produces water (or a horse) (*Met.* 6.80f; *Lib.* 3.14.1; Serv. *ad Aen.* 7.128; *Georg.* 1.12f and Serv. ad loc.). LEUCOTHOË's buried body, when warmed by the rays of her lover Apollo, puts forth a frankincense tree (*Met.* 4.254f). ROMULUS hurls a spear from the Aventine Hill to the Palatine, where it puts forth branches and leaves (Serv. *ad Aen.* 3.46; *Met.* 15.560f).

In the grasp of MENELAÜS et al. is one of Proteus' transformations (*Od.* 4.458); of PELEUS is a transformation of Thetis (*Met.* 11.244f). See also entries on DRYOPE and PHYLLIS, below.

Changed into trees. CYPARISSUS, as he grieves for the death of his pet stag (*Met.* 10.136f). DAPHNE, by her river-god father Peneus, to save her from pursuing Apollo (*Met.* 1.502f). DRYOPE, as her nursing baby and her sister cling to her (*Met.* 9.338f). The three HESPERIDES, after Heracles has killed the guardian snake and made off with the golden apples, vanish from sight when the Argonauts appear carrying the *Argo;* they reappear as three trees in response to Orpheus' request for help (*Argo.* 4.1423f). LEUCE, abducted by Hades, becomes a poplar in Elysium (Serv. *ad Ecl.* 7.61). MAENADS, by Dionysus because they tore Orpheus to pieces (*Met.* 11.67f). MYRENE, for having married in violation of her duty as priestess of Aphrodite; her bridegroom dies (Serv. *ad Aen.* 3.23). Pregnant MYRRHA (Smyrna), by Aphrodite or another deity in response to her prayer; baby Adonis is born when the trunk opens (*Met.* 10.503f; *Lib.* 3.14.4; Serv. *ad Aen.* 5.72, *ad Ecl.* 10.18). PHAETHON's SISTERS as they weep at his tomb (*Fab.* 154; *Met.* 2.346f; *Argo.* 4.596f). Old PHILEMON and BAUCIS, beside the shrine of Zeus that they have served as custodians (*Met.* 8.712f). PHILYRA, after giving birth to a Centaur (*Fab.* 138). PHYLLIS, after hanging herself, becomes a leafless almond, which breaks into leaf when embraced by Demophon (Serv. *ad Ecl.* 5.10).

Chopped or felled. CINYRAS cuts into the tree into which his pregnant daughter Myrrha has been turned, whereupon Adonis is born (Serv. *ad Aen.* 5.72). CYBELE cuts down the tree to which the fate of Sagaritis is bound, thus killing her because she seduced her devotee Attis (*Fasti* 4.221f). ERYSICHTHON's axe draws blood from a sacred oak; he beheads a man who tries to stop him (*Met.* 8.741f) and is ordered to stop by a dove (Serv. *ad Aen.* 3.466). HALIRRHOTHIUS is chopping a tree sacred to Athena when the axe blade flies off and beheads him (Serv. *ad Georg.* 1.18). PARAEBIUS' FATHER cuts down an oak despite the resident dryad's prayers (*Argo.* 2.474f).

Cut or pierced. AENEAS tries in vain to pull his spear free from a tree; Aphrodite does it for him (*Aen.* 12.766f). PARIS carves Oenone's name (a verse?) in a beech (*Heroïdes* 5.21f). PHYLACUS, when the bloody knife with which he is gelding rams terrifies his small son, sticks it in a tree that grows around it; Melampus subsequently retrieves it (*Lib.* 1.9.12).

Bent over to apply force. ALEXANDER has the treacherous Persian Bessus dismembered between two trees (Plut. 33.43). THESEUS treats Sinis similarly (Paus. 2.1.4) or uses one as a catapult to fling Sinis to his death, as Sinis himself has done to others (Plut. 1.8; *Lib.* 3.16.2; *Met.* 7.440f). (See also the entry on PENTHEUS, below.)

As hiding place. The Dioscuri are found in an oak (*Cypria* 2; Schol. on Pind. *Nem.* 10.114). Pentheus spies on Maenads' rites from a pine tree after Dionysus has bent it to the ground for him to get into (Eur. *Bacch.* 1064f).

Uprooted by Centaurs to use as weapons in the battle with the Lapiths, especially against Caenus (Hes. *Sh. Her.* 188f; *Met.* 12.510f; *Argo.* 1.59f; *Fab.* 14; *Ep.* 1.22); by Heracles, with which to make an oar (*Argo.* 1.1190f); by Maenads, when they discover Pentheus spying on them from it (Eur. *Bacch.* 1106f).

Traps in a crack the hands of mighty Milo, rendering him defenseless against an attacking lion (Val. Max. 9.12b.9).

Lying beneath a palm, Leto gives birth to Artemis and Apollo (*Lib.* 1.4.1) attended by Eileithyia et al. (*H. to Ap.* 115f; cf. Serv. *ad Aen.* 3.73, where it is recorded that Artemis assisted at the birth of her twin). Beneath an olive tree on the shore of Ithaca, Odysseus sleeps after being deposited there by the Phaeacians; he is awakened by a shepherd (Athena) (*Od.* 13.102f, 13.219f).

Bearing fruit. The seer Calchas challenges his rival Mopsus to divine the number of figs on a tree (*Ep.* 6.3). White mulberries are stained dark by Pyramus' spurting blood (*Met.* 4.122f). Tantalus reaches in vain for fruits that elude his grasp (*Met.* 4.457f; *Ep.* 2.1; *Fab.* 82; *Od.* 11.588f). (See also **Apple.**)

Gives birth to baby Adonis when a boar gashes the bark of the tree into which pregnant Myrrha has been metamorphosed, or when Cinyras cuts it (Serv. *ad Aen.* 5.72) or Lucina touches it (*Met.* 10.510f).

Growing from a cliff supports Odysseus when the whirlpool Charybdis sucks his improvised raft from under him, until it reappears to receive him (*Od.* 12.431f).

TRIAL

(See also **Judge.**)

Appius Claudius unsuccessfully defends himself against charges of having demanded illegally that Verginia be surrendered to his lust; the girl was killed by her father to save her from him (Livy 3.56).

Ares is tried by the gods for killing Poseidon's son Halirrhothius and is acquitted (Lib. 3.14.2).

Oppia, a Vestal, is condemned for unchastity (perhaps an innocent scapegoat needed by the priests) (Livy 2.42).

ORESTES, accused by Tyndareus of murdering Clytemnestra, is exiled by the people of Mycenae (*Fab.* 119).

PHRYNE wins acquittal by her judges by baring her breasts (Athenaeus 13.590e; Quint. *Inst.* 2.15.9).

TRIDENT

(See also **Fighting.**)

Attribute of Amphitrite; Nereus (*Aen.* 2.418); Poseidon; Tritons. Leaning against a pedestal that has a bust on it: Terminus.

Forged by the CYCLOPES for Poseidon (*Lib.* 1.2.2).

Pulled from a rock by AMYMONE, after her seduction by Poseidon, producing a stream of water (*Fab.* 169A).

Used by POSEIDON to kill Erechtheus (Eur. *Ion* 282); to shatter Troy's walls (*Aen.* 2.609f); to split the rock on which shipwrecked Ajax Oïleus has found temporary safety (*Od.* 4.502f; *Ep.* 6.6); to produce water from the ground (*Met.* 6.76f; *Lib.* 3.14.1; *Fab.* 169); to produce the first horse (*Georg.* 1.12f); to loose flood waters (*Met.* 1.276f); to calm waves (*Met.* 1.330f); to free Trojan ships grounded on rocks (*Aen.* 1.142f); to stir the two Ajaxes et al. to the defense of their camp and ships (*Il.* 13.59f).

TRIPOD

A three-legged, portable bronze altar used for sacrifices. The Pythian priestess sat on one when giving oracular responses. In pictorial art it often serves to place the scene at Delphi. It was a common prize for winners of athletic and dramatic contests, and frequently a gift in token of hospitality given or received.

Attribute of Apollo.

AENEAS et al. receive oracular instructions from the tripod (and priestess?) in Apollo's shrine at Delos (*Aen.* 3.90f).

COROEBUS, carrying a tripod, falls to the ground where he is to build a temple to Apollo (Paus. 1.43.7).

HERACLES carries off the Delphic tripod; Apollo fights him for it until Zeus parts them with a bolt (*Lib.* 2.6.2; Paus. 10.13.4; *Fab.* 32).

The HYLLEANS bury the tripod given them by Jason, since possession of it guarantees their safety (*Argo.* 4.526f).

TRITON in the likeness of a youth appears at the tripod set up by the Argonauts; he disappears into the sea with it after pointing out their course

PYTHIAN PRIESTESS ON THE ORACULAR TRIPOD

(*Argo.* 4.1547f; cf. Herod. 4.179, where Triton sits on the tripod and speaks prophetically).

Some of the more dramatic consultations of the Delphic oracle were by BRUTUS and the sons of Tarquin (Livy 1.56); by CADMUS (*Met.* 3.8f); by OEDIPUS (*Lib.* 3.5.7; *Fab.* 67); by ORESTES (Eur. *Iph. Taur.* 972f; *Ep.* 6.24, 6.26; *Fab.* 120). Several Delphic utterances are recorded in Herod. 1.47, 1.55, 1.65, 1.66, 1.67, 1.85, 1.174.

TROUSERS

Dress characteristic of many peoples to the east and north of Greece and Rome, occasionally of Amazons (q.v.; see also **Barbarian**).

TRUMPET

(See also **Musical Instruments.**)

Attribute of Misenus (*Aen.* 6.233); Muses; Sirens.

Sounding trumpets and clashing arms in the sky portend CAESAR's murder (*Met.* 15.784f).

Blown by ODYSSEUS causes a girl (Achilles) to seize a weapon from among the gifts offered by him to the daughters of Lycomedes, thereby betraying his sex (*Lib.* 3.13.8; *Fab.* 96).

TUB

(See **Barrel; Bathing; Vessel: Cooking, Large.**)

Filled with ice and snow: attribute of Aquilo.

TUNIC

(See **Garment.**)

TUNNEL

(See also **Cave.**)

ODYSSEUS and DIOMEDES enter and leave Troy by way of a sewer (Serv. *ad Aen.* 2.166).

ROMAN SOLDIERS burst from a tunnel into a temple in Veii (Livy 5.21).

TURTLE

(See also **Tortoise.**)

Waits in the sea and devours the victims kicked from a cliff by SCIRON (and presumably eats Sciron himself after Theseus hurls him down) (Paus. 1.44.12; *Ep.* 1.2).

TWINS

Baby twins (see **Baby**).

Adult twins. The DIOSCURI (Castor and Polydeuces) are the most prominent. Their usual representation is as two horsemen (q.v.) wearing conical hats and carrying spears.

Siamese twins. EURYTUS and CTEATUS (the Moliones or Actoriones) are two men joined (Schol. *ad Il.* 11.709), but see **Chariot** [Racing] for other descriptions of the pair. They are killed by Heracles (*Lib.* 2.7.2).

UNDERWORLD

Elysium is included here as well as other paradises not in the underworld.

ACHILLES lives in bliss with Helen on the White Isle (Paus. 3.19.13; Quint. Smy. 3.766f) or with Medea on the Isles of the Blest or in Elysium (*Argo.* 4.814f; *Ep.* 5.5).

PERSEPHONE is installed as Hades' queen, with the river goddess Arethusa as witness (*Met.* 5.501f).

Conducted to or from, by Hermes. IXION, whom he binds to a wheel (*Fab.* 62). Mute LARA, whom he seduces on the way down (*Fasti* 2.599f). PENELOPE'S SUITORS, slain by Odysseus, encounter Achilles and Agamemnon (*Od.* 24.1f). PERSEPHONE in a chariot to rejoin her mother Demeter (*H. to Dem.* 340f). PROTESILAÜS, to be reunited briefly with Laodameia and then returned to Hades (*Fab.* 103). SISYPHUS, allowed to return to earth to punish his wife, has to be carried back forcibly (Eust. *ad Il.* 6.153).

Invaded or visited by AENEAS and the Sibyl, who encounter various terrifying creatures (*Aen.* 6.268f; the following ten citations are from the *Aeneid*): souls awaiting passage across the Styx (6.298f), Palinurus (6.337), Charon the boatman (6.384f), the dog Cerberus (6.417f), judge Minos, casting lots (6.426f), Dido, who silently turns her back (6.450f), and Deïphobus, with his wounds still showing (6.494f); they pass by the gate to Tartarus, guarded by Tisiphone (6.548f) and enter the Elysian fields, where they see heroes of the past (6.637f), and meet Anchises, who points out future heroes (6.679f); by ALEXANDER, who meets many terrible creatures (Ps.-Cal. 209, 224, 258); by DIONYSUS, to fetch his mother Semele to Olympus (*Lib.* 8.5.3; Paus. 2.37.5); by HERA, to ask the Furies to hound the house of Cadmus (*Met.* 4.447f); by HERACLES, who fights Hades or Thanatos to win the release of Alcestis (*Lib.* 1.9.15; Eur. *Alc.* 843f, 1142f), drags the dog Cerberus to the upper world (see **Dog** [Three-headed]), and rescues Theseus (*Lib.* 2.5.12; *Ep.* 1.24); by ODYSSEUS, where he converses with Achilles (*Od.* 11.473f) and speaks to Ajax, who turns silently away (*Od.* 11.541f), sees Minos, Orion, souls in torment, and Heracles (*Od.* 11.568f); by ORPHEUS to get Eurydice; she is taken from him on the journey upward when he turns to look at her (*Met.* 10.11f; *Lib.* 1.3.2); by THESEUS and PEIRITHOÜS to abduct Persephone; they are made prisoners (*Ep.* 1.23.4).

URINATING

A bull's hide is watered by HERMES (*Fab.* 195); by OENOPION, instructed by Zeus et al. (Serv. *ad Aen.* 1.535); by ZEUS, POSEIDON, and HERMES (*Fasti* 5.531f). After the hide is buried, Orion is born from it.

URN

(See **Lots; Vessel, Bottle.**)

VEIL

Covering the body: attribute of Lucina. Falling down the back from a crown: Hera; Jupiter; Rhea. Shoulder length, framing the face: Hera, Saturnus.

PENELOPE veils her face, indicating to her father her decision to leave him and go with Odysseus (Paus. 3.20.10).

Given to HERACLES by Hesione as ransom for her brother Podarces (Priam) (*Lib.* 2.6.4); to ODYSSEUS on his raft, by the sea nymph Ino (Leucothea) (*Od.* 5.346f); it supports him when his raft breaks up (*Od.* 5.373f); he puts it into the sea to return to Ino (*Od.* 5.458f).

VESSEL

(See also Boat; Box; Chest; Helmet; Raft; Ship; Wineskin.)

Two-handled drinking cup (calix, cantharus): attribute of Dionysus; Ganymede; Hebe; Silenus. Dish with a single handle or no handle (patera): Concordia; a genius; Hagno (with a pitcher in her other hand); Hebe; Plutus. (A patera is also a symbol of plenty.) Jar from which water pours: Oceanus; river gods. Urn held in the hand: Notus; Pandora; Psyche; Skiron (the urn is inverted). Pitcher: Hagno (holding a patera in her other hand); Hebe; Iris. Bottle or phial: Asclepius; Triptolemus. A tub of ice or snow: Aquilo. A vessel emitting flames: Helius.

CUP, DISH, OR BOWL

Used or intended to be used for drinking. ALEXANDER, when offered water in a helmet on a march through a desert, refuses it because there is none for his men (Plut. 33.42) or pours it onto the sand (Arrian 6.26.2); ill in bed, he drinks medicine while his trusted physician reads a letter he has already read, warning him that the physician will poison him (Plut. 33.19; Arrian 2.4.8); he receives wine from Queen Cleophas (Q. Curt. 8.10); he drinks a poisoned cup at a party (Ps.-Cal. 266; Arrian 7.21.1f) or while sick in bed (Arrian 7.21.1f). APOLLO gets the Moirai so tipsy that they agree to modify Admetus' fate (Schol. on Eur. *Alc.* 12). ARTEMISIA drinks wine containing the ashes of her husband Mausolus (Val. Max. 4.6, ext. 1). AURA drinks a drug and is then seduced by Dionysus (Nonnus 48.599f). CALCHAS, holding a cup in his hand, is told by a soothsayer that he will die before he drinks; convulsed by the absurdity, he chokes and dies (Serv. *ad Ecl.* 6.72). CYBELE is poisoned by a cup intended for Charicleia (*Aeth.* 8). DEMETER, receiving a drink at an old woman's hut, throws it at a rude boy, turning him into a lizard (*Met.* 5.446f). ION is handed a cup at a banquet that he empties on the ground; a dove drinks and dies (Eur. *Ion* 1184f). M. CURIUS DENTATUS is found by an embassy that has come to bribe him, in a humble hut drinking from a wooden bowl (Val. Max. 4.3, 5). MATUSIUS offers King Demophon a bowl of wine containing the blood of his daughters (*Poet. Astr.* 2.40). MELAMPUS scrapes the rust from a knife into a cup of wine, which he gives to Iphiclus to drink (*Lib.* 1.9.12). ODYSSEUS plies the Cyclops Polyphemus with wine (*Od.* 9.347f; *Aen.* 3.630f), helped by Silenus (Eur. *Cycl.* 412f); he gives Silenus wine (Eur. *Cycl.* 153f). ODYSSEUS' MEN drink Circe's brew and are turned into animals (*Met.* 14.273f; *Od.* 10.316f). The OLYMPIAN GODS are served nectar by Hebe (*Il.* 4.1f) or by Hephaestus (*Il.* 4.586f). PITTHEUS plies Aegeus with wine in order to get him into his daughter Aegina's bed (*Lib.* 3.15.7). PROCRIS gives Minos a drug to drink before she lies with him (*Lib.* 3.15.1). SHEPHERDS drink the wine provided by Icarius; becoming intoxicated, they kill him (*Lib.* 3.14.7). THESEUS is handed a cup by Medea; Aegeus knocks it from his hand (Plut. 1.12; *Ep.* 1.6; *Met.* 7.406f). ZEUS gives the heart of Dionysus, whom the Titans have dismembered, to Semele in a drink (*Fab.* 167).

Used in revelry by DIONYSUS, SILENUS et al. (*Fasti* 1.393f); by MAENADS and BACCHANTS (*Met.* 3.528f); by PENELOPE'S SUITORS (*Od.* 1.109f, 1.144f, 17.356f, 18 pass., 20.247f). (See also **Eating** [Formal banquets].)

Used for taking poison by AESON, who kills himself by drinking bull's blood during a sacrifice (*Lib.* 1.9.27); by HANNIBAL, to evade capture by the Romans (Plut. 20.20; Livy 39.51); by PHILOPOEMEN in prison; his jailer hands him the cup (Plut. 19.20); by PHOCION in prison, with friends attending (Plut. 35.36); by SOCRATES in prison, with friends around him (Diog. Laërt. 2.5.42); by Carthaginian SOPHONISBA, who drinks the poison sent by her husband to save her from the captivity demanded by Scipio (Livy 30.15); and by THEMISTOCLES in exile, with friends around him (Plut. 7.31).

Used for making libation (usually a patera) by ACHILLES as he prays to Zeus for Patroclus' safety (*Il.* 16.228f); by AENEAS, at the funeral rites for Polydorus (*Aen.* 3.67f), at the tomb of Anchises, from which a snake appears (*Aen.* 5.77f, 5.98f), before entering the underworld with the Sibyl (*Aen.* 6.249f), and before the final battle in Latium (*Aen.* 12.174f); by ALEXANDER, from the bow of a ship (Arrian 6.3.1); by DIDO, who pours it on the head of a heifer, seeking divine favor toward her love for Aeneas (*Aen.* 4.60f); by any GOD who swears an oath on water from the river Styx (Hes. *Theog.* 793f);

by HERACLES as he stands at an altar wearing the robe that Deïaneira has unknowingly poisoned (*Met.* 6.190f); by MENTOR (Athena) at Telemachus' arrival at Nestor's palace (*Aen.* 3.67f); by ODYSSEUS et al. at the feast before his departure from Phaeacia (*Od.* 13.50f); by the TROJANS at their first meal after reaching the Tiber (*Aen.* 7.133f). (See also **Altar** and **Eating,** since pouring a libation is a part of many rites and the proper commencement of most meals.)

Thrown or dropped by ALEXANDER at Attalus (Plut. 33.9) and at the jester Lysius (Ps.-Cal. 57–8); by DIOGENES, discarding it as superfluous when he sees a child drinking from his cupped hands (Diog. Laërt. 6.2.37); by THESEUS, when Aegeus knocks it from his hand because he has suddenly realized that the stranger who is about to drink Medea's poison is his son (Plut. 1.12; *Ep.* 1.6; *Met.* 7.406f); by XERXES into the sea before his army starts across the Hellespont bridge (Herod. 7.54).

Taken from a box and polished by ACHILLES, before he pours a libation to Zeus (*Il.* 16.221f).

Stolen by ALEXANDER, dressed as Ammon, at Darius' banquet; recognized, he has to flee (Ps.-Cal. 180f).

Given by ARTAXERXES to a poor man who has no gift to offer but water in his cupped hands (Paus. 48.5).

Cups filled with gold are offered as a bribe by RHOESACES to Cimon, who rejects them (Plut. 25.10).

BOTTLE, BASIN, BOWL, JAR, PHIAL, PITCHER, OR URN

A vessel designed to contain or transport liquids or solids. For other uses, see **Lots, Voting,** and **Washing.** For urns containing the ashes of the dead, see **Funerary Urn,** below.

Carried or being filled. APOLLO dispatches a raven to fetch water in a bowl; it returns with a snake (*Fasti* 2.251f). ARGONAUTS race carrying jars on their shoulders (*Argo.* 1766f). DANAÜS' DAUGHTERS in the underworld are condemned to carrying water in vessels that leak (*Fab.* 168; *Met.* 4.462f). ELECTRA, returning to her hut with a water jar, is surprised by Orestes and Pylades (Eur. *Elec.* 55f, 107f, 215f). A GIRL (Athena) carrying a water jar meets Odysseus and leads him to the palace of Alcinoüs (*Od.* 7.18f). HERACLES inadvertently gives the boy who is pouring wine or water for washing his hands a light tap that kills him (Paus. 2.13.8; *Lib.* 2.7.6). HYLAS, as he draws water at a pool, is pulled in by the resident nymph (*Argo.* 1.1222f). IRIS brings water from the Styx for the gods to swear upon (Hes. *Theog.* 784f). PANDORA releases the evils contained within an urn (Hes. *W. & D.* 90f; cf. *Il.* 24.527f, where Zeus is the dispenser of evils). TUCCIA carries water in a sieve to prove her chastity (Val. Max. 8.1a.5). A WOMAN, carrying a vessel on her head and spinning flax as she leads a horse along, catches King Darius' attention (Herod. 5.12).

Dropped by a SERVANT when a footstool thrown at a beggar (Odysseus) strikes it (*Od.* 18.394f).

Containing snakes is handed to Sterope by HERACLES (*Lib.* 2.7.3); many such jars are lobbed from HANNIBAL's ships into those of the enemy (Nep. *Han.* 10–11).

Contains blood, which DEIANEIRA sprinkles on a garment for Heracles, thinking it to be a love charm (*Fab.* 34; *Lib.* 2.7.7).

From two vessels on the ground, ZEUS dispenses evils and blessings to mankind (*Il.* 24.527f).

Flour is poured from a jar under ALEXANDER's direction to mark out the walls of Alexandria (Arrian 3.2.1).

FUNERARY URN

A round jar or a square container, made of earthenware or metal, in which the bones and ashes of the dead are placed after cremation.

Receives the ashes of ACHILLES; the vessel is provided by Thetis (*Od.* 24.73f); of ACHILLES and PATROCLUS together (*Ep.* 5.5); of HECTOR (*Il.* 24.792f); of PATROCLUS (*Il.* 23.252f).

Being carried or placed. AGRIPPINA lands at Brundisium with the ashes of Germanicus and his children (Tac. *An.* 3.1). APOLLO places the bones of Python in his shrine (*Fab.* 140). The EPIGONI bring the bones of their fathers, who fell at Thebes, to their widows, Theseus, and Adrastus (Eur. *Suppl.* 1114f). ORESTES brings an urn to Electra and Chrysothemis, who do not recognize their brother; he tells them that the ashes in it are his own (Soph. *Elec.* 1098f). ORPHEUS' ashes are in a jar on top of a pillar; it falls to the ground and breaks open when a crowd jostles the pillar (Paus. 9.30.5). PELOPS' bones are brought to the Greeks at Troy (*Ep.* 5.10–11). PHOCION's ashes are buried by his wife at their hearth (Plut. 35.37). POMPEY's ashes are delivered to his wife Cornelia (Plut. 32.80). PYLADES brings an urn to Clytemnestra which, he falsely states, contains Orestes' ashes (*Fab.* 119).

COOKING AND MIXING VESSEL

ACHILLES' ATTENDANTS heat water with which to wash Patroclus' body (*Il.* 18.343f).

ATREUS cuts up and cooks the sons of Thyestes to serve to their father (*Ep.* 2.13; Sen. *Thy.* 818f).

CIRCE prepares a magic brew (*Met.* 14.261f).

HELEN puts a drug that banishes care into the wine bowl at the banquet for Telemachus (*Od.* 4.219f).

M. CURIUS DENTATUS, while cooking a frugal meal, refuses a bribe offered by a Samnite embassy (Plut. 18.2).

MEDEA prepares a magic brew (*Met.* 7.262f); she cooks an old ram and a lamb jumps from the pot, a miracle that encourages Pelias' daughters to cut up and cook their aged father in an attempt at a similar rejuvenation (*Lib.* 1.9.27; *Fab.* 24; *Met.* 7.312f).

POLYPHEMUS cooks two of Odysseus' men (Eur. *Cycl.* 391f).

PROCNE boils her son Itys to serve to his father Tereus, to avenge his rape and mutilation of her sister Philomela (*Lib.* 3.14.8).

TANTALUS cooks his son Pelops and serves him to the gods, who put the pieces back in the pot and draw him out whole, except for the shoulder Demeter has eaten (*Ep.* 2.3).

The TITANS dismember and boil Dionysus (Diod. Sic. 3.62.6).

LARGE VESSEL

With a figure inside. ARES is incarcerated in a brazen jar by Otus and Ephialtes (*Il.* 5.385f). DAMOCLES leaps into a cauldron of boiling water to escape from Demetrius (Plut. 43.24). EURYSTHEUS hides in fright in a storage jar when Heracles brings him the Nemean Lion (*Lib.* 2.5.1) and the Erymanthian Boar (Diod. Sic. 4.12.1). Little GLAUCUS, chasing a mouse or while playing ball, falls into a jar of honey, where Polyidus finds him (*Lib.* 3.3.1; *Fab.* 136). HELIUS and his horses are transported nightly from his set-

HERACLES DELIVERS THE ERYMANTHIAN BOAR TO TER-
RIFIED EURYSTHEUS; IOLAÜS HOLDS HIS CLUB AND
ATHENA LENDS SUPPORT

ting to his rising in a golden goblet (Pherecydes, in Athenaeus 9.39). HERA-
CLES borrows Helius' goblet to transport Geryon's cattle (*Lib.* 2.5.10). INO
leaps into the sea carrying her child in a jar (*Lib.* 3.4.3). (See also **Cooking
and Mixing Vessel,** above.)

VINE

(See also **Branch; Garland; Grapes.**)

Attribute of Dionysus; Hebe; Maenads.

DIONYSUS discovers the grapevine (*Lib.* 3.5.1). He presents it to Icarius
(*Lib.* 3.14.2; *Poet. Astr.* 2.4); to Oeneus, husband of Althaea, after seducing
her (*Fab.* 129; *Lib.* 1.8.1); to Oeno, giving her the power to produce wine
and her sisters the power to produce oil and grain (*Ep.* 3.10; *Met.* 13.632f).
He causes a vine to entwine the ship on which he is a captive (*H. to Dion.*
38f; *Met.* 3.622f). With his ivy-wreathed staff he kills a Giant (Eur. *Ion*
215f). He causes the tapestry woven by Minyas' daughters to turn into vines;
the daughters become bats (*Met.* 4.389f).

HEPHAESTUS makes a vine of gold for Zeus to give to Laomedon in
payment for the loss of Ganymede (Schol. on Eur. *Troad.* 822).

LYCURGUS, whom Dionysus has made mad, slashes vines and cuts off
his own foot (*Fab.* 132; cf. 3.5.1, where he kills his son, thinking him a vine).

MAENADS (q.v.), armed with wands of ivy, rout armed men (Eur.
Bacch. 758f).

PRIAM gives a golden vine to his sister Astyoche (Schol. *ad Od.* 11.520)
and to Tithonus, who in return sends his son Memnon to fight for Troy
(Serv. *ad Aen.* 1.493).

SILENUS, in bonds of ivy, entertains his companions with song (*Ecl.*
6.16f).

TELEPHUS trips on a vine as he runs from Achilles (*Ep.* 3.17).

VOLCANO

AENEAS' fleet reaches a harbor from which Etna in eruption is visible (*Aen.*
3.570f).

AMPHINOMUS and ANAPIUS carry their aged parents through the fires
of Etna (Val. Max. 5.4b.4; Paus. 10.28.2).

EMPEDOCLES leaps into the crater of Etna (Diog. Laërt. 8.2.11).

PLINY THE ELDER perishes in the eruption of Vesuvius (Pliny the
Younger 6.16).

VOMITING

Of his offspring by CRONUS, after eating them to eliminate competitors for his power (Hes. *Theog.* 495f; *Lib.* 1.2.1); by THYESTES, when he realizes he has dined on their flesh (Aes. *Agam.* 1590f).

VOTING

Black pebbles, cast into an urn to convict MYSCELUS, become white when he appeals to Heracles (*Met.* 15.41f).

Votes are cast whether to ostracize Aristides from Athens; he marks a shard (ballot) against himself when asked to do so by an illiterate voter (Plut. 17.7); whether to acquit or condemn Orestes for killing his mother Clytemnestra (Eur. *Elec.* 1258f).

VULTURE

(See **Bird.**)

WAGON

(See also **Chariot.**)

A two- or four-wheeled vehicle used to carry persons or cargo.

Drawn by Centaurs: attribute of Ariadne and Dionysus.

ALEXANDER cuts an intricate knot tied on a wagon pole at Gordium (Plut. 33.18; Arrian 2.3.1).

Drawn by horses or mules. ALCIBIADES forces a wagon to stop by lying in front of it, in order that a dice game in the roadway may not be interrupted (Plut. 11.2). ALEXANDER holds a party on a huge wheeled platform (Plut. 33.67). ALEXANDER's body is transported to Alexandria in a huge, magnificent, wheeled bier (Aelian 12.64). ANDROMACHE is driven with Astyanax to the Greek camp (Eur. *Troad.* 568f), where the child is taken from her by Talthybius (Eur. *Troad.* 764f). GORDIUS drives with his wife and son to a town, where he is acclaimed by the people as their destined king (Justin 11.7.5). ICARIUS and ERIGONE, traveling in a wagon, meet some shepherds to whom they give wine; when drunk, the rustics kill Icarius (*Fab.* 130; *Poet. Astr.* 2.4). IDAEUS drives a four-wheeled wagon loaded with ransom for Hector's body, accompanied by Priam in his chariot (*Il.* 24.322f); they meet Hermes who, driving the chariot, brings them safely to Achilles' quarters (*Il.* 24.440f); there the ransom is exchanged for the body (*Il.* 24.589f); Hermes then accompanies them most of the way back to Troy (*Il.* 24.690f). MEDEA rides with her box of drugs to Hecate's temple (*Argo.* 3.838f). NAUSICAÄ et al. drive to a washing-place by the sea; she drives back with Odysseus following on foot (*Od.* 6.57f, 6.255f). THEBANS load their wagons and flee when the Epigoni take the city (*Lib.* 3.7.3). TULLIA drives over the body of her father, whom her husband Tarquin has had assassinated (Livy 1.48). VESTALS remove themselves and the temple's sacred objects to safety when the Gauls invade Rome (Livy 5.40; Plut. 8.21).

Drawn by oxen. CLAUDIA leads the team that is pulling Rhea's statue into Rome (*Fasti* 4.333f). HERACLES takes one of a countryman's team and cooks and eats it, for which he is cursed (*Lib.* 2.5.11, 2.7.7). ZEUS, to play a trick on Hera, drives along with a woman in bridal dress beside him; Hera tears the figure's clothes off and finds a statue (Paus. 3.9.1).

Drawn by men. CLEOBIS and BITON take the place of missing oxen and pull their mother to a temple ceremony (Herod. 1.31; Plut. 5.26; *Fab.* 2.5.4).

Forming a barricade. ALEXANDER storms the defensive barricade an Indian force has made out of its wagons (Arrian 5.22.4). SPARTAN WOMEN dig wagons in as defense against Pyrrhus and his elephants (Plut. 21.27).

Wagons are launched down a slope by THRACIANS against Alexander's phalanx (Arrian 1.1.7).

WALL

(See also **Falling; Fighting; Ladder; Leaping.**)

A wall is built by AMPHION, who moves the stones into place by the music of his lyre while his brother Zethus has to labor at the same task (*Argo.* 1.735f; *Lib.* 3.5.5); by APOLLO and POSEIDON for Laomedon at Troy (*Lib.* 2.5.9; *Met.* 11.199f; *Fab.* 89), or by Poseidon alone (*Il.* 21.446f) and with the help of Aeacus (Pind. *Ol.* 8.30[40]f); by the GREEKS at Troy to defend their camp and beached ships (*Il.* 7.336f, 7.435f); by ROMULUS, who kills his brother when he tauntingly leaps over before it is finished (Plut. 2.10; Livy 1.7; cf. *Fasti* 4.841f, where Celer is named as the slayer of Remus).

Fighting at the Greek wall. APOLLO, bearing the aegis, breaks down the wall to help Hector and the Trojans get at the ships (*Il.* 15.355f). HECTOR leads the Trojan assault on its ditch and gate (*Il.* 12.81f). SARPEDON and GLAUCUS breach the wall and are met by the two Ajaxes (*Il.* 12.307f).

Separates the lovers PYRAMUS and THISBE, permitting them to communicate only through a crevice (*Met.* 4.65f).

WAND

(See also **Caduceus; Sceptre; Staff; Stick; Thyrsus.**)

Having magical power. With a touch, ATHENA transforms Odysseus into a beggar (q.v.) (*Od.* 13.429f, 16.454) and from a beggar back into his proper form for the reunion with Telemachus (*Od.* 16.172f); CIRCE turns Odysseus' men into pigs or other animals (*Od.* 10.237f; *Met.* 14.273f) and back into human shape (*Met.* 14.279f).

Used as a weapon. CIRCE strikes Odysseus, at which he threatens her with his sword (*Od.* 10.293f, 10.319f). DIONYSUS kills a Giant with his ivy-wreathed wand (Eur. *Ion* 215f).

WARRIOR

(See also **Arms and Armor; Bow and Arrow; Chariot; Fighting; Horseman; Killing; Officer; Phantom; Shield; Spear; Stone; Sword; Underworld; Wounded Figure.**)

WARRIORS GAMING

Most scenes in which a warrior appears will be found elsewhere, under headings that seem more appropriate, such as those above.

MALE

Transformed into. ANTS are changed into fighting men by Zeus at Aeacus' request (*Met.* 7.624f; *Fab.* 52; Serv. *ad Aen.* 2.7). CAENIS, at her request, is changed into a man who is invulnerable, by her seducer Poseidon (*Met.* 12.201f). DRAGON'S TEETH sprout into armed men, when sowed by Aeëtes (*Argo.* 3.413f); by Cadmus (*Met.* 3.106f; *Lib.* 3.4.1); by Jason (*Argo.* 3.1354f; *Lib.* 1.9.23; *Met.* 7.128f; *Fab.* 22).

ACHILLES talks with Clytemnestra and Iphigeneia (Eur. *Iph. Aul.* 819f, 899f, 1345f); he addresses angry soldiers in an attempt to save Iphigeneia from being sacrificed (Eur. *Iph. Aul.* 1347); he has Patroclus hand Briseïs to the heralds who have come for her (*Il.* 1.229f); standing by his ship, he and Patroclus watch the fighting and Nestor's rescue of Machaon (*Il.* 11.599f);

he comes from the underworld with Agamemnon et al. to speak with Odysseus (*Od.* 11.385f); he is surrounded by the spirits of Penelope's suitors, whom Hermes has brought to Hades (*Od.* 24.1f); he meets Helen through the contrivance of Aphrodite and Thetis (*Cypria* 1, in Proclus 1); he and Helen live together with other heroes on the White Isle (Paus. 3.19.13; Quint. Smy. 3.766f). (See **Underworld**.)

HECTOR chides Paris in Helen's presence for leaving the battle to be with her (*Il.* 6.312f); he spends a touching moment with his wife and child before returning to battle (*Il.* 6.390f); he sets off to battle with Paris (*Il.* 6.503f, 7.1f); standing between the seated armies, he issues Paris' challenge to Menelaüs to settle the war by single combat (*Il.* 3.75f), and he challenges any Greek to single combat (*Il.* 7.54f); he sends Dolon clad in his wolfskin to spy on the Greeks (*Il.* 10.303f).

MELEAGER wrathfully withdraws from the defense of Calydon and joins his wife (*Il.* 9.553f).

MENELAÜS rebukes the Greeks for their reluctance to accept the challenge to single combat issued by Hector (*Il.* 7.94f).

POLYNEICES, entering Thebes under safe-conduct, meets his mother Jocasta and Eteocles, his brother and enemy (Eur. *Phoen.* 263f).

FEMALE

ARTEMISIA speaks her mind at a Persian council of war presided over by Xerxes, before the naval battle at Salamis (Herod. 8.68) and after it (Herod. 101–102).

ATHENA fights off Hephaestus to defend her virginity (*Fab.* 166); she attacks Ares (*Ep.* 7.34, n. 7, Loeb edn.).

BERENICE on horseback rallies Ptolemy's troops (*Poet. Astr.* 2.24).

CAMILLA leads her cavalry troop to join Turnus' forces (*Aen.* 7.803f) and into battle (*Aen.* 11.597f); she is tricked into dismounting by a Ligurian horseman, who then tries to flee, but she outruns his horse and pulls him down (*Aen.* 11.699f); attracted by an enemy's finery, she stalks him but falls to Arruns' spear (*Aen.* 7.768f).

DEÏANEIRA is trained in chariot fighting (*Lib.* 1.8.1).

ENYO, together with Ares, leads the Trojans to battle (*Il.* 5.590f).

HARPALYCE, in defense of her father, routs Neoptolemus (*Fab.* 193).

LEMNIAN WOMEN prepare to repel the landing of the Argonauts (*Argo.* 1.627f).

SEMIRAMIS quells a rebellion in Babylon (Val. Max. 9.3b.4); she leads an assault on a citadel (Diod. Sic. 2.1f).

TELESILLA leads the women of Argos in repelling a Spartan force (Paus. 2.20.7–8).

Queen TOMYRIS, of the Massagetae, defeats the Persians and kills Cyrus; when she finds his body, she fulfills her threat by putting his head in a pool of blood (Herod. 1.214).

AMAZONS

AMAZONS are the war-loving daughters of Ares and Harmonia (*Argo.* 2.990f); they are attacked and beaten by Bellerophon (*Il.* 6.186f; *Lib.* 2.3.2); they attack Athens but are defeated by Theseus (Plut. 1.27; *Ep.* 1.16); they try to break up the wedding of Theseus and Phaedra (*Ep.* 1.17); several in succession are killed in combat by Heracles (Diod. Sic. 4.16.2); they are courted by and marry Scythians (Herod. 4.110); they are visited by Alexander (Q. Curt. 6.5; Ps. -Cal. 258).

ANTIOPE boards Theseus' ship to welcome him and is carried away by him (Plut. 1.26); she fights at his side in repelling the Amazon attack on Athens (Plut. 1.27); she bears him a son, Hippolytus (Plut. 1.28); she is killed by Theseus when out of jealousy she and others try to break up his wedding to Phaedra (*Fab.* 241; Plut. 1.27). N.B.: Antiope by some writers is called Hippolyte, Melanippe, or Glauce.

HIPPOLYTE is taken captive by Heracles (Diod. Sic. 2.46.4) or killed by him in order to secure her belt (*Lib.* 2.5.9; *Fab.* 30); she leads an attack on Athens to recover her sister Antiope from Theseus (Paus. 1.41.7); she is killed inadvertently by her sister Penthesileia during a hunt (*Ep.* 5.1 and n. 4, Loeb

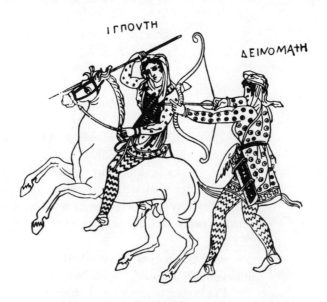

AMAZONS

edn.; cf. *Ep.* 5.2, where Hyginus says her death occurred at Athens during the brawl at Theseus and Phaedra's wedding, but owing to the confusion of Antiope and Hippolyte's names, this is doubtful).

PENTHESILEIA accidentally kills Hippolyte (q.v.); fighting for Troy (Quint. Smy. 1.225f), she kills Machaon but is killed by Achilles, who regrets her death and kills Thersites for jeering at him or for mutilating her corpse (*Ep.* 5.1; Quint. Smy. 1.536f).

WASHING

(See also **Bathing; Drinking; Vessel; Water.**)

Old EURYCLEIA, as she washes a beggar's (Odysseus') feet, recognizes him by an old scar (*Od.* 19.386f).

HELEN, while doing her washing, is seized by Furies (Polyxo's slaves in disguise) because of her responsibility for Tlepolemus' death at Troy (Paus. 3.19.10).

HERACLES diverts a river to cleanse the cattle pens of Augeas (*Fab.* 30; *Lib.* 2.5.5); as his hands are being washed, he inadvertently touches the boy holding the vessel with a movement that is enough to kill one who is so much less powerful (*Lib.* 2.7.6).

King MIDAS washes off his "golden touch" in a stream (*Fab.* 1.9.1).

NAUSICAÄ et al. do their washing near the place where Odysseus has crawled ashore and lies sleeping (*Od.* 6.85f).

While PELOPIA is doing her washing, she is seized by Thyestes and raped (*Fab.* 88).

PERSEUS washes off the blood of the sea monster from which he has saved Andromeda (*Met.* 4.740f).

SCIRON kicks the man who is washing his foot into the sea (*Ep.* 1.2).

WATER

(See also **Bathing; Drinking; Flood; River; Sea; Seashore; Ship; Swimming; Vessel, Urn; Washing.**)

Personified: OCEANUS or a river may be represented by a male figure holding a jar from which water pours and by "watery" garment, hair, and beard. The river SCAMANDER attacks and routs Achilles, but is overcome by fire (Hephaestus) (*Il.* 21.233f). (See also **River God; Sea Deity.**)

A form assumed by CASTALIA as she tries to escape from Apollo (Schol. on Statius, *Thebaïd* 1.697f); by PROTEUS in the grasp of Aristaeus (*Georg.* 4.410) or of Menelaüs et al. (*Od.* 4.458); by THETIS in her efforts to escape from Peleus' grasp (*Lib.* 3.13.5).

Transformed into water. ALOPE's body is turned into a spring by Poseidon (*Fab.* 187). ARETHUSA, hidden from Alphaeus in a mist provided by Artemis, dissolves into a stream (*Met.* 5.632f). BYBLIS is changed into a spring by nymphs, because her love for her brother is not requited (*Met.* 9.663f). CYANE, when she tries to stop Hades as he is carrying off Persephone, is touched by his sceptre and dissolves into her pool (*Met.* 5.411f). DIRCE is made into a pool by Dionysus (*Fab.* 7).

Grieving figures become water. CANENS, grieving for Picus (*Met.* 14.426f). EGERIA, for Numa, is transformed by Phoebe (Artemis) (*Met.* 15.547f). HYRIE, for her son Cycnus, a swan (*Met.* 7.380f). PEIRENE, for her son Cenchrias, whom Artemis has killed (Paus. 2.3.3). The shepherd SELEMNUS, because Argyra has left him; Aphrodite causes the change (Paus. 7.23.2). (See also **Tears.**)

Figures beside or in water. AENEAS, while sacrificing, falls into the Numicius River and becomes a god (Serv. *ad Aen.* 4.620). HERMES' SON goes swimming in the pool of Salmacis, who embraces him; when he resists her, their bodies merge into one who is named Hermaphroditus (*Met.* 4.297f). As HYLAS is filling his water jar, the nymph of the pool pulls him in (*Argo.* 1.1221f). MIDAS places himself under a gushing spring to wash away the "golden touch" (*Met.* 11.134f; cf. *Fab.* 1.9.1, where he is said to bathe in a river). NARCISSUS falls in love with his reflection in a pool and becomes a flower (*Met.* 3.407f); or he falls into the pool and drowns (Paus. 9.31.6). While he is fishing, PALAMEDES is pushed in by Odysseus and Diomedes and drowns (Paus. 10.31.1). When TANTALUS, standing in water to his waist or neck, tries to drink, the water recedes from hand or lips (*Od.* 11.582f; *Fab.* 82; *Met.* 4.458f). (See also **Falling; Leaping.**)

Flows from the grave of ACIS and becomes a horned river god (*Met.* 13.885f); from the rock that ATALANTA strikes with her spear (Paus. 3.24.2); from the hiding place of a goose when CORA (Persephone) pulls it out (Paus. 9.39.2); from beneath a rock when HERACLES stamps his foot (*Argo.* 4.1445f); from the earth where the winged horse PEGASUS' foot strikes; the Muses point it out to Athena (*Met.* 5.254f; Paus. 2.31.12); from the spot that POSEIDON strikes with his trident (*Fab.* 169).

Poured onto the sand by ALEXANDER because he is unwilling to drink when there is not enough for his men (Arrian 6.26.2); by IPHIMEDEIA into her lap makes her pregnant by Poseidon (*Lib.* 1.7.4).

Thrown by DEMETER at a rude boy while she is drinking, turns him into a lizard (*Met.* 5.451f; Ant. Lib. 23); by XANTHIPPE, the shrewish wife of Socrates, at her husband (Diog. Laërt. 2.5.36).

A lake made noxious by PHAETHON's fall into it, poisons birds flying over it; it is visited by the Argonauts (*Argo.* 4.594f). The lake of Avernus, bordering the cave through which Aeneas and the Sibyl enter the underworld, is similarly fatal to birds (*Aen.* 6.237f).

WAVE

A huge wave frightens the ARGONAUTS, but their helmsman steers over it safely (*Argo.* 2.169f, 2.579f).

WEAPON

See the identifiable weapon or object used as a weapon. Keep in mind that the artist may have depicted a weapon different from the one given in a literary source; accordingly, be prepared to look under other possible instruments. If the weapon that was probably used is not identifiable, refer to the action that seems to have taken place (e.g., **Beheading, Fighting, Killing,** etc.).

WEASEL

GALANTHIS, attending Alcmene at the birth of Heracles, is turned into a weasel by Eileithyia because she tricked the goddess into changing her pose, thereby breaking the spell that was preventing Alcmene's delivery (*Met.* 9.306f).

WEAVING

(See **Distaff; Garment, Robe; Loom; Spindle; Spinning.**)

WEDDING

Of ALEXANDER to Roxane (Plut. 33.47) and to Statira, at which ceremony several of the Companions also take Persian brides (Plut. 70); of CADMUS to Harmonia, which the gods attend (*Lib.* 3.4.2); of CUPID to Psyche, attended by the gods (Apuleius 9); of DAPHNIS to Chloë, in a pastoral setting (Longus

3); of JASON to Medea, attended by nymphs and Argonauts, outside their bridal cave (*Argo.* 4.1128f); of ORPHEUS to Eurydice, at which Hymen's torch smokes (*Met.* 10.1f); of PEIRITHOÜS to Hippodameia turns into a battle between Lapiths and their Centaur guests, who get drunk and try to abduct the bride and her attendants (*Met.* 12.210f; *Fab.* 33); of PELEUS to Thetis, which Hera and the gods attend, except Eris, who throws in a golden apple that each of three goddesses claims (*Argo.* 4.805f; *Fab.* 92; *Ep.* 3.2; *Lib.* 3.13.5); of PERSEUS to Andromeda, solemnized by torch-bearing Eros and Hymen (*Met.* 4.758f); of TEREUS to Procne, attended by torch-bearing Furies and an owl (*Met.* 6.430f); of THEAGENES to Charicleia, at which the Ethiopian king presides (*Aeth.* 10); of THESEUS to Phaedra (see **Warrior, Amazons**).

WEEPING

(See **Grieving; Tears.**)

WEIGHTS

Hand-held: attribute of Agon, the personification of contests. These weights, called *halteres,* are used by participants in jumping contests to improve performance.

Attached to the ankles of HERA (see **Anvil**).

WELL

(See also **Chasm; Grave; Pit; Vessel; Water.**)

An OLD WOMAN (Demeter), on her search for Persephone, sits by a well to which four women come to draw water (*H. to Dem.* 98f; *Lib.* 1.5.1).

PALAMEDES is put into a well by Odysseus and Diomedes, where he is stoned to death (Dictys 2.15).

TIMOCLEIA pushes the soldier who has raped her into a well (Plut. 33.12).

WHALE

ALEXANDER'S MEN land on a whale, thinking it to be an island until it submerges (Ps.-Cal. 224).

WHEEL

Attribute of a charioteer (see **Chariot**); Fortuna (blindfolded and winged); Nemesis; Triptolemus (seated on it, *Lib.* 1.5.2, n. 2, Loeb edn.); Tyche. With a griffin: Minerva. Suspended by chains held by Apollo and Diana: the Graces. With paddles on it, attached to a marine vehicle or shell: Amphitrite; Galatea; Poseidon; Venus.

Attached to the legs of an artificial cow or horse (qq.v.).

A wheel-like object carried on a woman's head (see **Crown**).

Used to punish AURA, whom Nemesis strikes with a wheel and a snake whip at Artemis' order (Nonnus 48.375f, 48.458f); IXION, who is bound to a wheel, sometimes fiery, in Hades (*Aen.* 6.616f; *Met.* 4.461; *Fab.* 62; *Ep.* 1.20).

WHIP

Attribute of Bellona; Furies, especially Tisiphone (*Aen.* 6.570f); Hecate; Jupiter; Justitia; Luperci; Nemesis.

Mad AJAX whips one ram and beheads another (Soph. *Ajax* 232f).

BOYS run about almost naked, whipping women to make them fruitful (Plut. 2.21).

The BOYS OF FALERII whip their schoolmaster back to their town after Camillus scornfully rejects his offer to hand them over as hostages (Plut. 8.10; Livy 5.27).

NEMESIS lashes Aura, on Artemis' order (Nonnus 48.458f).

A PRIEST whips unfruitful women (*Fasti* 2.443f).

TLEPOLEMUS, while beating a servant, accidentally strikes Licymnius and kills him (*Lib.* 2.8.2).

XERXES has the Hellespont scourged because its waves broke up his bridge of boats (Herod. 7.35).

WHIRLPOOL

(See **Raft; Ship, Storm-tossed.**)

WHIRLWIND

(See also **Mist.**)

In this form, Zeus carries off GANYMEDE (*H. to Aph.* 202f).

Carries off MEDEA after her attempt to poison Theseus is thwarted by Aegeus (*Met.* 7.424).

WINDS

(See **Cave; Flying; Storm; Wings** [Winds].)

WINESKIN

(See also **Bag; Bundle; Vessel, Jar.**)

Attribute of Silenus.

Given by DIONYSUS to Icarius and Erigone and by them to shepherds, who become drunk and kill Icarius (*Fab.*130; *Poet. Astr.* 2.4); by ODYSSEUS to Polyphemus, who drinks and falls asleep (*Od.* 9.347f).

Are carried by donkeys; the wine spills and is dipped up by the guards of a headless corpse. When the guards fall asleep, the donkey driver makes off with the body (Herod. 2.121).

WINGS

(See also **Flying.**)

ON HAT OR SANDALS (HEAD OR FEET) OR ON BOTH

Attribute of Destinus; Discordia (sometimes also on shoulders); Fatum (also on shoulders); Fortuna; Kairos (also holding scales); Mercury; Winds (though on shoulders usually; see below).

Attribute of HERMES. He finds Aeneas supervising construction and tells him he must leave Carthage and Dido (*Aen.* 4.259f) and, appearing to him while he sleeps, tells him it is time to sail (*Aen.* 4.556f). He warns Aegisthus not to kill Agamemnon and marry Clytemnestra (*Od.* 1.35f). He tells Calypso to let Odysseus go (*Od.* 1.81f, 5.55f). He instills in Dido hospitable feelings toward the strangers (Trojans) who are about to appear (*Aen.* 1.297f). He takes Helen from Paris, substituting her wraith, and takes her off to Proteus, king of Egypt (*Ep.* 3.5). He sells Heracles as a slave to Omphale (*Lib.* 2.6.3). He conducts Orestes from Delphi to Athens (Aes. *Eumen.* 89f). He brings Pandora with her jar of evils to Epimetheus (Hes. *W. & D.* 83f). He flies to Troy to help Priam recover Hector's body from Achilles (*Il.* 24.339f; see **Wagon**). He visits Prometheus, chained to a cliff in the Caucasus (Aes. *Prom.* 943f). For his activities as a baby, see **Baby,** and as guide for the dead, see **Underworld.**

Attribute of PERSEUS. He receives Hermes' winged sandals from some nymphs and returns them to Hermes after beheading Medusa, escaping from her sisters, rescuing Andromeda, and dealing with Phineus and Polydectes (*Lib.* 2.4.2–3; Hes. *Sh. Her.* 220f; cf. *Met.* 4.614f, where Perseus flies to his adventures on "whirring wings," not winged sandals; see also **Gorgon; Head**).

ATHENA ties on winged sandals to fly from Olympus to Ithaca (*Od.* 1.96f).

THETIS puts wings on the feet of her son Achilles; she has been given them at her wedding to Peleus by Zeus, who got them from Arce, sister of Iris (Ptolem. Heph. p. 152 a. 15).

AFFIXED TO SHOULDERS (MALE FIGURES)

Attribute of Comus (frequently with a drum at a symposium); Destinus; a genius; Horus; Kairos (with scales); Jupiter Pluvius (generally "watery" in appearance); Oneiroi (Dreams); Sigalion.

Attribute of EROS (often with bow and arrows, q.v. for instances of his marksmanship). Eros himself and Erotes generally are attributes of Aphrodite and of lovers. Eros with his head turned symbolizes love unrequited. Artists of all ages have illustrated details of his career that are not recounted in classical literature (e.g., his upbringing by Aphrodite and Ares; his being punished by various victims of his mischief; his flight to various protectors; his fight with Pan; his playing the armed conqueror; his triumphal procession). On instructions from Aphrodite, Eros lays aside his wings in order to impersonate the boy Ascanius, who has taken Dido's fancy; nestled in her embrace at a banquet, he infects her with love for Aeneas (*Aen.* 1.663f).

Attribute of HYMEN. His torch smokes at the wedding of Orpheus and Eurydice (*Met.* 10.1f).

Attribute of HYPNOS. At Hera's request, he puts Zeus to sleep after he makes love to his wife, to keep him from noticing Poseidon's help to the Greeks (*Il.* 14.231f, 14.286f); he tells Poseidon that he is free to provide such help (*Il.* 14.354f). Sent by Hera, he puts Zeus to sleep to keep him from seeing Heracles being buffeted by a storm at sea (*Il.* 14.249f). He causes the helmsman Palinurus to fall overboard while Aeneas sleeps (*Aen.* 5.838f). With Thanatos, he carries Sarpedon's body from the battlefield (*Il.* 16.671f).

Attribute of MORPHEUS. He flies to Alcyone's chamber, appearing to her in her sleep as her drowned husband Ceÿx (*Met.* 11.635f).

Attribute of THANATOS (sometimes an old man with a staff). Armed with a sword, he insists on his right to the life of Alcestis despite Apollo's objection (Eur. *Alc.* 24f). With Hypnos he carries Sarpedon's body from the battlefield (*Il.* 16.671f). He is captured and imprisoned by Sisyphus, but is released by Ares (Schol. *ad Il.* 6.153).

Wings are an invention of DAEDALUS. He makes some out of feathers and wax to enable him and his son Icarus to escape from Crete (*Met.* 8.189f; *Fab.* 40; *Ep.* 1.2).

DAEDALUS MAKING WINGS FOR ICARUS

(WINDS) Attribute of Winds (sometimes at head and feet; all with flying draperies). Other distinguishing attributes: Apheliotes (booted and carrying fruits in his robe); Aquilo (tub of snow); Boreas (triton shell); Eurus (face hidden in his robe); Libs (part of a ship); Notus (unopened urn); Skiron (upended urn); Zephyrus (unbooted and carrying fruits in his robe).

AQUILO blinds Phineus and sets the Harpies to tormenting him (Serv. *ad Aen.* 3.209f) and rescues Leto from the dragon Python (*Fab.* 53, 140).

BOREAS carries off Oreithyia (*Argo.* 1.216f; *Met.* 6.702f; see also **Pyre.** Paus. 5.19.1 records that in one picture he has serpent tails instead of feet).

NOTUS causes a flood (*Met.* 1.264f).

STORM WINDS are confined in a cave under the control of Aeolus—until Hera persuades him to turn them loose against Aeneas' ships (*Aen.* 1.50f); they are released from the bag in which Aeolus gave them to Odysseus to ensure fair winds; they blow up a storm (*Od.* 10.46f; *Met.* 14.223f).

ZEPHYRUS chases Chloris and seduces her (*Fasti* 5.201f; see also **Pyre**).

ZETES and CALAÏS, the sons of Boreas, stop the Harpies from tormenting Phineus and pursue them until Iris halts them (*Argo.* 2.262f, 2.426f); they are slain by the arrows of Heracles (*Argo.* 1.1298f; *Fab.* 14, 19).

(FEMALE FIGURES) Attribute of Eris; Eumenides (see **Furies**); Gorgons (q.v.); Graeae (Phorcides) (Schol. on Aes. *Prom.* 793); Harpies (q.v.); Hebe; Moirae (Parcae; see **Fates**); Nemesis; Nike (often a small-scale figure held in the hand); Nyx; Sirens (q.v.); Sphinx (q.v.); Victoria.

Attribute of EOS. She is seduced by Ares (*Lib.* 1.4.4) and tries to seduce Cephalus, to whom she gives valuable gifts with which to test the faithfulness of Procris (*Fab.* 189). She asks Hephaestus to make arms for her son Memnon (*Aen.* 8.384) and asks Zeus to honor Memnon, as he lies on his pyre, with a sign; this he does by making birds out of the smoke (*Met.* 13.583f). She carries off the hunter Cephalus (*Lib.* 1.9.3; *Met.* 7.700f), beautiful Cleitus (*Od.* 15.250f), Ganymede (Schol. *ad Argo.* 3.115), the body of Memnon (Serv. *ad Aen.* 1.493; Quint. Smy. 2.555), the hunter Orion (*Lib.* 1.4.4; *Od.* 5.121), and Tithonus, to be eternally her lover (*H. to Ap.* 218f; *Lib.* 3.12.4).

Attribute of the hag FAMES. She visits Erysichthon and makes him an insatiable glutton, forever gorging himself (*Met.* 8.814f).

Attribute of IRIS (often carrying a messenger's staff). She is sent by Hera to Achilles to tell him to rescue Patroclus' corpse from Trojan hands (*Il.* 18.165f); to Dido to free her soul as she lies dying in Anna's arms (*Aen.* 4.693f); to Heracles, taking Lussa (Madness) with her to goad him into killing his wife Megara and their children (Eur. *Her.* 815f); to Hypnos in his somnolent kingdom to have him send a dream (Morpheus) of Ceÿx to Alcyone (*Met.* 11.589f); to Thetis, Hephaestus, and Aeolus in turn with instructions to help the *Argo* get past various dangers safely (*Argo.* 4.753f); to the Trojan women to persuade them to set fire to their ships (*Aen.* 5.605f); to Turnus to tell him to assault the Trojan camp (*Aen.* 9.2f). She is sent by Zeus to stop Athena and Hera from leaving Olympus in their chariot to aid the Greeks against the Trojans (*Il.* 8.397f); to encourage Hector as he drives into battle (*Il.* 11.185f); to tell Hera to get Turnus out of the Trojan camp (*Aen.* 9.801f); to tell Poseidon to stop fighting for the Greeks (*Il.* 18.157f); to tell Priam to go to Achilles and ransom Hector's body (*Il.* 24.143f); to bring

THE WIND GOD NOTUS

water from the Styx for the gods to swear on (Hes. *Theog.* 784f). She brings the Winds Zephyrus and Boreas to Patroclus' pyre to make it burn (*Il.* 23.198f). Taking the form of Laodice, she brings Helen from her loom to the battlements to watch Paris fight Menelaüs (*Il.* 3.121f).

Attribute of OPIS (Upis). Sent by Artemis, she avenges the death of Camilla by shooting Arruns (*Aen.* 11.532f, 11.595f, 11.836f).

Attribute of SELENE. She visits her beloved Endymion, who is eternally asleep (*Argo.* 4.57f; *Lib.* 1.7.6).

Attribute of a SOUL, when represented as a small-scale figure rising from a corpse (see **Ascension; Corpse; Dying Figure**).

Wings of bees: attribute of the THRIAI, who are the prophetesses that reared Apollo and who practice divination by throwing stones into an urn; they feed on honey (*H. to Her.* 552f).

Wings of a butterfly: attribute of PSYCHE.

The MUSES don wings to escape from Pyreneus, who falls to his death when he tries to follow them (*Met.* 5.287f).

AFFIXED TO CREATURES OR OBJECTS

(See also the particular animal; **Monster.**)

Attribute of FAMA, a fanciful, feathered monster personifying Rumor, having many eyes, ears, and tongues. She spreads gossip throughout Africa about the growing passion of Dido and Aeneas for each other (*Aen.* 4.173f).

Affixed to a ball or a globe: attribute of Fortuna; Volupia. To a horse: Pegasus (see **Horse** [Winged]). To a staff or wand: Anubis; Venus (see also **Caduceus**).

WINNOWING FAN

(See also **Oar.**)

Serves as a cradle for baby DIONYSUS (Serv. *ad Georg.* 1.166); for HERMES, born in a cave to Maia (*Lib.* 3.10.2).

WOLF

(See also **Dog; Fox.**)

Attribute of Bellona; Mars; Tiber (a she-wolf).

Suckles ACACALLIS' BABY by Apollo (Ant. Lib. 30); PHILONOME's TWINS, after a river god rescues them (Plut. *Parallela Minora* 36); the twins ROMULUS and REMUS (Livy 1.4; Plut. 2.2; *Fasti* 2.412f).

Attacking. A wolf fights a BULL, observed by Danaüs (Serv. *ad Aen.* 4.377; Paus. 2.19.3); another slaughters the CATTLE of Peleus (*Met.* 11.365f) and, in the act of killing a HEIFER, the wolf is turned to marble by Psamathe (*Met.* 11.401f). Wolves attack the SHEEP of Evenius while he sleeps (Herod. 9.93); kill MILO of Croton, whose hands are held fast in a cleft in a tree (Paus. 6.14.8; cf. Val. Max. 9.12b.9, where it is a lion that attacks him).

Changed into wolves. LYCAON, by Zeus for serving him human flesh (*Met.* 1.232f; *Lib.* 3.8.1; *Fab.* 176; *Poet. Astr.* 2.4); THEOPHANE's SUITORS, by Poseidon because they are attacking the cattle into which he has changed the men of Crumissa (*Fab.* 188).

In this form, APOLLO kills the Telchines and mates with the huntress Cyrene (Serv. *ad Aen.* 4.377f).

Wolves are driven off by HIPPOLYTUS from Troezen (Paus. 2.31.6); by SHEPHERDS from sacrificial offerings into a cave (Serv. *ad Aen.* 11.785).

Brings a laurel branch to APOLLO after he has dispatched Python (Serv. *ad Aen.* 4.377).

WOLFSKIN

(See **Skin, of Animal.**)

WOMAN

(See **Human Figure.**)

WOODPECKER

(See **Bird.**)

WOUNDED FIGURE

(See also **Bed; Blood; Corpse; Dying Figure; Phantom;** and weapons by which wounds may be inflicted.)

Warriors are aided. ACHILLES, though mortally wounded in the heel, fights on; he pulls out Apollo's arrow and dies (Quint. Smy. 3.80f, 3.135f). AEMILIUS PAULUS declines to escape to safety even though Lentulus offers his horse (Plut. 10.16; Livy 22.49). AENEAS, after being dropped by Aphrodite as she carries him from the field, is taken up by Apollo and brought to Leto and Artemis to be healed (*Il.* 5.343f); attended by Achates, Ascanius, et al., he is healed by Aphrodite after she removes the arrow (*Aen.* 12.383f). ALEXANDER shows to those near him that his arrow wound drips blood, not a god's ichor (Plut. 33.28); an arrow is extracted after he is carried to safety (Plut. 33.64). ARES, complaining to Zeus about Diomedes' excessive violence, is tended by Paeëon and Hebe (*Il.* 5.864f). DIOMEDES is healed by Athena after Sthenelus pulls out an arrow (*Il.* 5.121f); an arrow is pulled from his foot by Odysseus (*Il.* 11.375f). EPAMINONDAS does not allow the spear to be drawn from his body until victory is assured and he can die unconquered (Nep. *Epam.* 9). ETEOCLES and POLYNEICES, after mortally wounding each other, speak with their mother Jocasta and sister Antigone before dying (Eur. *Phoen.* 1428f). EURYPYLUS, hit by an arrow in the thigh, is tended by Patroclus (*Il.* 11.804f, 11.842f, 15.390f). HADES, wounded by Heracles' arrow, retreats to Olympus to be treated by Paeëon (*Il.* 5.395f). HECTOR, stunned by a rock thrown by Ajax, is carried off by Sarpedon, Aeneas, et al. and revived with water (*Il.* 14.423f, 15.9f). HERACLES is rescued from battle by Zeus (*Lib.* 2.7.1) and is healed by Asclepius (Paus. 3.20.5). LEONYMUS, wounded in the chest by Ajax Oïleus, is later healed by the ghost of Ajax on an island where dwell the ghosts of Achilles and Helen (Paus. 3.19.12, 3.19.13). MENELAÜS' arrow wound is tended by Agamemnon, Machaon, et al. (*Il.* 4.148f). Wounded MEZENTIUS is reclining against a tree when the corpse of his son Lausus is brought to him (*Aen.* 10.833f). PARIS, hit by Philoctetes' arrow, begs his wife Oenone, whom he has abandoned for Helen, to heal him, but she refuses (Quint. Smy. 10.275f). SARPEDON is carried to a tree, where Tlepolemus' spear is withdrawn (*Il.* 5.663f); felled by Patroclus' spear, he appeals to Glaucus for help (*Il.* 16.482f). THEAGENES, among other wounded and dead warriors, is found by Charicleia, as pirates approach (*Aeth.* 1, 5).

Others wounded. ANTONY, after stabbing himself, is drawn up on a litter to Cleopatra's chamber, where he expires (Plut. 44.77). APHRODITE, while trying to protect Aeneas from Diomedes, is cut on her hand; Iris takes her to Dione, who heals her (*Il.* 5.352f); she is scratched on the breast by one of Eros' arrows, which causes her to love Adonis (*Met.* 10.519f). King DARIUS' damaged foot is treated by Democedes, who has been brought from prison in chains (Herod. 3.129). HEPHAESTUS, crippled or lifeless after his fall from Olympus, is found and cared for by the women of Lemnos (*Lib.* 1.3.5; *Il.* 1.590f). An arrow falls on PHILOCTETES' foot; the wound gives off such a stench that he is banished to a desert island (Serv. *ad Aen.* 3.402). PROCRIS, accidentally wounded by Cephalus while they are hunting, dies in his arms (*Met.* 7.845f). TELEPHUS' wound is healed by Achilles with rust from the point of his spear (*Ep.* 3.20).

Self-inflicted wounds. PEISISTRATUS shows them to a crowd of Athenians to gain their protection, claiming that his political enemies were responsible; old Solon sees through the deception (Plut. 5.30).

WREATH

(See also **Crown.**)

Held in the hand: attribute of Libertas; Nike (often a small figure standing in a larger figure's hand). Made of ivy: Hebe.

On the head: attribute of Libertas. Made of corn: Demeter. Of flowers: Flora. Of grapevine: Dionysus; Fidius; Silenus. Of ivy: Melpomene; poets; Thaleia. Of laurel: Apollo; poets; victors. Of lotus: Horus; Isis.

Awarded or given to CORIOLANUS for saving a life, by his commanding officer (Plut. 12.3); to MENELAÜS by Helen, to indicate her choice of a husband (*Fab.* 78); to THEMISTOCLES by the Spartans, for his services in the repulse of Persia (Plut. 7.17); (made of gold) to THESEUS by Amphitrite in her abode in the deep; he presents it, together with a ring she has given him, to Minos on his ship (Paus. 1.17.3).

Taken from a casket or cradle by ION as Creüsa watches; its presence there proves to him that she is his mother (Eur. *Ion* 1433f).

Worn. CIPUS wears a wreath to conceal the horns on his head as he addresses an assembly (*Met.* 15.590f). HERACLES in the underworld crowns himself with poplar, into which Hades' beloved Leuce has been changed (Serv. *ad Ecl.* 7.61), or which he finds on returning to earth (Serv. *ad Georg.* 2.66, *ad Aen.* 8.276); he wears an olive wreath as a memorial to man's great benefactor Prometheus, whom he has set free (*Lib.* 2.5.11).

WRESTLING

ACHILLES tries to strangle Cygnus; his opponent escapes by becoming a swan (*Met.* 12.72).

ALCIBIADES bites his opponent during a wrestling match (Plut. 11.2).

ARCHELAÜS grabs King Cisseus and hurls him into the fiery pit intended for himself (*Fab.* 219).

ARISTAEUS holds fast to Proteus, the Old Man of the Sea, in spite of his changes into a boar, tiger, snake, lioness, fire, and water (*Georg.* 4.387f). (N.B.: This Protean tactic may be represented by a composite creature or by the presence of the shapes assumed as a visual "aside.")

ATALANTA defeats Peleus at the games in honor of Pelias (*Lib.* 3.9.2).

HERACLES wrestles for the hand of Deïaneira against the river god Acheloüs, who takes the form of a snake, a bull, or a bull-headed man and has one of his horns torn off (*Met.* 9.62; Soph. *Trach.* 9f, 499f; *Lib.* 2.7.5); against Antaeus, whom he subdues by lifting him clear of contact with his strength-giving Mother Earth (*Lib.* 2.5.11); against Autolycus, who is teaching him the art (*Lib.* 2.4.9); against fire-breathing Cacus, who has stolen his cattle (*Aen.* 8.256f); against Eryx, to recover his stolen bull from among Eryx's herd (*Lib.* 2.5.10); against Menoetes, guardian of Hades' cattle, for whom Persephone intercedes (*Lib.* 2.5.12); against the Nemean Lion, which he strangles and carries off to Eurystheus (*Lib.* 2.5.1); against Nereus, who changes into various shapes in the vain effort to avoid being tied up (*Lib.* 2.5.11); against Periclymenus, who assumes the shapes of lion, snake, and bee before he is killed (*Lib.* 1.9.9); against Polygonus and Telegonus, who challenge him and are killed (*Lib.* 2.5.9); against Thanatos (Death) to win the release of Alcestis from her tomb (Eur. *Alc.* 843f, 1142f).

ILUS wrestles for and wins the prize of fifty youths and fifty maids at the Phrygian games (*Lib.* 3.12.3).

MENELAÜS et al. hold fast to Proteus throughout his transformations into lion, leopard, snake, boar, water, and tree (*Od.* 4.454f; *Fab.* 118).

ODYSSEUS defeats Philomeleides (*Od.* 4.341f, 17.132f); he and Ajax draw at the games for Patroclus (*Il.* 23.708f).

PELEUS subdues Thetis after she tries to escape by turning into a tree, bird, tiger and other wild animals (*Met.* 11.235f; *Lib.* 3.13.5).

TARCHON tears Venulus from his horse and rides off with him still struggling (*Aen.* 11.741f).

THEAGENES defeats the Ethiopian champion (*Aeth.* 10).

THESEUS takes on murderous Cercyon at his own game and kills him (Plut. 1.11; Paus. 1.39.3; *Ep.* 1.3).

TROJAN HEROES compete at games celebrating their arrival at Actium (*Aen.* 3.281f).

ZEUS wrestles with the monster Typhon and is carried off to the Corycian cave (*Lib.* 1.6.3).

WRITING

(See also **Book; Inscription; Letter.**)

ARISTAGORAS reads the message written on a slave's scalp after his hair is shaved off (Herod. 5.35).

CANACE, as she writes, holds in her other hand the sword with which she will kill herself (*Heroïdes* 11.5f).

DEMETRIUS, sworn not to speak to his friend who has come under suspicion, traces in the sand with his spear, "Fly, Mithridates" (Plut. 43.4).

DEMOSTHENES, pretending to write, bites on the poisoned reed he is using and so escapes from his enemies (Plut. 41.29).

A SCRIBE takes dictation from Seneca as he and his wife sit with opened veins awaiting death (Tac. *An*. 15.60).

The SIBYL of Cumae writes prophecies on pages that are scattered about her cave by the wind (*Aen*. 3.441f).

YOKE

Used as harness (see **Chariot; Plow; Wagon**).

Symbol of submission, consisting of two spears fixed in the ground and a third forming a crossbar, under which defeated enemies of Rome are forced to pass with bowed heads. HORATIUS passes under a yoke as penance for the murder of his sister; his valor in killing the three Curiatii has mitigated the usual penalty for this crime (Livy 1.26). ROMANS are sent under the yoke by barbarian Helvetii (Caesar *B.G.* 1.7.4); by the Tigurini (Caesar *B.G.* 1.12.5).

BIBLIOGRAPHY

The reference works that have been most useful in the preparation of this volume are:

Daremberg and Saglio. *Dictionnaire des antiquités grecques et romaines*. 5 vols. Paris, 1877–1919. (Illustrated. Excellent on antiquities. Not all mythological figures are treated.)

Pauly-Wissowa, eds. *Real-Encyclopädie der classischen Altertumswissenschaft*. 70 vols. Stuttgart, 1894–1978.

Peck, Harry Thurston. *Harper's Dictionary of Classical Literature and Antiquities*. New York, 1896. Repr. 1923, 1965. (Based on William Smith's work.)

Roscher, Wilhelm Heinrich. *Ausführliches Lexikon der griechischen und römischen Mythologie*. 6 vols. and supp. Leipzig, 1884–1937. Repr. 1965.

Smith, William. *A Dictionary of Greek and Roman Antiquities*. London, 1842. Repr. 1977. (Illustrated.)

Smith, William. *A Dictionary of Greek and Roman Biography and Mythology*. 3 vols. London, 1880. (This has been indispensable.)

Tripp, Edward. *Crowell's Handbook of Classical Mythology*. New York, 1970. (An excellent work.)

The following, along with Smith, are the sources of the attributes assigned:

Cartari, Vincenzo. *Imagini delli dei de gl'antichi*. Walter Koschatzky, ed. Graz, 1963 (repr. of the Venice 1647 edition).

de Tervarent, Guy. *Attributs et symboles dans l'art profane, 1450–1600*. 2 vols. Geneva, 1958–1959; supp. and index, 1964.

Hirt, Aloys Ludwig. *Bilderbuch für Mythologie, Archäologie und Kunst*. 2 vols. Berlin, 1805–1816.

Pigler, Andor. *Barockthemen*. Rev. ed. 3 vols. Budapest, 1974. (Lists of seventeenth- and eighteenth-century paintings in European museums that have classical subjects.)